Catering & Hospitality

NVQ SVQ 1+2

Food Preparation & Cooking

Anthony O'Reilly

Nelson

Thomas Nelson and Sons Ltd
Nelson House Mayfield Road
Walton-on-Thames Surrey
KT12 5PL UK

Thomas Nelson Australia
102 Dodds Street
South Melbourne
Victoria 3205 Australia

Nelson Canada
1120 Birchmount Road
Scarborough Ontario
M1K 5G4 Canada

First published by Thomas Nelson and Sons Ltd 1996

I(T)P Thomas Nelson is an International Thomson Publishing Company

I(T)P is used under licence

ISBN 0-17-490005-8
NPN 9 8 7 6 5 4 3 2 1

Publishing team:
Acquisitions: Alex Bridgeland
Administration: Jenny Goode
Staff editorial: Gaynor Roberts
Freelance editorial: Martin Noble/David Francis
Marketing: Jane Lewis
Production: Liam Reardon
Staff design: Eleanor Fisher/Maria Pritchard
Design: Ian Foulis & Associates

Printed in Spain

Contents

Section 3 Food Preparation and cooking

Section 4

Dedication

To Julie, my wife.

Acknowledgements

The author and publishers would like to acknowledge with thanks:

The staff and students of Milton Keynes College and Thames Valley University and Roland Allen Catering Suppliers for their participation in the photo shoots.
Alex Ward and Ursula Vaughan for their professional advice on the development of this book.
Further Education Consortium p.15, p.19
S C Johnson Professional p.49, p.317
The Controller of HMSO p.20. Crown copyright is reproduced with the permission of the Controller of HMSO.
Graham Lewis, The Upper Crust Bakery, Woburn Sands
Derek Andrews, The Meat and Livestock Commission

The author would like to thank the Sea Fish Industry Authority for permission to reproduce information from their fish preparation pamphlet for caterers: pages 172-177, Preparing flat fish, preparing round fish and preparing oily fish
© The Sea Fish Industry Authority.

Photographs

Brian and Cherry Alexander p.323
Roland Allen Catering Suppliers p.210, p.330, p.331, p.341,
Baker's Pride Europe Limited p.345
Barilla UK Ltd p.216
Ian Blackwell p.275
Anthony Blake p.6, p.8, p.68, p.91, p.94, p.95, p.96, p.219, p.270, p.287, p.305, p.307, p.315, p.319, p.322, p.341
Carol Bowen/Chancellor Press p.222
GGS Photographic p.295, GGS Photographic/Zanussi p.2
Lockhart Catering Equipment p.330, p.341
The Meat and Livestock Commission p.154
McDougall's Catering Foods Ltd p.257, p.267, p.337
Sainsbury's The Magazine © Nigel James p.106, p.136
UN/IPI p.214

All other photographs David Sparrow for Thomas Nelson

Cover design and Photography Simon Battensby

Illustration Samantha Bale

Introduction

'A chef is only as good as the food they put on the plate! After all, the food presented on the plate is an expression of the chef's abilities.'

The skills and expertise necessary to become a good chef are gained through hard work, boundless energy, total commitment, dedication and a sound underpinning knowledge. There are no short cuts. These skills cannot be taught alone, however, they are achieved through self-discipline, the right attitude, guidance and encouragement. Once these skills are acquired, the chef of tomorrow will succeed in fulfilling his or her full potential and will continue to progress well in his or her chosen profession.

WHAT ARE NVQS?

In simple terms, NVQs (National Vocational Qualifications) are nationally recognised qualifications. They are awarded in specific areas of industry for showing competence in practical skills and an understanding of the theory behind those skills. The Catering and Hospitality industry offers a wide range of NVQs/SVQs (the Scottish equivalent of NVQs) covering all types of jobs and at all levels.

NVQs have been available for the Catering and Hospitality industry since 1992 and are regularly reviewed and updated to ensure that they remain relevant to the industry's needs.

NVQs and SVQs show and prove that you can do specific tasks and activities and that you fully understand why they are done in a specific way. To achieve one of these qualifications it is necessary to collate evidence for each unit (which consists of a number of elements) undertaken, which is then recorded in an Evidence Diary. The Evidence Diary should describe in detail the tasks necessary to cover the performance criteria and range of each unit in order to achieve an NVQ/SVQ. Once sufficient evidence is gathered, it is checked and signed off by an Assessor and countersigned by an Internal Verifier as a true record of the individual's competence.

Assessment is divided into two main areas:

Theoretical

The underpinning knowledge may be tested through questionning, assignments, projects or a combination of these.

Practical skills

These are measured against a Performance Criteria and Range Checklist to ensure that the tasks have been carried out and completed in the appropriate manner.

When theoretical and practical skills are proven a certificate is awarded to show competence. Once the required number of units is obtained for the appropriate NVQ level, an additional certificate is awarded acknowledging the individual's successful completion of the qualification.

How long does it take to achieve an NVQ/SVQ?

This varies considerably and depends entirely on the individual. To gain the qualification it is necessary to complete the stated range of skills in the units. If you are in full-time employment, there should be ample opportunities to learn skills and prove competence in those skills which will enable you to quickly achieve an NVQ/SVQ. If you are attending college full-time, it will probably take longer to complete the criteria. However, working part-time in the industry will help to supplement the skills learnt on your programme.

Awarding body

Catering NVQs are awarded by City and Guilds who work closely with the HCIMA (Hotel Catering Institute Management Association). The HCTC (Hotel Catering Training Company) is the Lead Body whose role it is to ensure that the framework of NVQs/SVQs is regularly reviewed and updated.

To the trainee

Industry places heavy emphasis on education and training so it is important that the right package of qualifications, coupled with high quality practical skills are achieved. Certificates may be awarded for all areas of food preparation and cooking - from chef apprentice to fast food apprentice.

This book is designed specifically for trainees who are studying for a National Vocational Qualification (NVQ) or a Scottish Vocational Qualification (SVQ) level 1 and 2, Preparing and Serving Food or a Food Preparation and Cooking programme. It gives a thorough coverage of the cooking processes as well as essential information about the industry, conditions, hygiene, safety, commodities and equipment.

This book will not only provide the essential underpinning information necessary to complete all the units undertaken, but it will help the reader to develop a professional attitude and understanding, in preparation for his or her chosen career. It will prove to be an invaluable source of reference throughout the training programme and will continue to assist the trainee when working in industry as a self-support handbook.

Each unit has an activity section consisting of a number of activities which might include questions, explorative tasks, crosswords, wordsearches, or investigations, all of which will aid the learning process. The units also contain key words and tips for reference.

Illustrations have been supplied by representatives of leading national and international companies in the hospitality trade and supporting industries.

How to use this book

Nowadays, with less time devoted to structured theoretical classes, trainees need to be able to find relevant information quickly. This book is divided into four main sections for ease of use.

Section 1
The first section explores various aspects of:

- the culinary industry;
- equipment, large and small;
- basic social and practical skills;
- safety;
- security;
- hygiene.

Section 2
The second section covers the following skills at NVQ/SVQ level 1:

- preparing foodstuffs;
- primary cookery processes;
- assembling food for serving.

Section 3
The third section deals with fundamental kitchen tasks such as receiving, handling and storing food, cleaning and maintaining equipment as well as more complex culinary skills and specialist areas at NVQ/SVQ level 2. The following shows how Section 3 is divided:

- main kitchen work - soups and sauces; cooking meat, poultry and offal; cooking fish and shellfish; cooking vegetables; pulse, rice and pasta dishes; vegetable protein dishes and egg dishes;
- pastry work - cold and hot desserts; dough making; pastry dishes; cakes, sponges and scones; decorating methods;
- larder work - food for cold presentation; salads;
- specialist areas - cook-chill; cook-freeze; pizzas; fish and chips.

Section 4
The fourth section contains a comprehensive glossary of culinary terms plus an in-depth index to help locate the information required.

How to find information

There are three ways in which you can find the information you need in this book:

- by using the contents list at the front;
- by looking it up in the index at the back;
- by following the cross-reference buttons to other sections.

Buttons in the margins direct you to the relevant sections. They are a cross-referencing system which allows you to access additional information on the topic you are studying. When you are looking something up in another section, don't forget to mark your place in the book so that you can get back to it.

To the lecturer/trainer

This book is designed to support the trainee and may be used as a support to the structured programme of delivery, both as a course textbook and as a reference text. It will facilitate the flexible candidate-centred ethos of Vocational Qualifications by enabling those whose preferred style of learning is self-supported study to work at their own pace, providing the necessary underpinning knowledge and instructions of processes and simple recipes to try.

1 General

The first section of the book covers the more general aspects of catering, including kitchen equipment, the various branches of the industry, health and safety in the work environment, working relationships, cleaning and hygiene. The elements included cover both Levels 1 and 2.

CONTENTS

Equipment: a guide to identifying, maintaining and using large equipment in the kitchen environment

INTRODUCTION

Kitchen equipment is one of the most expensive outlays for the caterer and it is the responsibility of all users to make sure that when operating it, care and attention is taken. Equipment must never be abused and should be regularly cleaned and routinely serviced to ensure that it is kept in a safe operating manner at all times.

It can be hard work starting a new job and familiarising yourself with new surroundings and working practices, so it is important that you learn to operate equipment as quickly and safely as possible. To operate specific items of equipment the operator must be appropriately trained, as they are covered by the Prescribed Machines Dangerous Order Act 1964. These pieces of equipment can be identified by appropriate notices.

Figure 1 Large item of kitchen equipment from Zanussi

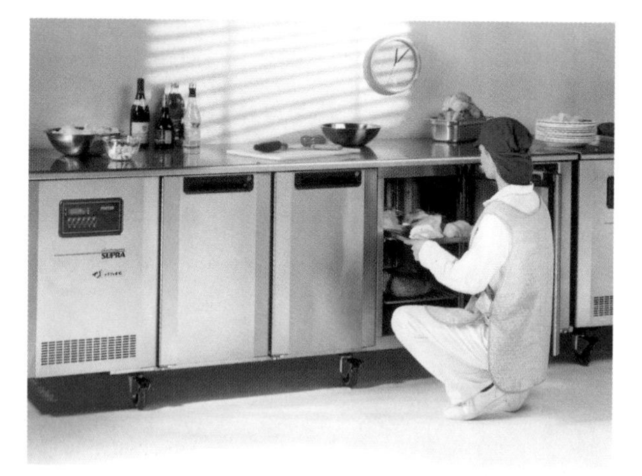

Figure 2 Large item of kitchen equipment from Foster

GENERAL GUIDE TO KITCHEN EQUIPMENT

Ovens

Combination ovens These ovens can have a *combination of convection* with the assistance of *steam* or *microwave*. They are multi-purpose and can be used for roasting, braising, poaching, fast steaming, baking and regenerating chilled or frozen foods.

Convection ovens The convection oven has a circulating current of air rapidly forced around the inside of the oven by means of an electrically operated fan or blower which distributes the heat evenly around the oven. Fast, hot-air circulation reduces evaporation loss, keeping food shrinkage to a minimum. With its even temperature distribution, the full capacity of the oven may be used.

General purpose stoves/ovens These are for roasting, baking and braising and are operated by electricity or gas (gas ovens can have an automatic pilot – lighting mechanism). A disadvantage of a conventional oven is that the temperature fluctuates around the oven.

Mealstream ovens Mealstream ovens are a combination of convection and microwave ovens, giving them the advantage of being able to cook rapidly and to brown (colour) at the same time.

Microwave ovens Microwave ovens cook by using high-frequency radio waves that disturb the molecules or particles in the food and agitate them, which heats the food up and cooks it. The disadvantage of microwave ovens is their low capacity, uneven cooking and an inability to brown foods.

Additional features of the more complex microwave oven include a revolving turntable for more even cooking, a browning element and stay-hot controls.

Pastry ovens These ovens are specifically used for large output baking of breads, pastry and cakes. Pastry ovens may be purchased as single or tiered on a stand, with each oven independently heated from top, bottom, front and back. An average oven height is 127 mm to 135 mm and they have a drop-down door. Some have the addition of steam injection to assist baking. An important feature is the even temperature control throughout the oven.

Pizza ovens These are multi-deck, rapid-recovery ovens used to bake pizzas. They reheat more quickly than conventional ovens.

Proving ovens These are low-temperature ovens operating at between 27° and 32°C. They are used for proving – or fermenting – dough. They provide a warm, moist atmosphere essential for successful fermentation of dough. Proving ovens are self-contained units fitted with a vapour-generating pan and water feed tank.

Other large items of kitchen equipment

Boiling pans These are usually made from stainless steel and are available in various sizes between 10 and 40 litres. Basic shallow pans with a tilting mechanism can only be used for boiling, but models surrounded by a steam jacket can be used for stewing.

Bain maries Bain maries are water wells and heated water baths which are used to hold containers of food during the food service period without burning.

Bratt pans Bratt pans are shallow pans with a tilting mechanism usually made from cast iron or stainless steel. Bratt pans are multi-purpose and are used for shallow frying, boiling, poaching and stewing.

Computerised fryers These highly advanced fryers are programmed to control the cooking temperature and cooking time precisely. When the food is cooked, the basket is automatically raised from the fryer.

Contact grills These are also referred to as infra-red or double-sided grills because they have two heating surfaces arranged facing each other. The food to be cooked is placed on the bottom surface and covered by the top surface.

Deep fryers These are basic fryers with a thermostatically controlled trough filled with oil or fat, heated by electricity or gas. They have a cool zone below the heat source for collecting waste food particles which would otherwise burn and shorten the life of the oil.

Griddle plates Sometimes known as dry plates, they have a solid base with side draining channels and are used for shallow frying. The heat source is from below and can be electric or gas.

Hot cupboards These are thermostatically controlled, heated cabinets into which hot food can be placed during the service period.

Induction plates These are solid top plates made with vitroceramic material. Special saucepans are placed on the plates and a generator below the plates creates a two-way magnetic field which passes a current of magnetic energy directly to the pan which, in turn, heats the contents. There is minimum energy loss as only the immediate area under the saucepan is heated and as soon as the saucepan is removed from the plate it switches off. The disadvantage is the price – the unit far exceeds the price of normal heating plates.

Pressure fryers Pressure fryers have an air-tight seal allowing the food to be fried in a shorter time than a conventional fryer and at a lower temperature.

Salamanders Also known as overfired grills, salamanders have gas burners that heat ceramic bricks or a metal mesh. They can also be electrically heated. When the salamander is heated properly it should heat up the movable bar rack which will mark the food and aid the cooking process.

Steamers There are three types of steamer: atmospheric, pressure and pressureless (*see* combination ovens). Pressure steamers cook much more quickly than atmospheric steamers.

Underflare grills These have heat source from below. Burners are located underneath a bed of lava rock or manufactured ceramic bricks. Underflare grills are so called because cooking juices and fat fall onto the heated bricks/rocks which then 'flare up'. The combination of the smoke and flame gives the food a unique flavour.

The industry: a look at all areas of the catering trade

INTRODUCTION

The catering industry is one of the major employers with an estimated 500,000 vacancies to be filled every year – that's a lot of job opportunities!

In traditional kitchens, chefs are divided into sections (parties). Trainees may enter as commis chefs, spending several months in each area learning 'on-the-job' from more experienced staff. After gaining experience in each section, a commis chef might be promoted to the chef in charge (*chef de partie*), running a particular section and supervising the work.

An experienced party chef may progress to second chef (*sous chef*), running the kitchen, supervising the work of the section heads and deputising for the head chef.

The head chef (*maître chef de cuisine*) controls the work of all the kitchen, ordering and buying supplies, planning menus and work rotas and may be responsible for on-the-job training of junior chefs.

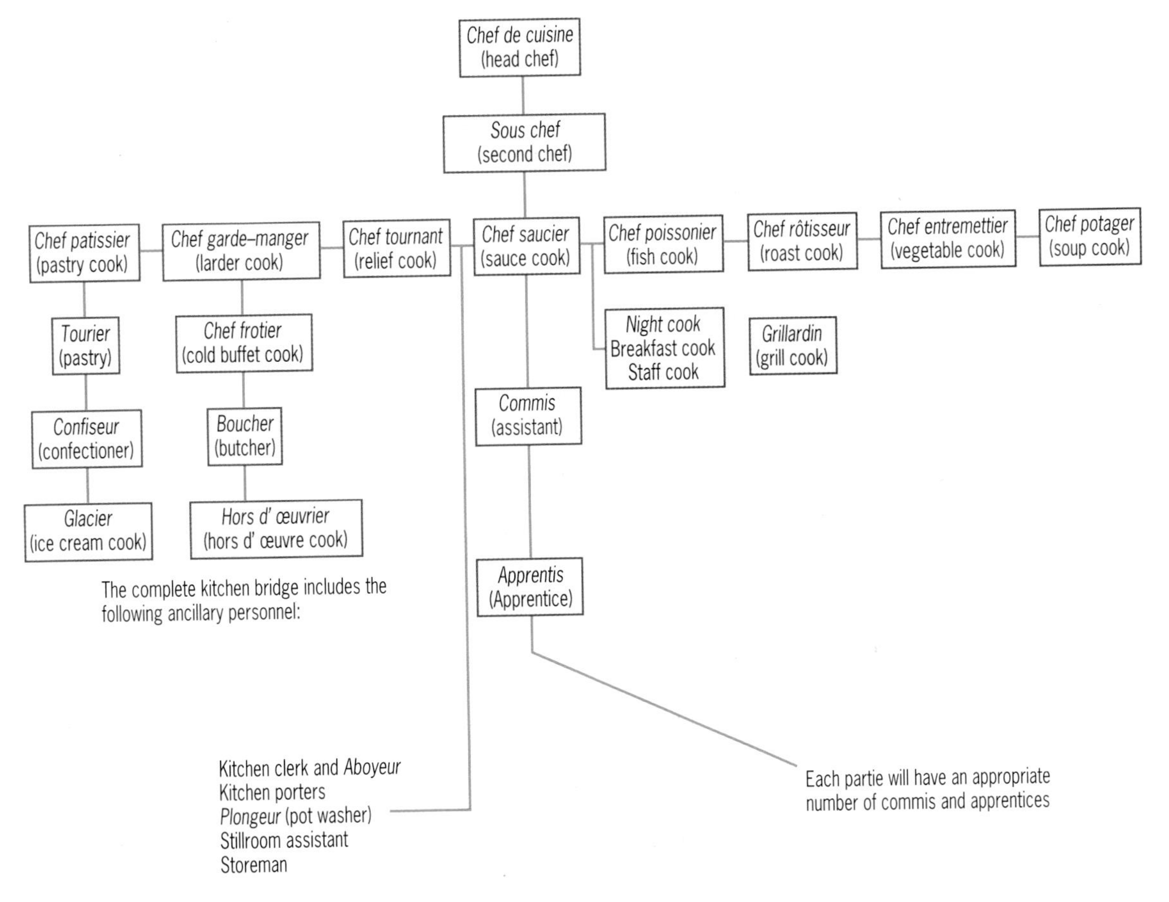

Figure 3 The traditional kitchen brigade

SECTORS OF THE CATERING INDUSTRY

Chefs may work in a wide variety of outlets, from hotels and restaurants in the commercial sector, to a works canteen, and hospitals in the welfare sector of the industry. Whatever area of catering you enter you will need to be committed, be willing to work as a member of a team and work in conditions that are often hot, steamy and stressful, especially at peak times. Some areas of the trade have conventional working hours, i.e. Monday–Friday 08.30 a.m. – 5.30 p.m. In the main, however, the hours may be unsociable, e.g. early morning, late nights, split shifts (combination of early morning and late nights), weekends and bank holidays. In fact, whenever people want to eat or to celebrate there will be a need to prepare, cook and serve meals.

Figure 4 Trainees working in a college kitchen

Figure 5 Hotel exterior

Hotels

Hotels provide a wide variety of services ranging from breakfast, lunch and dinner to meals 24 hours a day. Chefs need to be prepared to cover a wide range of shifts and be able to work in all areas of the kitchen.

Restaurants

Restaurants need to be able to cater for: regional, international, ethnic, vegetarian, fish and steak house cuisines. Experience is gained from working in reputable establishments.

Wine bars

Wine bars have become more popular since the 1970s and usually serve light meals: lasagne, chilli, bolognaise and salads at lunch and dinner times. Most establishments require a basic training (NVQ/SVQ I & II Food Preparation and Cooking) and the job training can be in-house styles and standards.

Public houses/steakhouses

There was a time when public houses were renowned for only offering a limited menu: crisps, sausage and chips, and steak and kidney pie.

However, nowadays the choice might include anything from a sandwich to a large selection of appetising dishes, for example, stuffed wild trout with dill sauce, port wine pheasant. Increased competition from major 'chain' restaurants, public demand for meals throughout the day and the extended opening hours have resulted in food being served throughout the day. *Sous vide* or 'second life' food is prepared food prepacked into special plastic pouches which are then vacuum sealed.

(See p. 309.)

Steakhouses are generally themed, i.e. decorated in a particular style, e.g. an old barn or American Wild West, and the main section of their menu usually consists of grilled meats, poultry and fish. Most establishments give on-the-job training and qualifications (NVQ/SVQ I & II).

Fast-food operations

Fast food is professional in its marketing and presentation, but there is little scope for creative cooking techniques. A choice of quick snack meals are readily available throughout the day ranging from fish and chips, burgers, pizza, fried chicken or sandwiches. Experience offered is limited as is the menu which might considerably hinder the development of cooking experience for some. However, a great deal of experience will be gained in handling and storing food, timing etc.

Industrial

Catering for everything from staff canteens to directors' dining rooms, industrial catering offers a wide choice of careers. The menus are sometimes subsidised by the company and offer a range of dishes of a high standard that would not be out of place in a high-class restaurant. As for public houses and steakhouses, most give on-the-job training and qualifications (NVQ/SVQ I & II); there are also many opportunities within catering companies to gain experience and promotion.

School meals

Gone are the days of 'stodgy puddings' and 'runny stews'. School meal cooks now have to consider nutritional balance as well as catering for a number of dietary requirements. Working hours are Monday to Friday, daytime during term. However, educational establishments and schools with boarders that are open throughout the year will need to produce meals outside term times. Experience is gained from on-the-job training.

Welfare

Welfare catering includes provision for hospitals, hostels and prisons. Good quality food must be produced three times a day from a limited budget. Many large institutions have opted for the cook-chill system of food production (see p. 309).

The services: army, navy, air force, police

Cutbacks have resulted in there being fewer positions for caterers within the services. However, it is still a worthwhile career. Many posts, due to the nature of the work involved, require working away from home – sometimes for long periods or travelling around the world. Working in the services you will be given the opportunity of learning to cook in field kitchens as well as conventional kitchens. Key positions include looking after important military personnel and members of government. This is an excellent opportunity to gain experience while seeing the world!

Airline catering (in-flight catering)

High-class food is prepared in bulk from a central kitchen. The cooked food is portioned on a conveyor belt into individual containers which are then chilled and reheated if required on board the aircraft in special ovens.

Some central units cook and freeze their portioned products.

Railway

Railway transport chefs might be expected to prepare anything from breakfast to an evening meal in very tight/cramped conditions for the first-class rail travellers. The food is usually cook-chilled and reconstituted on the train. Some meals – for example, steaks – are cooked to order on the train.

Figure 6 Serving food on a train

Ships' cooks

Catering at sea might involve anything from being a crew cook on a cargo ship, freighter or tanker to a head chef/*chef de partie* on a large cruise liner. A crew cook would be expected to be able to prepare good, wholesome, nourishing food for hard-working seamen and officers. Some freighters carrying passengers would normally have a second galley/kitchen for preparing their meals.

Cruise liners may be likened to 'floating first-class hotels' and are renowned for their excellent cuisine. To apply for a position aboard a cruise liner it would be necessary to have had comparative experience on land beforehand.

Contract catering

Contract catering has become popular with many sectors of industry. An organisation contracts a caterer to supply all of their catering needs. In recent years, schools, colleges, hospitals, police canteens and prisons have seen it as a way of standardising their running costs, maintaining standards and relieving themselves of the worry of running a canteen. Cooking jobs involve working early morning, late evening and early hour shifts. The jobs available are diverse and can involve anything from working on a very tight budget for prison services, to a directors' dining room in prestigious offices. Working for a contract caterer will give valuable insight and experience and the opportunities to travel locally, nationally and even in some situations abroad.

Event/outside caterers

There are many venues where event/outside caterers are employed, ranging from a wedding in a marquee to an international show or exhibition.

The cuisine is usually part-prepared at a base kitchen and transported to the venue where it is finished. There was a time when outside catering meant having to compromise with equipment and storage. However, with developments in satellite kitchens an empty room can very quickly be transformed into a functioning kitchen in no time at all. Satellite kitchens are units where the final stage of the cook-chill/cook-freeze process is carried out before the food is served to the customer. There are also complete mobile kitchens with walk-in fridges and freezers. These can be located at most venues and be up and running within a very short time after arriving on site. Certain large companies already own a number of these units or alternatively they may be hired through specialist equipment companies.

Cook-chill/cook-freeze operations

In cook-chill/cook-freeze operations chefs prepare and cook dishes in bulk in a central kitchen in near sterile conditions. The food is then portioned, chilled or frozen to be distributed to satellite units for regeneration.

Chefs need the NVQ/SVQ I & II in Food Prepation and Cooking. Junior positions offer on-the-job training while more senior positions will require the chef to have had experience from working in hotels or event catering and have additional qualifications in food handling.

Maintain a safe and secure working environment

ELEMENT 1

Maintain personal health and hygiene

INTRODUCTION

Food hygiene is an issue of considerable public concern and it is the responsibility of all food handlers to ensure that high standards of hygiene are maintained at all times. All food handlers must comply with the 1995 Food Safety (General Food Hygiene) Regulations (Schedule 1).

The regulations set out basic hygiene principles to be adhered to throughout the European Community: Directive (93/94/EEC). The regulations apply to all types of food, drink and ingredients and outline basic hygiene practices. One of the most important factors of the regulations requires that all food businesses identify individual staff needs and instruct, train and supervise their staff in food hygiene.

The regulations focus strongly on how to identify and control food safety risks at each stage of the process of preparing and selling food. They allow the food handler to assess the risk of food safety and then apply controls relevant to each specific situation.

For further information regarding current Health and Safety legislation contact the local authority's Environmental Health Inspector.

The 1995 Food Safety (General Food Hygiene) Regulations outline the responsibility of individual employees to report to their employers should they suffer from certain medical conditions. These are broken down into two categories:

1. If you are suffering from or known to be a carrier of a disease likely to be transmitted through food, e.g. typhoid fever; paratyphoid fever, any salmonella infection, amoebic/bacillary dysentery, staphylococcus infections.
2. If you are afflicted with an infected wound, skin infection, open sores, diarrhoea or have a similar medical condition.

Symptoms

These include:

- diarrhoea/vomiting;
- septic cuts/sores/boils/whitlows (inflammation of fingers);
- discharges from the ear/eye/nose.

PERSONAL HYGIENE

All food handlers must maintain a high standard of personal hygiene at all times. Bacteria and germs are present on all parts of the body and may be easily transferred to food, risking infection.

How to help reduce the spread of bacteria and germs

- Bathe or shower daily/wash hair regularly.
- Tie hair back to prevent loose hairs falling into food.
- Brush teeth at least once a day.
- Keep nails clean and short – avoid wearing nail varnish.
- Men should shave daily and trim moustaches.
- Cosmetics should be used sparingly (perfumes might taint the food).
- Wear minimum jewellery (wedding rings acceptable) – jewellery harbours dirt and germs.

All the above are commonsense and are most likely already part of your daily routine.

COVERING CUTS AND OTHER WOUNDS

Cuts, burns and other sores should be covered with blue coloured regulation waterproof dressings that are easily visible should they fall into food. Finger stools or gloves, which must be worn over cuts to the fingers or hands will need to be replaced regularly as they have a tendency to encourage perspiration.

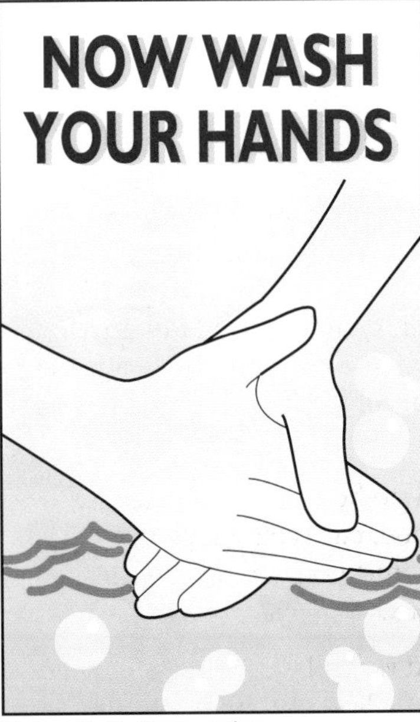

Figure 7 Hygiene notice

NOTE: Smoking is strictly prohibited in food preparation and cooking areas.

PREVENTING CROSS CONTAMINATION

- Hands and fingernails should be kept scrupulously clean.
- Fingernails should be kept short.
- Avoid wearing nail varnish (it chips easily and may fall into food).

Always wash hands with a bacterial soap, hot water and a nail brush:

- before commencing work;
- after handling waste;
- after handling raw or cooked food;
- as often as possible in between tasks;
- after using the toilet;
- after smoking.

Always:

- avoid touching the mouth/ears/nose when handling food;
- use a clean sterilised spoon when sampling/tasting each food;
- avoid wearing kitchen attire anywhere other than in the kitchen.

CLOTHING

The Food Hygiene (General) Regulations 1970 state that sufficient clean and washable overclothing must be worn when handling open food to protect the food from bacteria brought in from the outside.

Food handlers clothes must:

- be clean, lightly starched and well-ironed (the starch acts as a protective barrier should hot liquids fall on them);
- protect the body from the excessive heat of the kitchen and be adequate enough to protect from burns and scalds.

Clothes and footwear must comply with the following:

- They should be light in colour to reflect the heat, show up dirt easily and absorb perspiration.
- Sleeves should be long enough to protect the arms.
- Aprons should be worn to just below the knee to protect the trunk area and legs.
- Neck ties act as a band to soak up perspiration from the base of the neck (otherwise the perspiration would run down the back causing discomfort).
- Footwear should have non-slip soles and sturdy tops to protect the feet.

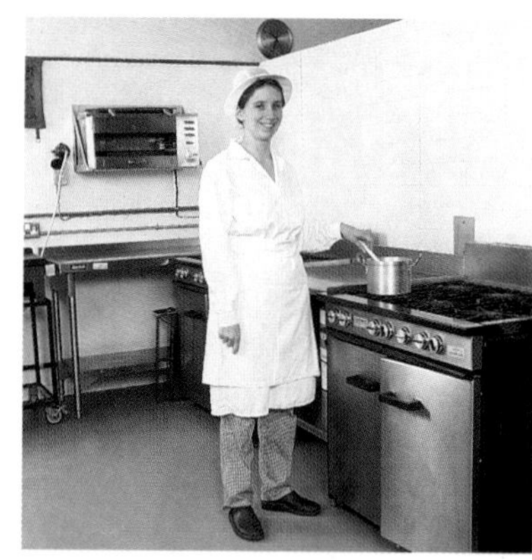

Figure 8 Front view of uniform

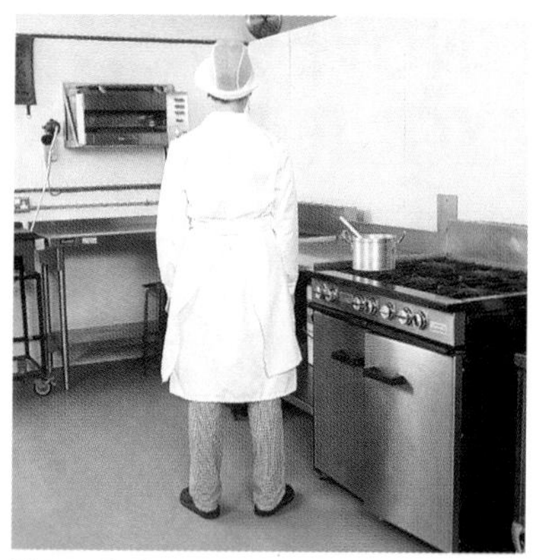

Figure 9 Rear view of uniform

Figure 10 Front view of uniform

Figure 11 Rear view of uniform

Activities

1. List six points of personal hygiene that should be observed to avoid the risk of bacteria contaminating food in the workplace
   (a)
   (b)
   (c)
   (d)
   (e)
   (f)
2. In your own words briefly outline your responsibilities under the Food Safety (General Food Hygiene) Regulations.
3. Find out where and from whom the 1995 Food Safety (General Food Hygiene) Regulations are available in your establishment:
4. In your own words, explain why it is important to:
   (a) shower/bathe regularly;
   (b) keep nails short and clean;
   (c) keep hair covered and tied back if long enough;
   (d) refrain from smoking in the kitchen;
   (e) always wash your hands after smoking.
5. What is the purpose of deodorant?

ELEMENT 2

Carry out procedures in the event of a fire

INTRODUCTION

A fire can easily start in a food preparation and cooking area and can result in serious injury or even death. It is therefore vital that appropriate steps are taken to prevent a fire occurring.

Every employer/employee should be fully aware of the correct procedures to be taken in the event of a fire and the appropriate course of action to be taken if they are to tackle the fire themselves. Never tackle a fire if there is any risk to yourself or others.

Fire procedure notices must be prominently displayed throughout the building which should include a route map for evacuation and clearly show the assembly point(s).

What to do in the event of a fire

- *Do not* panic – try to remain calm.
- Warn other people that there is a fire.
- Sound the fire alarm.
- If possible, turn off gas and electrical supplies.
- Close (do not lock) all doors/windows – this will help to slow the fire down.
- Evacuate in an orderly fashion, using the nearest safest exit to the assembly point.
- Do not use lifts.
- Contact the fire brigade. Do not wait for the fire to get out of control before calling the emergency services.
- If the fire is small and localised and can be extinguished quickly and safely, without risk to yourself or others, use the appropriate fire-fighting equipment to extinguish it .

Fire needs three components to spread

1. Fuel – something to burn
2. Air – oxygen to help burning
3. Heat – a source to create the flame or smoke

FIRE-FIGHTING APPLIANCES

Fire extinguishers

To extinguish a fire one or all of the above components must be removed. The most effective way to do this is to use the correct fire extinguisher. The most basic type of extinguisher is a water hose, though its use may be limited because:

(a) water conducts electricity (risk of electrocution);

(b) water would spread a fat fire – it is only suitable for fires involving wood, fabric or paper.

Requirements of fire extinguishers

- They must be manufactured in accordance with British Standards specifications (BS 4547).
- They must be colour-coded to indicate the type of fire they are best suited to extinguish.
- They must have instructions for use printed on the side.
- They must be checked regularly by trained personnel.

Figure 13 below shows types of fire extinguisher and their uses.

Extinguisher selection chart: types and uses
Fire classes according to BS 4547:1970

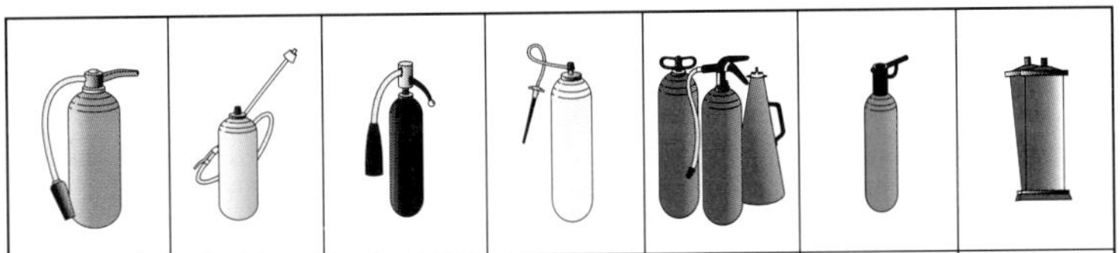

Dry Powder (blue*)	Dry Powder (special blue*)	CO_2 (Carbon Dioxide) (black*)	Foam (cream*)	Water (red*)	Halon (BCF§) (green*)	Fire blanket BS 6575: 1985
Class A: fires involving solid materials usually of organic nature in which combustion normally takes place with the formation of glowing embers, wood, papers, textiles etc. Extinguishing principles: water cooling or combustion inhibition.						
YES Excellent	NO	NO	YES	YES Excellent	YES	NO Small fires only
Class B: fires involving liquids or liquefiable solids, burning liquids, oil, fat, paint, etc. Extinguishing principles: flame inhibiting or surface blanketing and cooling.						
YES Excellent	NO	YES	YES Excellent	NO	YES	YES Excellent
Class C: fires involving gasses. Extinguishing principles: flame inhibiting.						
YES	NO	YES	YES	NO	YES	NO
Class D: fires involving metals, magnesium, sodium, plutonium, zirconium. Extinguishing principles: exclusion of oxygen and cooling.						
NO	YES Excellent	NO	NO	NO	NO	NO
Fires involving electrical hazards. Extinguishing principles: flame inhibiting						
YES	NO	YES Excellent	NO	NO	NO	YES

§ Bromochlorodifluoromethane.

Figure 12 Fire extinguishers

Sprinkler systems

Some establishments have automatic sprinkler systems that are situated at ceiling level to release water when the ceiling temperature rises above a pre-set level. Sprinkler systems are not practical in a kitchen because the extreme heat from cookers/hobs might inadvertently set them off.

Activity

1. Locate and read the Fire Notice in your establishment. In your own words, write your interpretation of it in the space below.

2. Sketch a map of your kitchen area in the workplace illustrating the shortest and safest route, from where you work, to the nearest assembly point.

3. Without looking at page 14, what would you do if a fire broke out in the kitchen.

ELEMENT 3

Maintain a safe environment for customers, staff and visitors

INTRODUCTION

Safety is paramount in the working environment and everyone should do their utmost to prevent accidents occurring. The Health and Safety at Work Act (HASAWA) (1974) states that both employers and employees must be aware of and comply with specific regulations. Its aim is to help prevent accidents happening while ensuring a safe working environment for staff, visitors and customers.

Many accidents are caused through negligence or unprofessional practices by the employer or employee which might be a result of insufficient or inadequate training. All employers/employees should have a sound knowledge of health and safety issues and have the appropriate training.

Every establishment should elect a Health and Safety Executive or representative and/or a committee whose job it is to make regular safety inspections of the building to ensure that there are no potential safety hazards. In the event of a safety hazard, it must be immediately reported to the appropriate personnel who must then take the appropriate action to rectify it.

In order to enforce the law, local authorities appoint Health and Safety Inspectors who have the authority to, for example, erect Prohibition Notices on the premises of persons who disregard the regulations and rules of the Act.

THE HEALTH AND SAFETY AT WORK ACT

Employers' responsibilities

Employees must, as far as is reasonably practicable:

- provide and maintain plants and systems of work that are safe and without risks to health;
- make arrangements to ensure safety and the absence of risks to health in connection with the use, handling, storage and transport of articles and substances;
- provide such information, instruction, training and supervision as will ensure the health and safety of employees, customers and visitors;
- maintain any place of work under their control in a safe condition without risks to health and provide at least statutory welfare facilities and arrangements.

Employees' responsibilities

As an employee you also have responsibilities and must:

- take reasonable care of your own health and safety;
- take reasonable care for the health and safety of other people who may be affected by what you do or neglect to do at work;
- cooperate with the establishment in the steps it takes to meet its legal duties;
- report any physical conditions or systems which you consider unsafe or potentially unsafe to a supervisor.

Safety hazards

If an area is deemed hazardous, for example, when there is liquid spilt on a floor or when there are loose tiles, the area should be cordoned off and an appropriate notice erected preventing people from using the area and causing harm to themselves.

When equipment/utensils are deemed a potential safety hazard, they must be removed and clearly labelled to prevent them from being used.

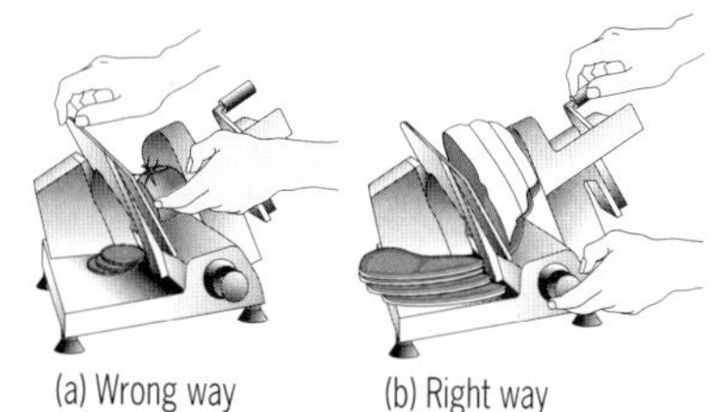

Figure 13 Using a gravity feed slicer

Safety

Before lifting, consider the following:

- Inspect the item for rough jagged edges, splinters, grease or other slippery surfaces.
- Wear the correct sized gloves for protection.
- Plan your route before you lift – know exactly where you are going.
- Clear any obstacle(s) from your path.
- Check the weight of the load.

To lift a heavy item

- Bend your knees, keeping your back and neck straight and your chin tucked in.
- Grasp the load firmly with your fingers and palms.
- Draw your arms in, close to the body.
- Stand slowly and lift smoothly, using your legs.

Never change your grip or twist your body when lifting heavy items – you might damage your back.

To unload a heavy item

- Bend the knees and place the load carefully on the floor or shelf (not on your fingers). Make sure that it is secure before letting go of your grip.

Figure 14 Placing saucepans on a stove – Right way

Figure 15 Placing saucepans on a stove – Wrong way

First aid

Should you be injured at work you must take immediate action. If it is a minor incident and can be dealt with by yourself, do so immediately. If not, your supervisor must be informed and you must go directly to the first-aider. If your injury is such that you are immobilized, a member of staff will summon immediate assistance for you.

Legal responsibilities of employers

- They should provide adequate first-aid equipment and facilities in the workplace.
- They should have trained personnel to administer first aid.
- They should ensure that first-aiders are kept up to date in their knowledge and skills and that they are regularly tested.

NOTE: In all instances an accurate record must be kept of any injury, occurrence or case of disease. This should include:

- **the date, time and place where the accident happened;**
- **personal details of affected person(s);**
- **description of event.**

Reporting hazards

As an employee in the hotel and catering industry you are governed by the Reporting of Injuries, Diseases and Dangerous Occurrences Regulations 1985 (RIDDOR) which came into effect in April 1986. The enforcing authority must be notified, without delay, of the following:

1. fatal injuries to employees or other persons in an accident connected with your business,
2. major injuries to employees or other persons in an accident connected with your business including:
3. any of the dangerous occurrences in the regulations. (These deal mainly with other industries.)

Prohibition
(No smoking)

WARNING
(Electrical hazard)

SAFE PROCEDURE
(first aid)

MANDATORY
(Now wash your hands)

FIRE
(Emergency exit)

Figure 16 Examples of hazard signs to be found in kitchen areas

For further information on current Health and Safety legislation contact your local authority or the Environmental Health Executive who will be able to help and advise.

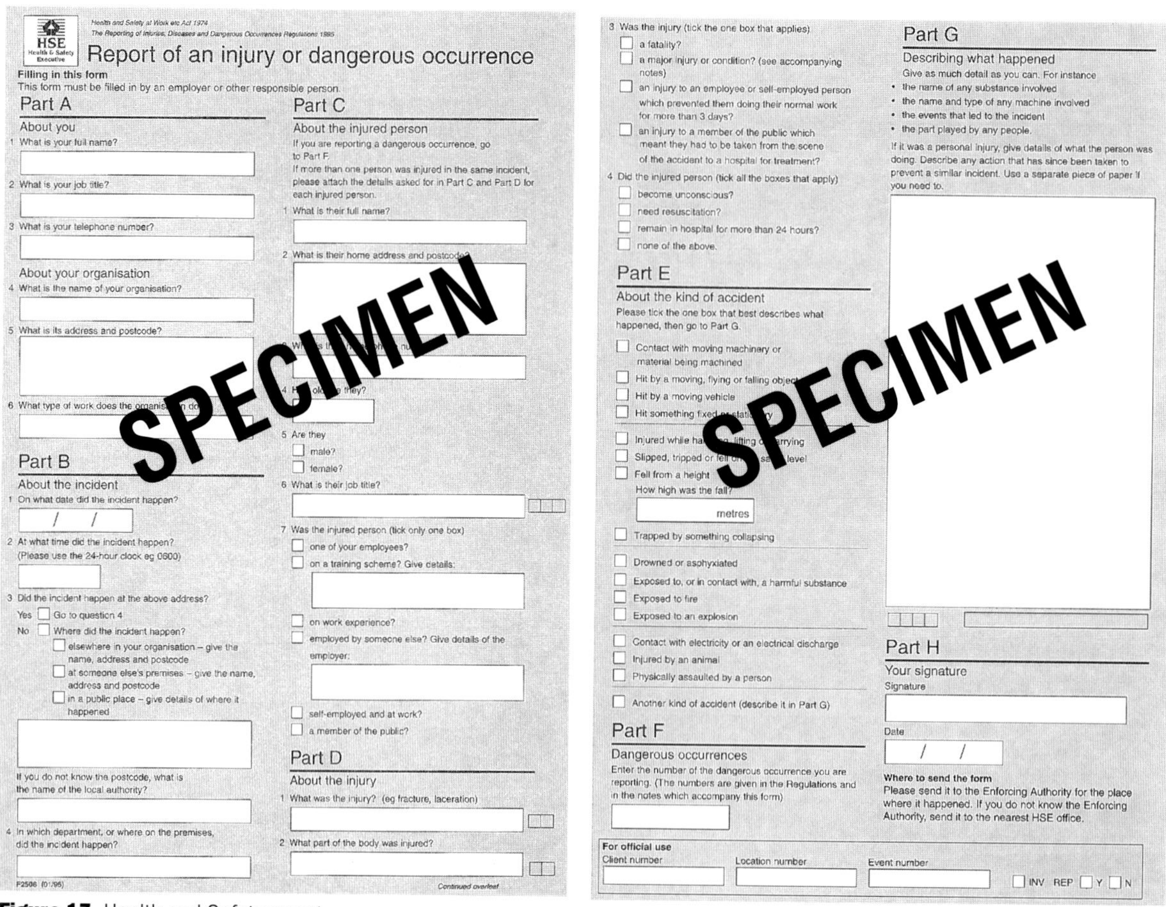

Health and Safety at Work etc Act 1974
The Reporting of Injuries, Diseases and Dangerous Occurrences Regulations 1995

HSE Health & Safety Executive

Report of an injury or dangerous occurrence

Filling in this form
This form must be filled in by an employer or other responsible person.

Part A

About you
1 What is your full name?
2 What is your job title?
3 What is your telephone number?

About your organisation
4 What is the name of your organisation?
5 What is its address and postcode?
6 What type of work does the organis... do?

Part B

About the incident
1 On what date did the incident happen? / /
2 At what time did the incident happen? (Please use the 24-hour clock eg 0600)
3 Did the incident happen at the above address?
Yes ☐ Go to question 4
No ☐ Where did the incident happen?
☐ elsewhere in your organisation – give the name, address and postcode
☐ at someone else's premises – give the name, address and postcode
☐ in a public place – give details of where it happened

If you do not know the postcode, what is the name of the local authority?
4 In which department, or where on the premises, did the incident happen?

F2508 (01/96)

Part C

About the injured person
If you are reporting a dangerous occurrence, go to Part F.
If more than one person was injured in the same incident, please attach the details asked for in Part C and Part D for each injured person.
1 What is their full name?
2 What is their home address and postcode?
3 What is their ... number?
4 How old are they?
5 Are they
☐ male?
☐ female?
6 What is their job title?
7 Was the injured person (tick only one box)
☐ one of your employees?
☐ on a training scheme? Give details:
☐ on work experience?
☐ employed by someone else? Give details of the employer:
☐ self-employed and at work?
☐ a member of the public?

Part D

About the injury
1 What was the injury? (eg fracture, laceration)
2 What part of the body was injured?

Continued overleaf

3 Was the injury (tick the one box that applies)
☐ a fatality?
☐ a major injury or condition? (see accompanying notes)
☐ an injury to an employee or self-employed person which prevented them doing their normal work for more than 3 days?
☐ an injury to a member of the public which meant they had to be taken from the scene of the accident to a hospital for treatment?
4 Did the injured person (tick all the boxes that apply)
☐ become unconscious?
☐ need resuscitation?
☐ remain in hospital for more than 24 hours?
☐ none of the above.

Part E

About the kind of accident
Please tick the one box that best describes what happened, then go to Part G.
☐ Contact with moving machinery or material being machined
☐ Hit by a moving, flying or falling object
☐ Hit by a moving vehicle
☐ Hit something fixed or stationary
☐ Injured while handling, lifting or carrying
☐ Slipped, tripped or fell on the same level
☐ Fell from a height
How high was the fall? metres
☐ Trapped by something collapsing
☐ Drowned or asphyxiated
☐ Exposed to, or in contact with, a harmful substance
☐ Exposed to fire
☐ Exposed to an explosion
☐ Contact with electricity or an electrical discharge
☐ Injured by an animal
☐ Physically assaulted by a person
☐ Another kind of accident (describe it in Part G)

Part F

Dangerous occurrences
Enter the number of the dangerous occurrence you are reporting. (The numbers are given in the Regulations and in the notes which accompany this form)

Part G

Describing what happened
Give as much detail as you can. For instance
- the name of any substance involved
- the name and type of any machine involved
- the events that led to the incident
- the part played by any people.

If it was a personal injury, give details of what the person was doing. Describe any action that has since been taken to prevent a similar incident. Use a separate piece of paper if you need to.

Part H

Your signature
Signature
Date / /

Where to send the form
Please send it to the Enforcing Authority for the place where it happened. If you do not know the Enforcing Authority, send it to the nearest HSE office.

For official use
Client number | Location number | Event number
☐ INV REP ☐ Y ☐ N

SPECIMEN

SPECIMEN

Figure 17 Health and Safety report

Activity

1. Make a chart of your kitchen area to include equipment, power points, gas valve and the electricity switch-off point.
2. List the hazard signs in your kitchen.
3. What procedures are taken in your working environment to report safety hazards?
4. The first-aider in my establishment is ....

   and can be contacted at ....
5. The Health and Safety Officer in my establishment is

   .... and can be contacted

   at ....

ELEMENT 4

Maintain a secure environment for customers, staff and visitors

INTRODUCTION

Security is vital on all premises and particularly in public places, for example, hotels and restaurants. Effective security practices help to reduce losses through theft and fraud. Theft may be stock, equipment, money or personal belongings. It is everyone's responsibility, as far as possible, to do their best to maintain a safe and secure working environment.

Sometimes, security personnel are employed specifically to protect staff, visitors, customers and premises.

SIMPLE SAFETY PROCEDURES

Protect your guests from dangers.

- Keep keys at the front desk or with authorised personnel.
- Return lost keys to the front desk.
- Recommend that guests remove valuables from cars.
- Report any suspicious persons.
- Don't remove duplicated keys without proper authorisation.
- Don't give out information about guests.
- Don't allow packages to be sent to guest rooms – deliver packages yourself.

Personal safety tips:

- Use the right tool for the job, and use it properly.
- Wear protective clothing and use appropriate equipment.

Unauthorised persons might be identified/recognisable by:

- not having the appropriate identification, e.g. name badges;
- asking for directions/access to restricted areas;
- carrying company property, e.g. computers, televisions, videos, or customers' property, e.g. clothes, suitcases, briefcases, in a area restricted to them;
- tampering or fiddling with locks to doors or windows.

If a person appears suspicious:

- approach them with caution;
- confront them in a polite manner and enquire as to whether you can help them;
- if, after confronting them, you still have your suspicions – report the incident to your supervisor.

Figure 18 Secure stores

SECURE AREAS

All kitchens have secured areas where food is stored. Freezers, fridges and dry stores should be kept locked and food should only be drawn from stores by the storekeeper with written permission from senior kitchen personnel. In the event of there not being a storekeeper, there should be an appointed person responsible for drawing stores.

Food is an expensive item and any pilfering will reduce profits, which may in turn result in the loss of jobs or, in extreme cases, be the cause of the business having to close down.

In the workplace there should be secure areas where staff can keep their personal belongings while they are working. These might be:

- secure lockers;
- a suitable room or cupboard.

NOTE: Always check windows, shutters, doors and any other rooms, for example, toilets, when locking up for the night. It only takes a moment for a thief to hide and lay in wait for an opportunity to commit a crime undisturbed.

KEYS

Hotels and restaurants all have some type of security system which might be a conventional lock and key or a computer-entry keycard. The following could help to reduce thieving;

- Never leave keys lying around or in locks.
- Always lock stores, fridges and freezers when leaving the premises.
- Only issue keys to responsible, authorised members of staff.
- Limit the number of, and keep a record of, all key holders.
- Never lend keys to unauthorised persons (staff or customers).

Figure 19 Lost property book

RECORDING LOST PROPERTY

If property is lost or mislaid there should be standard in-house procedures for reporting the incident. The following information is required:

- a full description of the missing item;
- the actual location of the item when it was reported missing;
- date and time loss was discovered;
- details of any action already taken to locate the missing item.

SUSPICIOUS ITEMS OR PACKAGES

Always be vigilant and cautious, and even more so in public areas. Be on your guard for any potentially suspicious packages/items which might be a dangerous device, for example, a bomb.

Reporting a suspicious item or package

If you have any suspicions regarding a package or item you should always:

- remain calm and do not panic, it might be an innocent situation; evacuation in a panic might result in injury to people;
- report it immediately to your supervisor who will take the necessary action, e.g. call the emergency services;
- if possible move people away from the area.

Never:

- under any circumstances attempt to move, touch or open a suspicious item or package

NOTE: If the emergency services are called they will ask:

- **for a description of the item/package;**
- **its exact location;**
- **what precautions, if any, have been taken (they might also offer immediate advice);**
- **the existence of any known hazards in the area, e.g. gas or oil;**
- **the reason for your suspicion;**
- **if there were any witnesses to the placing of the item/package.**

Activity

1. Find out what the security policy is in your establishment for:

   (a) customers' possessions

   (b) issuing keys

   (c) staff possessions

   (d) food stores

2. What security notices are posted in your workplace?
3. Does your establishment have set procedures for recording lost property and what are they?

NVQ 1+2

Create, develop and maintain effective working relationships

ELEMENT 1
Develop, establish and maintain working relationships with other members of staff

INTRODUCTION

The essence of an effective team is a good working relationship which is reflected in an effective operation and job satisfaction which in turn are reflected in the team's attitude and approach towards customers.

A good team member will:

- share information and learn from others;
- share the workload;
- work in an efficient and organised manner;
- be willing to share special skills and experience;
- achieve success and job satisfaction;
- be supportive, offer encouragement and give confidence to others.

DEVELOPING WORKING RELATIONSHIPS

Team members share a goal and should work together to achieve success. A team will only be successful if all members are totally committed and play their part. The golden rule to a successful harmonious team is to 'behave to others as you would like them to behave towards you'.

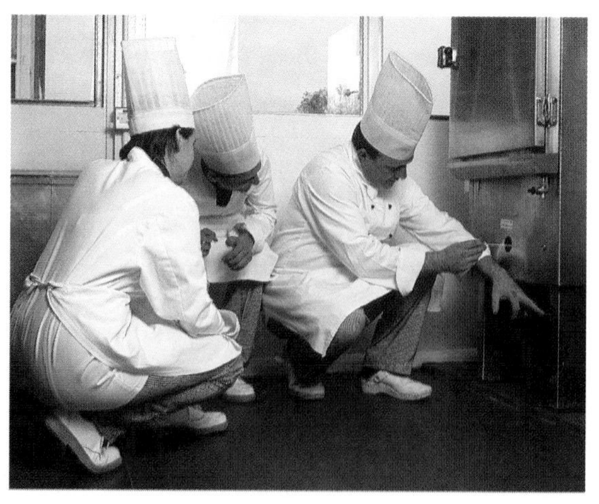

Figure 20 Chef explaining to 2 juniors

On occasion team members may disagree:

- about someone who is not pulling their weight;
- about working methods;
- about standards;
- because of personality clashes.

It is important that these situations are dealt with immediately. If not, they might disrupt the efficiency and standard of the work.

If there is a problem find out:

- exactly what the problem is;
- if it can be resolved by you;
- who can mediate.

If the standard of your work is questioned, i.e. it is not up to the required standard, would staff development help?

If the speed of the work is criticised, could the workload be too heavy?

If it is not your work schedule, are you happy with your job? Do you have personal problems?

Unhappiness makes it very difficult to concentrate. If the problems are at home, try to leave them there. Let the enjoyment of doing a good job take over.

If possible, you should always try and discuss your problems with your supervisor. Don't be afraid to ask. There are many employers who have trained counsellors who will be able to give you confidential, independent and professional advice.

Informal relationships of teams

Failing to work as a team may be due to:

- a breakdown in informal relationships;
- a clash of personalities.

Could it be because a member is:

- shy?
- noisy?
- thoughtless?
- annoying?
- interfering?
- standoffish?
- bad tempered?
- generally difficult to work with?

If you are the offender, you should try to 'play down' your worst points and consider others' feelings. If the behaviour of the group is not your style and you don't personally approve of it, don't be afraid to stick to your principles and conduct yourself according to you own standards.

Problems with the supervisor

These may arise:

- because of a personality clash;
- because you are not acting upon direct requests from the supervisor;
- because you have difficulty accepting constructive criticism.

TIP: If you are shy or find it difficult to mix with others, why not try and:

- **take up offers of friendship;**
- **if possible, make the first move, smile and say 'hello';**
- **listen to what others have to say and try to remember their interests;**
- **look friendly and interested.**

There is a solution to every problem so problems should always be dealt with immediately – don't leave them to escalate!

What can be done to rectify the problem? It may be necessary to seek the assistance of someone to mediate for you.

Figure 21 Preparation of meals in a team enviroment

MAINTAINING WORKING RELATIONSHIPS

Once you have developed and established a good working relationship with peers and supervisors, you should work at maintaining it.

Never:

- let your standards slip;
- be malicious or spiteful;
- take people for granted.

Always:

- show respect for others;
- look enthusiastic;
- be helpful.

Problems

If you do have a problem talk it over with someone – don't bottle it up. If a colleague has a problem, offer support. If they tell you personal information, never discuss it with others.

In all situations deal with problems in a professional and mature manner.

DISCRIMINATION

Discrimination can be defined as 'the unfavourable treatment of one person in relation to another'. It is an offence to discriminate.

Race relations Act 1976

Under the Race Relations Act it is unlawful for an employer to discriminate against any potential employee or job applicant on the grounds of race, colour, ethnic or national origins. It also applies to employees' conditions of employment, promotion opportunities, provision for training, transfers to other departments in the company, or in relation to benefits, facilities or services that are normally available to employees.

The Sex Discrimination Act 1975

The principles underlying the act are essentially similar to that of the Race Relations Act. Discrimination against individuals on the grounds of gender is unlawful in the areas of recruitment, terms of service or dismissal.

Activity

1. Write down what you consider to be your good points and your bad points. Make suggestions for rectifying the bad points.
2. How best do you think you could improve your performance in a team?
3. Find out from your company documents the disciplinary and grievance procedures in your establishment.
   - What are the standard procedures for discipline/dismissal?
   - What procedures do you follow in the event of a grievance?

ELEMENT 2

Receive and assist visitors

INTRODUCTION

Working in traditional kitchens there will probably be little contact with visitors. However, occasionally there will be times when you will come into contact with visitors, either on the telephone or in person. Visitors might include: company representatives, environmental inspectors, the Health and Safety Executive, visiting personnel or potential new staff.

When the first contact that the visitor has with the establishment is yourself, it is important that they be made to feel as welcome as possible. A good first impression will leave the visitor with a good lasting impression.

TELEPHONE SKILLS

Figure 22 Answering the telephone in restaurant reception

How to answer the telephone

Always answer the telephone in a professional and friendly manner as you will be reflecting the establishment's image and it is important to make a good impression.

You should be:

- efficient;
- courteous;
- attentive;
- responsive to the caller's needs and requests.

What to say

On answering the telephone greet the caller with 'Good morning/afternoon/evening', followed by the establishment's name and then your name.

At the end of your conversation always remember to thank the caller for telephoning.

Dealing with telephone calls/messages

Taking the time to write the message down accurately will help to avoid unnecessary confusion. There should be a system for recording telephone calls/messages, e.g. pre-printed telephone message pads.

Always find out the following details:

- the caller's name and telephone number;
- the time and date of the call;
- the actual message.

It is advisable to read back the details to the caller for confirmation before they ring off. Finally, sign or initial and date the message before passing it on to the appropriate person.

A point to note is that a message is no use if it is not passed on, e.g. an important visitor calling, a table reservation not being passed on or entered in the diary. This would cause embarrassment to both the visitor and the management and would make the establishment appear unprofessional. Always check that the message has been seen and actioned.

Figure 23 Greeting visitors at restaurant reception

VISITORS

Visitors should always be spoken to in a courteous manner and treated with respect. Good communication skills and confidence come with experience. Always refrain from using bad language, especially in the presence of guests.

Greeting visitors in person

Always acknowledge the visitor's presence. Make them feel important and welcome in your establishment.

Your personal appearance and communication either verbally or non-verbally, when greeting visitors, is of the utmost importance.

Always:

- be well groomed;
- appear confident;
- smile directly at visitors as you greet them.

A friendly smile, followed by 'Good morning/afternoon/evening, how may I help you?', should be used if the visitor is not known to you. Once you know the visitor's surname you can begin to use it. First names should be avoided though, as this may be considered 'over-familiar'.

Bidding the visitor farewell

Bidding the visitor farewell is as important as greeting them.

You should always say goodbye and thank the visitor for dining with you as they leave after a meal. A simple 'Goodbye (use surname/name if known), I hope to see you again' or 'I look forward to seeing you again' is sufficient.

Visitors who have communication difficulties

Addressing visitors with communication difficulties usually requires patience and tact.

When addressing a visitor who is hard of hearing, speak slowly and clearly and look directly at them – do not shout! You and the visitor may be able to lip read, but you should be prepared to repeat yourself if the visitor is unable to understand you the first time.

If a non-English-speaking visitor visits your establishment it is advisable, in the first instance, to check to see if any other member of staff speaks their language. Failing this, you should speak slowly and make gestures to indicate what you mean.

Always be attentive to your visitors and listen to what they have to say and do not be afraid to ask them to repeat themselves if you are unclear as to what was said the first time.

Figure 24 People seated in restaurant

DEALING WITH EMERGENCIES

The procedures for dealing with emergencies must be clearly documented and adhered to by all staff. If you are responsible for a visitor you must ensure that they are escorted from the building in the event of an emergency, e.g. a fire.

Never compromise visitors' safety.

COMPLAINTS

When dealing with complaints, particularly with aggressive or awkward visitors, it is essential that you use effective communication from the start as this may prevent the situation escalating into more serious issues. You should therefore choose the right words with care. Remember: all visitors should be treated with respect.

One of the main reasons for complaint is human error – and mistakes occur in all establishments from time to time.

TIP: Be patient – it takes time as well as tact to resolve problems.

Under no circumstances should any complaint, regardless of how insignificant it may appear, be taken lightly or in a flippant manner. All complaints must be taken seriously and must be dealt with politely and efficiently.

You must always:

- respond immediately and remain calm;
- listen carefully to the visitor – do not interrupt (even if you know the complaint should be dealt with by another member of staff);
- collect the facts and thank the visitor for bringing it to your attention;
- report the incident to the appropriate staff member.

In order to help prevent complaints arising treat all your visitors as VIPs.

Activity

1. Explain how you greet visitors on arrival to the establishment.
2. Practise with a fellow trainee in a role-play situation.
3. What are the procedures for dealing with aggressive visitors?
4. Compile a list of visitors who might call at your workplace and say who would greet and look after them.
5. Make a list of various types of incidents and where they might take place. Also list where they might occur in your establishment.
6. How would you deal with a visitor who has lost their property?

Clean food-production areas, equipment and utensils

ELEMENT 1
Clean food-production areas

INTRODUCTION

As with all food-related work it is essential that a high standard of hygiene be maintained at all times. All food-production areas: floors, walls, hand-basins, drains, gullies, taps and overflows, must be kept scrupulously clean, and shelves, cupboards and drawers should be thoroughly cleaned on a regular basis. All food-production areas require to be cleaned after each session to guard against the risk of contamination of food.

Personnel should be aware of the correct cleaning materials to use and their safe storage location. Debris and food wastage should be disposed of in accordance with the laid-down procedures for the establishment.

For further information contact the Department of Health (DoH) for a copy of their guidelines.

The principles of maintaining a safe and hygienic food-production area are mostly commonsense:

- clean the food-production area as frequently as possible and especially in between different jobs;
- only use the correct cleaning materials and detergents for their specific purpose.

CLEANING THE FOOD-PRODUCTION AREA

Certain food-production areas require cleaning at different times, for example, tables and work surfaces should be cleaned immediately after each use; whereas floors will normally require cleaning after the end of service or immediately after a spillage. There should be a regular schedule/rota for cleaning, which might be on a weekly or a fortnightly basis, to help reduce the build-up of bacteria. Kitchens should be 'deep-cleaned' during slack periods.

Figure 25 Cleaning surfaces

FOOD WASTE AND DEBRIS DISPOSAL

All food waste and debris must be disposed of in a safe and correct manner at regular intervals. Waste material may be divided into two categories, dry and wet, and should be disposed of in one of the following ways:

1. waste disposal units – food wastage;
2. rubbish/swill bins – wet wastage;
3. compactors – dry wastage.

Waste disposal units These are the most convenient and hygienic methods of disposal. They dispose of most rubbish with the exception of tough skins and bones.

Rubbish/swill bins These are usually situated outside the kitchen area. The waste material is stored, covered and collected on a regular basis. This method is somewhat outdated and is not recommended, due to the risk of contamination.

NOTE: All waste material must be stored in leak-proof containers ready for collection and the waste area must be cleaned regularly.

Compactors The compactor compresses materials, crushing the dry waste. This is a space-saving method, as the area necessary for storing waste is kept to a minimum.

All dry wastage (cans, tins, cardboard, paper etc.) should be bagged and collected by contractors.

CLEANING EQUIPMENT AND MATERIALS

Some cleaning materials contain harmful chemicals which might pose a health hazard. Cleaning materials must only be used for their specific job and the manufacturer's instructions must be read, clearly understood and followed at all times. It is essential that, where and when necessary, protective clothing is worn.

WARNING! Chemicals can be dangerous and must only be used according to the manufacturer's instructions and in a responsible manner. If chemicals are used incorrectly they could:

- **pose a health risk and be fatal;**
- **contaminate food.**

Activity

1. With the help of your supervisor, list the major cleaning agents used in your establishment and their specific use.
2. Fill in the chart below.

	Method of cleaning	Cleaning materials	Frequency
Walls			
Floors			
Tables			
Stores			
Cupboards			
Surfaces			
Drains/gullies			

ELEMENT 2

Clean food-production equipment

INTRODUCTION

Food-production equipment covers the larger items, for example, hobs, grills, deep fryers etc.

It is essential that all food-production equipment is kept as clean as possible at all times in order to minimise the risk of contamination.

Figure 26 Cleaning the hob/stove top

Figure 27 Cleaning the hob/stove top

Figure 28 Cleaning the grill

CLEANING OF FOOD-PRODUCTION EQUIPMENT

As with the cleaning of food-production areas the cleaning of food equipment is generally commonsense.

Always:

- follow the manufacturer's instructions (make sure they are clearly understood; if not, seek advice);
- check that the power source to the equipment is disconnected before cleaning
- clean any removable parts separately and carefully reassemble them after cleaning (when reassembled the equipment must be checked to ensure that it operates in a safe working manner);
- only use the cleaning materials for their specific job;
- clean equipment correctly and thoroughly; do not overlook legs, supports and pipes.

SAFETY

Particular items of equipment will require specialised cleaning, e.g. deep fryers and steamers. If in doubt, or unsure as to how to clean an item, always check with a supervisor or ask for assistance. The appropriate training must be given before staff are allowed to clean equipment.

- Always use the correct chemicals for the job – check to see if they must be diluted before use.
- Be vigilant when working with hot water and dishwashers.
- When necessary always wear the appropriate protective clothing.
- Report any defective equipment to a supervisor.
- Report any accidents immediately to a supervisor.
- Reassemble equipment properly and test to check that it is in working order before using it.

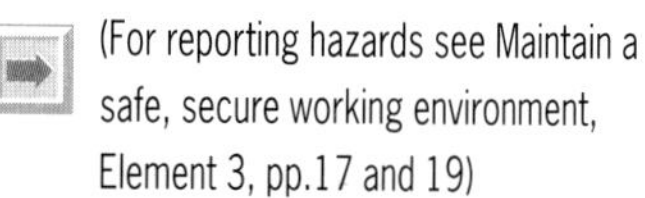
(For reporting hazards see Maintain a safe, secure working environment, Element 3, pp.17 and 19)

Activity

1. List items of equipment that require specialised cleaning.
2. Fill in the chart below.

	Method of cleaning	Cleaning materials	Frequency
Grills			
Hobs/stove tops			
Deep fryers			

ELEMENT 3

Clean food-production utensils

INTRODUCTION

As with the cleaning of food-production areas and equipment, it is essential that all utensils used in the production of food are kept and maintained in a clean and hygienic manner at all times. By doing so, the risk of cross-contamination is kept to a minimum.

Utensils cover the smaller items of equipment: pots, pans and cutlery etc.

UTENSILS

Kitchen utensils are made from a variety of materials. Some of the most common are:

- stainless steel
- aluminum;
- plastic;
- copper;
- cast iron;
- earthenware;
- plastic;
- wood.

WARNING! Never immerse utensils with wooden handles in hot water for excessive periods as this may cause splitting.

Figure 29 Range of utensils about to be cleaned

Chopping boards

Chopping boards are colour coded according to their uses as follows:

Red – raw meat

Blue – raw fish

White – bakery and dairy general

Green – salad

Yellow – cooked meat

Brown – vegetables

(For disposal of food waste see p. 33)

Cleaning utensils

Firstly, remove any excess waste from the utensil and dispose of it in a safe and hygienic manner. Then use one of the following methods:

1. two-sink method;
2. dishwasher method

The two-sink method The first sink is used for washing the utensils and the second sink for rinsing. The utensils are then allowed to dry. The sink used for rinsing should be kept at a temperature of between 75° and 85°C, to minimise the risk of contamination (the temperature also aids the drying process).

Dishwasher method The utensils are placed in special containers in baskets before being placed in the dishwasher. In the dishwasher they are sprayed with hot water and detergent, and then steam rinsed.

Figure 30 Two-sink method (A)

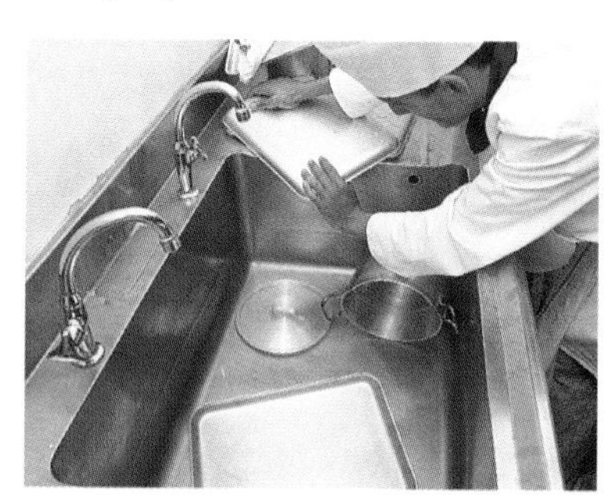

Figure 31 Two-sink method (B)

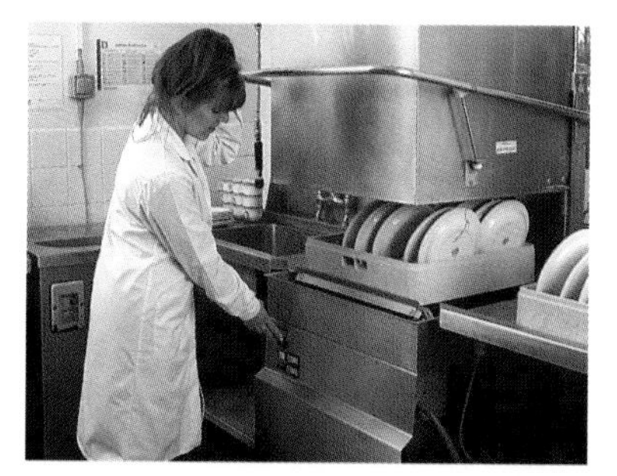

Figure 32 Dishwasher method

WARNING! Disinfectants should not be used when cleaning utensils. In their mildest form they will leave a taste which might taint food and in extreme cases could cause serious or fatal illness.

Drying/storing utensils

The best way to dry utensils is to leave them to dry naturally in a clean wire rack. A drying cloth might harbour dirt which could cross contaminate.

SAFETY

When cleaning utensils always:

- remove all excess waste with a scraper;
- use the correct cleaning detergents (when necessary, dilute them) and always read and follow the manufacturer's instructions;
- report and dispose of any defective utensils ;
- concentrate on the job in hand – especially when working with hot water or washing machines;
- check sinks for knives and sharp implements which might cause an accident;
- when necessary, wear protective clothing;
- report any potential dangers to the supervisor immediately.

WARNING! Be vigilant when working in hot/humid areas – it can be very tiring, and when tired, accidents are more likely to happen.

Activity

1. What is the best way to store utensils?
2. Fill in the chart below.

Equipment	Method of cleaning	Cleaning materials	Frequency
Spoons			
Ladles			
Whisks			
Cheese graters			
Sieves			
Saucepans			
Stock pots			

MAINTAIN AND HANDLE KNIVES

ELEMENT 1
Maintain knives

INTRODUCTION

Knives are the tools of the trade. Care should be taken to keep them sharp and in immaculate condition at all times. Knives are dangerous tools and it is therefore imperative that they are safely stored at all times and only used in a responsible manner.

CHOOSING A GOOD KNIFE

Knives should be purchased from a reputable and reliable manufacturer or dealer.

The most common material used for knives is steel, which is a mixture of at least 80% iron and up to 20% other elements.

Amongst metals, carbon steel takes the sharpest edge, and many chefs insist on it. However, carbon steel can rust, stain and pit easily. An alternative to carbon steel is high-carbon stainless steel, which takes almost as good an edge with the added bonus that it resists the corrosive effects of water, acid and salt.

Ideally, a knife blade should be forged, i.e. hammered into shape from hot metal – not stamped from a metal sheet. Forged blades take the sharpest edge if they have been expertly ground. The table below shows the advantages and disadvantages of various types of metal.

Metal	*Advantages*	*Disadvantages*
Carbon steel	Takes and holds an excellent edge	Discolours very easily, even while in use, e.g. on onions
Alloy or carbon steel		Not practical in a humid climate, especially salt air Not practical for use with high acid foods e.g. lemons
Stainless steel	Resistant to abrasion	Difficult to sharpen, does not take and edge easily
4% minimum and/or nickel	Resistant to corrosion and discolouring High tensile strength	Difficult to maintain an edge
High carbon stainless steel	Takes an edge better than stainless steel May be used in any climate and on all foods Does not rust or pit	Special care and attention must be taken to use the correct sharpening steel (hard)
Super stainless alloy steel	More for appearance than functional	Very hard, making it almost impossible to sharpen Not recommended

Finally, when choosing a knife make sure it feels comfortable in the hand. Mimic the motions of peeling, slicing and cutting; the knife should be comfortable and easy to manipulate.

PARTS OF THE KNIFE

Tang

The metal end that fits into the handle and balances and supports the blade is called the tang. A full tang, which conforms exactly to the shape of the handle, is the strongest type and is essential in heavy-duty cutlery, e.g. butchers' and chefs' knives. Some knives have 'rat-tails' tangs, which are as long as the handle, though only half its height. These are sufficient for small knives such as paring knives.

Check a knife by balancing it on a finger placed where the blade ends and the handle begins. The handle should feel heavy with the blade rising slightly, which indicates that the knife is balanced. The knife should then be comfortable to control. The handle should always be firmly secured to the tang with rivets – never purchase a knife if its tangs are held in place with an adhesive.

Both edges of the tang and the faces of the rivets should be flush with the surfaces of the handle. If these protrude the knife will be uncomfortable to hold and if they are recessed, the holes will collect grease and grime which is a health threat.

Figure 33 Plastic knife handle

Handle

Ideally the handle should be made of a non-slipping hardwood, which should not conduct heat and cold. Plastic, unlike wood, is impervious to germs and moisture. However, it may become slippery and can be damaged by intense heat. Some knives with wooden handles are impregnated with plastic which seals the pores, making the handles impervious to germs and moisture.

In order to comply with hygiene regulations all chefs' knives should have composition handles (plastic/plastic coated).

CARE OF THE CUTTING EDGE

Knives should be sharpened with either:

- a steel;
- a carborundum stone (flat whetstone);
- a rotary mechanical stone.

Figure 34 Steel

Steel

A steel is mainly used for the day-to-day sharpening of blades.

Where possible, use a steel with a guard. Hold the steel with the thumb safely tucked behind the guard. If using a steel with no guard, always draw the knife away from you. Use a feather-like stroke rather than a grinding action and work at a 45° angle drawing almost the entire length of the blade edge along the length of the steel evenly and consistently. Use five to six strokes on each side of the blade because 'over steeling' will damage the edge. Be careful not to hit the blade against the guard as this will damage the blade.

TIP: Always keep knives sharp, enabling them to carry out their job effectively. Sharp knives are less dangerous than blunt knives.

Carborundum stone

The carborundum stone is used for the periodic sharpening of blades, however it should not be used too often or it will wear down the blade.

Always draw the blade of the knife away from the hand holding the stone. Remember that not all stones have a safety guard. Proceed as for using a steel.

Rotary stone

The rotary stone is a round, wheel-shaped, mechanised version of the carborundum stone. Usually there are two wheels, one rough for making the initial edge and second smooth wheel for finishing.

Knives must always be wiped clean after sharpening or loose metal filings from the blade could contaminate food.

Cleaning

Knives should be thoroughly cleaned and sterilised as often as possible, especially between jobs, to minimise the risk of cross-contamination.

The blade should be wiped by hand using a damp cloth. Wipe from the back edge of the blade, not the cutting edge and wipe away from the body.

Carbon blades may be cleaned with scouring powder.

Never:

- leave a knife in a washing-up sink to soak; it is a safety hazard;
- put a knife in a dishwasher – the high temperature will damage handles;
- leave knives in a cluttered drawer .

COOKING TIP: Whenever possible, use separate sets of knives for cooked and uncooked foods. Colour-coded knife sets, along with colour-coded chopping boards, are the ideal solution.

Storage of knives

Knives should be stored in a case or box, out of harm's way; in a slotted holder; or on a magnetic rack in the kitchen.

Where possible, only have the knife you are using out on the work surface, with the others safely stored. Ensure that the working area is free from debris which could conceal the knife.

Activity

1. What is the ideal solution for preventing cross-contamination of foods when using knives?
2. How often should knives be cleaned?
3. Why are knives kept sharp?

INTRODUCTION

The tip, the centre of the cutting edge and the heel are each best suited to specific tasks.

- The tip of the knife should be used for delicate operations.
- The centre of the cutting edge should be used for general work and long strokes.
- The heel should be used for the heaviest tasks.

SAFE WORK PRACTICES

In order to prevent accidents with knives to yourself or others always:

- carry knives with the point facing downwards;
- concentrate on the task in hand;
- use the knive for its specific job;
- clean knives after use;
- store knives in a protective container;
- keep knives sharp and in a good, clean condition;
- use knives in a responsible manner.

Never

- leave knives unattended on kitchen surfaces;
- hand a knife to another person (place it on a flat surface for them to pick up)
- carry knives around the kitchen;
- try to catch a falling knife;
- run your fingers down the blade to check if it is sharp;
- allow a knife to hang over the edge of a work surface;
- attempt to cut an item of food in the palm of the hand;
- use a knife if feeling unwell.

TIP: If it is unavoidable to carry a knife in the kitchen, carry it by the side of – and away from – the body, ensuring that the point is facing down.

POSTURE AND POSITIONING

It is important to be properly positioned when handling a knife as it increases comfort and efficiency. Stand upright with both feet firmly on the ground and with the back straight. Never bend over as this can cause damage to the back.

CUTTING TECHNIQUES

When cutting with a knife there will be one hand which acts as the guiding hand. Always take care when positioning and moving the guiding hand for two reasons:

1. to prevent the item slipping while it is being cut and avoid harming yourself or others; the first cut on a round item of food should be to provide a flat base for stability.
2. to control the size of the finished item.

The first knuckle of the third finger of the guiding hand should touch the side of the knife blade after each end cut is made. The guiding hand should then move back; the distance moved will determine the thickness of the cut item. The process can then be repeated. See figure 35.

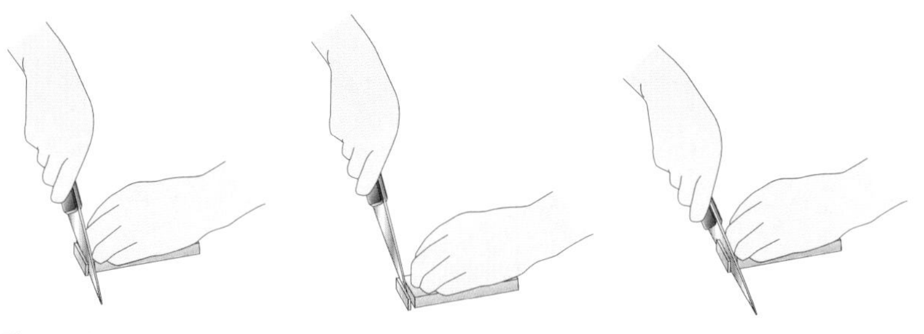

Figure 35 Guiding hand

Cutting surfaces

A cutting surface should be made from a resilient material. A hardened plastic is best. It should be completely flat and secure. Some chefs place a dampened cloth or kitchen paper underneath the cutting surface to ensure that it does not move when in use.

Hygiene and cleanliness

NOTE: Never place hot items on a plastic chopping board – it will warp or melt.

- Always have a clean, unlittered board to work on.
- Remove prepared food and set it aside.
- Keep prepared foods separate from unprepared foods.
- Chopping boards should not be put through the dishwasher or placed in very hot water; this will warp them.
- If boards warp they will become dangerous to use and must be discarded.
- Ensure that the work surfaces comply with hygiene regulations and are impervious.
- If damaged, boards should be discarded.

TYPES OF KNIVES

Boning knife. This is a razor-sharp knife with a curved point used for the boning of raw or cooked meat. All work carried out with this knife is done with or near the tip of the knife blade. The handle has a notch to prevent the user's hand slipping onto the blade.

Butcher's knife. The butcher's knife has a long scimitar-like blade and a sharp point. It is used to make incisions in larger cuts of meat, e.g. steaks.

Carving (slicing) knife. Hot and cold meats are sliced with the carving knife. It has a flexible, long and narrow blade which bends when carving poultry. The tip is rounded and blunt so that it does not tear thin slices.

The cook's knife. This is a rigid, irregular blade with slightly curved edges for chopping and dicing food. For effective chopping the knife is rocked, using the whole length of the blade. This is achieved by keeping the point of the knife on the cutting surface and rocking the cutting edge on the food.

Filleting knife. The filleting knife is used for skinning and filleting fish. It has a long flexible carbon steel blade, approximately 155 mm long.

Oyster knife. This is a short, rigid, sharp-tipped, dull-edged knife. The knife tip is placed in the crack near the mollusc's hinge and severs the muscle holding the shell closed. The knife is then twisted to open the shell. The dull edge of the blade is used to remove the flesh.

Palette knife. The palette knife has a rounded, non-cutting edge. It is used for scraping bowls, trays and slabs. It may also be used for turning, spreading, smoothing and finishing surfaces, e.g. icing cakes.

Serrated knife. The serrated blade is used for cutting bread, slicing soft fruits and carving meat.

Vegetable knife/paring knife. A small knife with a 9 cm to 10 cm blade. It is used for trimming and shaping vegetables.

Knives/Tools
1 Cleaver
2 Large chef's knife
3 Boning knife
4 Carving fork
5 Trussing needle
6 Small cook's knife
7 Turning knife
8 Vegetable knife
9 Boning knife
10 Steel
11 Serrated knife
12 Cook's knife
13 Filleting knife

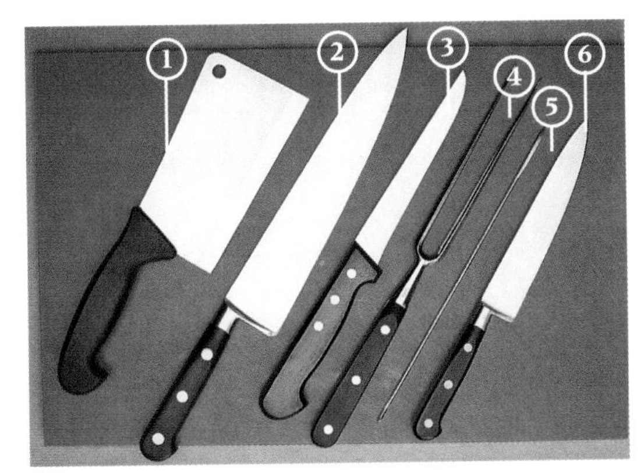

Figure 36 Knives–cleaver etc

Figure 37 Knives–cook's knives

MISCELLANEOUS TOOLS

Channel cutter/knife Used to make grooves in vegetables for decorating.

Parisienne cutter (parisienne). Half-moon-shaped cutters used for making ball-shaped vegetables and fruits.

Peeler. Used for removing the skin of vegetables and fruits.

Poultry secateurs/scissors. Special shears with curving blades, one of which is serrated for cutting through the cartilage and joints of poultry. Poultry shears should be at least 25cm long for use on large birds.

Roasting fork. A two-pronged fork used for lifting and steadying roast meats and poultry.

Steel. A carbon steel bar with a wooden or a polypropylene handle. The latter is preferred as it is considered more hygienic. It is used for sharpening all steel knives. A ring attached to the base of the handle enables it to be hung up when not in use.

Trussing needle. The trussing needle is used for securing joints of meat, poultry and game during cooking. It is a long steel pin with a pointed end and a hole in the other end for threading string through.

Zester. A sharp-edged holed instrument used to produce slivers of oranges and lemons.

1 Turning knife
2 Parisienne ball
3 Vegetable knife
4 Peeler
5 Zester

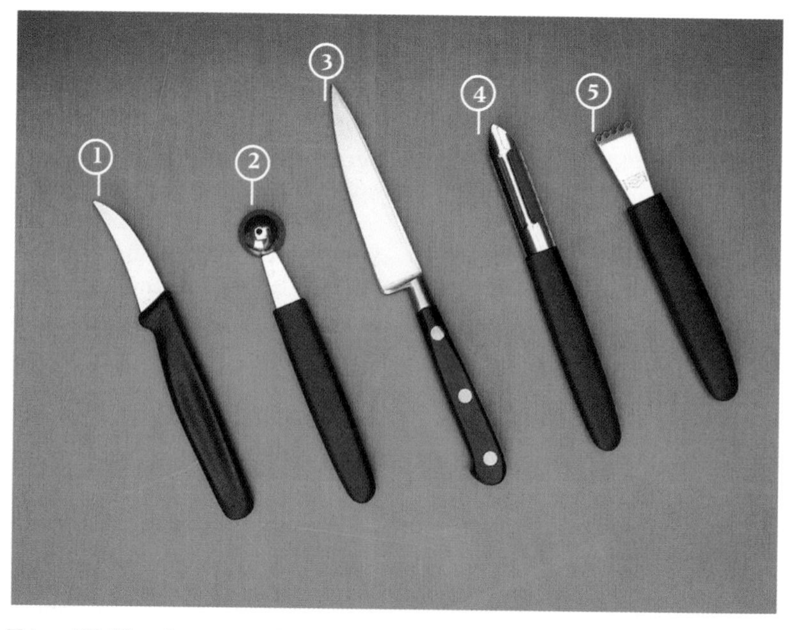

Figure 38 Miscellaneous tools

NOTE: Always take precautions, i.e. avoid dripping blood on to food to prevent the contamination threat from HIV, hepatitis etc.

FIRST AID FOR KNIFE ACCIDENTS

If a chef cuts his/her hand it is imperative to cease work and seek immediate first aid or medical assistance.

Figure 39 First-aid box (closed)

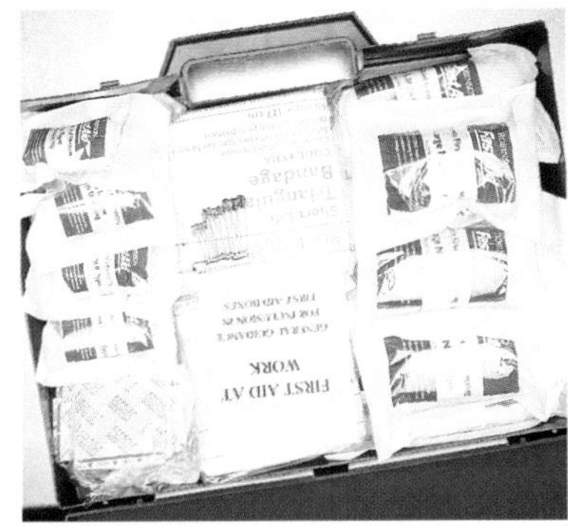

Figure 40 First-aid box (open)

Minor cuts

Wash the cut thoroughly under running water in a handwash basin. Dry with a clean cloth and apply antiseptic to the wound before covering with a blue (regulation) waterproof dressing. If necessary, re-dress.

Serious cuts

Wash the cut thoroughly, then cover with a dry, clean cloth. Apply pressure (direct or indirect) to the cut to stop or slow the bleeding and seek medical assistance immediately.

Activity

Choose four dishes from your cookery book and make a list of the tasks and the most suitable knife for the job.

Dish	Task	Most suitable knife/knives
1		
2		
3		
4		

Maintain and promote hygiene in food storage, preparation and cooking

ELEMENT 1

Maintain and promote hygiene in food storage

INTRODUCTION

Total commitment to high standards of hygiene must be maintained at all times by food handlers in preparation and cooking areas to prevent the possibility of cross-contamination.

PERSONAL HYGIENE GUIDELINES

Wash your hands frequently, but always wash your hands:

- after going to the toilet;
- in between jobs;
- after handling raw foods;
- before touching cooked foods;
- after smoking;
- after using chemicals, fluids and other cleaning materials;
- after handling and disposing of waste materials.

WARNING! Never allow raw food to come into contact with cooked food, otherwise it might contaminate the cooked food and poison it.

STORING FOOD

Food is an expensive commodity and is vulnerable to deterioration if it is not stored correctly. Deliveries should be checked immediately and correctly stored away – not left to spoil. If the food is unsatisfactory on delivery, return it to the supplier who will issue a credit for it. Always store food separately from cleaning materials.

Frozen foods

Check frozen food on arrival with a temperature probe to ensure that it has not started thawing; it should not be above –12°C. Provided it is at the correct temperature it can then be stored.

Chilled foods

As with frozen foods, chilled foods should be checked with a temperature probe on arrival (5°C or below). The food should be carefully organised in the refrigerator to prevent cross-contamination: raw foods on the bottom (not touching cooked foods) and cooked foods wrapped up, labelled, dated, given a brief description of contents and initialled, before being stored on the upper shelves.

(For further information see Cook-freeze food, p. 324)

TIP: Refrigerator temperatures should be checked at least twice a day, every day, with an appropriate thermometer and the details accurately recorded on a chart. Any faults must be immediately reported to the supervisor to action. (See Figure 42 below.)

Figure 41 Temperature probe

Week comm		Temp.	Init.	Temp.	Init.	Temp.	Init.	Temp.	Init.	Temp.	Init.	Temp.	Init.	Temp.	Init.	Temp.	Init.	Temp.	Init.	Temp.	Init.
MON	a.m.																				
	p.m.																				
TUE	a.m.																				
	p.m.																				
WED	a.m.																				
	p.m.																				
THUR	a.m.																				
	p.m.																				
FRI	a.m.																				
	p.m.																				
SAT	a.m.																				
	p.m.																				
SUN	a.m.																				
	p.m.																				

Figure 42 Temperature control chart

ORGANISING THE REFRIGERATOR

A fridge should never be overfilled, otherwise it will not function effectively. A fridge works on the principle of chilled air circulating around the unit. A chiller unit at the top cools the air which sinks to the bottom and warm air rises to replace it. If circulation is blocked, either by a large item of food or a large tray covering the entire surface of the shelf, the cold air becomes trapped and the food beneath the blockage will spoil, posing a health risk.

WARNING! Never place hot food in a fridge as this will warm up the other foods and spoil them. It may also burn out the fridge chilling motor.

Figure 43 Polycarbonate gastronorm containers in a fridge

Fresh fish storage. Ideally, fish should be stored in trays on ice in a separate refrigerator away from other foods.

Vegetable storage. Vegetable stores should be cool and well ventilated. Many establishments have specific stores that maintain a constant, even temperature.

Dairy product storage. Dairy products should be refrigerated as soon as possible.

CONTAMINATION

No animals, e.g. cats, dogs or birds, should be allowed into a kitchen area as they are carriers of harmful bacteria that will contaminate foods. Occasionally, vermin, such as mice, rats, cockroaches or flies find their way into food cartons and even into the food itself. Vermin also carry harmful bacteria and are a very serious source of food infection. Flies may be easily exterminated; however, other vermin are not. Any case of pest infestation should be dealt with by a professional pest control company.

Tell tale signs of infestation

- Rats and mice: Droppings, pungent odour of urine, holes, gnawing marks on food stock, grease marks on skirting boards.
- Cockroaches: Liquid droppings which give off a nauseating odour.
- Flies: Fly blow (eggs).

Activity

1. Why is it important to maintain high standards of hygiene in food storage areas?
2. Why are animals prohibited in kitchen areas?

ELEMENT 2

Maintain and promote hygiene in food preparation and cooking

INTRODUCTION

All foods must be handled carefully to prevent cross-contamination during preparation, cooking, cooling and storage. Food poisoning may occur even when the food has been prepared in clean kitchens. Cooked food must not come into contact with raw food, especially meat and poultry after cooking or during storage, nor should it come into contact with unwashed equipment or utensils that have been used for the preparation of raw foods. Under the 1995 General Food Hygiene regulations, individuals working in a food preparation and cooking environment must:

- maintain a high level of personal cleanliness and general hygiene throughout the preparation and cooking of food;
- routinely wash their hands;
- refrain from smoking in food areas;
- report any illness (infected wounds, skin infections, diarrhoea or vomiting) to a line supervisor/manager;
- be appropriately supervised and trained in food hygiene matters to a level appropriate to their job;
- wear suitable clean clothing and, where appropriate, protective clothing.

Figure 44 Uniform (front)

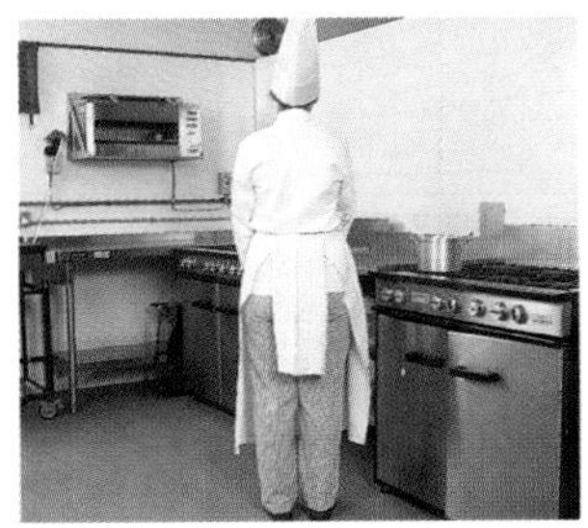

Figure 45 Uniform (rear)

HANDLING FOOD

Food should not be handled excessively, otherwise the risk of cross-contamination is increased.

To reduce unnecessary handling of foods:

- plan and organise your work, weigh ingredients, work to a recipe, work to a time plan;
- work to a routine.

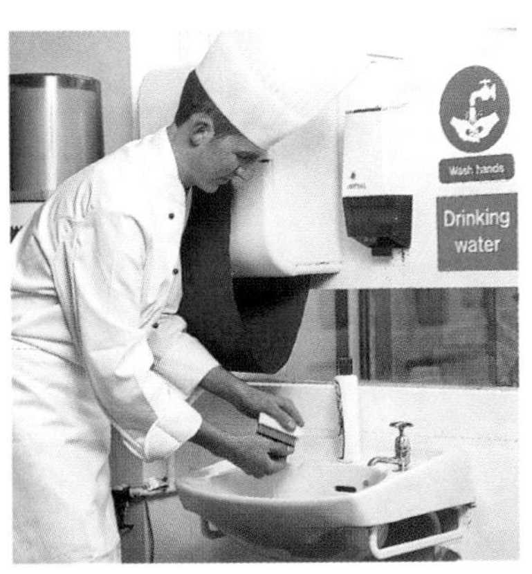

Figure 46 Washing hands

CORRECT METHOD OF WASHING HANDS

Always wash hands thoroughly, not just a quick rinse!

- Wash under warm, running water with an anti-bacterial soap.
- Be sure to clean all parts of your hands and wrists.
- Rinse thoroughly in clean water.
- Pay particular attention to fingernails and remove any food particles which collect underneath.

STORAGE OF FOOD IN THE KITCHEN

On no account should raw or cooked foods be left in the preparation and cooking area for longer than is required. Food left for any length of time in the extreme temperature of the kitchen will result in food poisoning bacteria multiplying rapidly. Only remove from the fridge what you require for immediate use. When preparing large quantities of food, do so in batches and return it to the fridge immediately, once it has been prepared and cooled sufficiently.

The 1995 Food Hygiene Regulations state that it is the individual's duty to protect food and ingredients against contamination, which is likely to render the food unfit for human consumption or pose a health hazard. If you have any suspicions regarding ingredients or food, report them to the supervisor/line manager who will be reponsible for disposing of the food.

CONTAMINATION THREATS/FOOD POISONING

Situations where food might be contaminated:

- excessive handling;
- bad storage;
- insufficient cooking.

See the food contamination chart on page 53 for full details on organisms causing food poisoning, types of food affected and symptoms.

COOLING COOKED FOOD

(For more information, *see* Cook-chill foods, pp. 309–18)

Cooked food to be stored should be cooled properly (below 5°C) within 45 minutes of removing it from the heat source, covered and labelled appropriately. Ideally cooked food should be cooled in a blast chiller.

The correct method of storing cooked food is in a fridge between 3°C and 5°C or in a freezer at –18°C or below.

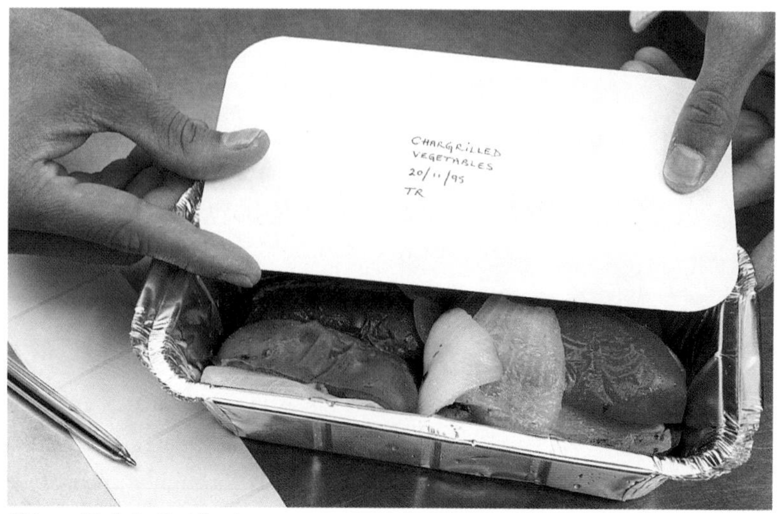

Figure 47 Labelling food

Food contamination conditions leading to food poisoning

Food poisoning organism	Incubation period	Symptoms	Duration of illness	Temperature required to kill	Dangerous practices	Foods involved
Salmonella	12 to 24hrs	Diarrhoea, abdominal pain, usually fever	1 to 7 days	70 °C for 15 min	Cross infection from raw to cooked foods. Poor personal hygiene. Infection from carriers. Inadequate defrosting of meat and poultry	Meat, poultry, eggs, unpasteurised milk, meat pie and left-overs
Clostridium perfringens	8 to 22hrs	Diarrhoea, abdominal pain, no fever	12 to 24hrs	Excess of 100°C	Meat dishes, gravies left to cool slowly. Inadequate reheating. Contamination from soil and from human carriers	Meat, poultry, meat dishes, particularly reheated dishes. Spices often contaminated
Bacillus cereus toxins	Two types: 1 to 5hrs	Nausea, vomiting stomach cramps	6 to 24hrs	Excess of 100°C	Holding cooked rice and meat dishes at warm temperatures for long periods	Rice, cornflour, meat dishes. Spices contaminated
	2.8 to 16hrs	Abdominal pain, diarrhoea	12 to 24hrs			
Staphylococcus aures	1 to 6hrs	Vomiting, stomach cramps	6 to 24hrs	70 °C for 15 min	Food handled by staff suffering from skin infections, uncovered cuts. Cross infection from raw to cooked foods. Coughing or sneezing near food. Dirty towels, equipment, piping bags	Food handled in preparation, cold sweets, cream fillings, custards, sandwiches, unpasteurised milk or cream
Clostridium botulinum	12 to 36 hrs	Double vision, difficulty in swallowing and breathing	Death in 1 to 8 days or slow recovery over 6 to 8 months	121 °C for 5 min	Using blown or damaged cans of food. Refreezing vegetables. Keeping smoked fish or vacuum packed fish or meat in warm temperatures	Insufficiently heat-treated, or defective commercially canned meat, fish or vegetables. Raw fish

THAWING FROZEN FOOD

Never allow food to thaw in the kitchen area. The correct method is to place the food on a drip tray and allow it to thaw slowly in a fridge.

When thawing frozen poultry or meat always follow the manufacturer's guidelines (on the packaging) or refer to a freezer manual.

Activity

1. Explain why good personal hygiene is essential when handling and storing food.
2. What checks are carried out in your establishment to ensure that commodities are in good condition on delivery?
3. Explain why food items should be defrosted properly.
4. Why is it important for a food handler to keep cuts and grazes covered at all times?
5. Explain why food should be handled as little as possible.

2 Level 1 Food preparation and cooking

This section of the book covers various cooking processes, such as baking, boiling, frying, grilling, microwaving, poaching and steaming. It also deals with the preparation of vegetables and fruit, sandwiches and rolls, and reconstituted and convenience foods. The units cover Level 1.

CONTENTS

Prepare and microwave food

ELEMENT 1

Prepare food for microwave cooking

COOKING TIP: Microwaves can only effectively penetrate 4cm into the food.

INTRODUCTION

Microwave cookery takes place in a specially designed electric oven. Food is cooked or reheated by microwaves (electro-magnetic waves) which penetrate the food causing water molecules in the food to oscillate (vibrate) and cook or reheat the food.

Microwave ovens come in different sizes with varying levels of power. Additions to the standard microwave model include browning elements, stay-hot controls, combination cookers (microwave plus forced air convection).

Combination ovens overcome the limitations of simple microwave ovens by cooking in a conventional mode at the same time. This allows the food to be browned and the surface to have a crisp finish, something an ordinary microwave cannot do. Combination ovens have gas burners, electrical elements and/or infra-red grills.

Microwave ovens are versatile and have many uses:

1. As a quick method of cooking raw foods.
2. To accelerate the defrosting cycle of frozen foods.
3. Reheating par-cooked, pre-cooked or pre-assembled foods.
4. As a fast method of heating liquids.

Never place the following in a microwave oven:

- china and earthenware with metallic decorative trimmings;
- ceramics containing oxide;
- lead crystal or antique glass;
- polythene bags;
- regular plastic wrapping film (high temperatures may release harmful substances into food); only use microwave wrapping;
- waxed paper;
- certain plastic and melamine (always check manufacturer's instructions before using);
- containers with glued handles.

Power and setting of microwave ovens

Microwave ovens can have as many as ten settings but the three basic settings are:

- **High power:** full power for general purposes to cook and reheat most foods quickly;
- **Low power:** a lower setting used to cook delicate foods;
- **Defrost:** used to thaw food. It is a full power setting but only in short bursts lasting approximately 30 seconds on then 30 seconds off with the cycle repeating according to the required setting.

NOTE: Always check the manufacturer's user manual to find the correct settings for the microwave oven.

Figure 48 Microwave oven

The power rating of a microwave oven is given in watts and kilowatts (1000 watts). Microwaves are produced by a component called a magnetron and the higher the wattage the more microwaves the magnetron will produce.

Power outputs range from 400 watts to 800 watts for the domestic or small industrial ovens, up to 1 kw (1000 watts) to 2 kw (2000 watts) used in larger catering units.

Every microwave oven has a metal plate or metallic sticker giving the output power in watts which corresponds to the power of the oven.

TIP: If you are unsure of the microwave oven power output, contact the manufacturer.

EQUIPMENT

Figure 49 Shallow microwavable dish

When using a microwave it is important to choose the right shaped container to enable microwaves to penetrate the food:

- plates and dishes with narrow rims and round sides;
- large shallow dishes to cook solid foods;
- jugs or tall containers to heat liquids only.

The following points should be considered when using equipment made from various materials.

Metal When microwaves come into contact with metal they are reflected. Microwaves cannot pass through metal so any food in a metal container will simply not be cooked.

Figure 50 Shallow dish

China, earthenware and glass China, earthenware and glass are very good transmitters of microwaves because the microwaves pass directly through to the food. China and earthenware should have no metallic or decorative edging.

Plastics and cardboard There are many forms of plastic and nearly all will transmit microwaves. Check to ensure that they are suitable for use in a microwave oven before using.

Cardboard is also a good transmitter of microwaves. Cardboard containers for microwaves are usually coated with plastic to make them more sturdy.

Plastic pouches Boil-in-the-bag pouches must be pierced to allow steam to escape; otherwise they will explode during heating.

Figure 51 Products used to cover microwave food

PREPARATION BEFORE USING A MICROWAVE OVEN

- Ensure the inside and the door is clean.
- Defrost the food (if necessary).
- Position the food evenly on the dish and cover, if appropriate.
- Pierce the skin/surface of the food, if appropriate.
- Space foods, if appropriate.
- Check microwaving times (pay particular attention to defrosting/cooking/re-heating times).
- Set the power and time (large pieces of food will need to be rotated and repositioned if there is no turntable in the microwave).
- Always use a probe to check the temperature of larger items.

Food may be covered with:

- greaseproof or kitchen paper;
- paper, cotton or linen serviettes;
- microwave plastic wrapping film.

Under-linings are sometimes placed between the food and dish to absorb any excess moisture, e.g. kitchen paper, cotton or linen serviettes.

Microwave roasting bags are made from specially treated plastics and are used to help brown foods cooked in a microwave.

Figure 52 Settings on the front of a microwave

SAFETY AND HYGIENE

Microwave ovens need to be maintained regularly, i.e. cleaned after every use as part of a regular cleaning programme and serviced as per manufacturer's recommendations (refer to instruction manual). A qualified technician should be called in to check around the perimeter of the door along with ventilation grilles for any microwave radiation leakage.

Microwave ovens must be cleaned immediately after use. Any spillages should be cleaned up at once. Use a soft cloth and a mild detergent water to remove any spilt food. Wash all surfaces, especially the roof and then rinse with a clean cloth.

Ensure that the door area is cleaned properly and that there is no build-up of spilt food as this might prevent the oven door from sealing properly and allow a microwave radiation leak.

Air filters should be removed and cleaned to prevent a build-up of grease

ADVANTAGES AND DISADVANTAGES OF MICROWAVE COOKERY

The advantages of cooking with microwaves are as follows.

- Food cooks rapidly saving time.
- Cooking time is reduced saving energy.

- It is labour-saving as food can be served straight from the dish.
- It defrosts meals straight from the freezer.
- A wide selection of dishes are readily available 24 hours-a-day.
- It is clean and hygienic.
- The controls and settings are relatively easy to use.
- The speed of cooking encourages flavour and the nutritional retention of food.
- It can re-heat to a higher temperature, reducing the chance of food poisoning.

The disadvantages of cooking with microwaves are as follows.

- It is not suitable for cooking all foods.
- It is unsuitable for foods that require to be cooked slowly.
- There are browning limitations (limited to certain models).
- Not all containers and utensils are suitable.
- Microwaves can only penetrate 4 cm into food.
- There is limited oven area.

KEY WORDS

COMBINATION OVENS
Microwave ovens that have an addition of an infra-red grill and/or electric elements or gas burners.

COVERING Covering food with absorbent kitchen paper or clingfilm speeds cooking time, helps to retain moisture, ensures a more even cooking and prevents spattering.

INPUT WATTAGE
The amount of electricity used in creating the microwave energy and operating the moving parts such as the fan and the turntable (optional).

MAGNETRON Component that produces microwaves

MICROWAVE Electro-magnetic wave

MOLECULES Very small particles of matter

OUTPUT WATTAGE
The energy measurement of an oven.

PIERCING To pierce the skin of certain foods to prevent a build-up of pressure and eventual explosion.

SPACING When possible, foods should be arranged in a circular pattern with a centimetre distance between each item.

THERMOPLASTIC DISHES
Special plastics that can withstand extreme temperatures.

WATTS/KILOWATTS
Measurements of electro-magnetic waves

ELEMENT 2
Microwave food

(*See* Prepare and cook basic meat, poultry and offal dishes, pp.153–70.)

INTRODUCTION

Most foods can be cooked by microwave. However, the best foods to cook by microwave are those with a high moisture content.

Meat and poultry

Microwave cookery is most effective with small pieces or individual portions of tender cuts of meat and poultry because the microwaves can penetrate the food successfully and therefore cook it rapidly. Larger joints of meat and poultry can be cooked provided they are turned regularly during cooking or placed on a rotating turntable to ensure even cooking. For details on cooking times see the table below (page 61).

If a browned effect is desired the following methods can be used.

- Shallow fry meat and vegetables prior to microwaving.
- Start a roast off in the oven before microwaving.
- Use a microwave oven that has a conventional cooking option (mealstream oven).
- Use microwave roasting bags.

COOKING TIP: Basic microwave ovens are not capable of browning meats, however you can purchase special dishes and roasting bags to encourage the browning process.

(*See* Prepare and cook basic fish dishes, pp.171–84;
Prepare and cook basic shellfish dishes, pp.233–42.)

Fish and shellfish

Fish and shellfish are ideal for cooking by microwave because of their high water content and less tough fibrous tissue, though extra care must be taken not to overcook.

(*See* Prepare and cook basic egg dishes, pp. 225–32.)

Eggs and cheese

Eggs and cheese have a high protein content, therefore special care must be taken not to overcook. Overcooking eggs in a microwave oven may mean that they explode. Both eggs and cheese tend to become rubbery when overcooked.

(See Prepare vegetables and fruit, pp.109– 20.)

Fruit and vegetables

Fruit and vegetables can be successfully cooked by microwave because they have a high water content. The advantages of cooking vegetables by microwave is that the speed of cooking and minimal liquid used means that vegetables retain more vitamins, minerals and natural flavouring than those cooked by conventional methods.

Potatoes can be cooked successfully by microwave and although other fibrous vegetables, e.g. cabbage and cauliflower can also be cooked by microwave, they are not really suited to this method of cookery because they do not cook evenly. As a rule, vegetables are usually cooked in the microwave on a medium setting and generally in a sealed container unless the recipe specifies otherwise. For times and setting instructions refer to the manufacturer's guidelines.

Figure 53 Putting a bowl of potatoes inside a microwave

Figure 54 Covered bowl of potatoes

COOKING TIP: Some fruits and vegetables need to be pierced before cooking (potatoes, apples), otherwise the rapid heating of water causes an expansion into steam which cannot escape, causing the food to burst during cooking.

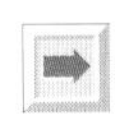
(*See* Prepare and cook basic pasta dishes, pp. 214–18; and Prepare and cook basic rice dishes, pp. 209–13.)

Pasta and rice

Pasta and rice have a low moisture content and absorb plenty of liquid during the cooking process. It is best to pre-cook pasta and rice in a conventional way and only use a microwave to finish the dish.

(*See* Prepare and cook basic pastry dishes, pp. 265–74.)

Pastry foods

Generally pastry foods tend to become soggy so this method of cookery is not recommended. However, shortbread can be cooked successfully in a microwave.

(*See* Prepare cook and finish basic cakes, sponges and scones, pp. 275–90.)

Sponges

Sponges can be cooked successfully in a microwave oven. A standard sponge takes between 4 and 5 minutes to cook.

COOKING TIP: Certain foods need to be taken out of the microwave underdone and allowed to complete cooking during *'standing time'*. The standing time allows the food to continue cooking without further addition of energy, e.g. fish turn from opaque to white, flaky and tender.

NOTE: Most chefs would not use a microwave for roasting but would use a more traditional method for a better cooked product.

Cooking meat and poultry by microwave

	Cooking times (min per kg)		*Special notes*
Roast beef	Rare Medium Well done	10 min 12–14 min 14–16 min	Place in a microwave roasting bag; allow to stand for 10–15 minutes before carving.
Minced beef	(40 ml liquid per 10 portions)	10 min	Stir throughout the cooking process.
Beef steaks	(min per 250 g) Rare Medium Well done	 2 min 2–4 min 4 min	Steaks must be browned on a pre-heated browning dish.
Roast chicken	12 to 15 min		Protect the wing tips and drumsticks with greaseproof paper. Place in a microwave roasting bag with a little stock to keep moist. Allow to stand for 15–20 min before carving.
Chicken portions	(min per 120 g portion) 3–5 min		Place the narrowest part to the centre of the dish. Brush with a little melted butter and season lightly. Cover with a buttered cartouche.
Roast lamb	Pink Medium	12 min 14–16 min	Place in a microwave roasting bag. Allow to stand for 15–20 minutes before carving.

Lamb chops Note: This also applies to lamb cutlets	(min per 2 × 100 g portion) - 1 portion 7–8 min 2 portions 8–10 min 3 portions 15–18 min	Chops must be browned on a pre-heated browning dish.
Roast duck	12–15 min	Protect the wing tips and drumsticks with greaseproof paper. Prick the skin thoroughly to aid the release of fat. Place in a microwave roasting bag with a little stock to keep moist. Turn occasionally through the cooking process. Allow to stand for 15 – 20 min before carving.
Roast pork	Well done 20–25 min	Score fat with a sharp knife and sprinkle with salt to get a crisp crackling. Place in a microwave roasting bag. Allow to stand for 15–20 minutes before carving.
Pork chops	(minutes per 150 g portion) 2–15 min	Chops must be browned on a pre-heated browning dish.

KEY WORDS

STANDING TIME
This is time allowed during which the food continues to cook after it has been removed from the oven.

STIRRING To move the food from the outside to the centre of the dish during cooking to equalise heat and speed microwaving.

WAVE GUIDE A channel within the microwave oven which guids the microwaves onto the stirrer

Activity

1. Check the microwave oven at work. Find out its power setting
2. Make a list of vegetables that can be cooked from raw in the microwave oven.
3. Why should microwaves be cleaned regularly?
4. Find the following words associated with microwaves:

- standing-time
- combination ovens
- output
- piercing
- magnetron
- microwave
- watt
- cover

W	C	L	S	T	A	N	D	I	N	G	T	I	M	E	R
C	O	M	B	I	N	A	T	I	O	N	O	V	E	N	S
J	R	V	R	O	X	E	Q	M	I	C	I	P	E	F	V
L	R	G	E	F	T	U	P	T	U	O	N	E	V	K	E
K	Y	I	A	G	J	L	H	D	O	S	R	U	A	C	N
R	O	T	Q	U	U	E	D	S	B	T	W	A	W	T	P
T	V	V	L	P	P	I	E	R	C	I	N	G	O	B	T
O	T	Y	C	Z	D	Y	D	F	E	R	D	F	R	H	U
Y	T	R	O	M	A	G	N	E	T	R	O	N	C	L	O
N	A	N	I	C	A	K	F	W	A	E	G	I	I	G	S
X	W	K	M	T	R	E	V	O	C	R	M	P	M	J	A
C	A	R	R	M	I	C	R	R	C	A	O	K	I	N	G

NVQ SVQ 1 | # Prepare and fry food

ELEMENT 1

Prepare food for frying

(See Prepare and griddle food, pp.101–5)

INTRODUCTION

Frying food provides a wide variety of dishes each with their own unique flavour and appearance.

The three principal methods of frying are:

1. **deep frying** food which is submersed in hot fat/oil at a preheated temperature;
2. **shallow frying** shallow frying is the cooking of pre-prepared food on a pre-heated surface, usually in a frying-pan or bratt pan with the food on a thin layer of fat or oil. The term *sauter* is used to describe the shallow frying of meat and poultry while the term meunière is used to decribe the shallow frying of fish.
3. **stir frying** is the fast frying of pre-prepared food (usually Chinese) using the minimum amount of oil.

COOKING TIP: It is important to have strict temperature control when shallow frying as the cooked food item should have an appealing golden brown exterior as well as being thoroughly cooked on the inside. Foods cooked by shallow frying are usually thin, evenly-shaped individual portions. This is because larger, thicker items would burn on the outside well before the food was cooked in the centre.

Figure 55 Cooking food in a frying pan

Temperature and time control

Deep frying temperatures vary from between 160 °C and 195 °C. As a rough guide, the fat or oil is ready for use when the surface is quite still and emits a faint, bluish tinge. Cooking times vary according to the size, structure and nature of the product being fried and the frying temperature. Use the table on page 65 as a guide to smoke points.

THE FRYING MEDIUM

With a wide variety of fats and oils available always take into account the flavour of the cooking medium, which needs to be compatible with the foods being cooked in it. Some oils, for example, sesame oil and olive oil, have a very distinct taste.

COOKING TIP: Nowadays it is strongly recommended that polyunsaturated fats are used as they are 'healthier' than saturated fats and reduce the risk of heart disease.

Guide to fat proportions of commonly used fats and oils and their smoke points

Type of fat/oil	*Proportion of polyunsaturated fats*	*Proportion of saturated fats*	*Smoke point*
Butter	Low	High	Low
Clarified butter/ghee	Low	High	Medium
Corn oil	High	Low	High
Dripping	Low	High	Medium
Ghee (from vegetable oils)	Depends on source	Depends on source	High
Lard	Low	High	Medium
Margarine	Low	Medium	Low
• Low-fat spread	Medium	Medium	Low
Olive oil	Low	Low	Medium
Sunflower oil	High	Low	High
Vegetable oil	Low	High	High

NOTE: Certain oils have a low smoke temperature while others are high.

(*See* Carry out procedures in the event of a fire, pp. 14–16.)

SAFETY

It is paramount that all staff are fully aware of the establishment's procedures in the event of a deep-fat-fryer fire. Deep frying is the most dangerous method of cooking and, should a fire occur, it must be prevented from spreading throughout the kitchen.

Always:

- act quickly and in a safe manner;
- turn the fryer off ;
- turn off at the mains;
- place a fire blanket or lid over the fire;
- inform the supervisor;
- if necessary, sound the fire alarm.

Never:

- switch a fryer on when it is empty;
- allow the oil/fat to overheat;
- use solid fats, e.g. lard in a fryer with electric immersion elements;
- leave other vessels used for frying, e.g. saucepan, unattended;
- cover ordinary deep fryers or saucepans containing oil/fat during cooking;
- use water, sand or earth to extinguish a fire.

To avoid the risk of accidents:

- do not allow oil or fat to overheat;
- check thermostats regularly.

HYGIENE

Check that all areas, equipment and utensils used for frying are clean and hygienic before use and during use.

Always:

- store food correctly during preparation;
- store raw meat and fish in a fridge separately from other foods (meat and fish are highly susceptible to contamination);
- store coatings, for example, egg batter, properly;
- discard seasoned flour used for coating meat, fish and poultry.

EQUIPMENT USED IN FRYING

Shallow frying

Bratt pan A multi-purpose item of equipment with a large cooking surface. It may be used for deep frying as well as shallow frying (also used for stewing, poaching and boiling).

Frying pan This multi-purpose pan is used for a variety of frying tasks.

Griddle plate This has a flat frying surface for cooking pancakes, eggs and individual portions of meat, fish and poultry.

Meunière pan An oval pan used for frying whole fish, it has a 'lip' so that juices or sauces made from the cooking juices may be easily poured off.

Omelette pan This is a special shaped pan with curved sides used for cooking omelettes.

Pancake pan This is a very shallow pan with sloping sides, used for cooking pancakes.

Sauté pan This pan has a straight vertical side and is used for shallow frying meat and potatoes. It is not to be mistaken for a sauteuse which has sloping sides and is used for reducing sauces.

Wok This Chinese pan is used for fast-frying food (stir-frying).

Deep frying

Automatic fryers These can be programmed. When the oil or fat is at the correct temperature the wire basket containing the food to be fried is lowered into the fat which keeps a constant temperature throughout cooking. When the cooking time is up, the basket is automatically raised and a buzzer sounds.

Continuous fryers These were originally used for frying doughnuts. They are now used for a variety of different foods and in particular for cook-freeze and cook-chill foods.

Deep fat fryers (Friture) These come in a variety of sizes and models and are specifically designed to allow the heat generated to circulate through the bath of oil or fat.

Enclosed fryers These are used mainly in small areas with no extraction system to remove fumes and odours. The fryer is enclosed in a steel box and has a built-in extraction system.

Pressure fryers These are for cooking foods that require longer cooking times, e.g. chicken pieces. The pressure inside the fryer is controlled by a pressure gauge and excess moisture given off by the food is vented off. The lid has a locking system which prevents the lid from opening until the pressure has been released. It is important to monitor cooking times carefully as it is not possible to view the food during the cooking process.

Figure 56 Deep frying equipment

FOODS SUITABLE FOR SHALLOW AND DEEP FRYING

COOKING TIP: Meat should always be fried in individual portions and sliced thinly to ensure thorough cooking.

Meat

Beef, pork, veal, offal

Poultry

Chicken, turkey

COOKING TIP: Coat with egg and breadcrumbs and serve with a rich sauce as chicken and turkey escalopes.

Fish

COOKING TIP: Most varieties of fish are suitable, however, oily fish are not usually deep fried.

Trout, John Dory, carp, skate, Angler fish (monkfish), sole/plaice

Figure 57 Frying bacon

Shellfish

Prawns, scallops, lobster, scampi

COOKING TIP: Most shellfish are suitable for frying.

Vegetables

Mushrooms, tomatoes, potatoes, onions, courgettes, peppers

Fruits

Apples, pineapples, pears

Nuts

All nuts are suitable for shallow frying

KEY WORDS

FRITURE A deep fat fryer.

RECOVERY TIME
The time it takes the oil or fat to return to the correct operating temperature after cold food has been placed into it thus lowering the temperature.

SMOKE POINT
The moment just before the fat or oil will burst into flames.

SPIDER A meshed tool used to remove food from a friture of hot fat or oil.

STANDBY TEMPERATURE
The temperature at which the oil is kept ready in a deep fat fryer. Temperature is generally no higher than 120 °C so as not to spoil the oil.

ELEMENT 2

Fry food

INTRODUCTION

Frying is the fast cooking of food either on a hot greased surface (shallow frying) or by immersing in hot oil (deep frying). Not all foods can be suitably cooked by the frying process and certain foods need to be protected during cooking, i.e. with a coating.

(*See* Maintain and promote hygiene in food storage, preparation and cooking, pp 48–54.)

HYGIENE

Fried food must be kept hot ready for use at a temperature in excess of 63 °C and should be served immediately. It should not be cooked too early, otherwise the moisture present in the food will turn to steam and the food will lose its crispness, the surface will become soggy and the food will have an unattractive appearance.

(*See* Carry out procedures in the event of a fire, pp. 14–16.)

SAFETY

Cooking in hot oil/fat is extremely dangerous and can cause serious accidents if the oil spills or catches fire.

Always:

- be on your guard when frying foods;
- dry items of food thoroughly before placing them in hot fat;
- work in an organised manner.

Never use water near a frying pan or deep fat fryer – it might splatter the immediate area with hot oil.

NOTE: The only liquid allowed near a friture (deep fat fryer) is a batter.

DEEP FRYING

Deep frying is cooking food by submerging it in pre-heated oil or clarified fat, in a friture or deep fat fryer at a temperature of between 165 °C and 190 °C. Frying temperatures vary according to the foods to be cooked. The fat must be hot in order to seal the outside of the food and prevent the food from absorbing fat. If the cooking medium is not hot enough the food is likely to absorb excess fat which will result in the surface being soggy in texture. Food to be deep-fried needs to be tender and of an even shape; however there are restrictions on food choice when particular foods are cooked from raw.

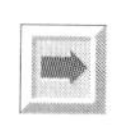

(*See* recipes p.337)

Coating foods for frying

Particular items of food need to be coated before frying to protect them. They might be coated in:

- flour seasoned with salt and pepper (plain flour for sweet preparations);
- milk and seasoned flour (*pané à la française*);
- seasoned flour, eggwash and breadcrumbs (*pané à l'anglaise*);
- seasoned flour and batter (*pané à l'Orly*).

Guide to recommended frying times

Food to be fried	*Suggested temperature*		*Recommended cooking time (minutes)*
	°C	°F	
Chicken pieces	171	340	6 to 12
Choux paste	182	360	1 to 2
Doughnuts	188	370	1 to 2
Fish (battered pieces)	177	350	2 to 4
Fruit fritters	177	350	2 to 4
Onion rings	177	350	2 to 4
Meat cutlets	177	350	3 to 6
Potato chips – straight through	188	370	4 to 5
Potato chips – blanching	166	330	4 to 6
Potato chips – browning	191	375	2 to 3
Prawns and scampi – battered	177	350	3 to 5
Sausages	177	350	1 to 2
Vegetables	182	360	1 to 2

COOKING TIP: Frozen foods will take slightly longer (approximately 1 minute) to cook.

Care of deep fat fryers

Always:

- maintain the recommended fat level within the fryer;
- set the thermostat to correct temperature, 165 °C to 190 °C;
- select correct temperature for food to be cooked;
- ensure that all foods are dry.

Cleaning deep fat fryers

(*See* Clean food-production areas, equipment and utensils, pp. 32–9.)

Always:

- switch off fryer at the mains and allow it to cool completely;
- remove wire basket and thoroughly wash and dry;
- drain the oil and filter the fat through a muslin cloth;
- remove and discard any food waste from the base of the oil chamber;
- close the draining tap and fill fryer with hot water and detergent solution;
- completely clean the fryer with the cleaning solution and bring to the boil;
- drain water off through the base tap and rinse thoroughly with clean water in the same manner until water runs clear;
- dry with a clean, soft cloth;
- close the outlet tap and fill with clean oil.

NOTE: Certain fryers are fitted with a filtration unit which recycles the oil and will extend the life of the oil. This particular variety of friture is often termed computerised and the processes of such fryers are automatic: Temperature, Timing, Heating and Filtration.

Never clean a deep fat fryer when it is hot.

SHALLOW FRYING

Shallow frying is split into three extensions:

1. Sweating
2. Sauté
3. Stir frying

Meunière

Meunière is the traditional term used to describe the shallow frying of fish. The word meunière means 'miller's wife', so named because the fish is passed through seasoned flour.

Sweating

This involves the slow frying of vegetables in fat, usually butter, using a lid and without colouring the food. It is used to cook vegetables for soups and sauces creating a distinctive flavour which is noticeable in the finished product.

Sauté

This is the cooking of tender cuts of meat and poultry. The term 'sauté' literally means to 'jump' and is also used to describe the frying of sliced potatoes.

Figure 58 Using a wok

Stir frying

Stir frying should be carried out in a traditionally-shaped wok (Chinese pan) using the minimum of fat. It is usually reserved for cooking Eastern-style dishes, but it has become increasingly fashionable and is considered to be a healthier method of cooking foods.

Shallow frying foods

1. Heat the oil on a moderately high setting.
2. Pass the food through seasoned flour or another coating.
3. Add the food and seal both sides.
4. Lower the heat and cook for the duration of the cooking time.
5. When cooked, drain on kitchen paper to remove any excess oil before serving.

NOTE: Use a splatter guard to prevent hot oil spitting out of the pan.

Dry frying

This is a healthier option to conventional frying as no cooking medium is used. This process relies on drawing out the natural fats in food which is achieved by placing meat in a cold frying pan or saucepan (preferably non-stick, which gives better results). The food is cooked over a low heat until some of the fat runs out, the heat is then increased to fry the meat for the recommended time. Any vegetables, e.g. onions, may be browned with the meat.

NOTE: Always follow the manufacturer's instructions regarding recommended temperature and cooking times for convenience foods.

FRYING CONVENIENCE FOODS

There is an extensive range of convenience foods readily available which require little or no preparation prior to cooking. Frozen foods are the most popular convenience food used for deep frying. The food is always individually portioned and is always cooked from its frozen state.

When shallow frying foods, ensure that they are cooked presentation side first: the fat will be clean and not spoil the overall appearance of the finished product.

Figure 59 Range of fried foods

WARNING! All chicken must be thoroughly cooked otherwise there is the risk of food poisoning.

FOODS SUITABLE FOR FRYING

Fish

Most varieties of white fish are suitable for frying and the most popular are cod, plaice and Dover sole. However, the oily types are not generally deep-fried with the exception of whitebait.

Large fish needs to be filleted before deep frying. The smaller variety such as plaice, whiting and carp are usually cooked whole and should have their eyes and gills removed, be gutted to remove the intestines and have their fins and tails trimmed before frying.

Larger varieties, such as cod and haddock, will need filleting and portioning before being fried.

Shellfish

Mussels (marinaded first), scampi, scallops and prawns are usually fried.

Meat and poultry

Chicken drumsticks and thighs are usually coated in breadcrumbs or batter before frying. Chicken supremes, turkey escalopes and veal are passed through seasoned flour for shallow frying. For deep frying they are usually coated in breadcrumbs.

Pastry

Sweets, for example doughnuts and balls of choux pastry, are deep-fried.

Cheese and eggs

Eggs can be shallow fried whole or scrambled. Scotch eggs are whole boiled eggs wrapped in sausage meat and coated in breadcrumbs and deep fried. Savoury cheese dishes and snacks may be deep-fried.

Vegetables

Onion rings, courgettes and mushrooms may be fried from raw. Most vegetable are suitable for deep frying once they have been boiled or steamed until they are tender but firm.

Classic deep-fried potato dishes

Name - (English and French)	***Description***
Chain (*en chaînes*)	Interlocking links approx. 7 mm × 2 mm thick
Chips, French fries (*frites*)	Sticks approx. 40 mm long × 10 mm thick
Collerette (*collerette*)	Thin rounds with grooved edges
Crisps (*chips*)	Very thin round slices
Cubes (*bataille*)	15 mm square
Fine straw (*chiffonette*)	Very fine strips
Matchsticks (*allumettes*)	Thin sticks 40 mm × 2 mm thick
Matchsticks, thick (*mignonnettes*)	Sticks 40 mm × 5 mm long
Pont Neuf (*Pont Neuf*)	Square batons 40 mm × 20 mm thick
Spiral (*bénédictine*)	Coiled strips 20 mm × 2 mm thick
Star (*étoile*)	Cubes cut into stars
Straw (*pailles*)	Fine strips
Straw, fine (*chiffonette*)	Very fine strips
Wafer (*gaufrettes*)	Thin slices cut into a trellis pattern
Woodchip (*copeaux*)	Thin lengths of varying widths cut like woodchips

Whole fried whiting (Merlan frit)

(× 4 portions)

Ingredients

600 g (Allow 150 g (approx.) whiting per portion)	whiting
	seasoned flour
	beaten egg
	white bread-crumbs
	Lemon wedges
	Parsley sprigs

Method

1. Prepare by removing the intestines, clean out head, remove gills, fins and the eyes and skin.
2. Wash thoroughly and drain.
3. Pass through seasoned flour, beaten egg and white breadcrumbs (pané) and shake off excess breadcrumbs.
4. Deep fry in a moderately hot fat (175 °C) until the coating is golden brown in colour. Drain on absorbent kitchen paper.
5. Serve with fried picked parsley, lemon wedges and an appropriate sauce, e.g. tartare.

Fried fish in batter (Poisson frit à L'Orly)

NOTE: Fried fish in batter usually refers to fillets of white fish, e.g. sole, plaice, haddock or cod etc.

Ingredients

100 g–150 g (Allow 100 g–150 g prepared fillet per portion)	fillet of white fish
	oil
	lemon juice
	chopped parsley
	seasoned flour
	batter (see p.336 for batter preparation)

Method

1. Place the fish in a dish and marinate in a little oil, lemon juice and chopped parsley for 3–4 minutes.and skin.
2. Drain, pass through seasoned flour and batter.
3. Deep fry in moderately hot oil (175 °C), drain well.
4. Serve with a suitable sauce, e.g. tomato.

KEY WORDS

BLANCHING Cooking of potatoes in deep fat until they are soft but not browned.

MARINADE Liquid that food is placed in prior to deep frying to enhance flavour.

PANÉ À L'ANGLAISE
Food passed through seasoned flour, with excess flour removed and the item then passed through eggwash, drained and passed through breadcrumbs. The breadcrumbs are lightly pressed onto the item of food.

PANÉ À LA FRANÇAISE
Foods too dry to be passed through flour are passed through milk first and then the flour. Once coated the food should be fried immediately.

PANÉ À L'ORLY
The marinaded food is passed through flour and then placed in batter.

SMOKE POINT Describes the dangerous stage when the fat or oil has become so hot that it starts to smoke. If heating continues it will burst into flames.

Activity

1. Give the French term for foods cooked in:

	French term
Batter	
Breadcrumbs	
Flour	

2. Name six deep-fried dishes and say how they are coated for cooking.

NVQ SVQ 1

Prepare and bake food

ELEMENT 1

Prepare food for baking

INTRODUCTION

Baking is the cooking of food in an oven by dry convection heat. The heat is usually generated by electric elements or gas burners, though in older ovens, charcoal or wood may be used. In some cases the ovens are modified to inject steam around the product being baked. This is mainly done for dough products.

Baking is widely used for all commodities. However, its main use is for confectionery, pastry and bakery items. The moisture within the food is heated sufficiently to produce steam which in turn modifies the dry air of the oven. The heat produced changes the structure of the raw foods and makes them edible. In the case of risen products, e.g. sponges, cakes and doughs, it is a chemical or biological action, caused by the heat, that gives aeration.

NOTE: Cooking by convection means that the food never comes into direct contact with the cooking source.

Figure 60 Baked cake on rack to cool

THE PROCESS OF BAKING

A cake is baked when the heat penetrates to the centre and then upwards to the crown of the product. Items baked go through a process of change during the time they are exposed to controlled heat in the oven and for a while afterwards.

In order to achieve the best possible results when baking and finishing, the following points should be adhered to.

- Preset the oven to the correct temperature.
- Use the specified size and shape of baking tins and trays.
- Place items to be cooked in the correct area of the oven.
- Do not open the oven frequently during cooking, otherwise the item will spoil.
- Test the item when cooked.
- Transfer cooked item to a designated area to cool completely.

To test if cooked: the item should be firm to the touch and when depressed lightly with the fingers it should spring back to its original shape. If the depression remains the item is not cooked and should be returned to the oven and checked at 10 minute intervals.

During the baking process the dry, brown, crusty surface formed on the food can be achieved by one or more of the following factors :

1. the high temperature of baking;
2. the caramelisation of sugar in cakes and sponges;
3. amino acids in foods, e.g. eggs in soufflés;
4. nitrogen compounds in foods, e.g. milk.

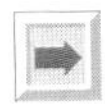
(*See* Maintain and promote hygiene in food storage, preparation and cooking, pp. 48–54.)

HYGIENE

In order to prevent the risk of cross-contamination the following points should be observed and adhered to.

- Hands must be kept scrupulously clean at all times. Sticky dough will draw out any dirt from the hands and from under the nails.
- All working surfaces and equipment must be clean before use and must be thoroughly cleaned down after use.
- Regular maintenance of ovens and baking trays is essential: they should be kept absolutely clean and free from pieces of food sticking to them; they should be greased to prevent food sticking to them.
- All food stuffs should be stored correctly in a safe and hygienic manner.
- All waste food and other debris must be disposed of in accordance with laid-down procedures.
- A good standard of personal hygiene must be maintained at all times.

PREPARATION OF WORK AREAS

All food production areas and relevant equipment to be used, for the range of dough products, should be correctly prepared. Doing so will enable the work to be carried out in an efficient and safe manner.

Preparation checklist

- Keep work surfaces clean and dry at all times.
- Ensure that all mechanical equipment is clean, safe and kept in full working order and has the necessary safeguards in place.
- Prepare and assemble in advance the necessary moulds, tins and baking sheets.

CONVENIENCE PRODUCTS

Pre-prepared dough

Pre-prepared dough should have undergone bulk fermentation and been knocked back to its original bulk with the finished result being a dry, easily stretched dough. During the weighing and shaping process it is essential that the dough is kept warm and covered with a clean cloth which should prevent a skin from forming on the surface.

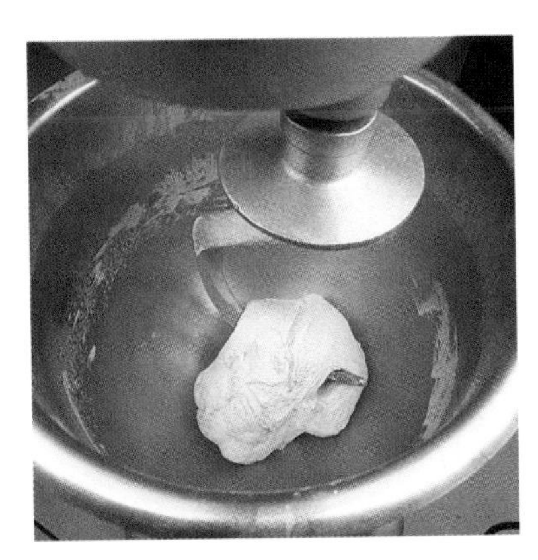

Figure 61 Dough being kneaded in kneading machine

Dough pre-mixes

A range of pre-mixes is available for both the domestic and industrial markets and may be purchased in small or bulk quantities. The catering industry tends to buy in bulk. Pre-mixes are highly beneficial to the busy caterer for a number of reasons.

1. They allow a greater range of doughs to be produced with the minimum of skill and labour.
2. They guarantee a standard result.
3. They are time-saving.

(*See* Prepare and cook basic dough products, pp. 254–64.)

When using pre-mixes (all types) always follow the manufacturer's instructions carefully. In real terms, the mixes need to be formed into a dough by adding a measured quantity of liquid. Both bulk fermentation and proving are necessary after the product has been formed, to achieve a similar product to that of traditionally prepared goods.

Foods suitable for baking

Pastry products. Pies, tarts, flans, sausage rolls, bouclées.
Bread products. Loaves, rolls, pizza.
Vegetables. Potatoes.
Fruit. Apples
Egg custards. Sweet egg custard, savoy egg custard.
Fish. Whole.
Sponges. Small, large.

Par-baked products

These are usually vacuum packed or frozen and are baked as and when required. No preparation other than brushing with egg, milk or dusting with icing sugar or flour is required.

EQUIPMENT USED IN BAKING

Baking sheets

Baking sheets, on which items are cooked in the oven, are usually made from black cast-iron, steel or aluminium. New baking sheets are made non-stick by heating them in a very hot oven, wiping them clean then lightly oiling them.

Care should be taken when cleaning as they are likely to lose their 'non-stick surface' so washing should be kept to an absolute minimum.

To clean baking sheets:

- wipe straight from the oven while still warm;
- if necessary, use a scraper to remove baked-on dirt;
- wipe dry.

If they are heavily soiled, wash in detergent water, rinse and dry thoroughly.

Cooling racks

These are special wire racks on which baked items are cooled.

Deck ovens

These special ovens used for baking bread, have top, bottom and front heat regulators.

ELEMENT 1
Bake food

Figure 62 Putting bread in oven

COOKING TIP: When a brown crust forms, this is usually an indication that the item is cooked.

(*See* Carry out procedures in the event of a fire, pp. 14–16.)

INTRODUCTION

It is essential that ovens are prepared properly and set to the correct temperature before beginning to bake. Accurate timing and temperature control is vital for successful baking. If the oven temperature falls below the required temperature in between bakes, the oven must be allowed to reach the set temperature again before continuing to bake.

TEMPERATURE CONTROL

Temperature levels are determined by:

- the size and thickness of the product;
- the humidity and area to be used in the oven.

SAFETY

When working in a hot area, accidents can easily occur. Caution must be taken when removing items from the oven as they will be exceptionally hot.

Always:

- use dry, thick oven gloves/cloths to handle hot tins and trays;
- balance baking sheets/trays properly;
- ensure that no part of the hand or arm comes into contact with hot baking sheets or trays;
- be aware of steam building up in ovens. Stand back when opening the oven door.

WARNING! Always follow the manufacturer's instructions when lighting gas ovens.

Never:

- overload the oven with dough products;
- use damp oven cloths, tea towels or cloths for removing items from the oven.

NOTE: Food intended to be sold hot within two hours of the end of the preparation period does not need to be kept at 63 °C for those two hours, provided it is reheated to at least 63 °C prior to sale. Any remaining food must be appropriately disposed of.

DISPLAYING BAKED ITEMS

Bakery products yield an appetising, appealing appearance and have mouth-watering aromas. Therefore all baked foods should be displayed to their full advantage taking into account their freshness, distinctive aromas and high quality.

COOKING TIP: Attractively displayed products will entice the customer to purchase the item.

(*See* Maintain and promote hygiene in food storage, pp. 48–50.)

STORAGE OF COOKED BAKED PRODUCTS

Baked products not for immediate sale should be:

- chilled as quickly as possible;
- stored in a refrigerator;
- labelled properly with the name of the product and dated.

Baked products should be stored:

- on trays in a refrigerator;
- kept separate from raw and strong smelling/flavoured foods.

KEY WORDS

BATCH COOKING
The splitting of large quantities of food dishes into batches for cooking because the cooking equipment is not large enough to process the entire quantity in one go.

BRUSHING To brush the items for baking with a wash before, during and/or after baking.

DECK OVENS Specially designed ovens for bread-making which have top, bottom and front heat regulars.

DOCKER A wooden disk with protruding points used to make small holes in pizza bases to prevent over-rising.

DREDGER A container with small holes used to dust dough items with flour or icing sugar.

FINISHING To finish baked goods for presentation, to coat with a glaze or dust with icing sugar or sieved flour. Sometimes the items are returned to a very hot oven to caramelise and give a gloss finish to the item.

GLAZING Glazing is done with a liquid made from boiled sugar and water and is carried out on some dough products to give them a gloss finish.

LOADING The term given to the organisation of oven space to maximise efficiency and economic use.

OVEN TRAYS Usually made from black wrought iron, steel or aluminium. They should not be washed, but scraped and wiped clean as washing removes the non-stick surface. New trays are made non-stick by coating with a thin layer of oil and then heated in a very hot oven.

PROVERS Steam cabinets used to ferment yeast products.

RIPE DOUGH A dough that has risen to the required size.

ROLLING Using a special rolling machine (also called a pastry brake) for rolling and shaping dough for pizzas.

Activity

1. Explain the process of baking in your own words.
2. During baking the dry brown crusty surface formed on the food can be achieved by one or more factors. Name three.

   (a)

   (b)

   (c)

3. List **two** advantages of using pre-mixes.

   (a)

   (b)

4. Why is accurate timing and temperature control necessary when baking?
5. How should baked items **not** for immediate consumption be stored?
6. How should baked items be stored in a refrigerator?
7. Baked items should be reheated to a minimum temperature. What is it?
8. List **two** points of safety to observe when working in a hot area.

   (a)

   (b)

Prepare, boil, poach and steam food

ELEMENT 1

Prepare food for boiling, poaching and steaming

INTRODUCTION

The boiling, poaching and steaming processes use conduction and convection to cook foods. Foods suitable for these processes vary, but in the main they are vegetables, fruits, fish, meat and poultry. The length of cooking time is determined by the type and structure of the food.

HYGIENE

A high standard of hygiene must be maintained at all times. All foods must be properly prepared and stored before cooking and all areas, equipment and utensils must be kept scrupulously clean. Food handling should be kept to a minimum.

NOTE: The term 'boiling' when applied to fish is not exactly true: if fish were to be boiled in the true sense, it would disintegrate.

BOILING

Boiling is either rapid and short, or simmering and long.

- Rapid boiling is where the surface is fiercely agitated.
- Simmering is identified when there is barely a motion on the surface.

The rate of cooking is determined by the needs of the item being cooked. Certain foods are cooked in rapidly boiling water, for example vegetables to preserve the colour, vitamins and mineral salts which are dissolved by prolonged cooking. Meat and poultry are best simmered otherwise they might cook unevenly, be stringy or even fall apart.

POACHING

Food to be poached may be either shallow- or deep-poached. Foods that may be cooked by this method are fish, eggs, farinaceous foods (e.g. gnocchi) and white meats, and in particular poultry. In some cases the food being poached is partly submerged in the cooking liquid. It is therefore necessary to use a lid or a cartouche to cover the food to ensure that an even heat is maintained within the cooking vessel.

STEAMING

COOKING TIP: The addition of an acid to the cooking liquid has a tenderising effect on the food being cooked and helps the setting or coagulation of the protein, consequently speeding up the cooking process.

Steaming is the cooking of food in vapourised water under varying degrees of pressure. The water is heated to 100 °C and above to produce the steam. When the steam comes into contact with the food it condenses. The heat is transferred from the steam to the surface of the food. Steaming causes the structure and texture to change by means of a chemical action.

Foods which can be cooked by this method are meat, poultry, fish, vegetables, potatoes, rice, sponge puddings.

Safety

When using a steamer be extra vigilant as not only are the components extremely hot but the steam produced could result in a nasty scald if due care and attention are not observed.

ELEMENT 2
Boil, poach and steam food

INTRODUCTION

Boiling, poaching and steaming are all classified as 'wet' cooking processes. Foods cooked by the 'wet' methods have an attractive appearance and often form the basis of healthy, appetising and nutritious meals.

Figure 63 Boiling chicken

BOILING

Boiling is carried out in salted water at a temperature of 100 °C. Some foods are simmered gently while others are boiled rapidly. The method chosen will depend on the type of food to be cooked.

The two techniques in boiling are as follows.

1. Placing the food into cold water and bringing it to the boil. This method is used to:

- soften fibrous materials in root vegetables such as potatoes, carrots and parsnips;
- extract the flavours in stock making;
- remove excess salt from cured and pickled meat;
- aid the removal of impurities and scum.

2. Placing the food directly into boiling water. This method is used to:

- seal in the flavour of fresh meats;
- reduce the overall cooking time;
- minimise vitamin loss;
- set the protein and colour in green vegetables.

Advantages of boiling

There are a number of advantages to cooking foods in this way which include the following.

1. It is labour-saving and requires little attention while cooking.
2. Because the liquid is in direct contact with the food being cooked, it is an inexpensive method of heat transfer.
3. If the cooking liquid is always covering the food item there will be minimum shrinkage or drying out.
4. It is nutritional: in the case of soups and stews, all the food is served.

Cooking equipment

Food items to be boiled are usually cooked in saucepans, boiling or bratt pans or stock pots with a lid. In large commercial establishments steam-jacket boilers are used.

POACHING

Poaching is the gentle cooking of delicate foods using the minimum quantity of simmering liquid. The cooking liquid should reach a temperature that is near boiling point without actually boiling, between 75 °C and 95 °F. There are two methods of poaching.

(See Poaching, p 182 for more detailis.)

1. Shallow poaching

Shallow poaching is usually reserved for small cuts of fish and is carried out in a sauteuse or a *plat à sauter* using the minimum amount of liquid. However, special fireproof china dishes ('sole dishes') or enamelled, cast-iron dishes can also be used. Small items of food, e.g. cuts of fish and poultry, may be shallow poached. They are placed in the cooking liquid which is brought to the boil, then simmered. The item of food then cooks in the liquid. The process may be completed in a moderate oven (180 °C), which will prevent the liquid from boiling and spoiling the food item. In shallow poaching the liquid is normally used to form the basis of the sauce which will accompany the cooked fish.

COOKING TIP: In poaching fish, if the water boils, the agitation of the liquid will damage the fish.

2. Deep poaching

Deep poaching is carried out in a *plat à sauter* or bratt pan and is mainly reserved for cooking eggs and large cuts of fish and whole fish. The term is a little confusing as it is also used to describe boiled fish.

The advantages of poaching

Poaching produces dishes which are delicate in texture and flavoursome as well as being a quick method of cooking. Fish is more suitable than meat for poaching for two reasons.

- Fish protein coagulates at a lower temperature than meat protein (41 °C).
- The collagen that is partly responsible for toughness softens to gelatin faster and at a lower temperature. Meat needs a temperature of at least 100 °C.

The disadvantages of poaching

- If the temperature of the poaching liquid is not monitored correctly or if food is left in the cooking liquor for too long, it might become overcooked and it will be ruined.
- There are a limited number of foods that can be poached successfully because of the relatively low temperatures and short cooking times involved.

(See Prepare and cook basic fish dishes, pp. 171–84.)

Poached fish

Fish may be poached in deep or shallow liquid. Whole fish should be cooked by placing in cold water, bringing to the boil and then reduced to simmering temperature until cooked (deep poaching). Small cuts of fish are placed in simmering liquid (short poaching). Cuts of fish are cooked in this way to prevent the juices from escaping and coagulating into a white coating on the cut surface.

COOKING TIP: An exception to the rule of starting whole fish from cold water is so-called 'blue' trout. The fish are placed in simmering liquid containing vinegar which turns the slimy layer blue while the heat makes them distorted. This effect can only be achieved with fish that are cooked within minutes of being killed and have not had the slimy surface washed off.

(See Prepare fruit, pp 116–20.)

Fruits

Fruits that may be poached include the following.

Apples and pears These are peeled, quartered, with their cores removed and then placed into a shallow poaching pan of simmering stock syrup. A cartouche is placed over the pan and the fruit is cooked until it is tender, for about 20 min.

Blackcurrants, gooseberries, redcurrants These are washed, their stalks removed and in the case of gooseberries the top which is not edible is also removed. The fruits are then placed into a shallow poaching pan and covered with boiling stock syrup and a cartouche. Simmer gentle for about 8 min.

Rhubarb The leaves are removed completely (they are poisonous) and stalks trimmed. The branch is then washed and cut into 4 cm lengths and placed into a shallow poaching pan and covered with boiling stock syrup. Simmer gently for about 8 to 10 min.

Stone fruits, e.g. apricots, cherries, damsons, greengages
These should be thoroughly washed and placed into a shallow poaching pan and covered with boiling stock syrup. Simmer gently for about 8 min.

COOKING TIP: Peaches are usually blanched in boiling water for about 10 seconds and then plunged into cold water to loosen the skin. They are then peeled and cooked in the same way as other stone fruit.

Poached eggs

Eggs are cooked in gently simmering water with a little vinegar and salt to help the albumen set and to add a little flavour.

COOKING TIP: Once the food is cooked it will need to be well drained especially if it is being served with the sauce as the cooking liquid residue will spoil the final appearance and consistency. Draining may be assisted by carefully placing the poached item on to absorbent paper or a clean cloth to dry.

Cooking equipment used in poaching

Shallow poaching is usually carried out in a sauteuse or a *plat à sauter* using a minimum amount of liquid. However, special fireproof china dishes called sole dishes or enamelled, cast-iron dishes can also be used.

Deep poaching is carried out in a *plat à sauter* or bratt pan with sufficient liquid to completely immerse the fish.

Figure 64 Fish kettle

Fish kettle Poached whole fish are generally cooked in a special 'fish kettle' which has a perforated drainer that fits into the bottom of the kettle with handles at both ends for ease of removal and has a tight-fitting lid. They are made from stainless-steel, aluminium or tin-lined copper.

Egg poachers This is similar to a frying pan with a lid. Egg poachers have small individual moulds for the eggs to fit into. The egg does not come into contact with the cooking liquid, only the steam, so this is not true poaching. It is referred to as *'oeuf moulé* (moulded eggs).

Cooking liquor

This is determined by the food item to be cooked and its size. Vinegar is added to some cooking liquors to aid coagulation of the protein. Although it is traditional to strain *court bouillon* prior to use, many chefs leave the liquor unstrained for maximum flavour.

When poaching eggs the quantity of vinegar used will depend on the condition of the eggs; fresh eggs need little or none because they hold firm and do not spread like older or stale eggs.

Fruits are poached in a liquor made with water, sugar, lemon juice and an additional flavour of a wine or liquor, depending on the finished dish.

To test if the food is cooked

(*See* Prepare and cook basic egg dishes, pp. 225–32.)

Eggs

These are the easiest of foods to test for over- or undercooking.

- Undercooked – the white is translucent and sloppy.
- Overcooked – eggs have a cloudy looking yolk and are hard to the touch.
- Cooked – the yolk is soft but firm and the white is set.

(*See* Prepare fruit, pp. 116–20.)

Fruit

The texture should be firm, so that the fruit retains its natural shape and should be tender enough to eat. Overcooked fruit will have a misshapen appearance and be soft.

(*See* Prepare and cook basic fish dishes, pp. 171–84.)

Fish

Whole fish Apply a little pressure with the thumb on the flesh. If it is cooked, it should yield with no sign of sponginess.

Portioned fish The skin and bone should leave the cooked flesh with ease. If over-cooked, it will fall to pieces and disintegrate into flakes.

(*See* Prepare and cook basic meat, poultry and offal dishes, pp. 153–70.)

Poultry

Make an incision with a knife into the thickest part of the breast and apply pressure with the thumb on the flesh. If it is cooked the juice will run clear; if not, return it to the oven and continue cooking for a further few minutes.

Factors that may affect the cooking time

The addition of an acid to the cooking liquid has a tenderising effect on the food being cooked and helps the setting or coagulation of the protein, thus speeding up the cooking process.

STEAMING

There are four methods of steaming.

1. **In a saucepan** A small amount of water is placed in a saucepan and the food is put into a hanging wire basket or on a metal trivet above the water line. A tight-fitting lid is applied. There are special steaming saucepans available with two compartments that sit one on top of the other above the saucepan.
2. **Atmospheric steamer** An atmospheric steamer uses a water bath in the bottom of a sealed cooking compartment. Water is replenished by means of a reservoir fed by a ball valve.
3. **Pressureless convection steamer** Combination ovens are based on pressureless steamers and are used to roast poultry and joints of meat because they keep the meat moist and minimise the loss of natural juices. This type of steamer uses an external generator to produce and replenish steam in the oven. A fan forces the air around the cooking compartment at 100 °C.

NOTE: Although called a pressureless steamer, there is a little pressure build-up (17kN/m_2) when the door of the steamer seals. This in turn rises the boiling temperature of water to 103 °C.

4. **High pressure steaming** Water is heated to between 115°C and 121 °C in a sealed cooking compartment at a steam pressure of between 70 kN/m_2 and 105 kN/m_2. A mechanism on the door prevents it from opening while in operation and before the pressure on the inside has equalled atmospheric pressure. To prevent the pressure from continuously building up, a safety valve allows steam to escape once the required pressure is achieved. In some models the steam is sprayed at a very high speed from jets onto the food, enabling much more rapid transfer of heat.

Steaming meat

Meat and poultry that are boiled can also be steamed. When steaming at low pressure the cooking times for meat and poultry are similar to boiling times. Plain steamed meats tend to be bland in flavour and lack colour, but this can be counteracted by serving with a flavoursome sauce or combining with another cooking process. Some establishments steam meat before roasting to prevent excess loss of moisture and thus ensuring a good ratio of return on portions.

Steaming fish

Whole fish and small cuts can be cooked by steaming. Fish should be lightly seasoned and flavoured with lemon juice and served in a similar way to poached fish. Steaming fish is an ideal way to cook fish for large banquets.

Figure 65 Cooked vegetables

Steaming vegetables and potatoes

Most vegetables can be steamed at low pressure, but green vegetables are best suited to steaming at high pressure to prevent spoiling their appearance. To prepare vegetables for steaming they should be lightly seasoned and placed on a perforated steaming tray.

The advantages of steaming

Steaming, especially high-pressure steaming, is rapid, thus cutting down on time and energy bills. Low-pressure steaming reduces the risks of overcooking fish. It is ideal for cooking vegetables with strong smells (caused by the release of hydrogen sulphide and ammonia) such as cauliflower, broccoli, turnip, cabbage and sprouts. The long and moist conditions of atmospheric steaming are excellent for tough meats such as diced beef used in steak and kidney pudding.

The disadvantages of steaming

Steamed food can lack the colour and flavour associated with other methods of cooking. For this reason foods cooked by this method have to be highly flavoured and seasoned and/or served with a sauce. Steamed foods have a tendency to 'pick up' flavours if the steamer is not thoroughly cleaned properly.

Points of safety

Once foods are placed in a steamer, ensure that the door is sealed firmly and when removing foods from the steamer always stand behind the door to shield yourself from the escaping steam. On no account stand in front of the door as you are liable to be scalded. Where high-pressure steamers are used ensure that the pressure in the steamer has equalised with that outside before opening the door.

A thorough maintenance and cleaning programme is necessary to prevent blockage of the steam escapes.

KEY WORDS

À LA CRÈME To coat with cream or cream sauce.

AL DENTE The Italian term used to describe the degree of cooking for vegetables and pasta, meaning 'to the tooth' where it is still firm when bitten into.

À BEURRE Brush with melted butter.

BLANC A mixture of water, flour, lemon juice and salt used for cooking vegetables that discolour easily.

BOUILLIR To boil.

FISH KETTLE Specially designed pans used to poach whole fish. They are long and narrow. They have a perforated drainer to remove the fish and a tight-fitting lid.

MIJOTER To simmer.

NATURE Served plain.

PLAT À SAUTER A pan with straight, vertical sides used to boil or poach food.

REFRESH To cool food after blanching by plunging into cold water or under cold running water.

SAUTEUSE Sloping-sided pan used to poach fish.

SIMMERING Gentle boiling action.

VAPEUR To steam.

Activity

1. Make a list of poached foods that are served in your workplace or training establishment.
2. Using the steaming equipment in your establishment and the chart below, work out the times required to cook **six** different foods.

Food and amount	Type of steamer	Time taken

3. In your own words, explain why steamers are dangerous if not used properly.
4. In your working establishment practise poaching eggs. Try cooking one in:

   (a) boiling water;

   (b) from cold water brought to the boil;

   (c) simmering water with vinegar added.

   Record your results.

Prepare and grill food

ELEMENT 1
Prepare food for grilling

INTRODUCTION

Grilling is the fast, dry process of cooking tender cuts of meat, poultry, offal, fish and vegetables by radiant heat. The heat may be directed from above or below and the origin of the heat may be charcoal (or charcoal effect), wood, gas or electricity. The speed of the cooking process enables maximum retention of nutrients and flavour. Grilling is so fast that there is only 1 mm of radiant heat penetration before conduction takes place. This makes the process unsuitable for tougher, coarser items that require thorough cooking to become digestible. The extreme heat and dryness of grilling would destroy the food before it was ever cooked.

Only use tender, good-quality meat and poultry with a reasonable fat content.

COOKING TIP: The American term for grilling is 'broiling'.

PREPARING FOOD FOR GRILLING

Before the grilling process begins the food must be properly prepared. Some foods, such as meats, can be marinaded to improve the flavour and to partially tenderise. Alternatively, meat may be flavoured with fresh herbs and/or spices. Generally, however, the item to be grilled is seasoned with salt and milled black pepper prior to cooking. All meats to be grilled are lightly brushed with a little oil to help keep them moist during cooking.

Food to be grilled should be:

- sprinkled liberally with salt and milled black pepper;
- brushed lightly with oil and/or butter to keep it moist and to prevent it from sticking to the cooking tray or surface;
- small cuts of meat (larger joints of meat should be cut into steaks or thin slices);
- suitably shaped, to promote even cooking.

Food to be grilled can also be marinaded to improve flavour and partially tenderised, and flavoured with fresh herbs and/or spices.

COOKING TIP: Certain cuts of meat may be cubed and threaded on skewers (kebabs). Other meat may be minced to make hamburgers and sausages.

Figure 66 Salt, pepper, oil, herbs

HYGIENE AND STORAGE OF FOODS FOR GRILLING

Storage and hygiene

The following rules *must* be followed at all times when storing raw foods for grilling:

- ensure a high standard of personal hygiene is maintained;
- all equipment, materials and areas must be clean;
- foods should be placed on stainless-steel or plastic storage trays and covered with cling film and stored in a refrigerator;
- all waste food and other rubbish should be disposed of in accordance with the laid-down procedure.

EQUIPMENT USED IN GRILLING

To achieve the best results when grilling:

- the grilling equipment should be preheated to the correct temperature;
- the grilling bars should be lightly oiled to prevent the food from sticking to them;
- use good quality trays under Salamanders. Trays which will not twist or bend.

Figure 67 Overfired grill

> **NOTE: Glazed fruits can be glazed by coating them in sugar and browning.**

KEY WORDS

AU GRATIN To cover with breadcrumbs and/or grated cheese and grill until brown under a Salamander.

(À LA) BROCHE Food cooked on an open fire.

BROCHETTE On a skewer.

GLAZING In the context of grilling this is to coat with an enriched sauce containing cream and/or egg yolks and browned under a salamander to give a glossy finish.

GRATINATING The food can be covered with a sauce and/or a grated cheese and breadcrumbs and then browned under salamander – it has a 'dull' finish.

SEARING The action of using fierce heat to create the initial colouring of the food's surface.

SKEWERS Thin lengths of wood, bamboo or stainless steel used to hold small pieces of meat, vegetables, fish and/or fruit to cook over a grill or under a Salamander.

TOASTING To brown with 'dry' heat (i.e. without the use of fat).

GRILLING TECHNIQUES

There are three techniques used to grill foods:

1. Cooking under radiant heat

(Over-fired grills such as gas or electric salamanders)

Steaks, cutlets and chops can be cooked on greased salamander bars. Food items, e.g. cuts of fish, sausages, tomatoes, mushrooms, bacon, and kidneys, are suited to being cooked this way. Salamanders are also used to brown certain dishes, e.g. macaroni au gratin, cauliflower Mornay, duchess potatoes, and also to glaze and gratinate fish dishes.

2. Cooking over radiant heat

(Charcoal barbecues or on gas or electrically heated grill bars, sometimes with special fire bricks to simulate real charcoal)

This technique is used to cook larger items such as steaks, chops and cutlets. It is unsuitable for small items which fall through the bars. The wire bars produce an attractive pattern and the oven flames on the food create a very distinctive flavour.

NOTE: There are specialised items of grilling apparatus used to cook specific foods:

- **continuous/rotary grills These are specially designed grills used in fast-food outlets for cooking burgers and in large hotels and restaurants for cooking toast;**
- **a conveyor belt This carries the raw food items past the heat source.**

3. Cooking between heat

(Specially designed electrically heated grill bars or plates, sometimes known as contact or infra grills)

This technique is suitable for smaller items of meat, e.g. minute steaks.

COOKING TIP: The process of grilling should not be confused with that of griddling. Griddling is in fact a form of shallow frying carried out on a griddle plate.

DEGREES OF COOKING

Most foods are usually cooked thoroughly for service. However, in the case of beef steaks, lamb and offal, they may be served according to the customer's wishes. Grilling items will vary according to the thickness and quality. The chart below can be used as a guide.

Au bleu (blue or very rare)	Sealed for a matter of seconds on each side. The meat looks nearly raw.
Saignant (bleeding)	The cooked meat has a reddish tinge (underdone or rare)
À point (just done or medium)	A slight pinkness of the meat
Bien cuit (well cooked or well done)	Thoroughly cooked throughout. No signs of pinkness in the meat

COOKING TIP: Grilled food must be cooked to the correct degree, if not, the customer may return it.

Figure 68 Steak

(*See* Prepare and cook basic meat, poultry and offal dishes, pp. 153–70.)

Cooking guide for grilled beef

Cut of beef	*Menu example*	*Weight per portion*	*Cooking time, Medium cooked*
Fillet (head)	*Châteaubriand grillé* Double fillet steak	400 g	15 to 18 min
Fillet (middle)	*Tournedos*	150 g	8 to 10 min
Fillet (middle)	*Fillet grillé* Fillet steak	200 g	10 to15 min
Sirloin, boned	*Entrecôte double grillé* Double sirloin steak	400 g	15 to18 min
Sirloin, boned	*Entrecôte grillé* Single sirloin steak	200 g	8 to 10 min
Sirloin, boned	*Entrecôte minute grillé* Minute steak	100 g	1 to 2 min
Sirloin with fillet	Porterhouse steak (T-bone)	600 g	15 to 18 min
Rump	Point steak, grilled Rump steak, grilled	200 g	10 to 12 min

NOTE: The above dishes can be garnished in the following ways:

à la maison – **in the style of the house**

bouquetière – **a bouquet of glazed carrots, turnips, buttered peas, beans, cauliflower coated with hollandaise sauce, and small château potatoes**

Henri IV – **Pont Neuf potatoes and watercress**

vert pré – **Parsley butter, watercress and straw potatoes**

Cooking guide for grilled lamb

Cut	*Menu example*	*Weight per portion*	*Cooking time, Medium cooked*
Chump chop	*Chop d'agneau grillée* Grilled chump chop	250g	15 to 18 min
Cutlet	*Côtelettes d'agneau grillée* Grilled lamb cutlets	100g	8 to 10 min
Double cutlet	*Côtelettes double d'agneau grillée* Grilled double lamb cutlets	200g	15 to18 min
Boned loin	*Noisettes d'agneau grillée*	100g	3 to 5 min
Noisette	Grilled lamb noisette		
Boned loin, rolled	*Rosette d'agneau grillée*	100g	5 to 8 min
Rosette	Grilled lamb rosettes		
Boned loin	Shish kebab/Brochette of lamb		

Note: The above dishes (with the exception of kebabs) can be garnished in the following way :

Dubarry	**–**	**Small florets of cauliflower coated with mornay sauce and château potatoes**
Fleuriste	**–**	**Tomatoes filled with jardinière vegetables and château potatoes**
Parisienne	**–**	**Braised lettuce and parisienne potatoes**
Princess	**–**	**Artichoke bottoms filled with asparagus heads and noisette potatoes**

Figure 69 Grilled Bacon

Cooking guide for grilled pork and bacon

Cut of pork/bacon	*Menu example*	*Weight per portion*	*Cooking time, Medium cooked*
Chop	Grilled pork chop *Côte de porc grillée*	200g	15 to 18 min
Bacon	Grilled bacon	100g	3 to 8 min
Gammon steak	Grilled gammon steak	150g	8 to 10 min

Cooking guide for grilled veal

Cut of veal	*Menu example*	*Weight per portion*	*Cooking time, Medium cooked*
Cutlet	Grilled veal cutlet *Côte de veau grillée*	250g	8 to 10 min
Escalope	Escalope de veau grillée	150g	8 to 10 min

Cooking guide for grilled poultry

Commodity	*Menu example*	*Weight per portion*	*Cooking time, Medium cooked*
Chicken	*Poulet grillé à la crapaudine* *Poulet grillée spatchcock* *Poulet grillée*	400g	8 to 10 min
Spring chicken		400g	20 to 25 min

Cooking guide for grilled offal

Commodity	*Menu example*	*Weight per portion*	*Cooking time, Medium cooked*
Liver calves and lambs	*Foie de veau/ d'agneau grillée*	200g	5 to 6 min
Lamb's kidneys	*Rognon d'agneau grillée*	75g	3 to 8 min

Figure 70 Grilled Fish

Cooking guide for grilled cuts of fish

Commodity	*Menu example*	*Weight per portion*	*Cooking time, Medium cooked*
Cod			
Fillet	*Filet de cabillaud*	100g	3 to10 min
Steak	*Darne de cabillaud*	150g	3 to 10 min
Suprême	*Suprême de cabillaud*	100g	3 to 10 min
Dover sole			
Fillet	*Filet de sole*	100g	3 to 10min
Haddock			
Fillet	*Filet de aigrefin*	100g	3 to 10 min
Steak	*Darne d'aigrefin*	150g	3 to 10 min
Suprême	*Suprême d'aigrefin*	100g	3 to 10 min
Hake			
Fillet	*Filet de colin*	100g	3 to 10 min
Steak	*Darne de colin*	150g	3 to 10 min
Suprême	*Suprême de colin*	100g	3 to 10 min
Halibut			
Steak	*Tronç de Flétan*	150g	3 to 10 min
Lemon sole			
Fillet	*Filet de sole limande*	100g	3 to 10 min
Plaice			
Fillet	*Filet de plie*	150g	3 to 10 min
Salmon			
Steak	*Darne de saumon*	150g	3 to 10 min
Suprême	*Suprême de saumon*	100g	3 to 10 min

Cooking guide for whole grilled fish

Commodity	*Menu example*	*Weight per portion*	*Cooking time, Medium cooked*
Herring	*Hareng*	200g	15 to 20 min
Kippers	*Craquelot*	200g	15 to 20 min
Mackerel	*Maquereau*	200g	15 to 20 min
Red mullet	*Rouget*	200g	15 to 20 min
Plaice	*Plie*	200g	15 to 20 min

Sole, Dover	*Sole Douvres*	200g	15 to 20 min
Sole, lemon	*Sole limande*	250g	15 to 20 min
Trout	*Truite*	200g	8 to 12 min
Whiting	*Merlan*	200g	8 to 12 min

Cooking guide for whole shellfish

Commodity	*Menu example*	*Weight per portion*	*Cooking time, Medium cooked*
Lobster	Homard (Lobster butter)	300 g (shell on)	10 to 15 min
Scampi	Langoustine (Hard butter sauce or sauce diable)	200g (shell on)	8 to 12 min

Figure 71 Grilled food on a plate

Hot sauces suitable for serving with grilled foods

Chasseur sauce – *Sauce chasseur*
Devilled sauce – *Sauce diable*
Piquant sauce – *Sauce piquante*
Robert sauce – *Sauce Robert*
Béarnaise sauce – *Sauce béarnaise*

Compound butter suitable for serving with grilled foods

Parsley butter – *Beurre maître d'hôtel*
Anchovy butter – *Beurre d'anchois*
English mustard butter – *Beurre moutarde à l'anglaise*
French mustard butter – *Beurre moutarde à la française*
Garlic butter – *Beurre d'ail*
Horseradish butter – *Beurre de raifort*
Colbert butter – *Beurre vin rouge*
Wine merchant's butter – *Beurre marchand de vin*
Lobster butter – *Beurre d'homard*

Mixed Grill (Panache grillé)

(× 10 portions)

Ingredients

200g	butter
50g	parsley
1 tspn	lemon juice
500g	straw potatoes (see deep frying)
10 × 100g	lamb cutlets
10	lambs' kidneys
10	chipolata sausages
10	grilling mushrooms
10	tomatoes
10 ×	slices back bacon

Method

1. Soften the butter.
2. Wash the parsley and remove the stalks. Chop finely. Add to the softened butter. Add lemon juice, season with salt and pepper, and roll into a cylinder on greaseproof paper and chill.
3. Cook the potatoes and keep warm.
4. French trim the lamb cutlets and season with salt and pepper. Brush with oil.
5. Remove the skin from the lambs' kidneys. Cut open and remove the core. Place on skewers to keep flat, season with salt and pepper. Brush with oil.
6. Place the chipolata sausages on a greased grilling tray. Brush with oil.

7. Remove the mushroom stalks, wash, place on the grilling tray. Brush with oil and season with salt and pepper.
8. Remove the eyes from the tomatoes, make an incision in the form of a cross on the top of the tomatoes. Place on the grilling tray. Brush with oil and season with salt and pepper.
9. Place the bacon on the grilling tray.
10. Grill all the ingredients under the salamander beginning with the cutlets and then every other item at 3 min intervals. The bacon takes 2 min to cook. The kidneys should be cooked slightly underdone.

Garnish: Small bunches of watercress

Grill in the order listed and then place on an oval platter. Garnish with deep-fried straw potatoes, watercress with a slice of parsley butter on the kidneys.

Grilled Turkish Kebabs (Brochette à la Turque)

× 10 portions

Ingredients

1 ½kg	fillet of lamb
6g	fresh/dried thyme
100ml	lemon juice
300g	onion
20	bayleaves

NOTE: Variations of red/green pepper, button mushroom and large pieces of onion may be added.

Method

1. Trim the fat and sinew of the lamb and cut into 1 cm slices. Place in a bowl.
2. Sprinkle the thyme over the lamb.
3. Pour the lemon juice over the lamb and allow to marinade for two hours.
4. Cut the onions into large dice.
5. Divide the lamb and onions into equal portions. Arrange alternative pieces of the lamb, onions and bayleaves on the appropriate number of skewers. Cook for the required time.

Serve on a bed of braised rice (*riz pilaff*) and accompany with a demi-glacé based sauce.

Grilled Stuffed Mushrooms (Champignons farcis)

Ingredients

300g	grilling mushrooms
15g	chopped shallots
50g	butter, margarine or oil
25g	breadcrumbs

Method

1. Peel and remove the stalk. Wash thoroughly and dry well. Retain 8 to 12 of the best mushrooms.
2. Finely chop the remainder with the washed peelings and stalks.
3. Cook the shallots, without colour in a little fat.
4. Add the chopped mushrooms and cook for 2 to 4 min (*duxelle*).
5. Place on a tray and season with salt and pepper. Brush with melted fat or oil and grill on both sides for 3 to 4 min.
6. Place the *duxelle* in the centre of each mushroom.
7. Sprinkle with a few breadcrumbs and melted butter.
8. Reheat in the oven under the salamander and serve.

Garnish: picked parsley

Whole grilled fish (Poisson grillé)

(× 10 portions)

Ingredients

10 × 200 g whole prepared fish

Method

1. Pass the fish through seasoned flour and shake off any surplus.
2. Brush the fish and the grilling tray with melted butter, margarine or oil. Warm the tray and place the fish on it presentation side down.
3. Place under the pre-heated salamander, presentation side first, and cook on both sides for the required time.
4. Serve on an oval flat garnished with fluted lemon and picked parsley. Serve with an appropriate compound butter.

Grilled tomatoes (Tomates grillées)

Ingredients

tomatoes

Method

1. Wash the tomatoes, and remove the eyes with a small knife.
2. Place on a greased, seasoned baking tray.
3. Make an incision 2 mm cross-shape on the opposite side to the eye and peel back the four corners.
4. Brush with melted oil or fat and season with salt and pepper.
5. Grill under a moderately hot salamander.

   Garnish: picked parsley

KEY WORDS

AU BLEU Blue or very rare.

AU GRATIN To cover with breadcrumbs and/or grated cheese and grill until brown.

À POINT Just done or medium.

BIEN CUIT Well cooked or well done.

BLANCH Cook without colouring.

(À LA) BROCHE Food spit roasted or cooked on an open fire.

BROUCHETTE On a skewer.

BROILING American term for grilling.

GLAZING Coating with sugar syrup during cooking.

PORTERHOUSE American term for T-bone steak.

SEARING The action of using fierce heat to create the initial colouring of the food's surface.

SKEWERS Thin lengths of wood, bamboo or stainless steel used to hold small pieces of meat, vegetables, fish and/or fruit to cook over a grill.

TOASTING To brown with 'dry' heat (i.e. without the use of fat).

Activity

1. Find a suitable recipe for a marinade for grilled meat.

   Ingredients:

   Method:
2. Why are some foods coated before grilling?
3. Why is it important to pre-heat the grill before beginning to cook?

Crossword

Across

1 Thin length of wood used for kebabs (7)

4 Brush with o_ _ _ before grilling (3)

5 A cut of meat (4)

8 Burnt wood used as fuel for a barbecue (8)

12 Term for covering with breadcrumbs and/or cheese and browning (2,6)

14 Various, m_ _ _ _ _ (5)

15 Use of fierce heat to create initial colouring(7)

Down

1 Type of grill used to glaze/brown dishes (10)

2 and 10 down w_ _ _ _ d _ _ _ _ e.g. steak (4,4)

3 American term for grilling b _ _ _ _ _ _ _ _(8)

6 Type of heat given off from a grill r _ _ _ _ _ _ _ (7)

7 French term for kebab b _ _ _ _ _ _ _ _ _ _ (10)

9 French term for almost raw (2,4)

10 See 2 down

11 Not over or under but b _ _ _ _ _ _ _ heat (7)

13 Mixed g _ _ _ _ _ (5)

NVQ SVQ 1 | Prepare and griddle food

ELEMENT 1
Prepare food for griddling

INTRODUCTION

Griddling is, in effect, a form of shallow frying and a versatile method of cooking. Many foods that cannot be grilled can be cooked on a griddle. As the food cooks very quickly on a griddle it should not be left unattended, otherwise it might overcook or burn.

A true griddle is a flat metal surface which can either be a modular, mobile piece of equipment, or a flat plate that can go on top of a stove. There is also an open-groove griddle which can be placed on top of a stove.

Griddled food is generally cooked to order, ensuring that when it reaches the customer, it is always at its best. It should be moist, succulent and fresh. Griddled food is popular because virtually no fat is used in the cooking process.

HYGIENE

The following must be observed at all times.

- There should be a high standard of personal hygiene.
- All areas, equipment and materials must be thoroughly cleaned before and after use and as and when necessary during cooking.
- Never leave food lying around in a warm kitchen environment.

(See Maintain and promote hygiene in food storage, pp. 48–50; and Store food deliveries, pp. 291–7.)

STORAGE

All foods must be stored properly before and during cooking. The following should be observed when storing raw foods.

- Food should be placed on stainless-steel or plastic storage trays and covered with cling film and stored in a refrigerator until required.
- Only remove food from the refrigerator for immediate requirements.
- All waste food and other rubbish must be disposed of in accordance with the laid-down procedures of the establishment as prescribed in the Food Hygiene Safety Regulations (1995).

NOTE: If the food is not cooked to the correct degree, the customer may return it!

DEGREES OF COOKING

Most foods are usually cooked thoroughly for service. However, in the case of beef steaks, lamb and offal, they may be served according to the customer's wishes. Griddling items will vary according to the thickness and quality. The chart below can be used as a rough guide.

TIP: For the best results all foods to be griddled should be of the finest quality.

Au bleu (blue or very rare)	Sealed for a matter of seconds on each side. The meat looks nearly raw.
Saignant (bleeding) (underdone or rare)	The cooked meat has a reddish tinge.
À point (just done or medium)	A slight pinkness of the meat
Bien cuit (well cooked or well done)	Thoroughly cooked throughout. No signs of pinkness in the meat.

Figure 72 Steak *au bleu*

Figure 73 Steak *saignant*

Figure 74 Steak *à point*

Figure 75 Steak *bien cuit*

FOODS SUITABLE FOR GRIDDLING

Meats: bacon, sausages, burgers, steaks

Vegetables: mushrooms, tomatoes, onions

Sweet: pancakes, flapjacks, dropped scones

Savoury: eggs

ELEMENT 2

Griddle food

INTRODUCTION

Griddling is a fast, dry method of cooking food on a pre-heated, lightly oiled flat metal plate surface. The surface of the griddle should be lightly oiled before placing food on the cooking surface. Some griddles have ridges to simulate the effect of being cooked on a charcoal grill. Food cooked by this process has a distinctive flavour and an attractive appearance, and retains more of its nutrients.

(*See* Maintain and promote hygiene in food storage, preparation and cooking, pp. 48–54.)

HYGIENE

- Thoroughly clean all work areas, equipment and implements before and after use.
- Ensure that frozen food for griddling is thoroughly thawed.
- Clean the griddle with specific degreasing agents and always follow the manufacturer's instructions. A wire brush or scraper should be used to remove deposits from the griddle. Never use pointed items, otherwise they will scratch and ruin the surface.
- Discard any food that cannot be safely stored or used again.

To avoid cross-contamination always:

1. keep raw and cooked foods separate;
2. wash hands after handling uncooked and cooked foods and as frequently as possible.

COOKING TIP: Small thin, evenly sized food items will cook far quicker and will look more appetising when presented.

GRIDDLING

Always work in an organised and safe manner. It is essential to be prepared before using the griddle which will reduce the risk of becoming flustered when cooking different food items to varying degrees.

Checklist for griddling:

1. Ensure that the griddle is preheated to the correct temperature.
2. Have all equipment to hand.
3. Check that work surfaces are clean and hygienic.
4. Arrange food on trays and try to keep it covered.
5. Ensure that food is prepared, e.g. seasoned, marinaded or coated.
6. Lightly brush the food with oil or butter before placing it on the griddle.
7. Turn and baste food as appropriate; use tongs so as not to puncture the food item.
8. Carefully monitor cooking food so that it does not overcook or burn.
9. When food is cooked to the correct degree, transfer it to a serving plate, garnish and serve immediately.

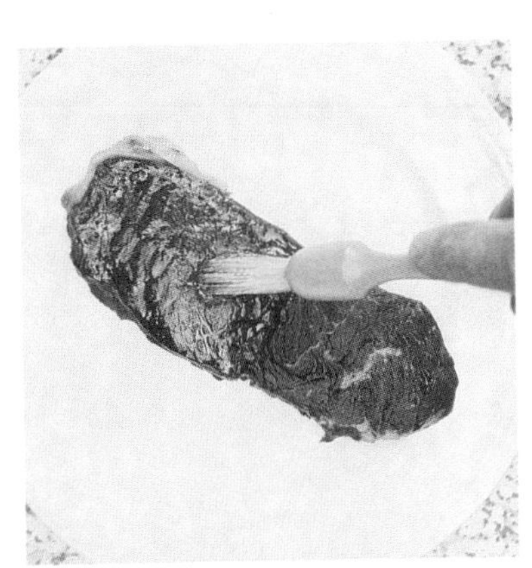

Figure 76 Brushing steak with oil

WARNING! Never leave a hot griddle unattended.

SAFETY

Extreme caution should be observed when using a griddle. Any food deposits or excess fat left on the griddle might:

- impair the efficiency;
- affect food cooked on the griddle;
- be a potential safety hazard.

Hamburg or Vienna steak Bitok

(4 portions)

Ingredients

15 g	chopped onion
250 g	lean minced beef
1	small egg
100 g	breadcrumbs
2 tbspn	cold water or milk

Method

1. Place the fat on a preheated griddle, cook the onion without colour. Allow to cool.
2. Add the onion to the remaining ingredients and combine well.
3. Divide the mixture in 4 even-sized ball shapes using a little flour. Flatten and mould into rounds.
4. Place on a preheated griddle and cook on both sides, reduce heat after the first few minutes. Ensure they are cooked through.

KEY WORDS

CHARRING To singe the surface of food to enhance the texture and flavour.

Activity

1. Explain why refrigeration is so important when preparing food for griddling.
2. Describe the types of foods that would be suitable for griddling and give examples of food items.
3. List the four stages of cooking meats and give a brief description of each stage.

   (a)

   (b)

   (c)

   (d)

4. Why is it important to keep preparation, cooking and storage areas and equipment hygienic?
5. Why is the temperature so important when griddling foods?
6. With the help of a supervisor or chef briefly describe any dangers associated with griddling.

....

....

....

NVQ SVQ 1

Prepare and finish reconstituted food

ELEMENT 1
Prepare reconstituted food

INTRODUCTION

Convenience food may be defined as those foods which have been carried to an advanced stage by manufacture and which may be used as a labour saving alternative to less processed products. Almost all food items involve some level of convenience, processing or manufacture.

NOTE: Some processing may involve the use of additives.

HYGIENE

All persons associated with the preparation of convenience food must have the appropriate training which should take into account:

- personal appearance and overall cleanliness;
- hygiene regulations;
- preparation of convenience food;
- cooking of convenience food;
- presentation of convenience food;
- holding/temperature control (hot and cold) of convenience food;
- storage of convenience food.

Figure 77 Range of convenience foods

STORAGE

When storing convenience foods the manufacturers'/processors' recommendations must always be followed carefully.

Never allow convenience foods to come into contact with raw or unprepared foods as they might cause cross-contamination.

REHEATING

Reconstituted food must be heated to a minimum temperature of 70 °C, but ideally to 75 °C. A temperature probe must always be used to check the core/centre temperature of the product.

ELEMENT 2
Finish reconstituted food

INTRODUCTION

There are many benefits from using convenience foods and they have many advantages over fresh products. Provided the manufacturer's instructions are always followed correctly, the caterer should encounter no problems when preparing and cooking such products. An important bonus of using convenience foods is that they offer precise cost and portion control.

Although costly, convenience foods allow the rationalising of staff and equipment. However, the chef must take into account the relationship of 'convenience foods' to the food-service operation: if everyone used only convenience foods there would be no individualism left in the art of cooking.

HYGIENE

WARNING! Never use stale, old or out-of-date convenience or pre-prepared food items

All persons involved in the cooking of convenience food items must:

- be tidy;
- be well-organised;
- maintain good hygiene practices at all times;
- ensure that all equipment, utensils and areas are thoroughly clean at all times.

STORAGE

Convenience foods can deteriorate and become a health hazard just like fresh produce and should therefore be treated as for fresh commodities.

Always:

- follow the manufacturer's instructions carefully;
- check the shelf life of the item.

Constituted pre-prepared or convenience foods that are not for immediate consumption must be cooled rapidly, preferably in a blast chiller, and stored at a safe temperature until they are required.

PRESENTING PREPARED CONVENIENCE FOOD

TIP: Remember, nobody wants to buy food that looks past its sell-by date!

All food must :

- be fresh;
- be attractively displayed;
- look appealing;
- be hygienically packaged.

Forms of convenience food

1. Dried, e.g. soups, sauces, fruit.
2. Frozen, e.g. vegetables, meat, cakes, tarts.
3. Canned, e.g. vegetables, soups, fruits, fish.
4. Chilled, e.g. pâté, smoked sausages.

KEY WORDS

CPU Central production unit for cooking food for distribution to pubs, hospitals, school meals and industrial sites.

RECONSTITUTE To regenerate food.

REGENERATE To return food to as near its pre-frozen/chilled state as possible by thawing or reheating to a safe temperature.

WARM HOLDING Keeping food warm over a period of time after it has been cooked and assembled for service.

Activity

1. With help from your supervisor or chef find out what the product information on a food label means.
2. Find out what the advantages and disadvantages of using convenience and pre-prepared food have over fresh.
3. Compile a list of convenience products that need reconstituting and which are used in your establishment.

NVQ SVQ 1 Prepare vegetables and fruit

ELEMENT 1
Prepare vegetables

INTRODUCTION

Vegetables are a vital part of our diet. They are good sources of essential vitamins, minerals and fibre and some provide carbohydrates for energy. They should be prepared correctly so as not to lose their nutritional value.

CLASSIFICATION OF VEGETABLES

The basic culinary classification for vegetables is: root for all those grown below the ground; and green for those grown above the ground. The expanded version of vegetable classification is shown below.

Figure 78 Vegetables on a board

Figure 79 Garlic

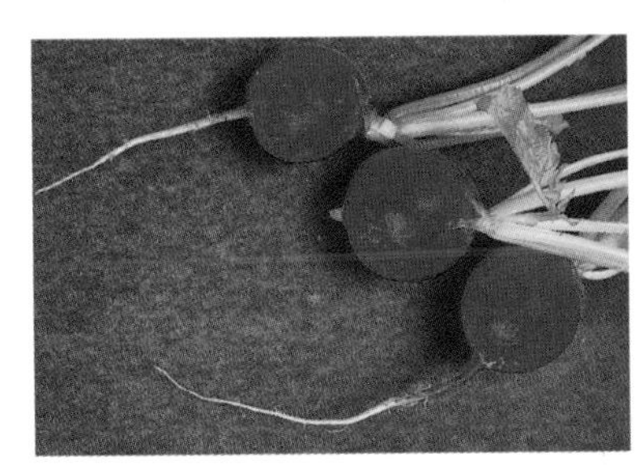

Figure 80 Radishes

Figure 81 Fennel

Culinary classification of vegetables
(The shaded classifications are not required to complete this unit)

Roots	Beetroot, carrot, celeriac, horseradish, mooli, parsnip, radish, salsify, swede, turnip
Tubers	Jerusalem artichoke, potato, sweet potato, yam
Bulbs	Garlic, leek, onion, shallot
Aqueous/Squash	Courgette, marrow, pumpkin, cucumber
Leaf	Chicory, Chinese leaf, lettuce, mustard cress, radiccio, sorrel, spinach, watercress
Fungi	Cepe, chanterelle, horn of plenty, morel, flat mushroom, beefsteak tomato, mushroom, button mushroom, cup mushroom, field mushroom, truffle
Brassica	Broccoli, cauliflower, kohlrabi, seakale, spring greens, Kale, Brussels sprouts, Savoy cabbage
Stem and shoot	Asparagus, celery, chicory endive, fennel
Fruit vegetable	Aubergine, avocado, courgette, pepper, tomato
Legume (pods and seeds)	Pea, French bean, broad bean, mange-tout, sweetcorn

QUALITY

Always check the quality of delivered vegetables. Some vegetables are more perishable than others and if they have not been stored properly, or have been stored for too long, they will be spoiled.

Always check that root vegetables:

- are free from soil and grit;
- are preferably pre-washed;
- have a good smell;
- are firm to the touch;
- are blemish free;
- are of even size and shape.

COOKING TIP: Vegetables, particularly root vegetables, can contain live food poisoning bacteria. Always scrub them thoroughly before and after preparation. Any soil finding its way to the preparation area, especially the chopping board, should be thoroughly cleaned immediately to prevent cross-contamination.

Always check that green vegetables:

- are bright in colour (first indication of freshness);
- are free from soil and grit;
- if root is attached, are soil-free;
- have crisp leaves;
- have tightly growing leaves; cabbage/sprouts must be compact.

GRADING

In Britain and Ireland the four main classes for vegetable produce are:

1. Extra class – top-quality vegetables
2. Class I – good-quality vegetables
3. Class II – reasonably good-quality vegetables
4. Class III – low marketable-quality vegetables

Each vegetable has its own set of standards from which they are graded.

HYGIENE AND STORAGE

The following rules must be adhered to at all times when preparing vegetables.

- Maintain a high standard of personal hygiene.
- Ensure that all equipment, materials and areas are clean before use.
- Store all fruits and vegetables in the correct manner.
- Dispose of all waste food and other rubbish in accordance with laid-down procedures as prescribed in the Food Hygiene Safety Regulations (1995).

(*See* Receive, handle and store food deliveries (Storage of fresh vegetables) p. 297 and Prepare and cook vegetables for basic hot dishes and salads, p. 185)

Prepared vegetables

After preparation fresh vegetables should only be stored for the minimum of time. They should be placed in a refrigerator in plastic or stainless-steel bowls and covered. Potatoes need to be submerged in cold water.

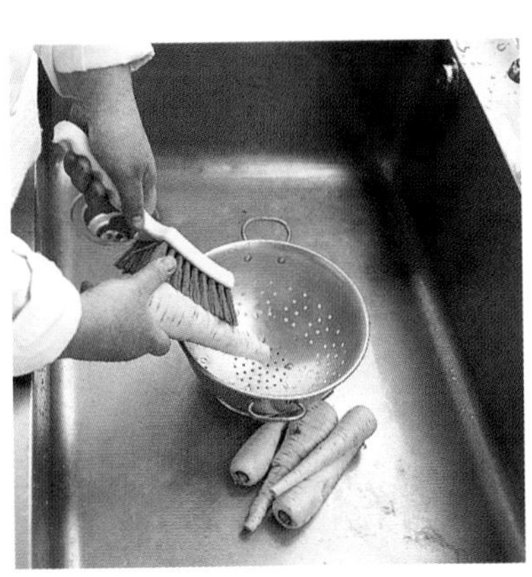

Figure 82 Brushing parnsips

Figure 83 Potatoes in cold water

PREPARING THE WORKING AREA AND EQUIPMENT

(See Handling and maintain knives pp. 40–7)

WARNING! Never have more than one knife out at any time.

Always:

- be properly prepared before beginning work;
- have the appropriate knife and equipment ready for the job in hand;
- use the correct colour-coded chopping board and make sure it is clean;
- work in a tidy and efficient manner;
- keep the preparation area clean and uncluttered at all times;
- have a receptacle, on or under the table, for peelings and discarded leaves;
- remove peelings and discarded leaves once finished;
- have a bowl ready for the prepared vegetables.

NOTE: In the main, root vegetables need not be stored in water, however, certain root vegetables (salsify) need to be placed in water with a little lemon juice to prevent discolouration

Basic preparation methods

Type	*Preparation*	*Special notes*
Roots	Wash and scrub thoroughly. Remove blemishes. Peel with a vegetable peeler. Re-wash and cut to required shape.	Turnips may be peeled using a small knife. Swedes require a cook's knife.
Tubers	Wash and scrub thoroughly. Remove any blemishes. Peel with a vegetable peeler. Re-wash and cut to required shape. Place in cold water and cover.	
Bulbs Onions/shallots	With a knife pull off the outerskin from the top to the root. Remove root close to the base of the vegetable. Cut to required shape and size.	
Garlic	To remove clove: lightly hit the head with the palm and use a knife to remove outerskin of clove from top to the root. Hit lightly with the flat of a knife and peel off skin.	
Leeks	Wash, remove discoloured/bruised leaves. Remove root close to bottom of the vegetable. Make an incision just above the root through to the top of the leek. Re-wash and cut to required shape.	
Leaves Lettuce/chicory	Remove any damaged/wilted leaves. Immerse in cold salted water to clean all leaves.	Leave in water for approx. 10 to 15 min. Do not wash under running water as this will damage the leaves.
Mustard cress	Cut 1 cm from the root and wash well.	
Watercress	Cut 1 cm from the root and wash well.	
Brassicas		
Brussel sprouts	Wash and remove any damaged/wilted or discoloured leaves. Trim and score the root in the shape of a cross and re-wash.	
Cabbage	Wash and trim the root. Remove damaged/wilted or discoloured leaves. Cut cabbage in quarters and remove centre stalk and any large leaf ribs. Re-wash.	

Type	Preparation	Special notes
Spring greens	Wash and trim the root. Remove damaged/wilted or discoloured leaves. Re-wash.	If small enough they may be cooked whole, if not, they should be quartered and any large leaf ribs removed.
Spinach	Wash thoroughly and remove all soil/grit. Remove centre stalk. Re-wash.	
Stems	Wash and cut the woody parts from the base of the stem.	
Asparagus	Remove spurs or tips from the leaves.	
	Peel the white section of the stem. Re-wash.	
Celery	Wash, remove the tough outer stalks. Trim the stem. Re-wash. Cut to required shape.	
Chicory endive	Remove outer leaves and any blemished leaves. Trim stem. Wash.	
Seakale	Wash and remove any damaged or discoloured leaves. Re-wash.	
Vegetable fruits Aubergines	Wash, peel, trim, slice or dice and place in a bowl of water with a little lemon juice added to prevent discoloration.	
Avocado	Cut in half and peel with a vegetable knife. Sprinkle with lemon juice to prevent discoloration.	
Courgettes	Wash, remove the top and base. Peel (if required). Cut to desired shape.	
Peppers	Wash, remove stalk and cut in half lengthwise. Remove pith and seeds. Cut to required shape.	
Cucumber	Wash and peel. Cut to required shape.	
Tomatoes	Wash, remove stalk and eye. Cut to required shape.	

Vegetable Cuts

Brunoise	Dice of Julienne (2 mm dice maximum)
Château	Barrel shapes
Jardinière	Baton shapes approximately 2 cm × 4 mm × 4 mm
Julienne	Thin, matchstick shapes, 2 mm × 36 mm long
Macedoine	Small ½ cm to 1 cm cubes
Matignon	Smaller cut of Mirepoix
Mirepoix	Roughly cut vegetables for stews, etc, which will not be used for presentation
Paysanne	Thin slices or pieces of vegetables which may be a variety of shapes, e.g. triangular, round, square or rough sided, approximately 1 cm in diameter.

KEY WORDS

BOUQUET GARNI
Bundle of herbs – bay leaf, parsley, thyme – wrapped in leek or celery.

ONION CLOUTÉ
An onion which has been studded with cloves and bay leaf.

CONCASSE Coarsely chopped.

FLORETS Small flowers, individual sections of flower head, for example, cauliflower and broccoli.

WILTED Not fresh, limp and drooping.

DUXELLE Type of stuffing which may be used for vegetables. Made from onions, mushrooms, butter, wine, garlic, breadcrumbs.

CHAFFANT Pot of hot salted water used for reheating vegetables.

Activity

1. Take a trip to the local supermarket and see how many varieties of the following vegetables you can find.

Commodities	Varieties
Potatoes	
Lettuce	
Tomatoes	
Onions	
Mushrooms	
Cabbage	

2. Using the weekly catering magazines find the market price for the following vegetables.

Commodities	£ per kg each as appropriate
New potatoes	
Old (main crop) potatoes	
Tomatoes	
Cucumber	
Cabbage	
Lettuce	
Onions	
Mushrooms	

ELEMENT 2
Prepare friut

INTRODUCTION

Fruit is used extensively in kitchens. It is extremely versatile and can be used on its own as a snack or dessert, as part of a hors d'œuvre or salad, to garnish or as the basis of a sauce for a meat, poultry or game dish, or as a sweet preparation. Most fruits are seasonal and although some are available from other parts of the world, purchasing will ultimately be determined by costs. Fruits contain nutrients such as vitamin C and are a valuable source of roughage.

Figure 84 Selection of fresh fruit

CULINARY CLASSIFICATION OF FRUITS

Fruit may be classified into the following groups.

(The shaded classifications are not required for completion of this unit)

Hard	Apple, crab apple, pear
Soft (stone)	Apricot, cherry, damson, greengage, nectarine, peach, plum
Citrus	Citron, clementine, grapefruit, lemon, lime, kumquat, mandarin, orange, tangerine, ugli
Berries (soft)	Blackberry, blackcurrant, blueberry, cranberry, gooseberry, loganberry, raspberry, strawberry, wild strawberry
Melons	Cantaloupe, charentais, gallia, honeydew, ogen, watermelon
Tropical fruits	Banana, cape gooseberries (physalis), carambola, date, feijoa, fig, guava, kiwi fruit, lychee, mangosteens, mangoes, passion fruit, papaya, paw-paw, pineapple, Sharon fruit
Other fruits	Fig, quince, plaintain, persimmon, pomegranate, prickly pear, rhubarb

Figure 85 Pineapple

Figure 86 Lemons

QUALITY

It is important to check the quality of fruit when it is delivered to the establishment. Fruit should have a good bright colour and appear fresh. It should be firm to the touch, clean and free of damage such as blemishes or bruises. Some fruits are liable to damage easily and if they have not been stored correctly or have been stored for too long, they will be ruined. Soft fruits are highly perishable. Try to ensure that fruits are not bought too ripe, otherwise they will deteriorate quicker.

GRADING

In Britain and Ireland (EEC guidelines) the four main classes for fruit produce are:

Extra class	top-quality fruits
Class I	good-quality fruits
Class II	reasonably good-quality fruits
Class III	low marketable-quality fruits

Each fruit has its own set of standards by which they are graded.

HYGIENE AND STORAGE

(*See* Maintain personal health and hygiene, pp. 10–13, *see also* Maintain and promote hygiene in food preparation and cooking, pp. 48–54.)

(For storage instructions *see* Receive, handle and store food deliveries, p 297.)

The following rules must be adhered at all times when preparing fruit:

- Maintain a high standard of personal hygiene.
- Ensure that all equipment, materials and areas are clean before use.
- Store all fruits in the correct manner.
- Dispose of all waste food and other rubbish is disposed of in accordance with laid-down procedures as prescribed in the Food Hygiene Safety Regulations (1995).

Prepared fruits

After preparation fresh fruit should only be stored for the minimum of time. It should be placed in a refrigerator in plastic or stainless-steel bowls and covered. Fruit absorbs strong odours which will taint it. Bananas should not be stored in a refrigerator as they might bruise. If soft, summer fruits are refrigerated for too long, the condensation encourages the growth of moulds and yeast.

PREPARING THE WORKING AREA AND EQUIPMENT

Always:

- be properly prepared before beginning work;
- have the appropriate knife and equipment ready for the job in hand;
- use the correct colour-coded chopping board and make sure it is clean and sterilised;
- work in a tidy and efficient manner;
- keep the preparation area clean and uncluttered at all times;
- have a bin, on or under the table, for peelings and discarded leaves;
- have a bowl ready for the prepared fruits.

WARNING! Never have more than one knife out at any time.

Figure 87 Bananas sliced in bowl of acidulated water

TIP: Some fruits may need to be placed in acidulated water to prevent discolouration.

Basic preparation methods

Type	*Preparation*	*Special notes*
Hard fruits	**For eating** Remove stalk. Wash in cold water. **For cold preparations and cooking** Wash, remove stalk. Peel, halve or quarter to remove the core. Place in acidulated water to prevent discolouration. Cut to required shape. to prevent discoloration	Place in acidulated water
Soft fruits	**For eating, cold preparation and cooking** Remove husks, tops and tails. Wash in cold water. Carefully remove the fruit and drain in a colander.	Do not over handle as soft fruit damages easily. Only wash the fruit being prepared as it deteriorates very quickly after washing.
Citrus	**For eating** Wash in cold water. If the fruit is to be cut for serving, remove centre core and pips. Free segments with a grapefruit knife. This makes for easier eating. For cold preparations and cooking Wash in cold water. Remove the skin and pith. Using a vegetable preparation knife remove each segment from all connecting tissue leaving only the flesh.	

CUTS OF FRUIT

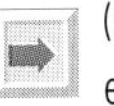
(See vegetable cuts in the previous element, p. 114)

The flesh of some fruits cannot be cut because of their delicate composition. However, others – in particular hard fruits – can be shaped.

Carrots, buttered *Carottes au beurre* or *Carottes glacées*

Ingredients

400 g	carrots
25 g	butter
	chopped parsley

Method

1. Wash and peel, the carrots. Rewash thoroughly.
2. Cut into even-sized pieces or turn barrel shape.
3. Place carrots in a saucepan with the butter, a pinch of sugar and a little salt. Just cover carrots with water.
4. Place a sheet of buttered paper (cartouche) over and allow to boil steadily until the water has evaporated.
5. Check that the carrots are cooked, if not, add a little more water and continue cooking. Do not overcook.
6. To glaze carrots: toss them over a fierce heat for approximately 1-2 min.
7. Sprinkle over chopped parsley and serve.

KEY WORDS

ACIDULATED WATER
A mixture of water and lemon juice used to prevent fruit from discolouring.

BLANCHE To plunge into boiling water then refresh to enable skin to be removed.

MACERATE To soak in sugar syrup and liqueur.

PITH The thick under-skin from citrus fruit.

REFRESH To plunge into cold water to arrest cooking.

ZEST The outer skin from citrus fruits.

Activity

1. Take a trip to the local supermarket/greengrocer and see how many varieties of the following fruits you can find.

Commodity	Varieties
Apples	
Pears	
Oranges	
Melons	
Berries	
Grapefruits	

2. Using the weekly catering magazines find the market price for the following fruits:

Commodity	£ per lb/kg
Eating apples	
Cooking apples	
Bananas	
Cherries	
Grapefruits	
Kiwi	
Lemon	
Mango	
Oranges	
Peaches	

3. Why is it necessary to store some prepared fresh fruits in covered stainless-steel or plastic bowls in the refrigerator?

Prepare cold and hot sandwiches and rolls

ELEMENT 1

Prepare cold sandwiches and rolls

INTRODUCTION

Sandwiches are the most popular convenience food in the UK and many companies make and package sandwiches for sale in thousands of retail outlets. Specialised packaging and improved refrigeration techniques have resulted in the use of an enormous variety of breads (traditional and continental) and a wide range of delicious fillings, from the exotic to the more conventional. Sandwiches are available either hot or cold and come in many shapes and sizes, some of which are variations or improvements on the traditional sandwich. Each country has its own particular way of preparing and filling this versatile 'quick and easy' snack.

HYGIENE

All fillings used in sandwich-making must be of a high quality and always fresh. Avoid cross-contamination by minimising the handling of foods. To guarantee total freshness of the product and avoid spoilage between preparation and consumption, sandwiches should be prepared quickly and, if required, packaged and refrigerated immediately to maintain hygiene standards. Potential dangers are from cooked fillings which might become infected and cause food poisoning.

Food hygiene regulations cover the temperature controls necessary for the preparation, packaging and storage of sandwiches and rolls. Preparation areas and all equipment and utensils used in the preparation of sandwiches must be kept scrupulously clean at all times.

(For more information see the Food Hygiene (Food Safety) Regulations 1995.)

STORAGE OF PREPARED SANDWICHES AND ROLLS

Prepared and packaged sandwiches made for commercial distribution must be kept at a temperature no higher than 8°C and should be sold within 24 hours of production, after which period they should be discarded. Refrigerated vans are used for transporting sandwiches for distribution between the assembly kitchen and the point of sale, in order to reduce the risk of spoilage and possible food poisoning.

BREADS

There is an enormous variety of different breads for sale that may be used in sandwich making and which come in a variety of shapes, sizes, flavours, textures and even colours!

Bagel This traditional Jewish bread roll is best served warm, classically with a cream cheese and smoked salmon or mackerel pâté.

Figure 88 Arrangement of breads

Baguette Sometimes referred to as 'French stick', it may be split lengthways, cut into various lengths or grilled. A variety of fillings may be used.

Brioche Rich, light and slightly sweet, this is an ideal base for open sandwiches when toasted.

Ciabatta A basic Italian dough flavoured with olive oil, it has a light texture and is available plain or flavoured.

Cottage loaf This crusty white loaf is ideal for toasted sandwiches.

Croissant Made from an enriched, laminated dough, it is best served warm and split before filling. It is delicious when spread with butter, sweet or savoury fillings.

Granary, onion bread, cheese and herb sticks These are a tasty base for any choice of appetising filling.

Pitta bread A popular unleavened bread available white or wholemeal, in rounds, ovals and mini shapes. It is delicious when filled with grilled meat and salads.

Pugliese This is a close textured bread made with olive oil.

Pumpernickel A black rye bread (heavy, close-textured) with a distinctive flavour, it is a suitable base for open sandwiches.

Quarten loaf This is a double-sized sandwich loaf.

Rye bread Available in light or dark rye or with sunflower seeds, it is delicious when served with a variety of fillings.

White breads. These are available pre-packaged and pre-sliced. Bakeries have their own particular varieties, some of which tend to be more flavoursome and have a better texture.

Wholemeal/wholewheat breads These are sometimes preferred to white breads for their distinctive flavour and texture.

SPREADS

Sandwiches can be spread with plain butter, flavoured butter or mayonnaise. Nowadays there are a number of 'healthy' options to choose from, such as low fat spreads and flavoured olive oil.

Butter Plain, tomato, mustard, onion or garlic flavoured, anchovy

Mayonnaise Plain or flavoured (tomato, tartare or anchovy)

Gravalax sauce Used with gravalax (Scandinavian marinated salmon), its piquant flavour also goes well with beef. Store in an airtight container in the refrigerator for up to two weeks.

Peanut sauce Suitable served with chicken, pork, duck or any vegetables, it may also be used as a 'dip'. Store in an airtight container in the refrigerator for up to one week.

SANDWICH FILLINGS

Sandwiches should be appetising, nutritious and enjoyable. There is a vast range of fillings for both cold and hot sandwiches, some of which include the following:

Vegetable and fruit

Avocado This gives a subtle flavour to sandwiches and mixes well with prawns or Brie.

Capers Ideal in dressings, they have a piquant flavour.

Cucumber Remove outer skin before using.

Lettuce Various types are used with a combination of fillings.

Olives These are delicious on toasted toppings.

Onion or shallot In slices or diced they complement most fillings.

Peppers These are a crunchy and colourful addition to sandwiches.

Tomatoes These are very versatile and may be used in numerous combinations.

Cheese fillings

Stilton Waldorf Spread a layer of mayonnaise on two slices of bread. Place slices of Stilton cheese, finely chopped walnuts, black grapes (halved) and shredded lettuce on top.

Figure 89 Cheeses

Blue cheese This is ideal mixed with fruit, particularly pear.

Gruyère or Emmenthal (Swiss) cheese These are usually melted under a grill.

Brie For the best flavour ensure that the centre is soft when used. Mix with avocado and tomato.

Cheddar cheese and pesto Mix mayonnaise with pesto sauce and spread over bread. Place a generous layer of grated Cheddar cheese over it and top with sliced tomatoes.

Cottage cheese and pineapple Mix cottage cheese with finely chopped pineapple. Spoon the filling into buttered roll.

Mozzarella Ideal for melting under the grill, it blends with sun-dried tomatoes and olive paste.

Chicken fillings

Coronation chicken Mix mayonnaise with a little curry paste and natural yogurt. Place strips of lettuce on the bread and place slices of chicken on top. Sprinkle with raisins.

Chicken and bacon Spread a thin layer of cranberry sauce on the bread before adding the chicken slices and bacon.

Chicken tikka Make a pocket in a pitta bread. Mix together natural yogurt with a little fresh mint and spread inside the pitta bread. Place slices of prepared chicken tikka in the bread with shredded lettuce and a little more of the yogurt and mint mixture.

Meat fillings

Figure 90 Meat fillings

Pork and cranberry Mix together cranberry sauce and natural yogurt (equal quantities). Spread the mixture onto a slice of bread before adding shredded lettuce, cold (cooked) pork slices.

Salami A vast range of smoked and unsmoked salami is available.

Grilled ham and Gruyère Slice a baguette in half lengthways (keep the base and top intact). Mix Dijon mustard and a little butter together and spread evenly on both sides of the baguette. Place a layer of sliced ham on the base with a layer of Gruyère cheese on top. Bake for 4 to 5 min, until cheese begins to melt.

Roast beef and horseradish Spread a layer of horseradish sauce over buttered bread and top with a layer of roast beef. Sprinkle over chopped spring onions.

Pastrami and watercress This is cured brisket of beef, smoked and is ideal with strong flavoured breads such as rye. Add chopped watercress to coleslaw and season with black pepper. Fill a roll with pastrami or smoked continental meat and spoon over the coleslaw mixture. Top with gherkins.

Parma ham This matured, cured ham is sliced thinly and used for delicate sandwiches.

Fish fillings

Figure 91 Fish fillings

Prawns and soft cheese This is ideal on crispbreads. Spread crispbread with a thick layer of soft cheese and arrange prawns on top. Place cucumber slices along the centre with a few prawns on top. Sprinkle with cayenne pepper and a twist of lemon.

Prawns /shrimp Always use the finest quality prawns and shrimps.

Smoked salmon and watercress Mix finely chopped watercress leaves with mayonnaise and a little lemon juice. Place chunks of cooked fresh salmon steaks between slices of bread and spoon over the mayonnaise mixture.

Tuna salad Drain and flake tinned tuna chunks, mix with a little horseradish sauce and natural yogurt. Place a layer of salad (lettuce, spring onions, radish, tomato) and add the tuna filling.

Crab and avocado Mix crab meat with spring onions, seasoning and mayonnaise. Cut the avocado into thin slices and brush with lemon juice. Spread the crab meat on buttered bread and cover with slices of avocado. Spread a little more mayonnaise over the top and cover with another slice of buttered bread. Remove crusts and cut into triangles. Garnish with endive leaves.

Rollmop herrings Pickled herring makes a tasty filling for open sandwiches.

Smoked salmon Ideal for open and pinwheel sandwiches, it may also be chopped and served with croissants.

Herring and apple Spread softened butter on rye bread and cover with lettuce leaves. Cut the herring fillets in half lengthways and place on top of the lettuce. Lightly brush the apple slices with a little lemon juice and arrange around the herring. Spoon over a dressing, e.g. fennel and soured cream, and garnish with fennel.

COOK'S TIP: Using various attachments on a food processor will save time in the preparation of fillings.

EQUIPMENT

The most essential item of equipment needed for making sandwiches is a good bread knife. The following, however, will also be needed and should always be kept close to hand:

Bread knife Always use a good quality bread knife for even cutting whole loaves into slices.

Cheese grater This is a must when preparing fillings. It may be used for vegetables as well as cheese.

Measuring cups and spoons These are used for standard portioning.

Mixing bowls These are essential for storing ingredients for fillings.

Palette knives These are ideal for spreading fillings evenly.

Pastry brushes Use them for brushing bread with melted butter and oils.

Saucepan Use it for melted and cooked fillings.

Spatula This should be flexible for spreading and transferring fillings from bowls.

PRODUCTION OF SANDWICHES

To produce large quantities of sandwiches in a hygienic and cost-effective manner the following rules should be observed:

- Have fillings prepared and in separate containers.
- Soften and cream the spread.
- Use sliced bread.
- Have containers on hand for crusts and trimmings.

PRE-PACKAGING SANDWICHES

When sandwiches are not consumed on the premises or are offered for sale from a vending machine or snack bar they should be packaged in a hygienic manner.

TYPES OF PACKAGING

- Hinged plastic boxes
- Clear heat-sealed triangles with cardboard sides
- Waxed paper
- Hinged waxed cardboard boxes
- Heat-sealed bags
- Polystyrene boxes

Mayonnaise

(1 cup/350 ml)

Ingredients

2	egg yolks
½ tspn/2.5 ml	Dijon mustard
300 ml	sunflower oil
2 tspn/10 ml	wine vinegar
	salt and pepper

Method

1. Place the egg yolks, seasonings and mustard in a mixing bowl, beat with a hand whisk. Gradually add the oil, drop by drop, whisking vigorously.
2. When mixture thickens, add the vinegar. Add the remaining oil in a steady stream, whisking continually. Add a little boiling water, if necessary, to thin the mixture.

Peanut sauce Suitable served with chicken, pork, duck or any vegetables. May also be used as a 'dip'. Store in an airtight container in the refrigerator for up to one week.

Peanut sauce

(1 cup/300 ml)

Ingredients

1 tbspn/15 ml	sunflower oil
1	onion, finely chopped
1 tspn/5 ml	ground cumin
1 tspn/5 ml	ground coriander
½tspn/2.5 ml	chilli powder
3 tbspn/45 ml	crunchy peanut butter
2 tspn/10 ml	soya sauce
1tspn/5 ml	lemon juice

Method

1. Heat the oil in a frying pan and fry the onion until it softens. Add the garlic and spices and fry for 1 min, stirring.
2. Add the peanut butter and mix, blend in 150 ml. water. Bring to the boil, stirring. Cover and cook for 5 min.
3. Transfer to a mixing bowl and stir in the soya sauce and lemon juice. If necessary, thin with a little water. Cool completely before using.

Gravalax sauce Used with gravalax, (Scandinavian marinaded salmon), its piquant flavour also goes well with beef. Store in an airtight container in the refrigerator for up to two weeks.

Gravalax sauce

(⅔ cup/150 ml)

Ingredients

2 tbspn/30 ml	German mustard
1 tspn/5 ml	caster sugar
1 tspn/5 ml	wine vinegar
2 tbspn/30 ml	oil
2 tbspn/30 ml	soured cream
1 tbspn/30 ml	fresh dill, finely chopped

Method

1. Place the mustard, sugar and vinegar into a mixing bowl and beat well. Gradually add the oil, beating well between each addition.
2. Slowly mix in the cream and chopped dill.

ELEMENT 2

Prepare hot sandwiches and rolls

INTRODUCTION

Though the basic idea of the sandwich has remained the same for more than two hundred years, there are now many permutations. The variety and availability of breads and ideas for creative fillings are endless. As well as the classic hot sandwiches – bookmaker and the Club, there are many more new and exciting sandwiches to tempt the – palate, all using a vast selection of mouth-watering ingredients, breads and dressing/sauces to create innovative snacks and wholesome meals.

HYGIENE

(*See* Maintain and promote hygiene in food preparation and cooking, pp.51–4.)

Sandwiches that are prepared to be served 'hot' must be stored as cold products, at a temperature of 5 °C or below to avoid spoilage between preparation and consumption.

Once sandwiches are 'warmed' they have a limited life, depending on the filling and bread used. They must never be cooled and reheated as this might cause food poisoning.

HOT SANDWICHES

Hot sandwiches consist of a single filling or variety of fillings placed between two or more slices of toasted bread (white/brown or white and brown), spread lightly with plain or flavoured butter, margarine or mayonnaise. For classic hot sandwiches, the crusts are removed and the sandwich cut into four triangles. Most modern hot sandwiches have the crusts left on.

Toasted sandwiches are served in most catering establishments and the fillings vary from scrambled egg, bacon and fried egg, cooked ham and cheese to the more traditional fillings of chicken breast and minute steak.

Hot sandwiches for the restaurant are served on a lined salver or plate. Traditionally, cocktail sticks are placed in the corner of each triangle to keep the bread and filling in position for service. Hot sandwiches for takeaway service are placed in hygienic containers.

SELECTION OF HOT SANDWICHES

Toasted sandwiches Toast two slices of bread, 'butter' and place the required filling in between the slices. Suitable fillings are cheese, scrambled egg, ham, bacon, sausage.

Bookmaker sandwich

(1 serving)

Ingredients

2 slices	bread, sliced
	butter
1 × 100 g	minute steak, prepared
	English mustard

Method

1. Grill or sauté the steak for 1 minute on either side.
2. Toast the sliced bread and butter.
3. Place steak on a slice of toast and spread lightly with English mustard. Cover with the other slice of toast. Remove crusts and cut into triangles.

   Serve immediately.

Club sandwich

(1 serving)

Ingredients

2 slices	bread, sliced
	butter
1	lettuce leaf
	egg, hard boiled
	tomato
100 g	chicken breast, cooked
2 slices	back bacon

Method

1. Toast the sliced bread and butter lightly. Spread with a little mayonnaise.
2. Wash and trim lettuce and place on one slice of toast.
3. Shell and slice egg and place on top of the lettuce.
4. Blanch tomato in boiling water for 10 seconds and refresh immediately. Remove skin and slice into thin strips. Place on top of egg.
5. Cut the chicken into slices and place appropriate amount on sandwich.
6. Place bacon under preheated salamander and cook for 2 to 3 min on either side. Cover with other slice of toast. Cut into triangles.
7. Complete sandwiches as follows: lettuce, sliced egg, tomato, chicken and bacon.

   Serve immediately.

Croque Monsieur sandwich

(1 serving)

Ingredients

2 slices	white bread, sliced
15 g	butter, softened
1 slice	ham, lean (thinly sliced)
30 g	Gruyère cheese
1	sprig parsley

Method

1. Lightly butter the sliced bread.
2. Lay the slice of ham on one slice of bread and place the slice of cheese on top of the ham. Cover with the other slice of bread.
3. Remove crusts.
4. Spread butter on top of the sandwich and place under the grill to cook for 2½ min.
5. Turn sandwich over, spread with a little butter and place under the grill for a further 2½ min, until it is golden brown and the cheese begins to melt.

   Serve immediately garnished with a sprig of parsley.

Danish hot tartare sandwich

(1 serving)

Ingredients

1 slice	toasted buttered bread
1 oz	clarified butter
4 oz	fresh minced steak
4	onion rings
1	tomato
2	gherkins
1	sprig parsley, garnish

Method

1. Toast bread on one side.
2. Spread minced beef on other side.
3. Fry in clarified butter until golden brown on both sides.
4. Transfer to a warm plate and garnish with onion rings, tomato quarters, gherkins and a sprig of parsley.

Köfte in pitta pockets (Turkish meat balls)

(4 serving)

Ingredients

4	pitta bread
1	slice bread
225 g	minced lamb
1 clove	garlic, crushed
	flour
	salt and pepper
1	onion (small), finely chopped
1	onion, sliced in rings
2	tomatoes, sliced
1 tbspn/15 ml	fresh mint, finely chopped
1 tspn/15 ml	ground cumin
1 tbspn/15 ml	pine nuts

Method

1. Soak the bread in water for 5 min, squeeze dry.
2. Place the minced lamb, chopped onion, cumin, mint, pine nuts and garlic in a mixing bowl. Add the soaked bread and mix throughly to combine all ingredients.
3. Shape into small balls, using dampened hands. Coat in flour.
4. Heat a little oil in a frying pan and shallow fry for 6 min, turning continually, until golden brown.
5. Heat the pitta bread in the oven until it puffs up. Cut a thin strip off one side of each pitta bread to make a pocket.
6. Fill with the köfte, onion rings and tomato slices.

Lamb in pitta pockets

(1 serving)

Ingredients

1	pitta bread
175g	lamb fillet
50ml	red wine
1 clove	garlic, chopped
1	bay leaf
50ml	olive oil

Method

1. Place the wine, olive oil, garlic, bay leaf, cumin and coriander and mix together.
2. Add the lamb fillet and marinade for at least 30 min.
3. Remove from marinade and grill lamb for 10 min, turning once to ensure even cooking. Slice thinly, stuff into the warmed pitta bread.
4. Add the lettuce, onion rings and tomato and spoon over tzatziki. Serve immediately.

Tzatziki: Mix together 100g Greek yogurt, 50g peeled and grated cucumber, 1 garlic clove (crushed), 1 1 tbspn/15ml, chopped fresh mint. Season to taste.

Figure 92 Tzatziki

Strammer Max Fry a slice of bread on both sides until golden brown. Place sautéed lardons of bacon on the bread and garnish with shallow fried egg and a sprig of parsley.

Pear and Stilton Soften cheese and mix in pieces of chopped ripe pear. Add chopped chives and season with black pepper. Bake in an oven for 5 min. This filling is suitable for croissants. Eat immediately.

Bruschetta al Pomodoro Rub crushed garlic on top of toasted bread and drizzle olive oil over. Spoon on top skinned, chopped or seasoned tomatoes and drizzle over a little more oil. Place under the grill. Garnish with basil sprigs. Eat immediately.

Pastrami on rye Butter rye bread and spread with a little German mustard. Place wafer-thin slices of pastrami on top and sliced (lengthways) gherkins. Place a slice of rye bread on top and press together firmly. Toast on both sides under the grill. Garnish with radish chrysanthemums and spring onions.

KEY WORDS

BAGUETTE French stick.

CHIFFONADE Thinly shredded lettuce or other leaf.

CROSS CONTAMINATION The transfer of bacteria from one food to another.

CUTTERS Many shapes and sizes are available and are especially useful for party sandwiches and canapés.

LARDONS Sliced bacon cut into thin strips.

QUARTEN LOAF Double-sized sandwich loaf.

PITTA BREAD A purse of coarse bread originally from India.

SMØRREBRØD Scandinavian open sandwich.

Activity

1. In your own words describe each of the following:

- Bookmaker sandwich
- Croque Monsieur sandwich
- Strammer Max sandwich

2. List four important points concerning hygiene when preparing cold sandwiches:

   (a)

   (b)

   (c)

   (d)

3. Name three types of bread suitable for making sandwiches:

   (a)

   (b)

   (c)

4. List four types of packaging used for cold sandwiches.

   (a)

   (b)

   (c)

   (d)

Prepare, cook and assemble food for service

ELEMENT 1
Prepare food and kitchen areas for service

NOTE: Some processing may involve the use of additives.

INTRODUCTION

Convenience food may be defined as those foods which have been carried to an advanced stage by manufacture and which may be used as a labour-saving alternative to less processed products. Almost all food items involve some level of convenience, processing or manufacture. For most products, the processing involves the use of one or more methods to inhibit or delay the onset of food spoilage, for example, cook-chill, cook-freeze and sous vide. All food purchased must be of prime quality.

HYGIENE

All persons associated with the preparation of pre-prepared and convenience food must have the appropriate training which should include:

(*See* Maintain personnel health and hygiene, pp. 10–13; *See* also Maintain and promote hygiene in food preparation and cooking, pp. 48–54.)

- personal appearance and overall cleanliness;
- hygiene regulations;
- storage of pre-prepared and convenience food;
- preparation of pre-prepared and convenience food;
- cooking of pre-prepared and convenience food;
- presentation of pre-prepared and convenience food;
- holding/temperature control (hot and cold) of pre-prepared and convenience food.

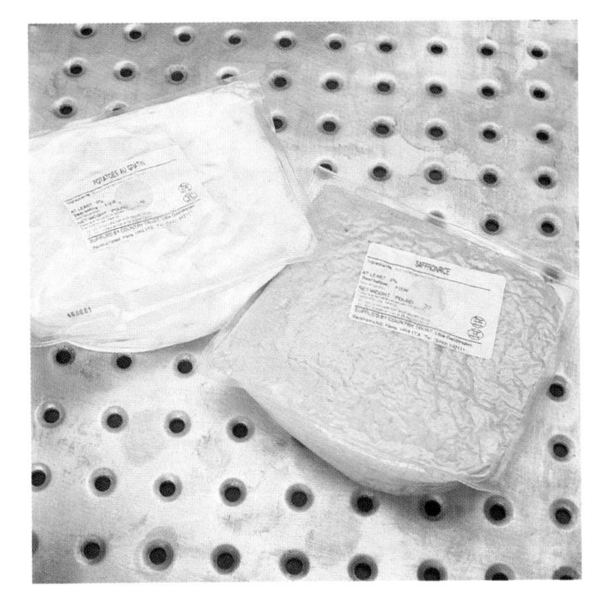

Figure 93 Sous vide food (vacuum-packed, prepared food)

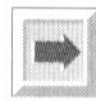
(*See* Maintain and promote hygiene in food storage, pp. 48–50.)

STORAGE

Always follow manufacturers' and processors' instructions regarding storage of pre-prepared and convenience foods. Never allow pre-prepared and convenience foods to come into contact with raw or unprepared foods as they might cause cross-contamination.

(*See* Cook-freeze food pp. 319–25.)

Cook-freeze foods

Cook-freeze products have a prolonged storage life allowing the product to be stored in stock in cases of emergencies and be available throughout the year. Some establishments use special computer-controlled rego-thermic ovens for regeneration.

(*See* Cook-chill foods, pp. 309–18.)

Cook-chill foods

These are available in single or multi portions. They are reheated in special ovens (infra-red, steamers, combi ovens and microwave ovens). The finished products may be stored for five to seven days.

Sous vide

Sous vide products are generally used in single portions for à la carte restaurants, but are also available in multi-portions. The sous vide system gives products a longer shelf-life than the cook-chill system (up to 28 days, check with your local EHO for guideline). All the natural juices, flavours and nutrients are retained, because the food is cooked in the sealed bags. Packaging is usually colour coded to help identify 'use by' date. The food is usually reheated in boiling water or microwave.

SAFETY AND HYGIENE

It is the responsibility of the establishment to:

(*See* Maintain a safe and secure working environment, pp 10–23; *See also* Maintain and promote hygiene in food storage, preparation and cooking, pp. 48–54.)

- ensure that good, safe working and hygiene practices are maintained at all times;
- ensure that all equipment, materials and areas are clean;
- place foods on stainless steel or plastic storage trays, cover with cling film and store in a refrigerator;
- ensure that all waste food and other rubbish is disposed of in accordance with the laid-down procedure.

REHEATING

Food must be reheated as quickly as possible to a minimum of 70°C, but ideally to 75°C. Always use a probe to check the core/centre temperature.

ELEMENT 2
Cook and assemble food for service

INTRODUCTION

Convenience or pre-prepared foods have many advantages over fresh products. Provided the manufacturers' instructions are followed correctly, the caterer will have no problems in preparing and cooking the products. They have the added advantage of offering precise cost and portion control.

There are many benefits to using convenience or pre-prepared foods. Although they are costly they allow the rationalisation of staff and equipment but the chef must take into account the relationship of 'convenience' foods to the food-service industry. If everyone used only convenience foods there would be no individualism left to the art of cooking.

ORGANISATION

People involved in the cooking of pre-prepared food items must be tidy and organised and maintain good hygiene practices at all times. All equipment, utensils and areas must be thoroughly clean at all times. Never use stale, old or out-of-date convenience or pre-prepared food items.

STORAGE OF RECONSTITUTED, PRE-PREPARED AND CONVENIENCE FOODS

(*See* Maintain and promote hygiene in food storage, pp. 48–50; *See also* Store food deliveries pp. 294–7.)

Pre-prepared and convenience foods can deteriorate and become a health hazard just like fresh produce and should therefore be treated in the same way as fresh commodities. Always follow manufacturers' instructions on storage and shelf life. Never keep food past its 'use by' date.

KEY WORDS

CPU Central production unit for cooking food for distribution to pubs, hospitals, schools and industrial sites.

RECONSTITUTE To return food to its pre-processed state.

REGENERATE To return food to as near its pre-frozen/chilled state as possible by thawing or reheating to a safe temperature.

WARM HOLDING Keeping food warm over a period of time after it has been cooked and assembled for service.

Activity

1. With help from your supervisor or chef find out what the information on a food label means.
2. Find out what the advantages and disadvantages of using convenience and pre-prepared food have over fresh.
3. Compile a list of pre-prepared and convenience products used in your establishment and categorise them under the headings 'frozen' or 'chilled'.

Figure 94 Convenience products

3 Level 2

Food preparation and cooking

This section of the book covers the preparation and cooking of foods and basic dishes including: fish, shellfish, meat, poultry, sauces and soups, eggs, vegetables, pulses, rice, pasta, vegetable protein dishes, hot and cold desserts, dough products, pastry dishes and cakes. It also covers cook-chill and cook-freeze foods, food deliveries, food for cold presentation, cutting equipment, fish and chips, and pizzas. The units cover Level 2.

CONTENTS

Prepare and cook basic sauces and soups

ELEMENT 1

Prepare and cook basic hot and cold savoury sauces

INTRODUCTION

A basic hot sauce is made from a liquid (stock or milk) and a thickening agent. Certain thickening agents such as flour need to be 'cooked out' in order to disperse the granules before mixing with a liquid. This is achieved by adding the flour to a melted fat/oil to form a roux and cooking to the required stage, depending on the type of sauce being made. Thickening agents, for example, blood and egg yolks are dissolved in a little cold liquid before being added to a simmering liquid and never reboiled as the sauce will curdle.

Originally sauces were used to moisten and mask the smell and flavour of stale foods. Today the purpose of sauce is to :

- add colour and improve the appearance of some dishes;
- complement the foods that they accompany;
- give nutritive value;
- bind dry foods;
- give flavour to dull foods;
- counteract the richness in some foods;
- aid digestion.

A definition of a good sauce is one that:

1. enhances and complements the flavour of the food, and does not overpower it;
2. has a good consistency – it should just coat the back of a spoon;
3. has a good appearance, e.g. colour must be distinct and not dull;
4. has a smooth texture and bright gloss. This is achieved by passing the sauce through a strainer or a tammy cloth, or by liquidising.

(*See* Maintain a safe and secure working environment, pp. 10–23, *See* also Receive and handle food deliveries, pp. 294–7.)

STORAGE AND HYGIENE

Cool all sauces quickly, preferably in a blast chiller prior to storing under refrigeration. Divide sauces into small quantities, preferably in 4 to 5 litre plastic, china or stainless steel containers with secure fitting lids. Carefully label with the date and contents' name before storage

Non-perishable sauces, e.g. convenience dried sauces, will keep for a considerable time provided they are stored in sealed, air-tight packets. When using convenience sauces always refer to the manufacturer's instructions.

FREEZING SAUCES

Some sauces with a roux base do not freeze well because they need a modified starch base or natural gum to stabilise the sauce.

WARNING! In order to minimise the development of food poisoning organisms, all sauces to be re-heated must be boiled for at least 5 min. Never add reheated sauces to remaining cold sauces.

RE-HEATING SAUCES

Boil a little stock in an appropriate sized, thick-bottomed saucepan, add the sauce and continue boiling for 5 min. The stock helps to prevent the sauce from burning on the base of the saucepan.

Never:

- leave any utensils in the sauce;
- store sauces close to raw commodities.

CLASSIFICATION OF SAUCES

Sauces are classified as follows:

1. roux-based;
2. starch-thickened;
3. egg based;
4. salad sauces and dressings.

(See sauce chart below.)

Roux-based sauces

There are three types of roux-based sauce as follows:

- **Béchamel** a basic white sauce made with a white roux and milk;
- **Velouté** a basic velvet sauce made with a sandy/yellow (blond) roux (stage 2) and white stock;
- **Espagnole** a basic brown sauce made from a brown (brun) roux (stage 3), mirepoix of vegetables, to purée and brown stock. When cooked it is further refined by adding an equal quantity of brown stock to the strained sauce and reducing by half.

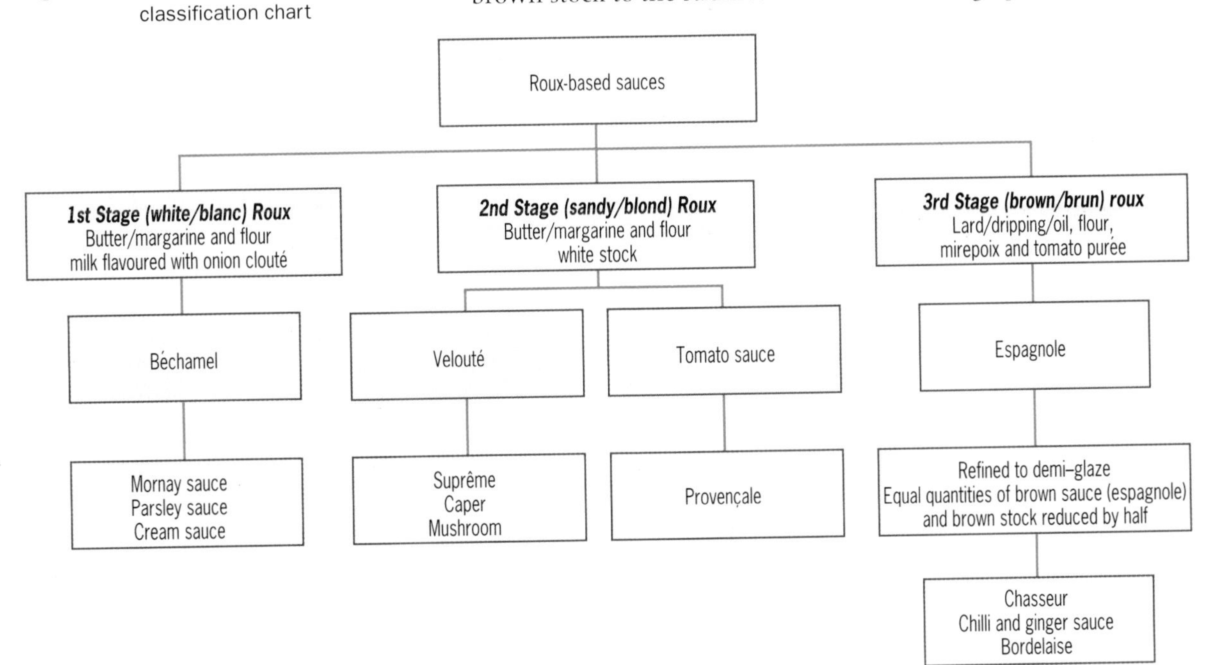

Figure 95 Roux-based sauce classification chart

COOKING TIP: Additional ingredients may be added to give a wide variety of finished sauces.

Starch-thickened sauces

Jus lié Basic light brown sauce made with meat or vegetable stock that can be flavoured with the juices of roast meat and thickened with cornflower or arrowroot.

COOKING TIP: Some chefs prefer to make most hot sauces with cornflour or arrowroot because they cook out more quickly, and are more economical with gas and electricity. Cornflour and arrowroot also make healthier sauces.

Egg-based sauces

Egg sauces are made by emulsification or foam. They can be hot as in hollandaise and béarnaise, or cold as in mayonnaise and tartare sauce.

Salad sauces and dressings

Salad sauces and dressings are all cold. They include mayonnaise, mint sauce, horseradish sauce and dressings: vinaigrette, French dressing, English dressing used with salads and hors d'œuvre.

THICKENING AGENTS

Roux

The classic method of making a foundation sauce is by thickening a liquid stock with a roux. A roux is made from equal quantites of fat and soft flour that is cooked to one of three degrees. It must always be cooked slowly, not rapidly, otherwise the starch granules would harden making it difficult to combine with the liquid. The heat is gradually increased so that the outer coating of the starch cells distend and swell and absorb the liquid.

The three stages of roux are:

1. White roux (*roux blanc*)

This is made with butter or margarine and flour, and is used to thicken béchamel sauce.

Method and preparation

Melt the required amount of fat over a gentle heat, add an equal amount of sieved flour and mix thoroughly. Cook for 2 to 3 min without colouring.

Figure 96–100 Five-stage sauce preparation

Melt fat

Add flour

Cook out and cool

Add liquid slowly

Cover with cartouche to prevent skin forming

2. Sandy roux (*roux blond*)

This is made with butter or margarine and flour and is used to thicken velouté, tomato sauce and certain soups.

Method and preparation

Melt the required amount of fat over a gentle heat, add an equal amount of sieved flour and mix thoroughly. Cook for 5 to 7 min allowing the roux to change to a sandy colour.

3. Brown roux (*Roux brun*)

This is made with dripping, lard or vegetable oil and is used to thicken espagnole and certain soups.

Method and preparation

Melt the required amount of fat over a gentle heat, add an equal amount of seived flour and mix thoroughly. Cook until the roux takes on a rich brown colour, stirring frequently. Do not overcook the roux as it will create a bitter flavour in the final preparation.

Arrowroot, cornflour and fécule (starch-based sauces)

Arrowroot – powdered maranta
Cornflour – powdered maize
Fécule – powdered potato
Rice flour – powdered rice

All the above thickening agents are diluted in a cold liquid before being stirred into the boiling liquid. They are then allowed to reboil and simmer.

Flour may also be diluted in water and added to a boiling stock for thickening purposes. This method is known as jay zee; the diluted flour must be strained carefully before being added.

Beurre manié

Knead three equal parts of flour to four parts of softened butter/margarine to a smooth paste. Roll it and slowly add as required to a boiling liquid. Beurre manié is mostly used in fish and vegetable dishes.

Blood

Mix blood with a little vinegar or red wine to prevent it curdling and carefully add to hot, not boiling liquid. The liquid must never boil after the blood is added as it will curdle.

Blood is used in jugged hare and other game dishes.

Figure 101 Making a sabayon

Egg yolks

Whisk the egg yolks with a little liquid to the ribbon stage. This is called a sabayon and is used in warm egg sauces, e.g. Hollandaise and Béarnaise. Sabayons are also used to aid the glazing process of a number of sauces.

Egg yolks are also used:

- in mayonnaise as an emulsification with oil;
- as a liaison incorporated with cream and added to hot liquid which must not be boiled.

Glazes

Glazes are concentrated essences of meat or fish that can be made into sauces by adding butter and/or cream or can be added to sauces whose flavour requires enhancing.

CONVENIENCE SAUCES

Frozen or chilled convenience sauces are available, the majority usually either condensed, tinned or dried sauce powders.

Convenience sauces ensure that some sauces which are dificult to produce in small amounts are available with the minimum of preparation.

They may be used because there is insufficient skilled labour or because the cost of skilled labour outweights the returns.

The disadvantages of convenience sauces are that:

- they lack the natural flavour of fresh sauces;
- they tend to have too strong a flavour and a bright colour.

COOKING TIP: When using convenience sauces always follow the manufacturer's instructions to reconstitute the sauce. To enhance and improve the flavour, cream, egg yolks, wine or spirits can be added.

BASIC SAUCE RECIPES

White sauce (*Béchamel*)

1 litre

Ingredients

100 g margarine or butter
100 g flour
1 litre milk (warmed)
1 studded onion

Method

1. Melt the margarine or butter in a thick-bottomed saucepan.
2. Add the sieved flour and mix well.
3. Cook over a gentle heat, without colouring for a few minutes.
4. Remove from heat and cool the roux.
5. Slowly add the warmed milk and stir till smooth.

6. Add the onion studded with a clove and simmer for 30 min.
7. Remove onion and discard. Taste, season and adjust consistency (if required). Pass the sauce through a conical strainer.

To prevent a skin forming cover with a film of margarine or butter.

Sauces made from béchamel

Sauce	*Served with*	*Additions per ½ litre (1 pint)*
Anchovy *Sauce anchois*	Poached, fried or boiled fish	1 tbsp anchovy essence
Egg *Sauce aux oeufs*	Poached fish or boiled fish	2 hard-boiled eggs diced
Cheese *Sauce Mornay*	Fish for vegetables	60 g grated cheese, 1 egg yolk. Mix well in boiling sauce and remove from heat. Strain, if necessary. Do not allow to reboil
Onion *Sauce aux oignons*	Roast mutton	100 g chopped or diced onions, boiled or sweated in butter
Soubise *Sauce Soubise*	Poached or boiled fish and vegetables	Onion purée and cream
Cream *Sauce crème*	Poached fish and boiled vegetables	Add cream, milk, natural yogurt or *fromage blanc* to give the consistency of double cream
Mustard *Sauce moutarde*	Grilled herrings	Add diluted English or Continental mustard to make a reasonably hot sauce

Velouté (chicken, veal, fish, mutton)

1 litre
(A basic white sauce made from white stock and a blond roux)

Ingredients

75 g margarine, butter or oil
75 g flour (soft)
1 litre stock (chicken, veal, fish, mutton)

Method

1. Melt the margarine, butter or oil in a thick-bottomed saucepan.
2. Add the sieved flour and mix well.
3. Over a gentle heat cook out to a sandy texture without colouring.
4. Remove from heat and cool the roux.
5. Slowly add the appropriate boiling stock and stir until smooth and boiling.
6. Pass the stock through a conical strainer.

A velouté sauce for chicken, veal or fish dishes is usually finished with cream and in some cases, egg yolks.

Supreme sauce (*Sauce suprême*)

½ litre

(A velouté made from chicken stock flavoured with well-washed mushroom trimmings)

Ingredients

½ litre	Chicken velouté
25 g	mushroom trimmings (white)
60 ml	cream
1	egg yolk
2 to 3	drops lemon juice

Method

1. Allow the velouté to cook out with the mushroom trimmings and pass through a fine strainer. Reboil.
2. Mix the cream and egg yolk in a basin (liaison). Add a little of the boiling sauce to the liaison.
3. Return all to the sauce taking care not to reboil.
4. Mix well and finish with lemon sauce and adjust seasoning.

Serve with hot boiled chicken, vol-au-vent, etc., or use as a base for white chaud-froid sauce.

A velouté sauce for chicken, veal or fish dishes is usually finished with cream and in some cases, egg yolks.

Sauces made from veloutés

Sauce	*Served with*	*Additions per ½ litre (1 pint)*
Caper sauce *Sauce aux câpres*	Boiled leg of mutton	2 tbsp capers per ½ litre of sauce 8 to 12 portions
Aurore sauce *Sauce aurore*	Boiled chicken, poached eggs, chaud-froid sauce etc.	Follow steps 1 to 3 for supreme sauce and add 1 tbsp tomato purée to the sauce. This will give a slightly tomato-flavoured, pinkish sauce 8 to 12 portions ½ litre
Mushroom sauce *Sauce aux champignons*	Boiled chicken, sweetbreads etc.	Follow steps 1 to 3 as for supreme sauce and add 100 g well-washed, sliced button mushrooms after the velouté has been strained. Simmer for 10 min and finish with egg yolk and cream 8 to 12 portions ½ litre
Ivory sauce *Sauce ivoire*	Boiled chicken	To the *sauce suprême* add a little meat glaze to give an ivory colour.

Brown sauce *(Sauce espagnole)*

1 litre (1 qt)

Ingredients

50 g	dripping or oil
60 g	flour (soft)
25 g	tomato purée
1 litre	brown stock
100 g	carrot } Mirepoix
100 g	onion } Mirepoix
50 g	celery } Mirepoix
Bouquet garni	

Method

1. Wash, peel, rewash and roughly cut the vegetables (Mirepoix).
2. Heat the dripping or oil in a thick-bottomed saucepan and brown the vegetables.
3. Add the flour and cook out slowly to a light brown colour, stirring continually.
4. Remove from heat and cool. Mix in the tomato purée.
5. Add warmed stock.
6. Drain off the fat and add to the sauce. Simmer gently for 4 to 6 hours. Skim when necessary. Strain.

Demi-glaze sauce *(Sauce demi-glace)*

1 litre

A demi-glaze is a refined espagnole.

Ingredients

1 litre	espagnole
1 litre	brown stock

Method

1. Simmer both liquids and reduce by half.
2. Skim off all impurities and pass through a fine conical strainer.
3. Reboil and adjust seasoning.

Sauces made from demi-glaze

Sauce Charcutière

(approx. 1 litre)

Ingredients

75 g	onions, finely chopped
50 g	butter
2 dl	white wine, dry
5 g	mustard, dry
1 litre	demi-glaze
10 g	sugar
110 g	gherkin, cut in julienne

Method

1. Melt the butter in a small saucepan, add the onions and cook without colouring.
2. Add the white wine and reduce by two-thirds.
3. Add the demi-glaze and simmer to a light coating consistency. Skim the surface.
4. Dilute the mustard with a little cold water and add, with the sugar, to the sauce. Do not reboil. Adjust seasoning and pass through a fine strainer.
5. Add the julienne of gherkins and simmer.

Served with grilled pork

Sauce chasseur

(approx. 1 litre)

Ingredients

250g	button mushrooms
50g	butter
50g	shallots, finely chopped
250g	tomato concassé
2dl	white wine, dry
1 tspn	tarragon, finely chopped
1 litre	demi-glaze

Method

1. Melt the butter in a small saucepan, add the mushrooms and cook without colouring. Season lightly
2. Add the shallots and cook gently for 2 to 3 min.
3. Add the tomato concassé, white wine and tarragon and reduce by half.
4. Add the demi-glaze and simmer gently to a coating consistency. Skim the surface and adjust seasoning accordingly.

Served with grilled and sautéed meat and poutry

Sauce Italienne

(approx. 1 litre)

Ingredients

50g	shallots, peeled and finely chopped
75g	butter
400g	mushrooms, finely chopped
100g	lean ham, finely chopped
4dl	demi-glaze
4dl	sauce tomato
1 tbsn	*fines herbes*, finely chopped

Method

1. Melt the butter in a small saucepan, add the shallots and cook without colouring (sweat).
2. Add the chopped mushrooms and cook gently until the liquid has almost evaporated.
3. Add the chopped ham, demi-glaze and sauce tomato and simmer gently for 5 min. Skim the surface and adjust consistency with stock if too thick
4. Add the herbs and adjust seasoning accordingly.

Suitable for grills and sautéed meat, poutry and offal

KEY WORDS

BOUQUET GARNI Thyme, bay leaf, parsley stalks and peppercorns wrapped in a small piece of muslin cloth or blanched leek and celery, tied with string and used to flavour sauces.

CARTOUCHE A circular piece of greaseproof paper cut to the diameter of the saucepan and brushed with butter or margarine.

ONION CLOUTÉ Also known as onion piqué. It is a small, peeled whole onion that has a bayleaf attached with three cloves and is used to flavour liquid.

COULIS A sauce which is thickened by its main ingredient (vegetable or fruit) and served as a purée.

EMULSION The term used for the suspension of one liquid in another.

MIREPOIX Roughly cut carrot, onion and celery.

MSG Monosodium glutamate is a food additive used as a flavour enhancer in certain sauces and dishes.

Activity

1. Check and record the temperature of cooling sauce at 30 min intervals and make a chart plotting the temperature reduction.
2. Find out how many forms of convenience soups and sauces are used in your establishment.
3. Using the grid below classify the fresh sauces used in your establishment.

Foundation sauces	Finished sauces	Egg and butter sauces	Salad dressings and sauces

4. In your own words, what are the disadvantages of using convenience sauces over fresh sauces?

ELEMENT 2

Prepare and cook soups

INTRODUCTION

The main purpose of soup is to stimulate the appetite and start the gastric juices flowing. For this reason soups should have a delicate flavour and natural colour.

MENUS

Soups may be served with most meals but as a rule the thicker, heavier soups such as broths and purées are served with a light main course, whereas consommés, creams, veloutés and bisques are served with a heavy main course.

COOKING TIP: The choice of soup, i.e. colour, flavour and texture should complement the rest of the meal.

HYGIENE AND STORAGE

(*See* Maintain a safe and secure working environment, pp. 10–23; *See* also Maintain and promote hygiene in food storage, pp. 48–50; and Store food deliveries pp. 294–7.)

The following points should be remembered to ensure that soup does not deteriorate:

1. Hot soups not for immediate consumption must be cooled to a temperature of below 5 °C immediately after use.
2. Soup should be placed in stainless steel, china or plastic storage containers, labelled and dated with the contents and chilled as rapidly as possible. Ideally this should be done in a blast chiller, but alternatively it can be placed in a sink of iced water and refrigerated as soon as the required temperature is reached.
3. Never attempt to cool a hot soup in the refrigerator as this will raise the temperature of the other food items in the refrigerator and may cause them to go off. It could also cause damage to the workings of the refrigerator and even cause poisonous bacteria to grow on other foods.
4. Hot soups should be kept at a temperature of above 75 °C and preferably at 90 °C for serving. Never re-boil soup that has cream in it as it will curdle.
5. Fresh soups with a roux base do not freeze well. In order to freeze a velouté it should be thickened with a starch such as cornflour or arrowroot. Consommés, French onion soup and some purées freeze acceptably.

CLASSIFICATION

Soup may be divided into eight categories.

1. Broths

Broths are made from a well-flavoured stock containing vegetables cut in varying shapes, a cereal (barley, rice) or farinaceous cereal (spaghetti), diced meat or seafood and herbs. Broths should have the appearance of a thickened soup which is the result of the starch content of the cereal and some of the vegetables extracted during cooking. Broths can be sub-divided into three groups: those in which the vegetables are 'sweated' in butter or margarine, those in which the vegetables are added to the boiling liquid, and fish broths.

Figure 102 Soup ingredients

2. Purées

Purées are divided into two groups.
Those made from

(a) dried pulse vegetable;
(b) those made with fresh 'aqueous' (watery) vegetables.

Purée soups made from aqueous vegetables will need rice or potato added to correct the cohesion and consistency. Occasionally meat or poultry is added to the soup for flavour (e.g. pea and ham). Usually dried pulse vegetables are soaked overnight in cold water to speed up the cooking process.

Purées often appear on French menus under the heading *'Potage'*.

3. Veloutés

A velouté soup is best suited to a dinner menu. The word velouté is French meaning 'velvety'. A velouté is made with a meat, poultry, game, fish or shellfish or vegetable stock thickened with a blond roux and finished with a liaison of egg yolks and cream. This soup must be smooth and light in texture and have a delicate flavour.

4. Cream

Cream soups are a light, creamy and extremely smooth, classically made from stock, a purée of the named ingedient and thickened with a béchamel sauce. Nowadays cream soups are more likely to made from a velouté with the addition of fresh cream, or a purée soup also with the addition of fresh cream.

5. Consommés and boullions

These are clear soups made from good-quality stocks that are refined by cooking with a bound mixture of minced meat, rough-cut vegetables, herbs and egg white. During the cooking process the mixture coagulates, working like a sieve to trap meat particles. This action results in the clarification of the liquid giving a crystal-clear soup.

Figure 103 Bowl of soup

6. Cold soups

Cold soups can be cold, well-flavoured, lightly jellied consommés, a cream soup, or made from selected vegetables specially prepared. Some cold soups are associated with a particular country, e.g. gazpacho andalouse which originated in Spain, and bortsch, which can be served hot or cold, is a Russian beetroot soup.

7. Bisques

Bisques are shellfish soups thickened with a roux or rice, passed through a sieve and finished with cream.

8. Miscellaneous (unclassified)

Soups that do not fall into one specific category, usually because of their unique method of preparation. They include brown soups, potages and soupes.

Portion size

The portion of soup served will be governed by the type of meal.

The other consideration is the number of courses (if there are many courses then a small portion will suffice)

Usually a ½ litre of thin soup will produce two portions. For thick soups ½ litre of soup will produce three portions. For accurate portion control the appropriate sized soup ladle should be used.

GARNISHES AND ACCOMPANIMENTS

Garnishes

Most soups are cooked with garnishes, vegetables, cereals or a pasta to give them their unique flavour and consistency. However, others have garnishes added after cooking, just before serving. A simple garnish is fine-chopped parsley, herbs or pluches. Some soups, e.g. cream soups, are garnished with a small portion of the main flavouring ingredient, cut fine.

Figure 104 Packet soups

Accompaniments

An accompaniment might be parmesan cheese, croutons, a croûte de flute or a diablotin.

Convenience soups

Convenience soups ensure that some soups which are difficult to produce in small amounts are readily available with the minimum of preparation.

They may be used because there is insufficient skilled labour or because the cost of skilled labour outweighs the returns.

Condensed, frozen or chilled convenience soups are available, but the majority are usually either tinned liquids, dried soup powders or granules.

COOKING TIP: There are three types of convenience soup:

condensed soups	**Concentrated soups that need a measured amount of water added to reconstitute the soup.**
dried	**Powdered soups that need to be mixed to a paste in cold water and then added to a measured amount of boiling water to reconstitute**
tinned	**Made-up soups that simply require opening and heating.**

The disadvantages of convenience soups are that:

1. they lack the natural flavour of fresh soups;
2. they tend to have too strong a flavour and bright colour.

COOKING TIP: When using convenience soups always follow the manufacturer's instructions to reconstitute the soup. To improve the flavour, fresh stock instead of water, cream, liaison or wine can be added.

KEY WORDS

A CORDON A thin line/ribbon of cream or liaison.

CHIFFONADES Fine shredded leaves of lightly cooked spinach, sorrel or lettuce.

CROÛTE DE FLUTE A ½ cm thick slice from a French stick toasted on both sides.

CROUTONS ½ cm cubes of bread fried in clarified butter or oil, cooked until golden brown.

DIABLOTIN A ½ cm thick slice from a French stick toasted on both sides with parmesan cheese on one side.

PLUCHES Small sprigs of parsley, chervil or other herbs.

SAVOURY PANCAKES Thin pancakes flavoured with chopped herbs usually cut into fine julienne and served in consommés.

SIPPETS Thin slices of shallow fried bread served as an accompaniment to soup.

Activity

1. Find the words associated with soups.

J	R	B	E	P	B	Z	J	A	T	P	A	A	W	L	E	O	M
G	A	R	N	I	S	H	O	I	N	T	W	L	Z	C	E	T	M
W	R	O	P	T	O	E	G	A	Z	P	A	C	H	O	U	M	N
I	I	T	L	R	L	U	E	M	M	L	I	H	I	N	I	U	P
U	T	H	L	A	G	S	A	O	T	U	U	O	G	S	W	T	Z
S	U	Y	E	W	W	M	E	I	M	T	Z	W	I	O	T	S	L
C	L	I	H	P	S	W	I	A	T	I	N	D	I	M	T	S	G
L	E	S	I	P	P	E	T	S	U	E	N	E	N	M	P	G	G
Y	R	N	A	L	O	U	L	N	W	S	Y	R	C	E	I	D	L
P	O	Y	A	U	P	E	R	W	N	T	E	L	R	Y	S	E	T
D	S	P	G	C	L	E	V	E	L	O	U	T	E	R	E	R	R
D	R	P	A	H	P	R	Y	Y	M	C	E	Y	A	Y	S	R	O
R	O	R	R	N	T	S	S	D	I	K	M	T	M	I	S	O	D
F	R	E	N	C	H	O	N	I	O	N	B	I	S	Q	U	E	E
P	T	L	I	T	L	R	P	D	I	E	O	I	I	D	D	O	I
T	H	T	S	T	Y	W	O	K	L	Q	R	U	P	E	E	L	A
L	P	T	H	R	O	U	X	E	E	L	S	E	S	M	E	L	R
D	F	H	M	I	B	N	G	G	T	A	C	O	R	D	O	N	M
A	S	S	S	C	T	Y	W	O	K	L	H	Q	S	E	E	L	A
B	A	R	L	E	Y	E	D	J	M	A	Y	I	Z	O	P	P	I

2. List and catagorise the soups used in your establishment

Figure 105 Soup in saucepan

Classification	Name of soup			
Broth				
Purée				
Velouté				
Cream				
Consommé				
Cold soups				
Bisques and chowders				
Unclassified				

Prepare and cook basic meat, poultry and offal dishes

ELEMENT 1

Prepare, poultry and offal dishes

INTRODUCTION

Meat, poultry and offal provide a good source of energy and supply much of the protein required for growth and repair of our bodies. All meat, poultry and offal must be correctly prepared making them more manageable for cooking, portioning and consumption. Nowadays, more kitchens purchase their meat from reputable catering butchers who, using Meat and Livestock guidelines, prepare meat to specific requirements.

Establishments might decide to use catering butchers instead of preparing it themselves for a variety of reasons:

1. insufficient experienced staff;
2. the time factor involved in having a specialised member of staff to carry out preparation;
3. the size of storage and preparation areas required to store and prepare quarters of beef, sides of pork and bacon and whole lambs outweigh the advantages.

(For storage of prepared meat, poultry and offal *see* Receive, handle and store food deliveries, Storage of meat, poultry and offal, pp. 295–6.)

STORAGE

HYGIENE

The following rules of hygiene must be observed.

(*See* Maintain personal health and hygiene, pp. 10–13; *See* also Maintain and promote hygiene in food storage, preparation and cooking, pp. 48–54.)

- Only use knives and chopping boards designated for preparing meat and poultry.
- Handlers must have an excellent standard of personal hygiene.
- Avoid all risks of cross-contamination.
- Handle meat, poultry and offal as little as possible.
- Carry out all preparation in cool conditions.
- Make full use of refrigeration. Never leave raw meat, poultry and offal lying around the kitchen.
- Ensure that all equipment is clean and in good working order.
- Defrost oven-ready poultry correctly following the guidelines.
- Seek immediate first aid if any cuts or injuries occur.

MEAT

Meat is the collective term for domestic animals, cows, calves, pigs and lambs that are reared for human consumption.

Classification of cattle:	
(a) Entire:	Bull calf up to one year
	Yearly bull in first year
	Bull adult
(b) Castrated:	Steer calf (castrated young)
	Steer ox (castrated adult)
(c) Female:	Heifer calf
	Heifer (not calved)
	Cow – heifer (young female after calving)
	Cow (after calving)
Classification of pigs:	
(a) Boar:	Entire male
Hog:	Castrated young
Stores:	Young weaned pigs
Suckling pig:	Unweaned pig 6 to 8 weeks old

Preparing meat

Meat requires more preparation than poultry mainly because of its size. Preparation can be divided into the following processes.

Basic preparation

Basic preparation comprises three stages:

- Dissecting – dividing the carcass into more manageable joints;
- Boning – removing bones from the joints to allow for further processing of the meat;
- Trimming – removing as much excess fat, connective tissue and gristle as is possible so that the meat is made more palatable.

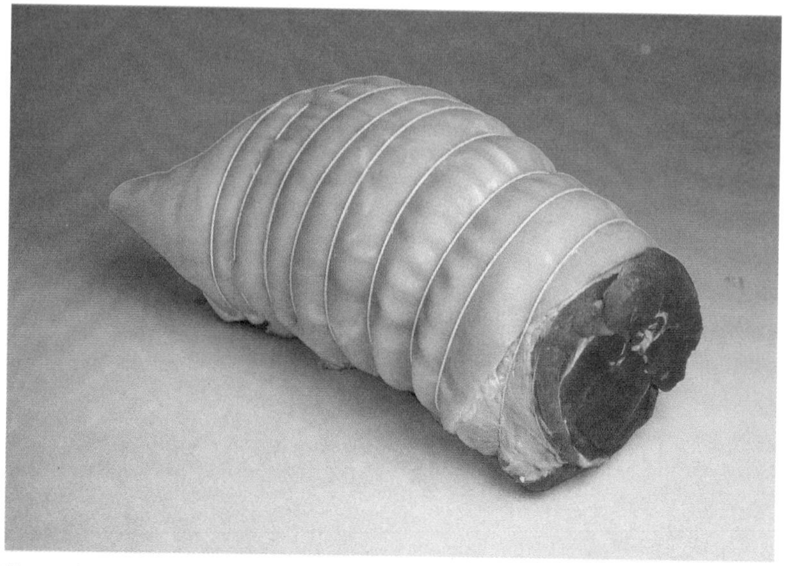

Figure 106 Boned rolled meat

For roasting

The following guidelines should be observed

- With the bone removed from the meat, it is reformed, rolled and tied securely to retain the shape during cooking and to facilitate carving.
- Roast meats for presentation/carving may have some bone(s) left to act as a steadying support when cutting.

For stewing

The stages are the same as for the basic preparation, then the meat is diced into regular, mouth-sized cubes.

For grilling, frying or braising

The stages are the same as for basic preparation, then the meat is cut into regular slices of even size and thickness ready for cooking. This can be done off the bone, e.g. with steaks, or on the bone, e.g. with lamb cutlets or pork chops.

Figure 107 Beef marinading

Marinading

Meat is often marinaded for between 2 and 24 hrs to add flavour and to assist in the tenderising process. A marinade might consist of wine or lemon juice, oil, vegetables and herbs or spices.

Beef

The best beef is home-killed and comes from Scotland, Norfolk and Devon. There are four classes:

(a) steer
(b) heifer
(c) cow
(d) bull.

Steer beef is considered to be superior.

Storage of beef

If beef is purchased in hind or forequarter it must be hung in a refrigerator with drip trays below at a temperature of between 0 °C and 2 °C for up to 14 days (to tenderise and improve the flavour). The tenderising process is a result of the action of enzymes of the flesh and the natural relaxation after rigor mortis.

	Approximate weight	Use	Good cuts	Medium cuts	Poorer cuts
Forequarter					
1 Neck or clod and sticking (le talon du collier)	8 kg	(18 lb) Sausages and prepared meat dishes			✓
2 Chuck ribs (les côtes du collier)	13.5 kg	(30 lb) Stewing and braising		✓	
3 Middle ribs (les côtes decouvertes)	9 kg	(20 lb) Roasting and braising		✓	
4 Fore ribs (les côtes)	7.25 kg	(16 lb) Roasting and braising	✓		
5 Shank or shin (le jarret)	5.5 kg	(12 lb) Consomme and beef tea			✓
6 Leg of mutton cut (l'epaule)	10 kg	(22 lb) Stewing and braising			✓
7 Brisket (la poitrine)	17.25 kg	(38 lb) Pickled boiled and pressed			✓
8 Plate (le plat)	9 kg	(20 lb) Stewing and sausages			✓
Hindquarter					
9 Wing ribs (la côte d'aloyau)	5 kg	(10 lb) Roasting, grilling, frying and steaks	✓		
10 Sirloin (l'aloyau)	9 kg	(18 lb) Roasting, grilling, frying and steaks	✓		
11 Rump (la culotte de boeuf)	10 kg	(20 lb) Grilling , frying and steaks	✓		
12 Silverside (le gîte à la noix)	14 kg	(28 lb) Pickled and boiled)		✓	
13 Topside (la tranche tendre)	10 kg	(20 lb) Braising, stewing and roasting	✓		
14 Leg or shin (le jarret)	7 kg	(14 lb) Consomme and stewing			✓

Figure 108 Diagram of beef A

	Approximate weight	Use	Good cuts	Medium cuts	Poorer cuts
15 Thin flank (la bavette)	9 kg	(20 lb) Stewing, boiling and sausages			✓
16 Thick flank (la tranche grasse)	11 kg	(24 lb) Braising, stewing		✓	
17 Fillet (le fillet de boeuf)	3 kg	(6 lb) Roasting, grilling, frying and steaks	✓		
Offal					
Heart (le cœur)	1–2 kg	(2–4 lb) Braising			
Kidney (le rognon)	1+ kg	(2–3 lb) Stewing and soup			
Liver (le foie)	5.5–6 kg	(12–14 lb) Braising and frying			
Sweetbreads (young animals only) (le ris de veau)		Braising and frying			
Tongue (la langue)	1.5–2 kg	(3–4 lb) Pickled, boiling and braising			
Tripe (la tripe)	3.5–5.5 kg	(8–12 lb) Boiling and braising			

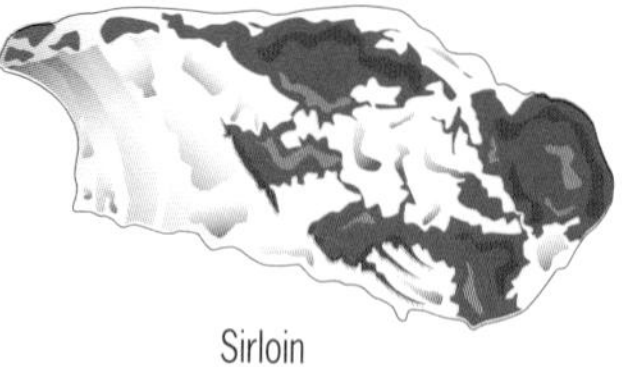

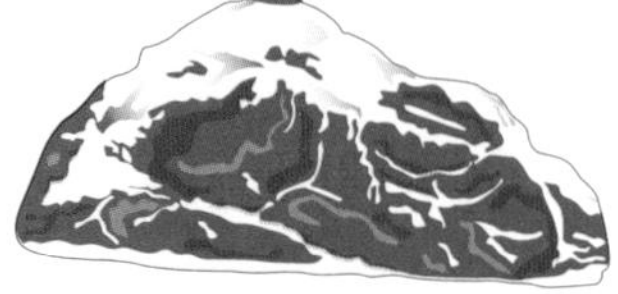

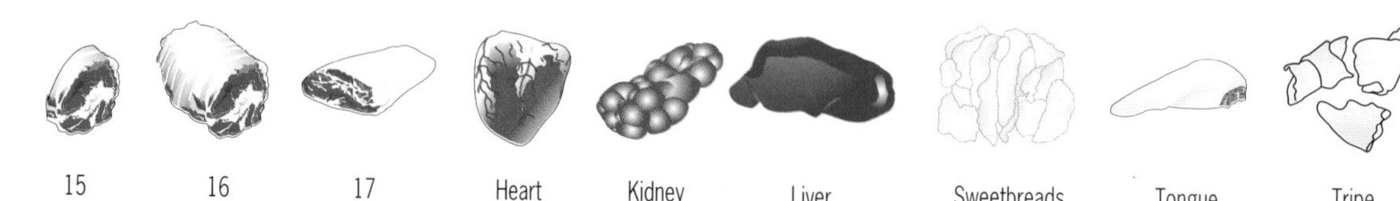

Figure 109 Diagram of beef B

Quality points to consider when purchasing beef

- The flesh should be moist, firm and bright red.
- There should not be excessive fat.
- The lean meat should be flecked with fat (which is known as marbling).
- The fat should be dry, creamy-white in colour and odourless.
- The bones should not be brittle and when cut should have a bloody interior.

Lamb

The classification of lamb is a sheep under 12 months old. A sheep over 12 months old is classed as mutton. Lamb is marked with light brown stamps on each joint and mutton is stamped purple.

	Approximate weight		Use	Good cuts	Medium cuts	Poorer cuts
	Lamb	Mutton				
Lamb and mutton 1 Leg (shank and fillet) (le gigot)	3 kg (7 lb)	5 kg (11 lb)	Boiling and roasting	✓		
2 Saddle (la selle) Loin and chump (la longe)	3 kg (7 lb)	5 kg (11 lb)	Grilling, frying, and roasting	✓		
3 Best end (le carré)	2 kg (4 lb)	3 kg (6 lb)	Grilling, frying, and roasting	✓		
4 Shoulder (l'epaule)	3 kg (6 lb)	4 kg (9 lb)	Roasting and stewing	✓		
5 Middle neck (le cou)	2 kg (4 lb)	3 kg (6 lb)	Stewing		✓	
6 Scrag end						

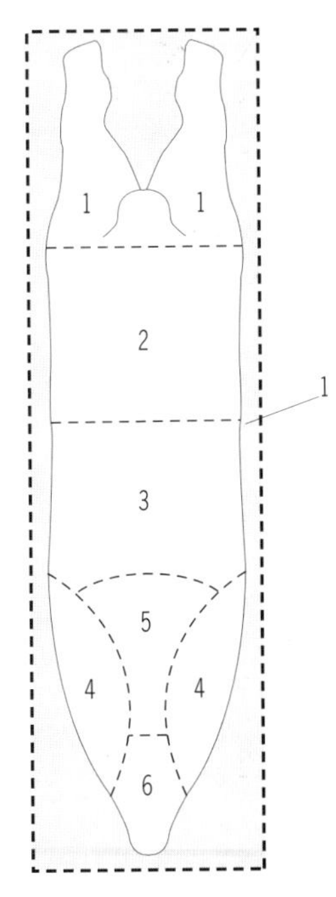

Figure 110 Diagram of lamb

Storage of whole lamb

Lamb bought whole should be hung by the legs for up to five days (to tenderise and improve flavour) at a temperature of between 0 °C and 2 °C with a drip tray placed below to catch any blood.

Quality points to consider when purchasing lamb

- The carcass should have a pleasant smell, crisp skin and be compact and evenly fleshed.
- The flesh must be moist, firm and dull red and have a fine grain or texture.
- The fat should be clear white, hard, brittle and flaky.
- There should not be an excessive amount of fat.
- Bones should be brittle and contain blood.

Pork

Pigs reared for consumption fall into two distinct categories:(a) porkers or (b) baconers. Baconers are bred to be lean-fleshed during the early stages whereas porkers tend to be fat-forming and need longer to mature for a lean flesh.

Item	Approximate weight	Use	Good cuts	Medium cuts	Poorer cuts
1 Leg: knuckle or fillet (le cuissot)	4.5kg (10lb)	Boiling, and roasting	✓		
2 Loin (la longe)	5.5kg (12lb)	Frying, grilling and roasting	✓		
3 Spare rib (la basse côte)	2kg (4lb)	Pies and roasting	✓		
4 Head (la tête)	3.5kg (8b)	Brawn			✓
5 Shoulder-blade or hand or spring (l'épaule)	3kg (6lb)	Pies, roasting and sausages		✓	
6 Belly or breast (la poitrine)	2kg (4lb)	Boiling and pickling		✓	

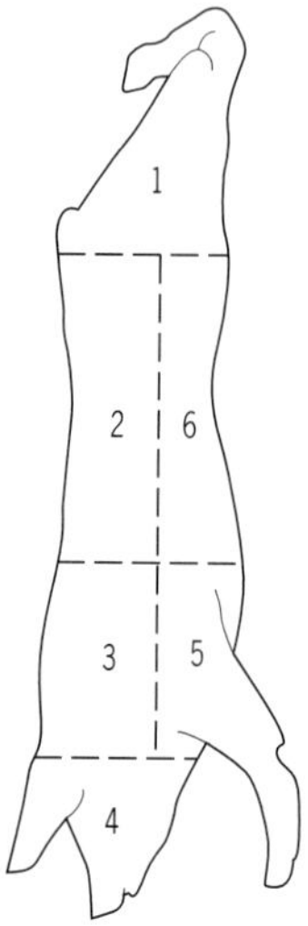

Figure 111 Diagram of pork

Storage of sides of pork

Pig production is mainly in factory-type buildings under strict conditions so the muscle tissue is not as tough as that of cattle and sheep, thus eliminating the need for hanging. Pork tends to deteriorate more quickly and should only be kept for a maximum of 2 to 4 days in a refrigerator.

COOKING TIP: If a refrigerator is used to keep both raw and cooked commodities, raw meat, poultry and offal should be placed on a tray, covered with cling film and labelled and stored at the bottom of the refrigerator to ensure that blood does not drip on prepared or cooked food and cross-contaminate it.

Quality points to consider when purchasing pork

- The carcass should have a pleasant smell.
- The skin should be smooth, hairless and undamaged with no bruises or lacerations.
- There should not be an excessive amount of fat.
- The flesh should be firm and pale pink.

Bacon

Bacon is produced from a breed of pig that is reared specifically to be lean-fleshed in the early stages of development. The traditional process of curing bacon can take anything from between twelve days and eight weeks. However, there are, modern, rapid methods available to cure bacon but they adversely affect its shelf life.

Item	Approximate weight	Use	Good cuts	Medium cuts	Poorer cuts
1 Gammon – corner, middle	6.3kg (14lb)	Boiling,frying or grilling	✓		
2 Back loin	7.25kg (16lb)	Frying or grilling	✓		
3 Collar, shoulder	3kg (7lb)	Boiling or grilling		✓	
4 Hock	3kg (7lb)	Boiling			✓
5 Streaky thick	3.5kg (8lb)	Frying and grilling	✓		
6 Streaky thin			✓		

Figure 112 Diagram of bacon

Green bacon

Green bacon is produced by one of two methods:

(a) Dry method

The bacon is cured in drying rooms that assist in removing some moisture which is replaced by a sufficient concentration of salt to prevent the growth of micro-organisms. The surface is rubbed with salt and saltpetre then layered with the curing mixture between. This takes about five to six weeks. The salt is then brushed away and the bacon left to mature for a further two weeks.

(b) The tank method

The meat is injected with a brine solution. It is then placed into a vat with a curing solution for four days and left to mature for a further seven days.

Smoking method

Bacon is smoked in large rooms where the temperature, humidity and density of smoke are carefully controlled to give the required effect. Smoked bacon tends to keep longer than green-cured bacon because the surface of the bacon is very dry.

Storage of sides of bacon

Sides of bacon should be hung in a refrigerator.

Quality points to consider when purchasing bacon

- It should have a pleasant smell.
- The rind should be smooth.
- There should not be excessive fat.
- The lean flesh should be deep pink in colour.
- The surface should not be sticky.

OFFAL

Offal is the term used to describe the edible organs and some other parts of animals, e.g. head, brain, tongue, sweetbreads, heart, liver and kidneys. Offal is inexpensive in comparison to main joints and mainly suited to luncheon dishes and garnishes for other dishes.

Offal from young animals, e.g. lamb and calf, produces the best quality and is best suited to grilling or shallow frying. Offal from an older, tougher animal is suitable for braising or stewing.

Preparing offal

Some types of offal require excess fat to be removed. The kidneys have the core removed and the bile bag is removed from the liver.

COOKING TIP: If a refrigerator is used to keep both raw and cooked commodities, it is essential that the raw foods be stored on the bottom shelves.

Offal chart

	Tongue	*Heart*	*Sweetbreads*	*Liver*	*Tripe*	*Kidneys*	*Ears*	*Tail*	*Head*	*Ears*	*Brain*
Beef	✔	✔	✔	✔	✔	✔		✔			
Calf	✔	✔	✔	✔	✔	✔			✔		✔
Lamb	✔	✔	✔	✔		✔			✔		✔
Pork				✔	✔	✔	✔		✔	✔	
Chicken				✔							

Kidneys

Lambs' kidneys are prepared by skinning, splitting and removing the centre core. Each kidney should be skewered to keep it flat during cooking.

COOKING TIP: Lambs' kidneys are grilled or shallow fried.

COOKING TIP: Ox and calves' kidneys are used for steak and kidney pies or puddings.

Ox and calves' kidneys are prepared by skinning, splitting and removing the centre core. They are then diced before cooking.

Liver

When preparing calves' and lambs' liver you should check that the bile bag has been removed. The bile bag/gall bladder is a small green sac attached to the liver that contains a brownish-yellowish bitter fluid which is used by the liver to aid digestion. If the contents of the bile bag leak onto the liver it will become sour and be ruined. Calves' and lambs' liver should be skinned and sliced very thinly, and grilled or shallow fried. Ox liver is prepared in the same way. However, it is tougher and should be braised.

POULTRY

Poultry is the term used to describe domestic birds reared specifically for human consumption, the most common of which are chicken and turkeys. Poultry is usually only hung for 24 hours as tenderising takes place quickly.

Poultry and food poisoning

More than 10,000 people suffer from food poisoning each year. Cases range from slight tummy upset to extreme illness and sometimes death. Unfortunately, the number of recorded food poisoning cases continues to rise.

Most food poisoning is caused by *salmonella* bacteria and poultry is one of the commonest sources of *salmonella*. *Salmonella* are killed by heat; however, if the heat is not sufficient the bacteria will multiply and cause food poisoning. Poultry can also be the indirect cause of food poisoning if proper care is not taken in its preparation and storage. Incorrect preparation and storage cause harmful bacteria to contaminate other food which is eaten without further cooking. It is therefore paramount that strict hygiene precautions should be adhered to when storing and handling raw poultry.

WARNING! Poultry should never be eaten undercooked.

Quality points to consider when purchasing poultry

- Chicken should have a pleasant smell and be dry to the touch.
- The skin should be white and unbroken.
- The breasts should be plump with a pliable breast bone with no bruises.
- The legs should be smooth and covered with small scales, have no bruises and the bones should be unbroken.

Poultry chart

English	*French*	*Weight*	*Number of portions*
Single baby chicken	*Poussin*	360 to 500 g	1
Double baby chicken	*Poussin double*	500 to 750 g	2
Small roasting chicken	*Poulet de grain*	0.75 to 1 kg	1½ to 2
Medium roasting chicken	*Poulet reine*	1 to 2 kg	2 to 4
Large roasting chicken	*Poularde*	2 to 3 kg	4 to 6
Turkey	*Dinde*	3.5 kg to 20 kg	Depends on size
Goose	*Oie*	4 to 7 kg	Depends on size
Duck	*Canard*	2 to 3 kg	3 to 4

Preparing poultry

Poultry is available 'New York' dressed (undrawn). That is to say, it has had the feathers removed, but still has the head, neck and innards intact. These will have to be removed and it is advisable to have a separate preparation area in order to reduce the risk of infection from harmful bacteria from poultry offal.

After gutting the inside, poultry will need to be washed to remove any loose intestines and then wiped with a clean cloth.

Basic preparation

When preparing whole poultry, you need to ensure that the edges of the winglets have been trimmed and the following have been removed:

1. the feet and spurs (the hard projection on chicken legs);
2. any hair or feathers;
3. the wishbone;
4. excess skin from the abdominal and neck area;
5. excess fat.

Marinading

Some recipes require poultry to be marinaded for between 2 and 24 hours to give flavour and to assist in the tenderising process. A marinade might consist of wine or lemon juice, oil, vegetables and herbs.

SAFETY: Always ensure that meat and poultry is properly thawed before preparing. Never attempt to prepare frozen meat and poultry.

For roasting (chickens, turkey and ducks)

The stages are the same as for the basic preparation, and then they are tied (trussed) with string to hold the shape and cooked whole.

For grilling (chicken only)

1. Follow the stages for basic preparation.
2. Split the bird down the back along the backbone, passing a knife through the body from the parson's nose to the neck.
3. Flatten with a cutlet bat, remove ribs and trim the backbone.

For supremes (chicken only)

1. Follow the stages for basic preparation and remove legs from the carcass by detaching at the joint socket.
2. Remove the skin from the breast and detach the breasts from the sides of the carcass.
3. Remove the sinew from the inside of each supreme and bat out lightly.
4. Trim and clean the end of the wing to expose the bone.
5. Cut a small pocket in the thick part of the breast flesh into which the fillet is inserted.

COOKING TIP: Turkey breasts can be filleted as for chicken supremes and cut into steaks or escalopes or diced for stewing.

For sauté (chicken only)

1. Follow the stages for basic preparation, remove the legs from the carcass by cutting through the skin between the thigh and the body till the joint socket is reached.
2. Pull the leg outwards.
3. With the point of the knife cut through the connective sinew along the fleshy part between sockets and the parson's nose and remove the leg from the carcass.
4. Divide the leg into its natural components – the thigh and the drumstick.
5. Repeat the process for the other side. These pieces are the dark meat.
6. Remove the ailerons (winglets) at the first joint of the wing and trim.
7. Remove the wings, cutting through the joint close to the body and along the breast.
8. Remove the breast from the carcass, then cut crosswise into two equal parts and trim.
9. The wings and the breast are the white meat.
10. This will result in four portions each consisting of a piece of white meat and a piece of dark meat. Normally the smaller piece of brown meat – the drumstick – would be served with the larger piece of white meat – the wing.

Cut	No of cuts	French term
1 Wings	2	Aile
2 Winglets	2	Aileron
3 Breast	2	Blanc/poitrine
4 Thigh	2	Gras de cuisse
5 Drumstick	2	Pilon de cuisse
6 Carcass	3	Carcasse

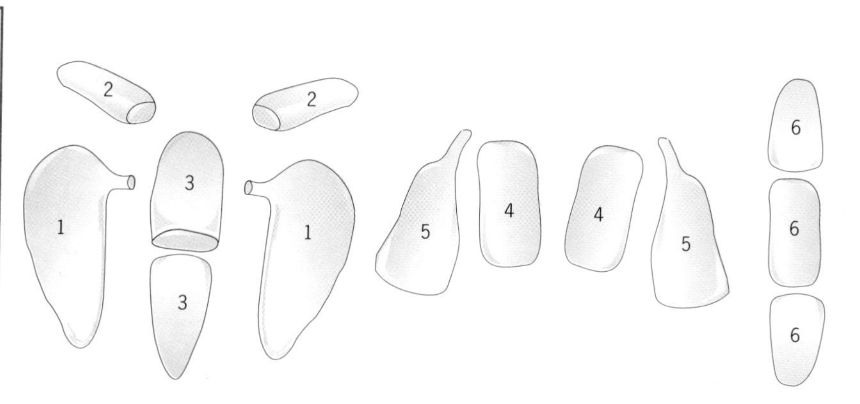

Figure 113 Diagram of chicken joints

KEY WORDS

AITCH BONE Portion of pelvic girdle.

BARDING Laying and securing a thin layer of pork fat or bacon over lean joints of meat before roasting to help retain the natural juices and protect the joint from overheating.

BATTING Using a cutlet bat or steak hammer to flatten and even out a piece of meat or poultry to a required thickness.

BRINE Solution of water, salt and saltpetre.

CARCASS Slaughtered, dressed animal.

CHINE Removal of back-bone.

CUTLET BAT An implement used to flatten and tenderise meat and poultry.

DICING Cutting pieces of meat, poultry or game into mouth-sized cubes.

DISSECTION Division of carcass into joints.

JOINTING Cutting meat or poultry into more manageable joints.

LARDING Insertion of strips of specially prepared pork fat into lean flesh using a larding needle.

PANÉ To coat with flour, eggwash and breadcrumbs.

PICKLED Steeped in brine.

SALTPETRE Nitrate of potash to colour and preserve.

SCORE To make shallow cuts in skin to facilitate heat penetration.

TRUSSING Trussing is the action of passing string through poultry and securing it with a knot to help keep a good shape during the cooking process.

TYING To secure the shape of a rolled piece of meat with string.

ELEMENT 2

Methods of cooking meat, poultry and offal dishes

INTRODUCTION

Meat, poultry and offal play an important role in most people's diet. They are a valuable source of protein which is essential for growth and repair of body tissues. All cooking methods can be applied to meat and poultry, however offal cooking is restricted by the nature of its structure.

DRY COOKING PROCESSES

Roasting

Roasting is a dry cookery process defined as the cooking of foods in an oven by convected heat. The heat either circulates naturally or is forced around the oven by an electrical fan.

Cooking vessel

The most common cooking vessel is a metal roasting tray with tall sides. The tray should just be large enough to hold the item being cooked. If it is too small, fat might spill over the sides and cause a fire and, if it is too large, fat in the tray will burn which will ruin the finished flavour.

Pre-roasting procedures

Meat is sealed/seared before roasting to give colour and add to the flavour by sealing in the juices. This can be achieved by either:

- frying all sides in hot fat in a frying pan; or
- placing the meat or poultry into a very hot oven 220 °C to 225 °C for approximately 15 min.

A trivet lifts the item being roasted off the bottom of the tray and prevents it being fried in fat. A trivet is a special metal rack, However, if this is not available an improvised trivet may be made from a bed of root vegetables and/or chopped bones. The essence from the bones/vegetables will flavour the gravy.

Process of roasting

The sealed joint of meat or poultry is placed on a trivet in a roasting tin with the largest cut surfaces exposed. Any fat on the top will baste the joint automatically. It should not be necessary to add extra fat during cooking.

NOTE: When using roasting bags always follow the manufacturer's recommendations.

For pork crackling, score the rind well, dry and brush the surface with oil and rub in a little salt. To ensure really crisp crackling, refrain from basting the joint during cooking.

Internal temperatures and roasting times

For hygiene reasons the internal temperature of meat or poultry needs to reach a minimum of 63 °C.

Approximate roasting time		*Ideal degree of cooking*		
Meat	**Cooking times**	**Degree of temperature**	**Final internal cooking**	**Oven temperature**
Beef	15 min per ½ kg and 15 min over	Underdone	63 °C to 65 °C	170 °C to 175 °C
Chicken	15 min per ½ kg and 15 min over	Cooked through	80 °C to 85 °C	165 °C to 170 °C
Pork	25 min per ½ kg and 25 min over	Well done	80 °C to 85 °C	170 °C to 175 °C
Lamb	15 min per ½ kg and 15 min over	Underdone	63 °C to 65 °C	170 °C to 175 °C
	20 min per ½ kg and 20 min over	Cooked through	63 °C to 65 °C	70 °C to 175 °C
Mutton	20 min per ½ kg and 20 min over	Cooked through	63 °C to 65 °C	165 °C to 175 °C
Turkey	20 min per ½ kg and 20 min over, cooked through	Cooked through	80 °C to 85 °C	165 °C to 170 °C
Veal	25 min per ½ kg and 25 min over	Cooked through	80 °C to 85 °C	170 °C to 175 °C

WARNING! Pork is more susceptible to salmonella food poisoning than other meats. It is also inclined to contain a parasitic worm called Trichinosis which can only be killed off under high temperatures.

Test for cooking

To check if the meat is cooked use the following methods:

1. **Appearance** This is usually best left to experienced chefs and even then it is not an accurate test. It should only be done in conjunction with one of the other methods of testing.
2. **Pressure test** Press the meat with the hand. Generally, the less resilient the meat is to pressure, the more cooked (well done) it is.
3. **Thermal needle** As well as being the most accurate method it is also the most hygienic. The food is pierced with a special thermal needle which records the internal temperature of the food. This is paramount when cooking meats that have been stuffed, as the stuffing must reach the required temperature in order to kill off harmful bacteria.

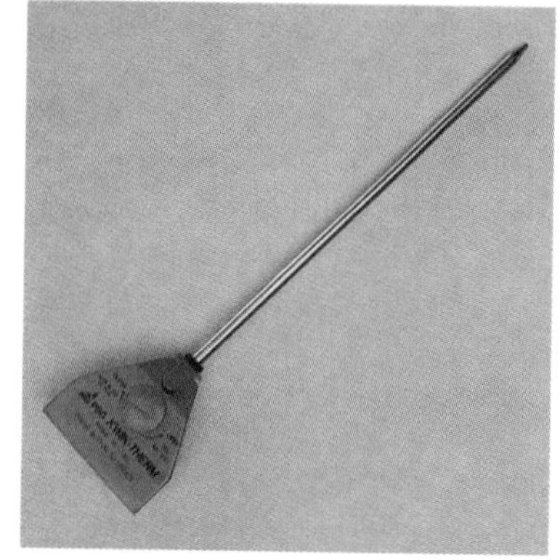

Figure 114 Thermal needle

Standard garnishes for roast meats and poultry

English term	French term	Garnish
Roast beef	*Boeuf rôti à l'anglaise*	Yorkshire pudding, roast gravy, horseradish sauce, watercress
Roast lamb	*Agneau rôti*	Mint sauce or redcurrant jelly, watercress and roast gravy
Roast mutton	*Mouton rôti*	White onion sauce, redcurrant jelly, watercress and roast gravy
Roast pork	*Porc rôti*	Sage and onion stuffing, apple sauce, roast gravy and watercress
Roast veal	*Veau rôti*	Thickened roast gravy, lemon parsley and thyme stuffing, watercress
Roast chicken (English style)	*Poulet rôti à l'anglaise*	Roast gravy, bread sauce, grilled bacon, game chips, watercress
Roast chicken with stuffing	*Poulet rôti farci*	Roast gravy, parsley and thyme stuffing, watercress
Roast chicken with stuffing, English style	*Poulet rôti farci à l'anglaise*	Roast gravy, parsley and thyme stuffing, bread sauce, grilled bacon, game chips and watercress
Roast duck/duckling	Canard/caneton rôti	Sage and onion stuffing, apple sauce, roast gravy and watercress
Roast turkey (young)	Dindonneau rôti	Bread sauce, grilled bacon, chestnut stuffing, grilled chipolata sausages, cranberry sauce, roast gravy and watercress
Roast turkey (female)	Dinde rôtie	

Figure 115 Pot roast

Pot roasting

Pot roasting (*poêler*) which is also known as cocotte cooking is similar to roasting because it involves the cooking of joints of meat and poultry in an oven where the food is basted with a fat. Traditionally, pot roasting should be carried out in a cast-iron pot. Where it differs from roasting is that the food is placed in a cooking vessel with a tight-fitting lid on a bed of vegetables and herbs and the fat for basting is always butter. A sauce is made from the thickened cooking juices and stock or demi-glace.

(For more details on grilling, *see* pp. 90–100.)

Grilling

Prepare meat and poultry for grilling by brushing with oil and seasoning with salt and pepper. Grilling can take place either under a pre-heated grill (salamander) or on a charcoal or charcoal-effect grill. Always brush the grill bars with oil to prevent the meat from sticking and turn meat and poultry regularly during cooking.

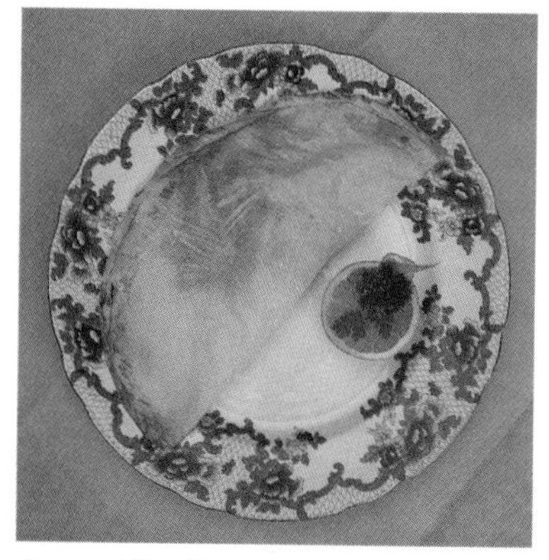

Figure 116 Chicken cooked en papillote

Baking

There are four ways of baking these dishes

(a) *'en croûte'*, i.e. wrapped in pastry, for example Beef Wellington;
(b) in pies, e.g. chicken or steak and kidney;
(c) in batter, e.g. toad in the hole;
(d) *'en papillote'*, i.e. cooking tender pieces of meat and poutry in special sealed silicon bags.

When meat or poultry is placed in the oven to cook it is usually called roasting or pot roasting, but some meat and poultry dishes may be baked. Normally the food has been partially cooked by another process and is just finished off in the bag which is served and opened in front of the customer.

Shallow frying, stir frying and griddling

(See Prepare and fry food, pp 64–75; Prepare and griddle food, pp 101–5.)

Shallow frying is carried out in a frying pan, sauté pan or sauteuse where the meat comes into contact with the lightly oiled hot cooking surface. Stir frying takes place in a special wok and is very quick. With griddling the cooking surface is an oiled, temperature-regulated solid metal plate onto which the food is placed to cook.

WET COOKING PROCESSES

Figure 117 Stirfrying

Stewing

Stewing is defined as cooking prepared food by moderate heat in liquid. The liquid can be water, wine, beer, stock or sauce. Stewing temperature is just below boiling and during cooking the slow, gentle process aids the extraction of flavours and helps to break down the connective tissue of meat and poultry into a gelatinous substance, causing the fibres to soften and become digestible. Stewing usually takes place on top of the stove, simmering gently on a low heat, but can also be carried out in the oven in an appropriate cooking vessel.

Stews are divided into three main categories:

1. brown;
2. white;
3. miscellaneous.

Brown stews

Classic brown stews are further divided into two categories:

1. *ragoût*;
2. *navarin*.

A *ragoût* is a brown beef stew though it is possible to have a veal, rabbit or kidney *ragoût*.

A *navarin* can be either a lamb or veal stew. These stews are usually thickened with a brown *roux* at the beginning of the cookery process.

The browning effect is created by shallow frying or briefly cooking (flashing) the meat in a hot oven. The flour used to thicken the liquid may also be browned under the grill or in the oven.

White stews

Classic white stews are also divided into two categories:

1. *fricassée;*
2. *blanquette.*

A *fricassée* is only suitable for tender cuts of either veal, chicken or pork. The meat is cooked in a white sauce which is made with sandy roux (blond) and the appropriate white stock.

A *blanquette* is normally made with a lesser quality, tougher cut of meat. The nature of the meat used has a direct effect on the cooking time which is longer than a *fricassée*. The meat is first brought to the boil in water; once boiled it is cooled down and refreshed. 'Refreshing' or ' blanching' is used to remove impurities and excess blood which form as a scum on the top of the liquid. The meat is then placed into stock and the cooking process takes place.

The strained cooking liquid is thickened using a blond roux to make *velouté* which is used as the serving sauce.

Miscellaneous stews

Miscellaneous stews cannot be classified into the other two main categories. They include curries, goulash, chilli con carne and Irish stew.

Braising

Figure 118 Braised beef

Introduction

Braising is a combination of pot roasting and stewing. Pot roasting because it is carried out in an oven in a cooking vessel with a tight-fitting lid and stewing because it is cooked in a minimum amount of liquid. Meat or poultry may be marinaded overnight in wine/vinegar, vegetables and herbs to give flavour.

Braising is suitable for meat and poultry that is too tough for roasting. The technique of braising is long and slow and the highly flavoured liquor or sauce becomes an integral part of the completed dish. Always use a tight-fitting lid on the cooking vessel to hold in the flavour and prevent excess evaporation.

There are two techniques used in braising :

- **White braising** Used to cook white meats such as veal and poultry. However it is rarely used these days for cooking joints.
- **Brown braising** Used to cook meats such as beef, mutton and offal (e.g. heart, tongue and oxtail). The process is initially started by browning the meat (shallow frying or flash roasting) to give it its distinct colour and flavour. The meat is then placed on a bed of roots and ⅔ covered with stock.

Cooking vessel

Braising is carried out in an oven-proof dish provided it has a thick bottom (to prevent burning) and a tight-fitting lid (to prevent evaporation).

A *daubière* is a special earthenware, stoneware or tin-lined copper casserole, traditionally used for braising and its use is known as cooking *en daube*.

(See Prepare, boil, poach and steam food, p 88 for recipes.)

Boiling

Tougher meats and older poultry are suitable for boiling. Fresh meats and poultry are immersed completely in boiling water to cook and pickled/salted meats are soaked overnight to remove excess salt, then placed in cold water to aid the extraction of salt and brought to the boil.

(See Prepare, boil, poach and steam food, p 88.)

Steaming

Steaming can take place in an atmospheric steamer, a pressureless convection steamer or a high-pressure steamer. The long and moist conditions of steaming are excellent for cooking tougher, coarser joints of meat and poultry.

KEY WORDS

BLANCHE Place in cold water, boil to refresh (to whiten).

BRATT PAN A large tilting pan with lid (modular).

BRAWN A jellied meat dish made from pig's head and feet.

DEMI-GLAZE Equal quantities of brown sauce and brown stock reduced by half.

FLASH ROASTING Quickly sealing in a pre-heated oven at a temperature of 250 °C (480 °F).

REFRESHING To wash meat under running water, blanching to clear impurities.

SKIMMING To remove fat and scum from surface of cooking liquor.

TRIVET A wire frame to keep roasting meat out of fat during cooking.

NVQ SVQ 2

Prepare and cook basic fish dishes

ELEMENT 1
Prepare basic fish dishes

INTRODUCTION

Fish is an exceptional source of protein and vitamins and has an excellent taste.

Fish is best bought fresh, daily and used on the day of purchase. Fresh fish supplies are subject to weather conditions and seasons for availability. Chefs must consider this when planning menus.

Fish is classified into two main groups: white fish, where the oil is concentrated in the liver; and oily fish, where the oil is dispersed throughout the flesh.

The techniques of skinning and filleting fish will be demonstrated to the trainee by the supervisor/tutor. The information here on these techniques is intended only as a back-up.

WHITE FISH

The flesh of white fish is high in protein and low in oils. White fish are divided into two groups; round and flat. Round fish live near the seabed while flat fish live on the seabed. Large round species, such as coley and cod, can be bought as steaks (*darnes*). Small round species, such as whiting and haddock, are sold whole or in fillets.

The larger flat fish varieties, such as halibut and turbot, are bought whole and in fillets or steaks (*tronçons*) and trimmed as required. Small flat fish, such as plaice, lemon sole and Dover sole, are usually bought whole, and trimmed or filleted as required.

COOKING TIP: Some fish are sold preserved or cured by salting, marinating or smoking. There are two methods of smoking fish: hot and cold. Cold smoked fish, like kippers, have a smoky flavour but they are still raw and must be cooked. Hot smoked fish, like mackerel, are smoked at higher temperatures, so they are cooked and ready to eat.

OILY FISH

Oily fish are both high in proteins and oils. All fish are important sources of essential nutrients, however the oily fish species such as herring and mackerel are particularly good sources of vitamins A and D. The oils found in these fish are mainly polyunsaturated fats which are proven to be beneficial to health. In fact the fatty acids in fish oils are believed to assist in preventing heart disease. The oils are stored throughout the flesh of the fish resulting in a dark or pinkish colour. Oily fish can be bought whole, in steaks or in fillets.

Quality points to consider when purchasing whole fresh fish

- Eyes are bright and full, not sunken.
- Gills are bright red in colour.

- Flesh is firm and resilient; when it is pressed with the finger the impression disappears quickly.
- Fish is not limp.
- Scales lie flat, and are moist and plentiful.
- Skin is covered with a fresh sea slime, or is smooth and moist.
- The smell is pleasant; stale fish smells of ammonia.
- Stale fish is dull and flabby and shows discoloration.

Quality points to consider when purchasing portioned fresh fish (may have been frozen previously)

- The flesh is white and translucent, firm and not ragged or gaping.
- There is no smell of ammonia or sour odours.
- There are no bruises or blood clots and no areas of discoloration.
- There is no excess moisture which indicates poor defrosting.

COOKING TIP: When defrosting fish and shellfish it is best to thaw them overnight in the refrigerator. Do not thaw fish in water as it loses texture, flavour and valuable nutrients. Frozen fish may also be defrosted in the microwave, using the defrost setting.

STORAGE OF FRESH AND FROZEN FISH

(*See* Receive, handle and store food deliveries, p. 296)

Whenever possible fresh fish should be used on the day of delivery. If this is not possible it should be stored at a temperature just above freezing-point and ideally be covered with crushed ice to prevent the surface from drying out.

Frozen fish should be stored at a temperature of no higher than –18 °C and used in strict rotation.

PREPARING FLAT FISH

Skinning whole small flat fish

- Wash thoroughly to remove natural slime.
- Cut slightly into the skin near the head (for lemon sole, plaice etc.).
- Using a clean cloth to grip the fish, loosen the skin by working the thumb around the length of the side fins towards the head.
- By grasping the freed side firmly the whole skin should be cleanly pulled diagonally across the fish until it is free.
- The head is usually left intact but neatly trim the tail and side fins either with a sharp knife or suitable pair of fishmonger's scissors.
- To complete the job remove the eyes, cut away the gills and wash out all the blood.

Skinning a dab is more difficult but, once the skin has been loosened at the tail end, it is just a question of getting a good grip.

Skinning Dover sole

- Cut slightly into the skin near the tail.
- Loosen the skin to get a good grip.
- Hold the tail firmly with one hand.
- Pull the skin away towards the head.

(For preparing darnes and tronçons see Steaking p. 175)

Skinning turbot (large flat fish)

This fish has a lot in common with other flat-fish classes but the skin is so firmly attached that it is not practicable to skin before filleting.

It is generally better to fillet as for other flat fish, then skin the fillets. The blade will often catch the back end of the spikes that characterise this variety, so you must take care.

Skinning skate

As whole fish or wings are usually covered in thick slime when freshly purchased, they need to be thoroughly cleaned. A little salt in the water helps counteract the slime.

When skinning a whole fish, the wings should be removed by cutting them free from the body, starting with the knife at the head end and following the natural body contour. This job should be done with the fish laid out on the block, with its dark side up.

Detach the skin from the thickest part of the piece with a sharp knife, ease the skin from the flesh until there is enough free to hold firmly with the fingers. Using a cloth in the hand for security, pull in one sharp stroke towards the edge of the fish, detaching with the point of a filleting knife any flesh that might stick to the skin.

Cross-cut filleting

This method produces two double fillets.

- Make a cut around the head and insert the knife horizontally against the backbone.
- Work carefully out towards the tail fin.
- When one side of the fish has been freed, continue cutting over the ridge bone to the other side, finishing off by cutting again to the fin and removing the whole fillet.
- Treat the reverse side in the same way.
- Finally, trim the fillets to remove any odd fine bones.

Filleting into quarters or four

- Always prepare white side first.
- Make the first cut by running the knife through the lateral line following the course of the backbone from head to tail.
- Then insert the knife at the shoulder end easing in under the fillet and working outwards and downwards to the tail. Several cuts may be required. To avoid waste, keep the knife against the bone.
- Rotate the fish and release the second fillet in the same way turning the knife slightly upwards when arriving at the junction of the side fins.
- Turn the fish over and repeat the process on the dark side.
- Clean and trim the four fillets in the same way as for the cross-cut fillets.

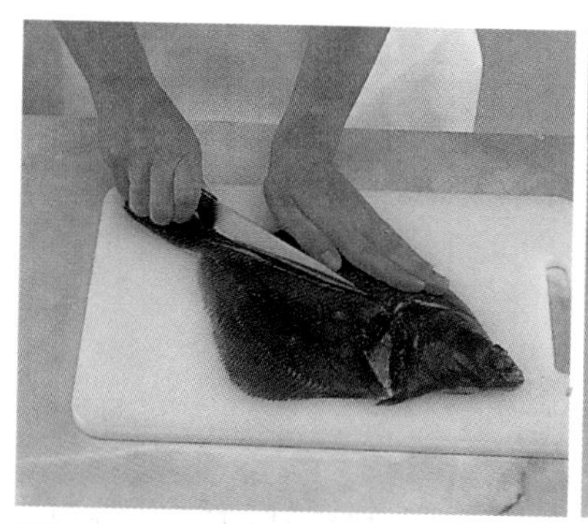
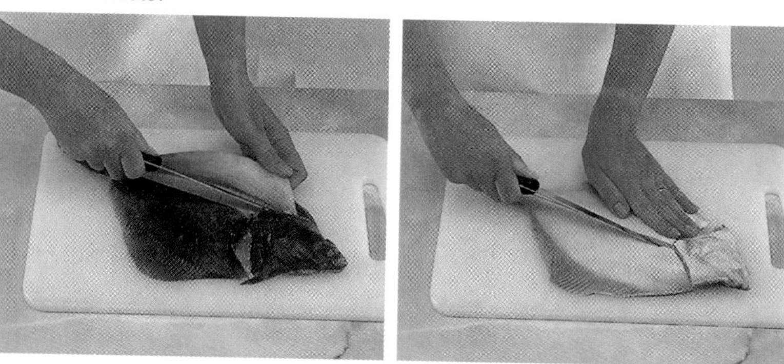

Figure 119 Quartering

Skinning fillets

- Lay the fillet on a flat surface, skin side down with tail end towards you.
- Insert the knife between the skin and flesh.
- Keeping the blade quite flat to the surface (if you don't there will be wastage), work it towards the thicker shoulder end using a gradual sawing motion.

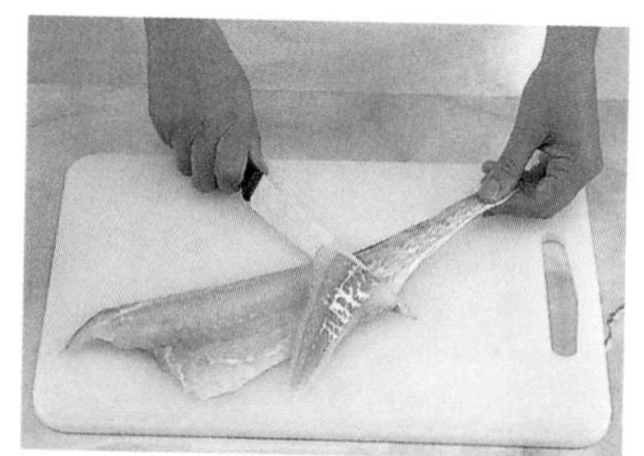

Figure 120 Skinning fillets

PREPARING ROUND WHITE FISH

- Wash thoroughly to remove natural slime.
- Remove scales.

Removing the head

- Insert the knife behind the gills.
- Cut deeply both sides, extending the cuts to include a little of the flap.
- Finally, cut through the bone to sever the head completely.

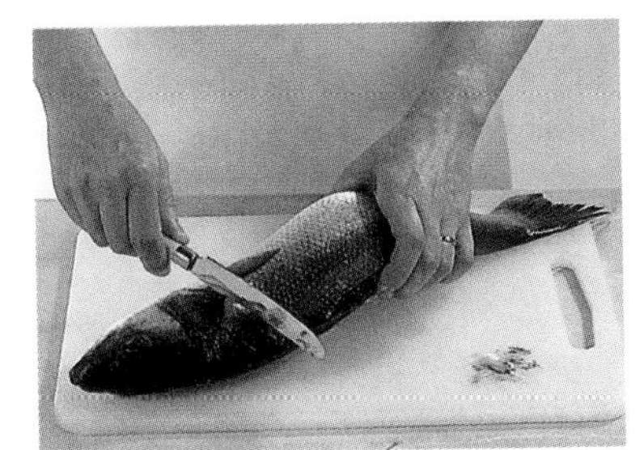

Figure 121 Scaling round fish

Scaling round fish

- Scale the fish under a running tap to prevent the scales making a mess.
- Using the back of a knife, skim neatly along the fish from tail to shoulder.
- The scales should come off the fish easily.
- Keep the skin intact as the appearance of the fish is important if it is to be steaked.

Cleaning round fish

- Remove the 'sound' (the thin membrane that lines the gut wall) by inserting a small knife at the centre of the fish at the shoulder and penetrating just below the membrane.
- Cut away the sound on one side by keeping the point of the blade still and cutting outwards by raising the handle and blade of the knife until the membrane is freed.
- Repeat the process to remove the other side but hold and pull away the sound as you cut.
- Insert the point of the knife in the vent and scrape out any blood towards the shoulder.
- Ideally whole fish should be washed thoroughly under cold running water. If using a bowl, change the water frequently.

Steaking (darnes: round fish; tronçons: flat fish)

- Keep the knife vertical and cut straight through.
- By standing over the knife and not to the side of it you should be able to avoid 'wedge cutting'.
- The backbone in cod, coley, hake etc. is of a harder texture so use a fishmonger's mallet to tap the knife through.
- Give the blow when the blade has been allowed to pass beyond the fish girth.

Filleting (round fish)

- Lay the fish flat on a block and insert the knife at the shoulder cutting cleanly to the backbone from the shoulder to the tail.
- Make a couple of strokes with the knife down the fish, between fish and bone, to free the fillet over the backbone.
- The last cut, once over the bone, should free the fillet.
- Trim the flap from the fillet and check for bones.
- Turn the fish over to remove the second fillet.
- Make the first cut in the backbone beginning from the tail and cutting back to the shoulder.
- Make a number of strokes with the knife to cut the fillet free at the centre of the fish and cut away from you to free the tail end.
- Reinsert the knife at the centre to free the fillet at the shoulder end. Trim the fillet and check for bones.

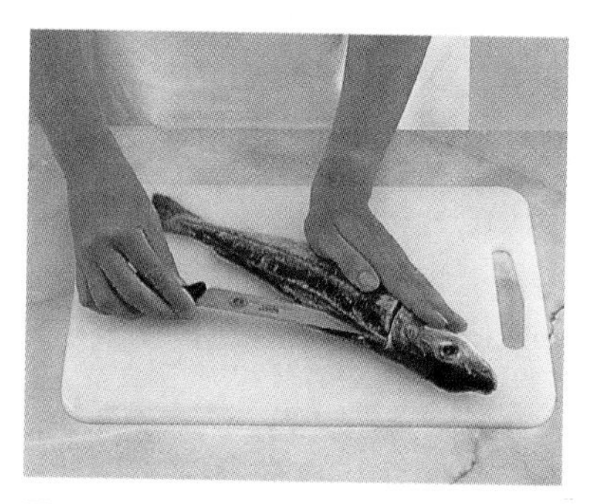
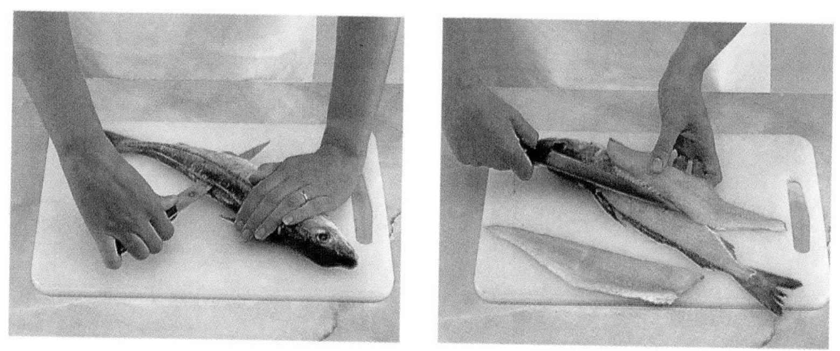

Figure 122 Filleting round fish

PREPARING OILY FISH

Splitting

Remove the head first. Split the fish from the head to the tail or the back to the belly, the former being more usual. Carefully place the roe or milt on one side.

Boning

It is impossible to remove all the fine lateral bones. However, if you are careful most will be out when you have finished boning the fish.

- Remove the head and lay the fish flat on the block and cut the belly.
- Carefully move the knife along beneath the backbone. Use a sharp knife to prevent hacking or pulling.

  When the fish is in an oily condition an alternative method may be used.
- Slit the belly and open the fish up, laying it on the board with the skin uppermost.
- Using your fingers and the heel of your hand, press firmly along the backbone.
- Turn the fish over and ease the freed bone out.

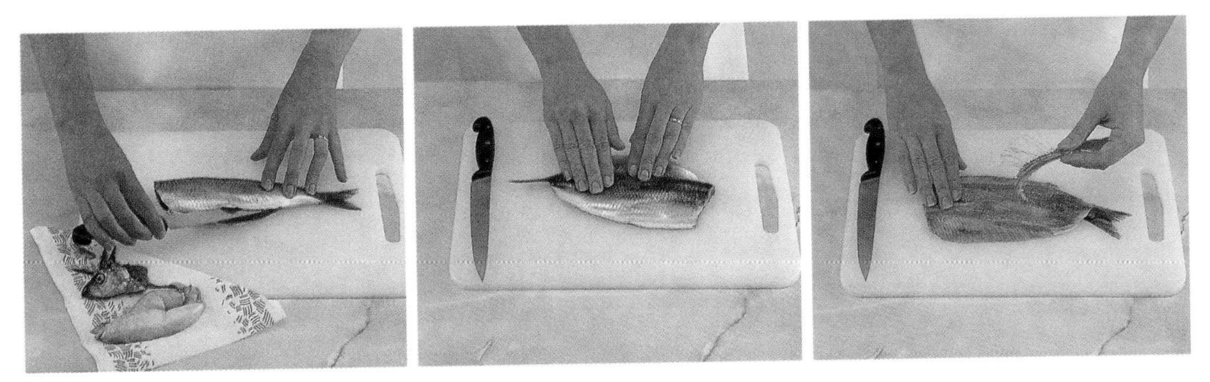

Figure 123 Boning fish

KEY WORDS

À L'ANGLAISE Coated with seasoned flour, egg wash and breadcrumbs.

À LA FRANÇAISE Coated with milk and seasoned flour.

À L'ORLY Coated with seasoned flour and batter.

BEURRE NOISETTE Nut brown butter.

BRANDING To mark with a hot poker.

CISELER To score.

DARNE Section of round fish cut across and through the bone.

DÉLICE A neatly folded fillet of fish.

FILLETS Flesh of fish removed from the bone

GOUJONS/GOUJONETTES Fillet of fish cut into thin strips. Goujonettes are smaller thin strips.

MEUNIÈRE Shallow fried fish.

PAUPIETTE Fillet of fish skinned, usually spread with fish forcemeat and rolled.

SUPRÊME Section of fish cut on a slant from a large fillet.

TRONÇON Section of large flat fish cut across and through the bone.

ACTIVITY

Find the market price and/or the retail price for the following whole fish and cuts of fish and their seasons

Fish species	Season availabilty	Unit and price			
		Whole steaks, £ per kg	Fillets £ per kg	Steaks,round £ per kg	Steaks, flat £ per kg
OILY FISH					
Conger					
Eel, common					
Herring					
Mackerel					
Pilchard					
Rainbow trout					
Sea trout					
Sprat					
Tunny					
Whitebait					
ROUND WHITE FISH					
Bass					
Catfish					
Cod					
Coley					
Dogfish					
Grey mullet					
Gurnard					
Haddock					
Hake					
John Dory					
Ling					
Monkfish					
Pollack/Pollock					
Red mullet					
Sea bream					
Skate					
Whiting					

FLAT WHITE FISH					
Brill					
Dab					
Dover Sole					
Flounder					
Halibut					
Lemon sole					
Megrim					
Plaice					
Turbot					
Witch					

Activity

1. How often should fresh fish be purchased?
2. Ideally, how should fresh fish be stored?
3. At what temperature should frozen fish be stored?

ELEMENT 2

Cook, basic fish dishes

INTRODUCTION

Every species of fish can be cooked in a variety of ways. Large fish are usually filleted and cut into suprêmes or cut through the bone for steaks (Darnes and Tronçons). However, the one golden rule when cooking fish is never overcook! When fish is cooked it appears white in colour or opaque and a fork or skewer will easily penetrate the flesh. It should also be noted that one species of the same type may almost always be substituted for another. For example, when following a recipe for cod, you may substitute coley or pollack etc.

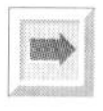

(*See* Prepare and fry food, (p.74) for deep-fried fish recipe.)

COOKING TIP: When cooking fish by dry processes the delicate flesh of the fish must be protected. Suitable methods of cookery for this unit are listed below.

DRY COOKING METHODS

Deep frying

The delicate flesh of fish needs to be protected from the high cooking temperatures when deep frying. This is done by coating the fish in a batter, breadcrumbs or simply milk and flour. Deep frying can take place in a fryer or friture at a temperature of between 175 °C and 196 °C.

(Meunière: (*see* Prepare & fry food, p72.)

Figure 124 Deep-fried fish

(*See* Prepare and fry food, pp. 64–75; *See* also p. 337 for recipes)

Shallow frying

Shallow fried fish should also be protected during cooking. After basic preparation the fish is usually passed through seasoned flour to protect it. Shallow frying is traditionally done in a meunière pan or alternatively a good frying pan may be used.

COOKING TIP: Protective coatings will not only safeguard the fish when cooking but will also:

- **prevent excess absorption of the cooking medium, provided the fat is at the right temperature;**
- **reduce moisture loss in the flesh;**
- **help retain the shape and natural flavours of the fish during cooking.**

(See Prepare and grill food, pp.90–100.)

Grilling

Grilled fish must be protected as with deep and shallow frying. Fish may be grilled in one of the following ways:

- under a salamander with the heat source from above;
- on a charcoal or simulated charcoal grill with the heat source below. This is for whole fish only;
- using an infra-red grill, with heat sources above and below.

(See Prepare and bake food, pp. 76–81.)

Baking

Fish may be baked as a dish in its own right or as an integral part of another dish, i.e. a quiche, flan, a stuffing, or in a soufflé. As with other dry methods of cooking, fish must be protected during the process. This may be done by:

1. cooking in a sauce;
2. cooking in a special pouch made from greaseproof paper and/or foil. This method is usually referred to as cooking *'en papillote'*;
3. wrapping the fish in a puff, brioche or filo pastry. This is known as cooking *'en croûte'* (in a crust).

(See Prepare, boil, poach and steam food, pp. 82–9.)

WET COOKING METHODS

Steaming

Fish may be steamed with excellent results whether it is carried out in a high pressure steamer, a pressureless convection steamer or a low-pressure steaming unit. The advantage is that the process is rapid with little loss of flavour or nutrients.

Figure 125 Steamed fish

Shallow and deep poaching

Poaching is cooking at a temperature below boiling, between 90 °C and 95 °C, with very little or no movement in the liquid, otherwise the fish might break up. Poaching is divided into two categories: deep poaching and shallow poaching.

Deep poaching

Deep poaching is carried out in a special salmon or trout kettle or a *plat à sauter*. In deep poaching the fish is completely immersed in the cooking liquid. Depending on whether the fish is oily or white, the liquid is either :

1. a vinegar court boullion (for oily fish) made from water, vinegar, carrots, onions, thyme, bay leaf, parsley stalk, salt and peppercorns or
2. a white wine or lemon juice bouillon (for white fish) made from water, dry white wine or lemon juice, onions, thyme, bay leaf, parsley stalks, salt and peppercorns.

Shallow poaching

Less liquid is used in shallow poaching; the liquid only ever covers two-thirds of the fish and the exposed area is covered with a cartouche to prevent the fish from drying out. The cooking process is only suitable for small cuts of fish and takes place in a special poaching pan, a sauteuse, an oven-proof, earthenware pan or a shallow saucepan. The cooking liquor is usually stock and wine. Once cooked the fish is removed from the pan. The cooking liquid is heated and reduced and used as part of the finishing sauce.

Recipes call for shallow-poached fish dishes to be glazed or gratinated. Glazing is done by enriching the finishing sauce with a sabayon or a liaison and browning under a salamander or in a pre-heated oven. Gratinating is done by sprinkling grated cheese and/or breadcrumbs on the fish and browning under the salamander or in a pre-heated oven.

Figure 126 Gratinated shallow poached fish

STORING COOKED FISH

Fish is a protein dish and as such is prone to the growth of food poisoning bacteria and should be stored either cold at a temperature of below 5 °C or hot at a temperature of above 65 °C.

Apart from the hygiene factor, the flesh of fish does not stand up to long holding periods and will deteriorate rapidly.

ACTIVITY

1. Using the key, fill in the most suitable methods of cooking.

KEY

BK	Baking	G	Grilling
SF	Shallow or stir frying	P	Poaching
DF	Deep frying	ST	Steaming

Fish species	*Method of cookery*
OILY FISH	
Herring	
Mackerel	

Pilchard	
Rainbow trout	
Whitebait	
ROUND WHITE FISH	
Bass	
Cod	
Coley	
Haddock	
Hake	
John Dory	
Monkfish	
Red mullet	
Sea bream	
Whiting	
FLAT WHITE FISH	
Brill	
Dab	
Dover sole	
Halibut	
Lemon sole	
Plaice	
Turbot	

2. What is added to a fish sauce to make it glazed?
3. Using your cookery book give **four** examples of glazed and **four** graninated fish dishes

Glazed	Gratinated
1	
2	
3	
4	

Prepare and cook vegetables for basic hot dishes and salads

ELEMENT 1

Prepare vegetables for basic hot dishes and salads

INTRODUCTION

As well as being an excellent source of vitamins and mineral salts, vegetables add variety, colour and interest to dishes and can form the basis of a well-balanced, nutritional, vegetarian diet. Vegetables can be used in soups, salads, garnishes, side dishes or as vegetarian main dishes, e.g. baked in pastry, vegetables stews, char-grilled vegetables. Extreme care should be taken when preparing and storing vegetables to minimise damaging their delicate structure and losing goodness.

(*See* Maintain personal health and hygiene, pp. 10–13.)

HYGIENE

The following rules must be adhered at all times when preparing vegetables.

- Maintain a high standard of personal hygiene.
- Ensure that all equipment, materials and areas are clean before use.
- Dispose of all waste food and other rubbish in accordance with laid down procedures as prescribed in the Food Hygiene Safety Regulations (1995).

COOKING TIP: Vegetables, particularly root vegetables, can contain live food poisoning bacteria. Always scrub them thoroughly before and after preparation. Any soil finding its way to the preparation area, especially the chopping board, should be thoroughly cleaned off immediately to prevent cross-contamination.

STORAGE OF FRESH VEGETABLES

Fresh vegetables should ideally be stored in a dry vegetable store in the following manner.

- Potatoes are best left in their sacks to prevent sprouting.
- Onions and shallots should be stored in nets or racks.
- Root and green vegetables should be stored on racks.
- Mushrooms should be stored in their containers in the fridge.
- Lettuce, courgettes, peppers and cucumbers should be left in their packaging and placed in the fridge at 1°C.

Figure 127 Onions and shallots in stores

STORAGE OF PREPARED VEGETABLES

After preparation, fresh vegetables should only be stored for the minimum of time. They should be placed in a refrigerator in plastic or stainless steel bowls and covered. Potatoes need to be placed in cold water.

NOTE: Always discard vegetables that are beginning to decay.

CLASSIFICATION OF VEGETABLES

The basic culinary classification for vegetables is:

- **root** for all those grown below the ground;
- **green** for those grown above the ground.

See the expanded version of classification of vegetables below.

(The shaded classifications are not required to complete this unit)

Roots	Beetroot, carrot, celeriac, horseradish, mooli, parsnip, radish, salsify, swede, turnip
Tubers	Jerusalem artichoke, potato, sweet potato, yam
Bulbs	Garlic, leek, onion, shallot
Aqueous/Squash	Courgette, marrow, pumpkin, cucumber
Leaves	Chicory, Chinese leaf, lettuce, mustard cress, radiccio, sorrel, spinach, watercress
Fungi	Cep, chanterelle, horn of plenty, morel, flat mushroom, beefsteak tomato, mushroom, button mushroom, cup mushroom, field mushroom, truffle
Brassicas	Broccoli, cauliflower, kohlarabi, seakale, spring greens, kale, Brussels sprouts, Savoy cabbage
Stems and shoots	Asparagus, celery, chicory endive, fennel
Fruit vegetables	Aubergine, avocado, courgette, pepper, tomato
Legumes (pods and seeds)	Pea, French bean, broad bean, mange-tout, sweetcorn.

AVAILABILITY

Whenever possible, fresh vegetables should always be used. Frozen vegetables should be kept for use in cases of emergency or in situations where it is not economical to prepare fresh produce.

The availability of reasonably priced, fresh vegetables will depend on the season of the year. Most vegetables are available throughout the year now, but at a price. As some vegetables will have to be imported from other countries this is an important factor to take into account when planning menus.

QUALITY

Always check the quality of vegetables that are delivered to the establishment. Some vegetables are more perishable than others and if they have not been stored properly, or have been stored for too long, they will be spoiled.

Always check that root vegetables:

- are free from soil and grit;
- are preferably pre-washed;
- have a good smell;
- are firm to the touch;
- are blemish free;
- are of even size and shape.

Always check that green vegetables:

- are bright in colour (first indication of freshness);
- are free from soil and grit;
- are soil-free, if root is attached;
- have crisp leaves;
- have tightly growing leaves: Cabbages and sprouts must be compact.

GRADING

In Britain and Ireland the four main classes for vegetable produce are:

1. **Extra class** top-quality vegetables
2. **Class I** good-quality vegetables
3. **Class II** reasonably good-quality vegetables
4. **Class III** low marketable-quality vegetables

PREPARATION METHODS

Washing

Vegetables should be washed thoroughly before beginning preparation. It is imperative that soil is removed from root vegetables and green vegetables should be washed thoroughly to remove all traces of insecticides.

Once prepared, vegetables should be rewashed to ensure that all the dirt is removed.

- Wash
- Prepare
- Rewash

(see Handling and maintaining knives, pp. 40.)

WARNING! Never have more than one knife out at any time.

Basic preparation methods

Type	*Preparation*	*Special notes*
Roots	Wash and scrub thoroughly. Remove blemishes. Peel with a vegetable peeler. Re-wash and cut to required shape.	Turnips may be peeled using a small knife. Swedes require a cook's knife.
Tubers	Wash and scrub thoroughly. Remove any blemishes. Peel with a vegetable peeler. Re-wash and cut to required shape. Place in cold water and cover.	
Bulbs	With a knife pull off the outer skin from the top to the root.	
Onions/shallots	Remove root close to the base of the vegetable. Cut to required shape and size.	
Garlic	Remove clove from bulb.	To remove clove: lightly hit the head with the palm of your hand and use a knife to remove the outer skin of the clove from top to the root. Hit lightly with the flat of a knife and peel off skin.
Leeks	Wash, remove discoloured or bruised leaves. Remove root close to the bottom of the vegetable.	

Type	*Preparation*	*Special notes*
	Make an incision just above the root through to the top of the leek. Re-wash and cut to required shape.	
Leaves	Remove any damaged or wilted leaves.	
Lettuce or chicory	Immerse in cold salted water to clean all leaves.	Leave in water for approx. 10 to 15 min. Wash each leaf separately, drain and dry thoroughly. Do not wash under running water as this will damage the leaves.
Mustard cress	Cut 1 cm from the root and wash well.	
Watercress	Cut 1 cm from the root and wash well.	
Brassicas		
Brussel sprouts	Wash and remove any damaged or wilted or discoloured leaves. Trim and score the root in the shape of a cross and re-wash.	
Cabbage	Wash and trim the root. Remove damaged, wilted or discoloured leaves. Cut cabbage in quarters and remove centre stalk and any large leaf ribs. Re-wash.	
Spring greens	Wash and trim the root. Remove damaged, wilted or discoloured leaves. Re-wash.	If small enough, they may be cooked whole. If not, they should be quartered and any large leaf ribs removed.
Spinach	Wash thoroughly and remove all soil and grit. Remove centre stalk. Re-wash.	
Stems	Wash and cut the woody parts from the base of the stem.	
Asparagus	Remove spurs or tips from the leaves. Peel the white section of the stem. Re-wash.	
Celery	Wash, remove the tough outer stalks. Trim the stem. Re-wash and cut to required shape.	
Chicory/Belgian endive	Remove outer leaves and any blemished leaves. Trim stem. Wash.	
Seakale	Wash and remove any damaged or discoloured leaves. Re-wash.	

Type	Preparation	Special notes
Vegetable fruits		
Aubergines	Wash, peel, trim, slice or dice and place in a bowl of water with a little lemon juice added to prevent discoloration.	
Avocado	Cut in half and peel with a vegetable knife. Sprinkle with lemon juice to prevent discoloration.	
Courgettes	Wash, remove the top and base. Peel (if required). Cut to desired shape.	
Peppers	Wash, remove stalk and cut in half lengthwise. Remove pith and seeds. Cut to required shape.	
Cucumber	Wash and peel. Cut to required shape.	
Tomatoes	Wash, remove stalk and eye. Cut to required shape.	

NOTE: In the main, root vegetables need not be stored in water. However, certain root vegetables (salsify) need to be placed in water with a little lemon juice to prevent discoloration.

Preparing the working area and equipment

Always:

- be properly prepared before beginning work;
- have the appropriate knife and equipment ready for the job in hand;
- use the correct colour-coded chopping board and make sure it is clean;
- work in a tidy and efficient manner;
- keep the preparation area clean and uncluttered at all times;
- have a receptacle, on or under the table, for peelings and discarded leaves;
- have a bowl ready for the prepared vegetable;
- remove peelings and discarded leaves immediately preparation is complete.

FROZEN VEGETABLES

In many modern kitchens some vegetables may be purchased frozen and need little or no preparation. Frozen vegetables are mainly used in situations where:

- there is insufficient trained staff available;
- there is a staff shortage;
- economics dictate their necessity.

Figure 128 Bags of frozen vegetables

SALADS

A vegetable salad can be produced from a vast range of ingredients and can be used as:

1. part of or a complete hors d'œuvre;
2. a side dish;
3. a main course.
4. a garnish for presentation.

Vegetables for salads must be thoroughly washed to remove any traces of chemicals (weed and insect killer), dirt, insects and worms that might contaminate the salad. Always handle salad vegetables carefully when preparing, as rough treatment will most likely cause bruising and spoil the overall appearance of the finished dish. Leaves should be separated by hand, and vegetables checked for bruising.

Always:

- wash and rinse in several changes of cold water;
- scrub to remove dirt from uneven surfaces;
- soak for a short time in salt water to help drive out live insects from cracks, crevices and in between leaves.

Cooked vegetables used in salads should only be lightly cooked and refreshed to preserve nutrients, flavour and colour.

WARNING! Never leave salad items at kitchen temperature for too long as they will deteriorate rapidly. Whenever possible they should be covered and refrigerated.

Salads can be divided into two basic groups: single/simple and compound/mixed salads.

Single/simple salads

Endive	Tomato
Chicory	Potato
Sorrel	Cucumber
Watercress	Beetroot
Lettuce	Haricot beans
French beans	Celeriac

Compound/mixed salads

Coleslaw	Potato and watercress
Russian	American
Bagatalle	Alice
Waldorf	Meat
Fish	Shellfish

Vegetable cuts

Brunoise	Dice of Julienne (2mm dice maximum)
Château	Barrel shapes
Jardinière	Baton shapes
Julienne	Thin, matchstick shapes
Macedoine	Small cubes
Matignon	Smaller cut of Mirepoix
Mirepoix	Large roughly cut vegetables
Paysanne	Thin slices or pieces of vegetables which may be a variety of shapes, e.g. triangular, round, or square or rough-sided, approximately 1 cm in diameter.

TIP: As a safety precaution, never stack sacks/bags of vegetables too high.

Moulding vegetables

Occasionally vegetables are used for moulding, as in terrines or timbales, either raw or cooked.

Health and safety

When lifting heavy sacks and bags of vegetables e.g. potatoes, it must be done in the correct manner to avoid possible injury.

(For further information regarding the correct lifting techniques see p. 18.)

ELEMENT 2

Cook vegetables for basic hot dishes and salads

INTRODUCTION

Vegetables play an important part in most people's diets and are no longer regarded as an 'accessory' to the main meal. Most vegetables need to be cooked only to the stage where they possess their authentic character and some degree of firmness (*al dente* – to the tooth – still firm after cooking). It is necessary to know how to cook vegetables correctly so as to retain the original colour, texture, taste and nutritional value.

Most vegetables may be cooked in several ways. When selecting a suitable method of cooking the following points must be considered:

- If vegetables are cooked in water, the water soluble vitamins are gradually leaked out into the cooking liquid.
- In most situations only use the minimum amount of water.

Is the vegetable to be served whole, in portions or passed?

This is to determine the cut or amount of preparation needed for cooking. If it is large, it might be better to portion and cut into even sizes.

Is it classified as a root or a green vegetable?

As a rule, when boiling vegetables, root vegetables which are dense and fibrous are normally placed in cold salted water which is brought to the boil, then simmered. Green vegetables which are delicate and have a distinct colour are plunged into boiling, salted water to cook. Green vegetables should be cooked uncovered to allow acids to escape in the steam.

COOKING TIP: The rich green colour which makes vegetables attractive and appetising comes from chlorophyll which is affected by acids and alkalis when heated. It used to be common practice to intensify the colour by using baking powder. However, this destroys the vitamin content and flavour and the vegetable becomes mushy.

Quality

It is not advisable to store cooked vegetables too long after cooking. Apart from the nutritional loss from reheating cooked vegetables they begin to deteriorate, some lose flavour and colour, while in others, chemicals present cause sour tastes and pungent odours.

Storage of cooked vegetables

Cooked vegetables should be cooled down properly as soon as possible for storage. This involves refreshing under cold water until the vegetables are cold to arrest the cooking process and set the colour. If there is any latent heat present in the vegetable, it will continue to cook, even after being removed from the heat source.

Hygiene

Vegetables should be drained well and placed on hygienic trays, covered, and labelled with the contents and dated before being placed in a refrigerator.

METHODS OF COOKING

Blanching

Blanching is the part-cooking of vegetables for reheating and serving at a later stage. There are two ways to do this:

- deep frying: chips are cooked at a temperature of 165°C to cook without colouring;
- boiling: carrots, broccoli, beans, peas are part-cooked and refreshed to preserve colour, flavour and nutritive value and speed up the finishing time.

Figure 129 Green vegetables in saucepans

Refreshed, blanched vegetables should be covered, labelled and stored in a refrigerator for no more than 48 hrs.

Boiling

Vegetables may be boiled in the following ways:

1. Place in cold water and bring to the boil to cook.
   - Young root vegetables should be placed in boiling, salted water to cook.
   - Mature root vegetables, e.g. carrots, should initially be placed in cold salted water and brought to the boil (which facilitates the leaching out of certain strong flavours), skimmed and cooked briskly until firm to the bite.
   - Dried pulses, e.g. lentils and peas, after soaking, should be placed in cold water, brought to the boil and all impurities skimmed from the surface. Salt and flavourings may be added before simmering gently until cooked.
2. Place in boiling salted water and return to the boil.
   - For green vegetables, rapidly bring the water to the boil and immediately add the vegetables, cover and bring back to the boil at once. Remove lid and any scum on the surface of the water and boil as required until cooked. Some green vegetables, e.g. cabbage, may be boiled quickly. However, more tender items, e.g. asparagus, will need to be simmered gently to prevent any damage.
3. Cook in a blanc preparation or acidulated water to maintain their colour.

(See boil, poach and steam food, pp. 82–9.)

CHEF'S TIP: Too little salt added to the cooking water may result in a loss of colour, poor texture and flavour (particularly green vegetables). Over-salting will degrade the taste and flavour of any vegetable even if refreshed under running water and then reheated.

Poaching

Poaching has little application to the cooking of vegetables. Most vegetables require the temperature of boiling liquid (or simmering) in order to cook them quickly and successfully. Particularly tender items, e.g. courgettes and young turnips, will finish cooking in their liquid if removed from the heat after minimal boiling or simmering.

Steaming

Steaming is a good method of cooking and helps to retain the nutritional value of food. Almost all vegetables can be steamed: potatoes can be steamed plain or in their jacket. Green vegetables are best cooked in a high-pressure steamer which reduces the cooking time, thus aiding colour and nutritional value.

Shallow frying

(See Prepare and fry food, pp. 64–75.)

Shallow frying is the cooking of vegetables in a cooking medium of refined animal fat, vegetable oil and/or butter or margarine through contact with a hot surface. Mushrooms, onions, aubergines and courgettes are shallow fried from raw whereas other vegetables are cooked by another method and can be finished or reheated by shallow frying. Potatoes can be shallow fried from raw (*sauté à cru*) or part-cooked by steaming or boiling first then finished by shallow frying.

Figure 130 Shallow fried vegetables

Figure 131 Shallow fried food

Deep frying

There are very few vegetables that can be deep-fried from raw as the process would cause considerable damage and result in the food being unsuitable for consumption. Most vegetables are par-cooked (boiled or steamed) then coated in batter or breadcrumbs. They should then be well drained before being deep-fried quickly until crisp.

Vegetables for deep frying are protected from the intense heat during cooking with a coating. This coating may be milk and seasoned flour, in flour and batter or seasoned flour, eggwash and breadcrumbs.

Raw vegetables, e.g. courgettes and onion rings, may be passed through milk and seasoned flour before being deep-fried. Alternatively, some vegetables may be passed through flour and beaten egg prior to deep frying.

Potatoes are excellent deep-fried and may be cut in a variety of shapes. They may be shallow fried from raw or part-cooked by boiling or steaming first.

(*See* prepared bake food, pp 76–81.)

Baking

Baking is only suitable for a limited number of vegetables. The dryness and the fierce temperature of the process damage most vegetables.

Vegetables suitable for baking include potatoes and stuffed tomatoes, marrows and courgettes.

Grilling

(*See* prepared and grill food, pp. 90–100.)

There are two grilling techniques that can be applied to vegetables:

1. cooking under the heat (salamander);
2. cooking above the heat (charcoal, electric or gas barbecue).

The fierce heat from grilling is only suitable for certain vegetables, though other vegetables can be finished by browning under a salamander. Raw vegetables suitable for grilling include tomatoes, mushrooms, aubergines, courgettes and peppers.

Roasting

Not all vegetables are suited to this dry and very fierce method of cooking. Vegetables for roasting tend not to have too high a water content. These include:

- tubers: potatoes, sweet potatoes, Jerusalem artichokes;
- roots: parsnips;
- bulbs: onions.

Figure 132 Roasted potatoes

Combination cooking

Some vegetable dishes require more than one method of cooking (e.g. sauté potatoes – steamed and shallow-fried). The vegetable is prepared, then cooked by the primary process and then made ready for service by a different method of cookery.

Cooking of vegetables

	Boiling	*Steaming*	*Poaching*	*Stewing*	*Braising*	*Grilling*	*Roasting*	*Shallow frying*	*Deep frying*	*Baking*
Cauliflower	✔	✔							✔	
Carrots	✔	✔								
Potatoes	✔	✔					✔	✔	✔	✔
Onions	✔	✔		✔	✔	✔	✔	✔	✔	
Leeks	✔	✔			✔					
Chicory	✔	✔			✔					
Broccoli	✔	✔								
Brussels sprouts	✔	✔								
Cabbage	✔	✔								
Spring greens	✔	✔								
Spinach	✔	✔								
Asparagus	✔	✔			✔					
Celery	✔	✔								
Seakale	✔	✔								
Tomatoes						✔		✔		✔
Aubergines	✔	✔		✔		✔		✔	✔	
Mushrooms	✔					✔		✔	✔	✔
Courgettes	✔	✔				✔		✔	✔	✔
Peppers	✔				✔	✔		✔		✔

FINISHING METHODS

Vegetables are reheated traditionally, by one of three methods:

1. plunged in a basket into a pan of boiling salted water (*rechauffé chauffant*);
2. tossed in butter (*rechauffé au beurre*).
3. in a microwave.

Ensure that reheated vegetables are seasoned well before serving, because refreshing will remove most of the seasoning that was present in the initial cooking.

Vegetables that are reheated in water must be drained well otherwise they will be soggy.

COOKING TIP: Some dishes might be finished with nuts or in a sauce and some sauces might need browning e.g. cauliflower, Mornay Sauce, Broccoli, Hollandaise sauce, Delmonico potatoes or gratinating under the salamander.

Holding cooked vegetables

For best results, reheated vegetables should be served immediately. If they are held for any length of time, they will lose their colour, flavour and nutritive value.

Blanc (*Blanc*)

(× 4 portions)

Ingredients

½ litre	water, cold
10g	flour
	juice of ½ lemon
	salt

Method

1. Whisk the flour and water together.
2. Add the salt and lemon juice.
3. Pass through a strainer.
4. Place in a saucepan and bring to the boil, stirring continuously. Used for globe artichoke, salsify, mushrooms.

Fried egg plant (*Aubergine frite*)

(× 4 portions)

Ingredients

2	aubergines
50g	flour, seasoned
75ml	milk

Method

1. Allow ½ aubergine per portion.
2. Remove alternative strips and cut into ½cm slices on the slant.
3. Pass through seasoned flour. Shake off excess flour.
4. Deep fry at 185°C.
5. Drain on absorbent paper and serve.

Ratatouille (*Ratatouille*)

(× 4 portions)

Ingredients

200g	courgettes
100g	aubergine
120g	tomato concassé
50g	onion, thinly sliced
2 clove	garlic, peeled and chopped
50g	green peppers, diced
50ml	olive oil
1 tspn	parsley

Method

1. Trim off both ends of the courgettes and aubergines. Remove skin and cut into 3 mm slices.
2. Heat the oil in a thick-bottomed saucepan. Add the onions, cover and sweat for about 5 min.
3. Add the garlic, cook for 5 min. and add aubergines, courgettes and peppers. Season with salt and pepper.
4. Cook gently for about 5 min, toss occasionally and keep covered.
5. Add the tomato concassé and cook for a further 20 to 30 min, until all ingredients are tender.
6. Sprinkle in the parsley and season with salt and pepper.

Grilled mushrooms (*Champignons grillés*)

(× 4 portions)

Ingredients

300g	flat mushrooms
50g	butter or margarine, melted
pinch	salt

Method

1. Wash and remove mushroom stalks, rewash and drain well.
2. Place on a baking tray, season with salt and pepper.
3. Brush mushrooms with the melted butter or margarine and place under a salamander for about 3 to 4 min each side.
4. To serve: sprinkle with picked parsley.

French fried onions (*Oignons frits à la française*)

(× 4 portions)

Ingredients

200 g onions
50 g flour, seasoned
75 ml milk

Method

1. Peel and wash the onions. Cut into 2 mm thick slices, against the grain. Separate into rings.
2. Pass through seasoned flour and milk and shake off excess flour.
3. Deep fry in hot fat (185°C). Drain well. Season with salt and serve.

Braised celery (Céleri braisé)

(× 4 portions)

Ingredients

2 heads celery
100 g carrots, thinly sliced
100 g onion, thinly sliced
½ litre white stock
salt and pepper
bouquet garni

Method

1. Trim celery heads and root, remove any outside discoloured stalks and cut heads to about 12 cm lengths. Thoroughly wash under cold running water. Portion into bunches and tie firmly with string.
2. Place in a saucepan of boiling water, simmer for about 20 min then refresh.
3. Place the sliced carrots and onion in a sauté pan or casserole to form a bed of roots.
4. Add the celery portions and place on the bed of roots.
5. Pour over the stock and season, add the bouquet garni.
6. Cover with a sheet of greaseproof paper and a tight-fitting lid. Cook in a moderate oven for about 2 hours or until tender.

Roast potatoes (*Pommes rôties*)

(× 4 portions)

Ingredients

500 g (3 to 4 pieces per portion) potatoes
oil or dripping
salt and pepper

Method

1. Wash, peel and rewash the potatoes. Dry thoroughly.
2. Heat the oil or dripping in a roasting tray.
3. When hot, add the potatoes and lightly brown on all sides.
4. Season with salt and pepper and cook in a hot oven for about 1 hour until they are golden brown. After 30 min turn the potatoes over.
5. Drain well and serve.

Braised potato dishes (*Pommes boulangères*)

(× 4 portions)

Ingredients

400 g	potatoes
100 g	onions
25 to 50 g	butter, margarine, melted
½ litre	white stock parsley, finely chopped
	salt and pepper

(For cooking temperatures see Prepare and fry foods, p71.)

Method

1. Cut potatoes into 2 mm slices on a mandolin, reserve best slices for the top.
2. Finely slice the onions.
3. Place potatoes and onions in a bowl and mix together. Season with salt and pepper.
4. Arrange in a buttered shallow ovenproof dish and just cover with the stock.
5. Neatly arrange overlapping slices of potatoes on the top and brush with the melted butter.
6. Place in a hot oven for about 20 min until potatoes are lightly coloured. Lower heat and allow to cook steadily, pressing down firmly from time to time with a platte knife.
7. When cooked, the potatoes will have absorbed the stock (approx. 1½ hours cooking time in all).
8. Transfer to a serving dish. To finish: sprinkle chopped parsley over the top and serve.

Baked jacket potatoes and cheese (*Pommes surprises gratinées*)

(× 4 portions)

Ingredients

4 large	baking potatoes
50 g	butter
75 g	grated cheddar cheese
25 g	Parmesan cheese

Method

1. Scrub potatoes well and make an incision round the potato. Place on a bed of salt on a baking tray and cook in a hot oven for about 1 hour. Turn potatoes over after 30 min.
2. Test by holding the potato in a cloth and squeezing gently. If cooked the potato should feel soft.
3. Remove potatoes and cut in half lengthwise. Spoon out the potato from the skin (retain skins) and place it in a bowl.
4. Add the butter, cheddar cheese and season accordingly and mash with a fork.
5. Refill potato skin with the mixture and place on a baking tray.
6. Top with the grated Parmesan.
7. Place in oven until top is golden brown.

Fried/chipped potatoes (*Pommes frites*)

(× 4 portions)

Ingredients

600 g potatoes

Method

1. Scrub potatoes, peel and rewash.
2. Cut into slices 1 cm thick and 5 cm long . Cut slices into strips 5 × 1 × 1 cm.
3. Wash, drain and dry in a clean cloth.
4. Place in a frying basket and cook without colouring in moderately hot fat.
5. When required, place in a frying pan and cook in hot fat until crisp and golden.
6. Drain thoroughly and season accordingly.

KEY WORDS

BLANCH To cook lightly in boiling water to retain colour.

BOUQUET GARNI Bundle of herbs, bay leaf, parsley, thyme wrapped in leek or lengths of celery tied with string.

CHAUFFANT Pot of hot salted water used for reheating vegetables.

CONCASSÉ Coarsely chopped.

DUXELLE Type of stuffing which may be used for vegetables. Made from onions, mushrooms, butter, wine, garlic, breadcrumbs.

FLORETS Small flowers, individual sections of flower head, e.g. cauliflower and broccoli.

FLUTING Scoring or marking in a pattern, for example, on a cucumber.

FLUTE To score or mark in a pattern.

ONION CLOUTÉ An onion which has been studded with cloves and a bay leaf.

SWEATING Cook without colouring.

WILTED Not fresh, limp and drooping.

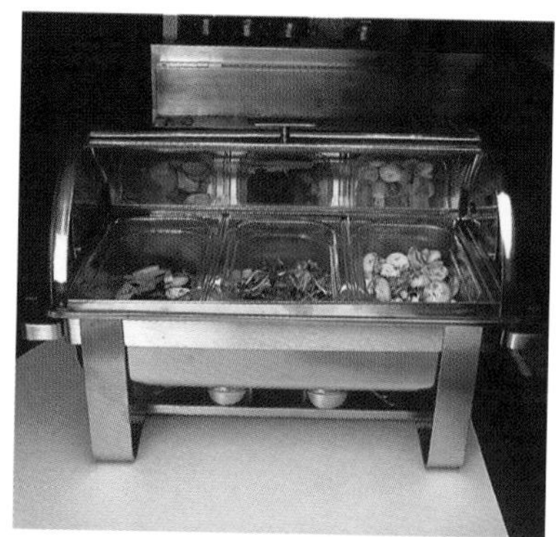

Figure 133 Cooked vegetables in heated display/service unit

Activity

1. With the aid of your cookery book, compile a list of vegetable dishes which are cooked by one method and finished by another (combination cookery).
2. In your own words, describe the following terms:

   Chauffante

   Sauté au beurre

   Lyonnaise

   Duchesse

   Croquette
3. Using the following headings make a list of salads for each group.

Compound salads

Vegetable	Fruit	Meat	Fish	Shellfish

Single salads

Vegetable	Fruit

4. Compile a list of four different fungi that may be used in the kitchen.
5. In your own words, explain the following preparation methods:

   Grate

   Shred

   Shell

   Trim

NVQ SVQ 2

Prepare and cook basic pulse dishes

ELEMENT 1
Prepare pulses

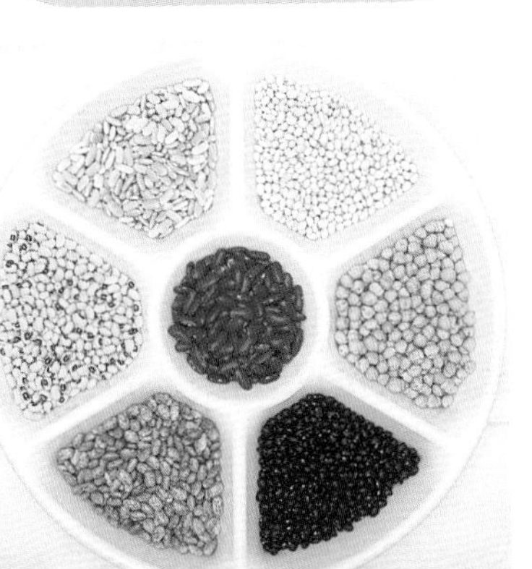

Figure 134 Various types of bean

INTRODUCTION

Beans and peas are used in cooking all over the world and increasingly more so today with the rise in awareness of healthy eating and the growth of vegetarianism. It is only recently that the full health benefits of eating pulses have been realised.

Beans are one of the best forms of carbohydrate available, full of dietary fibre and free of cholesterol. They are packed full of vitamins and minerals and they also form part of a complete protein diet when combined with grains, for example, rice and corn.

Many beans we consume in Britain are grown in America, where the climate, growing and harvesting conditions ensure a primary quality bean crop.

Beans are extremely versatile and can be used in a multitude of dishes. They have the added advantage that their flavour is improved and enhanced when they are reheated.

Every type of bean has its own unique taste and texture, and when combined with other ingredients provides an economical meal with the minimum of effort.

Storage of pulses

Canned pulses Should be kept in a cool, dry store.

Dried pulses These should be kept in a cool, dry airtight container, out of direct sunlight.

TYPES OF PEAS AND BEANS

Aduki beans These are small red beans, not unsimilar to kidney beans, with a strong nutty flavour. They are good for vegetarian burgers, baked loaves, stuffing vegetables and Chinese cooking.

Black-eyed peas These are a cream to light yellowish colour, oval-shaped bean with a purplish black eye. They are used in many African and Indian dishes and have a very subtle taste. Black-eyed peas have a thin skin and can be cooked without pre-soaking.

Black turtle beans These are small, shiny, black and spherical shaped with a mushroomy flavour. They do not require soaking.

Broad beans or fava beans These have a fine texture, and are whitish, beige or brown. They require soaking overnight.

Cannellini beans These creamy-white kidney beans have a fluffy texture and are slightly bigger than haricot beans.

Chick peas Known in Spain as Garbanzo beans, they are round, beige with a wrinkled-looking skin. It is advisable to soak chick peas for 24 hours as they are extremely hard. When cooked, they have a firm texture, nutty taste and are almost impossible to overcook.

Flageolet beans These are delicate pale green in colour with a nutty flavour and rather like a small kidney bean in shape.

Haricot beans Also known as pearl (small) haricots, navy beans, or pea beans, these are small, spherical and ivory-white in colour. They are probably best known in the form of canned 'baked beans'.

Mung beans Also known by their Indian name 'moong dal', they are small, bright green in colour and when sprouted are known as bean sprouts. Mung beans have a sweet pea flavour.

NOTE: Under certain conditions red kidney beans may be dangerous to eat. The toxic factor is a haemagglutinin which can lead to an acute gastric attack unless destroyed by adequate cooking. The soaking and rinsing process reduces the haemagglutinin by approximately two-thirds and the danger can be entirely eliminated if the beans are boiled for ten min before simmering for a further 30 min (minimum).

Peas, marrowfats Otherwise known as blue peas, they have a soft, floury texture and tend to have a tough skin.

Peas, split Yellow or green, these are skinless and have a soft, floury texture.

Pinto beans Oval shaped, beige in colour with streaks of brownish pink on the skin, the pinto bean has a succulent texture and savoury flavour. Used extensively in Mexican cooking, it was the original bean used in refried beans.

Red kidney beans These are deep to light red in colour, oval in shape and rich in colour and flavour. When cooking dry kidney beans, it is vital that they are cooked properly to kill toxins present in the bean. See the note.

Soybeans Available in a range of colours including black, red, green and yellow, they are more commonly known for being turned into soymilk, cheese, curd and textured meat substitute. They can also be used in soups and stews.

TYPES OF LENTILS

Figure 135 Lentils

Whole lentils The most common varieties are green or brown. Brown lentils are earthy in flavour while green lentils have a more delicate flavour. These lentils do not need soaking.

Split lentils Orange-red or yellow in colour, they are usually cooked to a purée and are popular in Indian cuisine (dal).

Preparing pulses

Dried pulses should be rinsed before soaking to remove any dust.

SOAKING DRIED PULSES

Pulses are soaked before cooking for two reasons:

1. to soften and return the moisture, thus reducing the cooking time.
2. to break down the indigestible sugars (oligosaccharides) that cause flatulence.

Beans should be soaked in plenty of water, generally three to four

Figure 136 Beans soaking in water

times their volume of water for a minimum of four hours. Some bean recipes call for beans to be soaked overnight. Usually soaking overnight is for convenience. It has been proven that beans absorb all the soaking water they can hold in a four-hour period.

NOTE: Lentils, split peas and black-eyed peas generally do not need soaking and may be cooked from their dried state.

NOTE: If beans are soaked for long periods, the water should be changed regularly to prevent fermentation.

Soaking beans reduces the cooking time by approximately half and retains vitamins, minerals and proteins, which can be destroyed during prolonged cooking.

COOKING TIP Never add salt to soaking pulses or to the cooking liquid until the pulses are as soft as you require them. Salt reacts with the seed coat, forming a barrier which prevents absorption of liquid. This in turn, halts the tenderising process.

Figure 137 Beans boiling in a saucepan of water

Soaking method 1

1. Place the washed and picked-over beans in a large saucepan and cover with two inches of fresh water.
2. Bring to the boil and continue boiling for 2 min.
3. Remove from heat, place aside and soak the beans, covered, for one hour.
4. Drain and discard soaking water and rinse the beans well. They are now ready for use.

Soaking method 2

1. Place the washed and picked-over beans in a large saucepan and cover with two inches of fresh water, or three times their volume.
2. Bring to the boil, reduce to medium heat and boil for 10 min.
3. Drain and cover the beans with 5 cm or three times their volume of fresh cold water.
4. Allow the beans to soak for 30 min. Discard soaking water. Rinse the beans thoroughly. They are now ready for cooking.

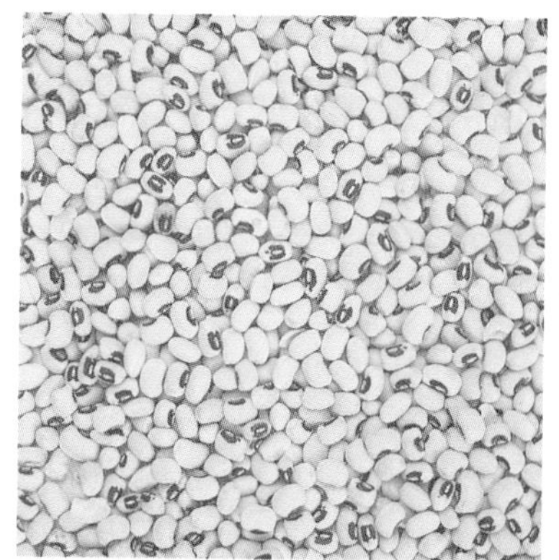
Figure 138 Black-eyed beans

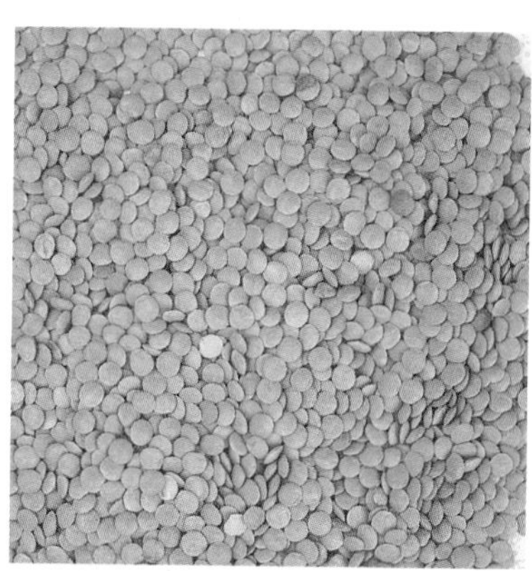
Figure 139 Green lentils

Figure 140 Red kidney beans

Soaking times for pulses

Variety	*Soaking time (hours)*
Aduki	4
Black beans	4
Black-eyed beans	N/A
Lima beans	4
Cannellini beans	4
Chick peas	4
Dals	—
Fava (broad beans)	12
Ful nabed (broad beans)	12
Great Northern beans	4
Brown lentils	—
Green lentils	—
Orange/red lentils	—
Mung beans	4
Split peas	—
Whole peas	4
Pigeon peas	
Pink, calico, red Mexican beans	4
Pinto beans	4
Red kidney beans	4
White kidney beans (cannellini)	4
Small white haricot (navy) beans	4
Soybeans	12

ELEMENT 2
Cooking of pulses

INTRODUCTION

It is advisable that initial cooking of pulses should be carried out in simmering water or stock with a variety of flavourings. Never hurry the process. The slower the beans cook the easier they will be to digest. Pulses can be flavoured with onions, garlic, celery, bay leaf, herbs and spices during cooking, but never season with salt. Salt reacts with the seed coat, forming a barrier which prevents absorption of liquid. This, in turn, halts the tenderising process.

Pulses should not be cooked in tomato juice, sauce, vinegar, lemon juice or any other acidic commodity. Acid tends to prevent the pulse from softening. Additional commodities should be added later when the pulses are tender.

Very old pulses may take longer to tenderise than fresher ones. To check if they are cooked, press the cooked pulse against the roof of the mouth with your tongue. If it mashes easily, it is ready. Pressure from a fork on a flat surface accomplishes the same test without the chance of burning your palate!

Cooking beans in a hard water environment

Hard water has an abundance of calcium and magnesium and can act like salt interfering with the tenderising process and lengthening the cooking time considerably. A little baking soda (¼ level teaspoon per 1 lb of beans) can help overcome this problem. Do not use any more baking powder than prescribed as this will turn the pulses mushy.

Frying pulses in oil

The flavour of beans can be improved by pre-frying them in a little olive oil after washing and soaking. They should then be cooked in the normal manner. The cooked beans will have a more creamy appearance and an improved flavour.

Cooking times (approximate)

Variety	*Cooking time*
Aduki	1 hour
Black beans	1½ hours
Black eyed beans	45 min to 1 hour
Lima beans	1 to 1½ hours
Cannellini beans	1 to 1½ hours
Chick peas	2 to 2½ hours
Dals	30 min
Fava (broad beans)	3 hours
Ful nabed (broad beans)	3 hours
Great northern beans	1 hour
Brown lentils	35 min
Green Lentils	40 min
Orange/red lentils	30 min
Mung beans	45 min to 1 hour
Split peas	30 min
Whole peas	40 min

COOKING TIP: The digestion of pulses can be improved by adding caraway, aniseed, fennel or asafoetida as part of the seasoning during cooking.

Pigeon peas	30 min
Pink, calico, red Mexican beans	1 hour
Pinto beans	1 to 1½ hours
Red kidney beans	1 hour
White kidney beans (cannellini)	1 hour
Small white haricot (navy) beans	2 hours
Soybeans	3 to 3½ hours

Uses for pulses

Pulses may be featured in the following courses on a menu:

1. hors d'œuvre;
2. salads;
3. soups/purées;
4. vegetable;
5. main course: vegetarian dishes.

They can also be used in stuffings and as a coulis.

Lentil and mushroom burgers with groundnut and sesame sauce

(20 portions)

Ingredients

1.5 kg	lentils
500 g	onion, finely chopped
2 cloves	garlic, chopped
250 g	sunflower margarine
2 kg	mushrooms, finely chopped
75 g	breadcrumbs, wholemeal
4-5	eggs
250 g	seasoned flour for coating
150 ml	oil for shallow frying
4 tbspn	parsley, finely chopped

Method

1. Place the lentils in a saucepan of cold water. Bring to the boil. Simmer until cooked.
2. Melt the margarine in a frying pan and add the onion and garlic, sweat until soft. Add mushrooms. Cook over a medium heat for 15 to 20 min until all the liquid has been evaporated and mushrooms are in a thick purée.
3. When cool, add the cooked lentils and mix thoroughly. Add breadcrumbs and parsley and bind with beaten egg. Mix together. If the mixture is too loose, add a few more breadcrumbs, if too dry, add a little beaten egg and season.
4. Shape into burgers and pass through seasoned flour.
5. To cook: fry quickly in hot oil (take care not to let to burgers break up) or alternatively, place on a baking sheet, brush with oil and bake in a pre-heated oven for approx. 20 min. Turn them over once during cooking.

Serve: Place on a bed of groundnut and sesame sauce.

Chick pea and potato curry

(20 portions)

Ingredients

2 kg	chick peas, cooked
8 cloves	garlic, crushed
6 tbspn	oil, vegetable or ghee
8 sticks	cinnamon
8	bay leaves
4 tspn	cumin seeds
4	onions, chopped
2 kg	tomatoes, chopped
10 tbspn	curry paste, hot
2 tspn	salt
550 g	potatoes, peeled and diced
850 ml	vegetable stock
6 tbspn	vinegar
4 fl.oz	lemon juice
1 bunch	coriander leaves

Method

1. Place the chick peas in a mixing bowl, add crushed garlic and mix.
2. Heat oil or ghee in a large frying pan, gently cook cinnamon, bay leaves and cumin to bring out flavours.
3. Add onion and cook until soft, do not brown. Stir in tomatoes with juice and curry paste, cook for 4 to 5 min.
4. Add lemon juice and vinegar. Adjust seasoning accordingly.

   Garnish: coriander leaves

Pasta con fagioli

(20 portions)

Ingredients

150 ml	oil, vegetable
6 large	onions, chopped
8 cloves	garlic, fresh
2 tspn	herbs, mixed
4 tb spn	basil, torn
3 kg	tomatoes, chopped
4 tspn	tomato purée
4 tspn	sugar, caster
3 kg	red kidney beans, cooked
2 kg	tagliatelle (allow 100 g dry weight per serving)

Method

1. Heat the oil in a large saucepan. Add the onion and garlic and cook until softened.
2. Add herbs, tomatoes with juice, tomato purée and sugar, mix well.
3. Bring to the boil, reduce heat and simmer uncovered for approx. 20 min.
4. Add red kidney beans and simmer for a further 10 min.
5. Cook pasta, drain and serve with tomato and bean sauce. Adjust seasoning.

Figure 141 Pasta con fagioli

Black bean salsa
(10 portions)

Ingredients

1 kg	black turtle beans
4 cloves	garlic, fresh
1.5 kg	tomatoes, skinned, seeded and diced
1 tspn	chilli paste
6 tbspn	coriander leaves, chopped
12	spring onions
4 tbspn	oil, olive
4	lemons or limes, juice only
	salt and pepper to taste

Method

1. Soak beans overnight. Drain and place in a large saucepan and cover with fresh cold water.
2. Bring to the boil for 10 min, reduce heat, add garlic and cook for 45 min or until the beans are tender.
3. Drain and remove garlic. Stir in the remaining ingredients (while still warm)and mix thoroughly.

   Serve cold as a first course or as a salad accompaniment.

Activity

Using your recipe manual, find recipe examples for the following:

1. hors d'œuvre;
2. salads;
3. soups/purées;
4. vegetable;
5. main course: vegetarian dishes.

NVQ SVQ 2

Prepare and cook basic rice dishes

Prepare basic rice dishes

INTRODUCTION

There are around 7000 different varieties of rice produced throughout the world in India, China, South America, USA, Italy and Japan. Rice can be combined with any number of other commodities, cheese, eggs, fish, shellfish, meats and vegetables, and flavoured with herbs or spices.

Figure 142 Different types of rice

VARIETIES

Rice may be divided into three broad groupings:

Long-grain rice

The characteristics of long-grain rice are as follows.

- It has a narrow pointed grain.
- Its length is four to five times its width.
- The grains are clear and translucent with little chalkiness.
- The grains remain separate and distinct after cooking.

Varieties grown include Patna, Blue Bonnet and Rexoro. Basmati rice is classified as long.

Medium-grain rice

The characteristics of medium-grain rice are as follows.

- The length is approximately three times the width.
- After cooking, separation characteristics are not as distinct as that of long-grain rice.
- It is slightly less expensive than long-grain rice.

Varieties grown include Calrose and Nato.

Short-grain rice

The characteristics of short-grain rice are as follows.

- The grains are stubby and round.
- Its length is one-and-a-half to two times the width.
- When cooked the grains may be a little more glutinous.

The most common variety grown is Pearl.

PRODUCTS AND BY-PRODUCTS OF RICE

Brown rice Usually long grain rice from which only the hulls have been removed and the bran (or most of the bran) remains. The advantage of retaining the bran is that it offers additional nutritional value (proteins, traces of iron, calcium and vitamin B).

Milled rice Milled rice is generally used in recipes calling for rice. It is white rice from which hulls, germ, outer bran layers and most of the inner bran layers are removed in the milling process.

NOTE: Cooked or uncooked rice in a recipe is white milled rice. Where another type of rice is called for, it should be stated in full, e.g. 200 g of uncooked brown rice or 200 g of cooked parboiled rice.

Note: Wild rice. Despite its name it is not rice, but a water grass native to North America. It is long grained with a 'nutty' flavour and is very expensive. It can be bought separately or mixed with long grain rice varieties.

Parboiled rice Rice that has been subjected to steam or water treatment prior to milling. It retains more vitamins and minerals using this process.

Pre-cooked rice Rice that has been completely cooked and the water removed. This reduces the preparation time.

Rice bran The first major by-product removed from the rice kernel during the milling process. It is relatively high in protein and is primarily used for livestock feed.

Polished rice This is what is left after the final layers have been removed from the rice kernel during the polishing process. The residue is finer and heavier than bran and high in fat and carbohydrate. It is blended in various process foods.

Rice oil The oil extracted from rice bran and polish. It is a stable, neutral oil which is adaptable to the manufacture of some margarine, cooking oil, salad oil, industrial oil, soap and an extensive range of other products.

Rice flour Milled rice which is ground into flour. Used in place of wheat flour in cakes and breads for those with allergies to wheat. Used in face powders and similar cosmetics. It is also used in frozen pies and other commercial baked goods and as a thickening agent.

Rice cereal Rice that has been converted into various forms. Rice flakes or puffs may be eaten cold or as pulverised rice which may be cooked in boiling water and served as a hot cereal.

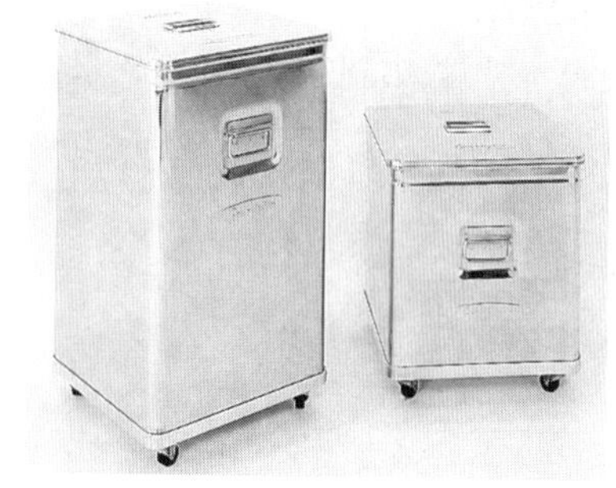

Figure 143 Rice bins

Storage of uncooked rice

For storage purposes rice is classified as a dry food and will keep almost indefinitely if stored correctly. It should be kept in easy-to-clean bin type containers with tight-fitting lids.

Portions

Use 50 g per person when using rice as a complete dish or 15 g to 25 g as a garnish or accompaniment.

ELEMENT 2
Cook basic rice dishes

INTRODUCTION

Although rice is a simple product, it is very easy to ruin it during cooking. Firstly, unless it is being boiled and refreshed the cooking time must be exact. Rice does not 'hold' for long after cooking and will soon become overcooked and the appearance of the finished dish will be spoiled.

Each type of rice is suited to a particular traditional cooking style: Japanese and Chinese cuisine requires a short-grain rice which can be shaped by hand and fingers; for Indian dishes a long-grained rice is required.

Rice appears in various ways on the menu. For example as:

- a breakfast dish (kedgeree);
- a separate course (farinaceous) served between the egg and fish course (pilaf/rissotto);
- moulded into a pedestal or ornamental stand for buffet work (*socle*);
- an accompaniment to a main course (curry/chilli), fish, shellfish;
- a garnish/thickening for soup(broth/fish soup);
- a stuffing for vegetables (tomatoes/peppers);
- a salad;
- a hot or cold sweet dish (rice pudding/Empress rice);
- with egg dishes, e.g. curried eggs.

METHODS OF COOKING RICE

Prior to cooking, rice needs to be washed thoroughly. The following methods are used to cook rice.

Plain boiled

This method usually applies to long-grained rice that is plunged into plenty of boiling salted water.

Braising

This method is otherwise known as pilaf and is suitable for long grain rice. The rice is cooked in the ratio of two parts stock to one part of rice in an oven.

Stewing

This method is otherwise known as risotto and is suitable for short grain rice. The rice is cooked in the ratio of three parts stock to one part rice on the top of the stove.

Stir frying

Stir-fried rice is boiled rice that has been refreshed, drained well and is then tossed in the minimum of hot fat in a wok.

Steaming

With this method rice is placed in a solid steamer tray with liquid and seasoned before placing in a steamer.

Figure 144 Stir-frying rice

HYGIENE AND STORAGE OF COOKED RICE

To avoid deterioration of cooked rice, follow these points.

- Store cooked rice not for immediate consumption in a refrigerator between 4° and 6°C on a covered tray or container for a maximum of 24 hrs. Cool rice by placing the saucepan in a sink, covering with a colander and allowing cold water to flow over it until it goes cold. If it is not completely cold any latent heat will continue to cook the rice.
- Place rice in stainless-steel, china or plastic storage containers, labelled and dated and chill as rapidly as possible.
- Never attempt to cool rice in the refrigerator as this will raise the temperature of the other food items in the refrigerator and may cause them to go off. It could also cause damage to the workings of the refrigerator and/or even cause poisonous bacteria to grow on other foods.
- Keep hot rice at a temperature of above 75°C.

RE-HEATING RICE

Cooked rice may be reheated by stir frying or in one of the following ways:

- placing the rice in a container with a cover and steaming;
- placing the rice in a shallow container and re-heating in a microwave.

Always ensure that the rice is reheated properly as rice is susceptible to bacillus cereus.

KEY WORDS

CARTOUCHE A circle of greaseproof paper used to cover a saucepan or frying pan.

REFRESHED Cooked, usually by boiling, and then cooled under cold water until completely cold.

SWEAT To cook without colouring.

SOCLE A cold decorative base made from rice.

STIR FRYING Usually associated with Chinese cooking this is lightly frying food in the minimum amount of oil by stirring constantly over a very high heat in a special frying pan called a wok.

Activity

1. In your own words, what is the difference between braised rice and stewed rice?
2. Make a list of dishes that are accompanied by boiled rice.
   (a)
   (b)
   (c)
   (d)
   (e)
   (f)
3. State what the ratio of rice to liquid is in the following:
   (a) braised rice
   (b) stewed rice
4. How can cooked rice be reheated?

Figure 145 Finished rice dish

Prepare and cook basic pasta dishes

ELEMENT 1

Prepare pasta dishes

Figure 146 Pasta in production in a factory

INTRODUCTION

The history of pasta

The origin of pasta is uncertain, however, it appears to have been influenced by many nationalities.

Pasta products are normally made from a high gluten wheat (Durum wheat). The wheat is milled to produce a fine semolina-type flour and mixed with salt, oil and water. The dough can also be coloured and flavoured with either eggs, tomato purée, cooked spinach or beetroot juice. It is estimated that there are in excess of 600 shapes and sizes of Italian pasta. Pasta on its own has little taste so it is therefore always served with butter, garlic, grated cheese or with a sauce.

Gnocchi are small, shaped savoury dumplings or cakes made from poached semolina or polenta, mashed potato or choux paste. They are served plain with melted butter and grated cheese or with a variety of sauces. They may be served as a main course on their own or as a traditional Italian accompaniment to grilled meats or roast chicken.

CLASSIFICATION OF PASTA

Pasta can be divided into four main classifications according to its size and shape:

1. **Long pasta** This group includes smooth rods such as spaghetti and vermicelli; tubular forms of which the outer surface may be smooth or corrugated, e.g. long macaroni, mizzoni; and flat forms such as noodles and lasagne.
2. **Short pasta** This group contains cut macaroni, ziti, tubetti lunghi and ditali.
3. **Pasta suitable for filling** There are two main types in this group:

- Those that are filled while the pasta is raw, e.g. ravioli, tortelli, and then cooked;
- Those that are partly cooked before being filled, e.g. cannelloni, and then finished off in the oven. Fillings can include meat, fish, vegetables or a vegetarian substitute.

4. **Small fancy pasta** This group consists of a large variety of small pastas which are used mainly for garnishing, e.g. *alfabeto* (alphabets), *numeri* (numbers) and *stellette* (small stars).

PURCHASING PASTA

Pasta falls into two main types:

1. factory-made;
2. home-made.

Figure 147 Different pasta shapes

Home-made pasta includes ravioli, tortelli, lasagne, cannelloni, tagliatelle and noodles. All other varieties are factory-made, however, home-made pastas can also be factory-made.

A good selection of pasta is available dried, tinned, chilled, frozen and vacuum packed, either in single or multi-pack portions.

To cook convenience products always follow the manufacturer's instructions.

Popular varieties of pasta

Anelli	Ring-shaped pasta pieces
Bozzoli	Cocoon-like shapes
Bucatini	Small whole wheat pieces of *macaroni* cut at a slant
Cannelloni	Large hollow pipe shapes
Cappelletti	Small hat-shaped pieces
Capellini d'angelo	The finest type of ribbon pasta. *Capelli d'angelo* means 'angel's hair'
Casareccia	Twisted lengths of 4 cm
Cavatappi	Twisted ridged pieces
Conchiglie piccole rigate	Small seashell shapes
Conchiglie rigate	Large seashell shapes
Creste de gallo	Elbow-shaped, ridged mane, cut *macaroni* pieces
Diamanti	Elongated diamond shapes
Ditali	Finger or thimble shape
Ditalini	Smaller version of *ditali*
Elicidali	Small hollow lengths with spiral line pattern
Farfalle	Butterfly-shaped pieces
Farfalline	Small butterfly-shaped pieces
Fedelini	Very fine cylindrical pasta similar to *vermicelli*
Festonati	Garland or festoon shapes
Fusilli	Corkscrew shapes
Fusilli bucati	Spring-shaped pieces
Gramigna	Small grass or weed-like shapes
Lasagne	Approx. 8 cm wide, flat ribbon-shaped
Lasagnette	Flat ribbon with ruffled edges. A smaller version of *lasagne*
Lumache	Snail-shell shaped
Macaroni	Hollow-shaped version of *spaghetti*
Orecchiette	Ear-shaped pieces
Pastina	General term used for a variety of various shapes, e.g. numbers, alphabets etc.
Pipe rigate	Ridged pipe-shaped
Raviolli	Small square-shaped envelope
Riccini	Stuffed
Rigatoni	Large hollow lengths with spiral line pattern
Ruotine	Wheel-shaped
Spaghetti	Available in plain, whole and buck wheat. Known as *vermicelli* in southern Italy. The word *spaghetti* means 'little strings'
Spirali	Lengths twisted together to form a spiral
Tagliarini	Flat 3 mm ribbon noodle
Tortellini	Small stuffed dumplings

Tubetti lunghi	Elbow-shaped *macaroni* shapes
Ziti	A large *macaroni* shape cut into pieces

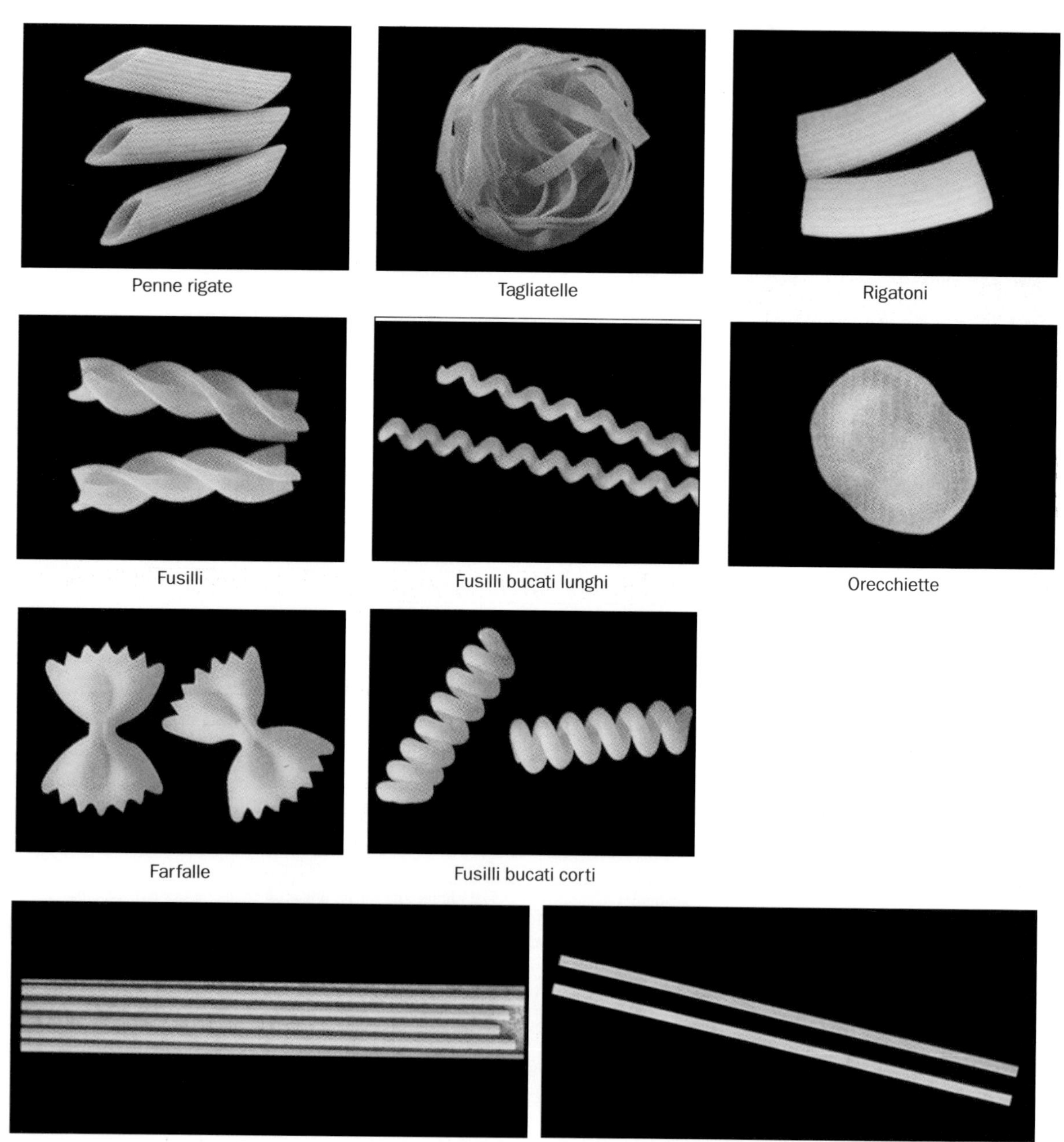

Figure 148 Pasta

ELEMENT 2
Cook pasta dishes

Figure 149 Cooking pasta

Figure 150 Macaroni cheese

(See Maintain and promote hygiene in food storage, pp. 48–50.)

INTRODUCTION

Pasta can be cooked and used in a variety of ways. Traditionally it is served on a luncheon menu, coming after the soup or instead of an hors d'œuvre item. Pasta may also be used as a garnish for soup, to accompany a meat, poultry or fish dish or as a sweet pudding, e.g. macaroni pudding. Some establishments serve pasta as a main course. When it is served as a starter course it is usually referred to as an *antipasto*.

To cook pasta it should be immersed in plenty of boiling salted water, with a little olive oil added to prevent it sticking. It should then be simmered for between 10 to 15 min. Pasta should be cooked to the stage known as 'al dente' (to the tooth), which means that there should be a slight firmness in the cooked dough.

Whenever possible pasta should be cooked to order or cooked in batches and refreshed rather than all together.

Cooking times

Spaghetti	10 min
Lasagne	12 min
Macaroni	20 min

HYGIENE AND STORAGE OF COOKED PASTA

The following points should be remembered to ensure that cooked pasta does not deteriorate:

1. Cooked pasta not for immediate consumption should be stored in a refrigerator between 2 °C and 4 °C in water in a covered tray or container labelled and dated for a maximum of 24 hours.
2. Pasta is cooled by placing the saucepan in a sink, covering with a colander and allowing cold water to flow over it until it goes cold. If it is not completely cold any latent heat will continue to cook the pasta.
3. Never attempt to cool pasta in the refrigerator as this will raise the temperature of the other food items in the refrigerator and may cause them to go off. It could also cause damage to the workings of the refrigerator and/or even cause poisonous bacteria to grow on other foods.
4. Hot pasta should be kept at a temperature of above 75°C.

RE-HEATING PASTA

Cooked pasta may be reheated by:

- frying in a little butter (*au beurre*);
- placing in a chauffant (*chauffant*);
- placing in a shallow container with a little water and re-heating in a microwave;
- in a steamer in a container and covered.

KEY WORDS

AL DENTE Term meaning 'to the tooth', just done.

CHAUFFANT Saucepan of boiling salted water with a basket into which pasta is placed and reheated.

DURUM WHEAT Hard wheat milled into a semolina-type flour.

ROULETTE Pasta cutting wheel.

Activity

1. Find out which pasta products are used in your establishment and whether they are fresh, frozen, tinned or dried.
2. Using a cookery book list **four** classic pasta dishes and give a brief explanation of each dish.
3. Find the names of pasta used in your establishment.

F	X	K	E	E	B	Z	D	I	T	A	L	I	N	I	I
G	B	E	C	C	H	I	R	L	A	A	D	S	Z	C	M
E	R	O	A	T	O	E	H	H	A	I	X	Q	U	O	R
S	I	T	N	I	O	U	E	B	U	C	A	T	I	N	I
P	T	H	N	A	G	S	A	B	U	D	A	N	I	N	I
A	U	Y	E	W	W	M	E	I	M	T	Z	N	T	O	G
G	L	I	L	P	S	F	I	A	T	I	N	D	T	I	R
H	E	S	L	P	P	E	T	S	U	E	N	E	N	I	A
E	R	N	O	L	O	S	L	N	W	S	Y	R	C	E	T
T	O	Y	N	U	P	T	R	W	N	T	E	L	R	Y	I
T	S	Z	I	T	I	O	V	E	L	O	U	T	E	R	N
I	S	P	A	O	P	N	Y	Y	M	C	E	Y	A	Y	A
I	P	R	R	R	F	A	R	F	A	L	L	E	M	I	T
F	I	E	N	T	H	T	N	I	O	N	B	I	S	Q	E
P	R	L	I	E	L	I	P	D	L	A	S	A	G	N	D
T	A	T	S	L	N	M	C	M	L	A	S	A	G	N	E
L	L	T	H	L	U	M	A	C	H	E	B	Y	S	R	I
R	I	N	I	I	L	N	E	U	O	N	G	R	A	E	M
A	S	S	S	N	S	T	A	G	L	I	A	R	I	N	I
A	C	K	M	I	Y	E	D	J	E	R	Y	I	Z	O	P

NVQ SVQ 2

Prepare and cook basic vegetable proteins

ELEMENT 1
Prepare basic vegetable protein dishes

INTRODUCTION

In the past decade, public concern regarding intense farming methods and a growing awareness of health issues, have resulted in an ever-increasing number of people not consuming any animal product or by-product. This may be for a variety of reasons: health, social or economic. In order to meet these requirements, a new hi-tec industry has began producing processed vegetable protein, as a substitute for animal, fish and shellfish flesh. Vegetable protein is manufactured from plant materials and in its natural state has a somewhat bland taste and needs to be flavoured and/or combined with fresh vegetables, fruit, cereals, nuts and seeds as part of a dish.

Figure 151 Field of wheat

TYPES OF VEGETABLE PROTEIN

Textured vegetable protein (TVP)

Protein derived from wheat, oats or cotton seed, but mainly from the soya bean. TVP is available in many forms: nuggets, granules, flakes, strips, chunks or finely minced.

There are two methods of texturing soya proteins:

1. extrusion;
2. spinning.

The different textures lend themselves to a range of uses. Spun threads of TVP are stretched and twisted into bunches giving a meat-like texture and flavour.

TVP is the oldest form of commercially manufactured meat substitute and the least desired because of its taste and texture. It was originally and still is occasionally, used to 'bulk up' real meat in inexpensive dishes.

FACT: In the UK TVP must, by law, be fortified with vitamin B12.

Tempeh

Tempeh is produced from whole soya beans that have been fermented by special bacteria for up to 36 hours before being flavoured with vinegar. Tempeh is low in saturated fats, high in protein, and cholesterol and is salt-free. It is used in soups, stews, stir-fries and salads.

Tofu (soya bean curd)

Tofu is widely used in Oriental cooking. Tofu curd is produced from pulverised soya beans which have been boiled with water and then filtered. The resulting thick curd is cooled, set and cut into blocks.

Fresh tofu is bland in flavour, however, this is not a disadvantage as it makes it suitable for either sweet or savoury dishes. Tofu is available:

1. soft;
2. firm.

Figure 152 Products made from vegetable protein

Soft (silken) tofu

Soft tofu is suitable for blending as it gives a smooth, creamy texture. When flavoured and sweetened, it is an ideal topping for desserts, ice-cream or puddings. It can also be used as a savoury for pie fillings or sauces.

Firm tofu

This is sliced or cubed and used in casseroles, pies, stews, kebabs, or stir-fry dishes. Can be purchased with a smoky flavour for use in sandwiches.

Tofu can be frozen, but, during the defrosting process it appears to completely change in texture, becoming chewy with a fibrous texture similar to meat.

Quorn (brand name)

Quorn originates from a member of the mushroom family. The fungi grow in a fermenter with the addition of carbohydrate in the form of glucose, oxygen, nitrogen and minerals. It is harvested when the liquid is pasteurised, to prevent further growth. The liquid is then removed by filtration leaving behind a sheet of quorn which is similar in appearance to uncooked pastry.

FACT: Quorn as a source of protein was discovered in the 1960s by Rank Hovis McDougall.

Flavouring is added along with a protein to set the quorn. Originally this protein was made from egg whites, but recently this has been replaced with a vegetable substitute. It is then cooked, sliced, diced or minced accordingly. Quorn absorbs flavours from other foods. It may be used in stir-fries, stews, pies, flans and as sandwich fillings.

HYGIENE AND STORAGE OF UNCOOKED VEGETABLE PROTEINS

Uncooked vegetable protein deteriorates quickly. Therefore it is important to observe the following rules of hygiene.

(*See* Maintain and promote hygiene in food storage, pp. 48–50.)

- Maintain a high standard of personal hygiene.
- Clean all equipment, materials and areas before use.
- Ensure good stock rotation.
- **Always** keep textured vegetable protein dry.
- Tempeh should be kept frozen (–18°C) and must **never** be refrozen (a fresh product).
- Tofu should be kept in a refrigerator in a covered bowl of cold water (a fresh product).
- Fresh quorn needs to be refrigerated and used as soon as possible (available fresh or frozen).
- Keep all vegetable proteins away from strong odours or flavours.

SAFETY

Always:

(See Maintain a safe and secure working environment, pp. 10–23.)

1. Ensure that all personnel are trained to operate the appropriate equipment;
2. Have equipment regularly serviced and checked to ensure that it is in safe working order.

ELEMENT 2

Cook basic vegetable protein dishes

INTRODUCTION

With the number of non-meat-eaters increasing yearly, there is an immediate need for a repertoire of vegetable protein dishes. In some cases dishes can be classic meat recipes using vegetable protein. Vegetarians, however, may be unhappy with this option.

Fresh vegetable proteins need minimum or no preparation and in some cases can be added straight to the dish in its final stages. Always follow the manufacturer's instructions for the best results when making up these dishes. Vegetable proteins absorb the surrounding flavours quickly and effectively therefore the amount of additional flavouring can be reduced.

Use 150g of fresh vegetable protein per portion (50 to 100g dried).

There are a number of companies producing preformed dishes, e.g. burgers, sausages and loaves.

ADDITIONAL INGREDIENTS

Additional ingredients can be added to balance the diet and improve flavour.

Figure 153 Nuts and seeds

Nuts

Almonds There are two types of almonds: sweet and bitter. The bitter are poisonous when eaten in their raw form. They enrich dishes and are high in protein.

Brazil nuts Originating from the Brazilian Amazon, these nuts quickly turn rancid due to their high oil content.

Chestnuts These soft textured nuts are low in fat and high in carbohydrates and may be purchased canned (whole or puréed) or vacuum-packed and dried.

Hazelnuts These are aromatic and sweet, adding flavour to both sweet and savoury dishes. They may be roasted.

Peanuts The most popular of nuts, they are not strictly a true nut. They have a distinctive flavour and are rich in protein.

Pecan These sweet and richly flavoured nuts are similar in appearance to walnuts.

Pistachio Bright green in colour, they are richly flavoured.

Walnuts These are the most versatile of all nuts and impart a rich full taste.

Pine nuts A soft creamy coloured nut, they are found at the base of a species of pine cone and have a delicate flavour.

Seeds

Poppy seeds These mild, sweet seeds from the opium poppy are free from narcotic properties.

Pumpkin seeds These flat green seeds from the pumpkin have a light, distinctive taste and are a good source of zinc, iron and protein.

Sesame seeds These very small, light brown or creamy coloured seeds have a sweet, mild and nutty flavour and are high in calcium and protein.

Sunflower seeds These have a very distinctive taste and are high in protein, iron, fibre and calcium.

USES OF VEGETABLE PROTEINS

Each vegetable protein has its own particular use.

TVP Soya

Used mainly in inexpensive dishes: curries, stews and pies. It normally requires soaking before use. The flavour lingers.

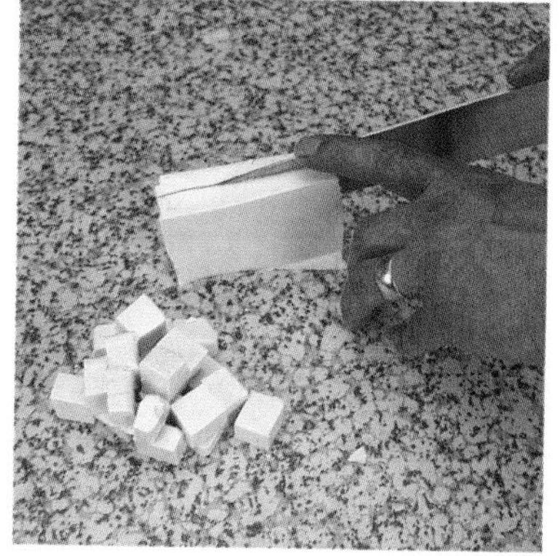

Figure 154 Cubing tofu

Tofu

This is already cooked and only really needs reheating. It is diced, stir-fried or sautéed, served in salads and used extensively in Chinese cookery. When added to sauce it will swell as it absorbs the liquid.

Tempeh

This is raw and needs to be cooked before using (30 min approximately). Used in Japanese cooking it can also be used in stews and salads

Quorn

This is already cooked so no preparation is necessary. It can be added directly to a dish in its final stages. There is no waste as all the product is used. Quorn can be marinaded (which takes approximately 1 hour) and absorbs flavours.

METHODS OF COOKING VEGETABLE PROTEINS

Boiling

(See pp. 138–52.) Follow the procedure as for soups and sauces.

(See Prepare and fry food, pp. 64–75.)

Deep frying

Vegetable proteins can be diced and minced, flavoured to taste as fish or chicken, and then coated in batter or breadcrumbs.

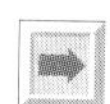

(See Prepare and grill food, pp. 90–100.)

Grilling

For the best results the product should be diced and marinaded before cooking.

Stir frying

Use as for meat dishes. The vegetable protein should be cut into thin strips. Do not overcook.

Stewing or braising

Cut into cubes. Vegetable proteins only need to be added to a sauce 15 to 20 min before conclusion.

Baking

Vegetable proteins can be minced for loaves and cubed for pies.

(See Maintain and promote hygiene in food storage pp. 48–80.

STORAGE AND HYGIENE

The following rules must be adhered to at all times when storing cooked vegetable protein dishes.

- Ensure that a high standard of personal hygiene is maintained.
- All equipment, materials and areas must be kept clean.
- Hot foods, not for immediate consumption, must be cooled to a temperature of below 5°C immediately after use.
- They should be placed in stainless-steel, china or plastic storage containers, labelled and dated with the contents and chilled as rapidly as possible.
- Ideally this should be done in a blast chiller, but alternatively they can be placed in a sink of iced water and refrigerated as soon as the required temperature is acheived.
- Never attempt to cool hot food in the refrigerator as this will raise the temperature of other food items and may cause them to go off. It could also cause damage to the workings of the refrigerator.
- Ensure all waste food and other rubbish is disposed of in accordance with laid-down procedures.

Bean and soya burgers

(Approx. 20 burgers)

Ingredients

1 kg	black beans or red kidney beans, cooked
1 kg	minced soya (soaked)
3 tspn	mixed herbs, dried
300 g	onion, finely diced
	salt and pepper

Method

1. Place all the ingredients in a food processor, process for a few seconds on a slow speed to bind them together. If necessary, scrape down and process again to ensure the mixture is even.
2. Divide the mixture into 20 equal pieces (scale at 100 g) and shape into burgers.
3. Shallow fry in oil or grill for approximately 6 min on each side. Adjust seasoning.

Meadow pie

(20 portions)

Ingredients

4 tbspn	sunflower oil
400 g	onions, diced
2 kg	minced soya, soaked
1 litre	vegetable stock
2 kg	baked beans in tomato sauce
2 kg	potatoes
	salt
100 g	butter, melted
	milk

Method

1. In a large frying pan, heat the oil and fry the onion until softened. Add soya and continue frying for 2 to 3 min, stirring frequently.
2. Crumble the stock cubes in 300 ml of boiling water and add. Add baked beans. Bring to the boil, reduce heat and simmer for 50 min, stirring occasionally.
3. Wash, peel and dice potatoes. Boil in salted water until tender. Drain and mash, add the melted butter and a little milk to achieve a piping consistency. Place in a large piping bag with a large star nozzle.
4. Place the cooked soya and beans into an ovenproof dish and pipe the mashed potato on top. Cook for 25 to 30 min or until the potato is browned.
   Adjust seasoning.

Bean and tofu balls in tomato sauce

(Approx. 20 portions)

Ingredients

3 kg	minced tofu
750 g	red kidney beans, cooked
8 tbspn	tomato purée
4 tspn	chives chopped, fresh
2 tspn	salt
1 tspn	pepper

Sauce

2 tbspn	sunflower oil
2 kg	tomatoes, chopped
1 tbsp	cornflour
1 tspn	marjoram, dried
1 tspn	salt
½ tspn	pepper

Method

1. Place the tofu, mashed beans, tomato purée, chives and seasoning in a large mixing bowl and mix together thoroughly.
2. Divide mixture into 20 golf-sized balls. Sprinkle sunflower oil into a shallow ovenproof dish and add the tofu balls. Place in the oven (180°C/Gas 4) for approximately 15 min.
3. Make the sauce: blend all the sauce ingredients together.
4. Remove the tofu balls from the oven and drain away oil. Turn soya balls over and pour the sauce mixture around them.
5. Return to the oven for a further 15 min.
   Adjust seasoning.

Activity

1. Name **four** Oriental dishes that can be made with tofu.
2. Find the price of cubed quorn per kg and compare it with that of boneless chicken breast.
3. Why should vegetable protein products be stored separate from foods with strong flavours and odours?

NVQ SVQ 2

Prepare and cook basic egg dishes

ELEMENT 1

Prepare basic egg dishes

INTRODUCTION

Eggs are one of the most versatile foods used in cookery and it is estimated that 30 million are consumed every day in the UK! The term egg applies to all edible eggs and the majority of eggs eaten in this country are laid by hens. Fresh hens' eggs are, in the main, supplied by British farmers. However, some are imported from European countries.

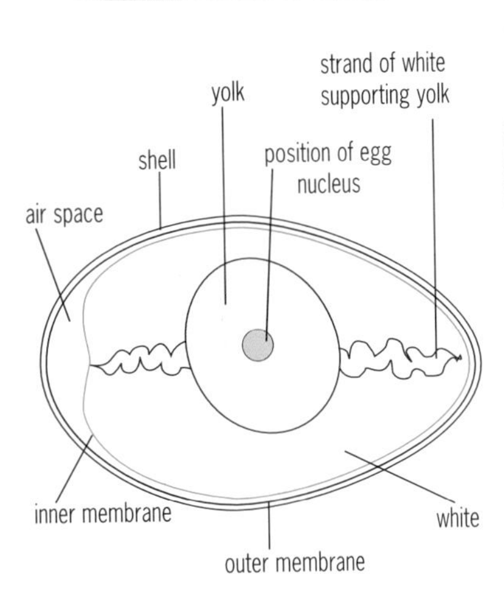

Figure 155 Make up of egg

FACT: The egg is 12% shell, 58% white and 30% yolk.

NOTE: Eggs contain: water, air, protein, fat, carbohydrate, minerals, vitamins A and D, thiamin, riboflavin and niacin, calcium, iron, phosphorous and are low in calories!

PRODUCTION

Eggs are produced by three methods:

1. free range;
2. deep litter;
3. battery.

Class A eggs are graded for size and weight in line with EEC regulations:

Grade	Size
1	70g+
2	65g
3	60g
4	55g
5	50g
6	45g
7	45g or less

NOTE: Only grades 1 to 5 are offered for public sale to the public. Grades 6 and 7 are used in manufacturing.

TIP: Standard egg size (size 3 to 4) weighs approximately 60g. It is advisable though to weigh the eggs.

QUALITY

The quality of eggs is indicated by the class:

Class A	Top quality
Class B	Second quality (used for preserved eggs)
Class C	Non-graded eggs (used in the manufacture of foodstuffs for human consumption)

Quality points when buying eggs

- The shell should be clean, well-shaped, strong and slightly rough.
- When broken there should be a high proportion of thick white to thin white.
- The yolk should be central, firm and have an even colour.

Do as follows to ascertain whether an egg is fresh.

- Place it in a 10 % solution of salt.
- A 2-day-old egg will float near the bottom of the solution (broad end upwards).
- The older the egg, the lighter it becomes and it will float closer to the surface of the solution.

As eggs deteriorate the yolk loses its strength and starts to flatten, water evaporates from the egg and is replaced by air.

Blood spots are usually found in the white and tend to decompose in a short time.

NOTE: All egg dishes should be consumed as soon as possible after preparation or immediately refrigerated.

HYGIENE

Salmonella food poisoning is associated with eating raw egg in uncooked foods or eating egg dishes that have not been cooked properly. The Department of Health issued the following advice to all Chief Environmental Health Officers in September 1988:

'To advise food manufacturers and caterers that for all recipes currently needing raw shell eggs, which involve no cooking, pasteurised egg (frozen, liquid or dried) should be used instead'.

NOTE: Do not consume cracked eggs, always discard them.

VARIETIES OF EGGS

The main varieties of eggs used in cookery are: hens', turkeys', ducks', geese', guinea fowl', gulls', quails' and plovers' (the latter two are protected species in the UK).

STORAGE

Eggs stored at a temperature of below 5°C immediately after laying will keep for three months before they become unusable.

COOKING TIP: Egg protein is complete and easily digestible. Used as a main dish eggs are a protective food and provide energy and material for growth and repair of the body.

Eggs should be:

- stored in a cool place, ideally a fridge but brought to room temperature before using;
- stored in their packing trays point down;
- kept separate from possible contaminates: raw meat;
- kept separate from strong smelling foods, e.g. cheese;
- rotated in stock: first in, first out.

Never leave raw eggs or raw egg preparations in the fridge for any length of time as they will easily become infected

PRESERVATION

Like all other protein foods, eggs will deteriorate and become infected if they are not stored properly. There are a number of methods used to preserve the life of eggs.

Cold storage Eggs are kept just above freezing point. The air conditioning is controlled. Eggs will keep for a maximum of 9 months under these conditions.

Frozen eggs These are sold in large tins in a variety of sizes. The eggs are washed, sanitised and broken into sterilised containers. When the yolks and whites are combined they are strained, pasteurised, packed and quickly frozen. They are usually used by bakers and confectioners.

Dried eggs The eggs are broken, mixed and spray dried at a temperature of approximately 71 °C . These are usually used by bakers and confectioners.

Pasteurised eggs The same conditions apply as for frozen eggs. The liquid eggs are heated to 63 °C for 1 min before being rapidly cooled.

Dried egg white These are suitable for meringues and royal icing etc.

Dried egg white substitute This may also be used for meringues, royal icing and similar albumen-based confections.

COMPOSITION OF HENS' EGGS

The white

The egg white is known as albumen, constitutes approximately 58% of the whole egg and contains a mixture of proteins. The two albumens, ovalbumin and conalbumin, account for 70% of the protein. The proteins produce a stiff foam when egg whites are whisked.

FACT: There is no difference between white and brown eggs. The food value and efficiency in dishes does not vary.

The yolk

The yellow is the egg yolk, constitutes approximately 30% of the whole egg and contains a complex mixture of proteins, including lecithin which is responsible for the emulsifying ability of the yolks. Egg yolks contain cholesterol.

Figure 156 Hen's eggs in eggbox

Prepare and cook basic egg dishes

ELEMENT 1
Cook basic egg dishes

INTRODUCTION

Egg cookery is based on the effect of heat on egg protein. Hens' eggs are one of the most versatile and widely used commodities used for both sweet and savoury dishes as well as being used for thickening as in sauces, emulsifying as in mayonnaise, coagulating as in setting, clarifying as in consommé and aerating as in soufflés and meringue.

DIGESTIBILITY

Raw and lightly cooked eggs are easily digested because unlike meat they have no tough connective tissue, and the fat is emulsified (distributed). Cooking at a high temperature or overcooking causes the proteins to become less digestible.

Figure 157 Pavlova

QUALITY

The quality of the finished item always depends on the quality of the basic ingredients.

- Only use the freshest eggs
- Cooked egg dishes need to be cooked and served immediately.

HYGIENE

Hens can pass salmonella bacteria into their eggs and thus cause food poisoning; however, the incidence of known infection is very small. Moreover, most infections cause only a mild stomach upset but the effects can be more serious in very young or elderly people weakened by other diseases.

All preparation surfaces, utensils and containers should be thoroughly cleaned before and after preparing eggs and always between the preparation of different dishes.

STORAGE

Cooked eggs ready for consumption must be kept at a temperature of 63°C or above, but this means that they have a limited life as they continue to cook, becoming rubbery and hard, and they eventually have to be discarded.

Figure 158 Soufflé

Figure 159 Whisking egg whites

Uses of eggs

Dish	*Examples*
Hors d'œuvre	Egg mayonnaise and in salads
Soups	Clarifying consommé, thickening soups and veloutés
Egg dishes	Soft and hard boiled, scrambled, omelettes, poached, *en cocotte*, *sur le plat*
Farinaceous	Used in many pastas: ravioli, noodles, cannelloni
Fish	Coating fish prior to crumbing and in the preparation of frying batter
Meat and poultry	Binding mixtures and coating cuts of meat and poultry prior to cooking
Sauces	Hollandaise, béarnaise, sabayon, mayonnaise etc.
Salads	Usually hard-boiled and used in many composed salads
Savouries	Scotch woodcock, savoury flans and cheese soufflés etc.
Sweets and pastries	Used in a wide variety of ways

EGGS IN COOKING

Coagulation

Apart from use in a number of dishes, eggs can be used for setting foods and this is done by coagulation.

The main protein in egg is albumen (egg white) which begins to coagulate at 60°C. Egg yolk begins to coagulate at between 65°C and 70°C. Careful control of cooking is vital. If an egg is overcooked the texture becomes tough and rubbery. If the mixture boils (as in making crème caramel) it will scramble and be useless.

COOKING TIP: For poaching, a firmer set is achieved at a lower temperature by the addition of salt, or an acid in the form of vinegar in the liquid used to cook eggs.

Aeration

Egg whites and whole eggs are whisked to a stiff consistency and can be used to aerate as in sponges and meringues. Stale eggs will not whisk properly.

Emulsifying

Emulsification is the suspension of one liquid in another. Egg yolks can be used as an emulsifier as in mayonnaise or hollandaise.

Scrambled eggs (*Oeufs brouillés*)

(× 1 portion)

Ingredients

2	eggs
30g	butter
1 tbspn	cream
	salt
	pepper

Method

1. Break the eggs into a mixing bowl, season with salt and pepper and whisk (do not allow the mixture to become frothy).
2. Melt 15g butter in a sauteuse and add the eggs. Cook gently, stirring until mixture is lightly set. Remove from heat source
3. Finish with remaining 15g butter and cream. Serve warm.

Figure 160 Bowl of scrambled eggs

Scotch eggs

(× 4 portions)

Ingredients

4	hard-boiled eggs
350g	sausage meat
25g	flour
1	beaten egg
50g	breadcrumbs

Method

1. Cover the eggs completely with sausage meat.
2. Pass through flour, egg and breadcrumbs. Shake off excess breadcrumbs.
3. Deep fry until they are golden brown. Drain.
4. Cut in half and serve hot or cold.

Plain omelette

(× 1 portion)

Ingredients

2 to 3	eggs
15g	butter
	salt and pepper

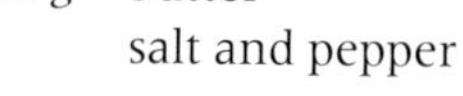

Figure 161 Plain omelette

Method

1. Break the eggs into a mixing bowl and season with salt and pepper.
2. Beat well until the yolks and whites are thoroughly combined.
3. Heat the omelette pan.
4. Wipe pan with a clean cloth. Place 10 g butter and heat until it foams and add the egg mixture. Cook quickly moving the mixture continuously with a fork until lightly set.
5. Remove from heat. Fold the omelette in half and gently tap the bottom of the pan to bring up the edge of the omelette.
6. Tilt pan to allow the omelette to fall carefully onto a serving plate. Serve immediately.

KEY WORDS

AERATING Meringues, soufflés, genoise. Eggs when whisked incorporate and trap tiny bubbles of air in their structure. This property of eggs can be used to produce a variety of dishes.

ALBUMEN A protein found in egg which is important for the production of a stiff foam.

BAVEUSE A wet texture associated with omelettes.

BEATING Whisking egg whites for use in meringue.

BINDING Croquette potatoes, rissoles, stuffings. Egg yolks used to ensure that the ingredients are held/bound together during cooking.

CLARIFYING A process by which consommé is made clear by using egg white.

COAGULATION Causing boiled egg custards to set during cooking.

COLOURING Egg wash on baked goods can also refer to glazing of poached fish dishes by including a sabayon (egg whisked to form a foam).

ENRICHING Sugar paste – improves the quality and texture. Velouté sauces and soups - added in the form of a liaison (egg yolk and cream) by incorporating into sub-boiling liquids not exceeding 70 °C.

EMULSIFYING Mayonnaise and hollandaise sauce. The lecithin found in the egg yolk has the ability to absorb and stabilise as a greater quality of fat/oil is present in the egg yolk. This property can be utilised in the preparation of the above sauces.

FOLDING To incorporate egg into sponge.

FRESH EGGS Eggs that are still sound and have not been preserved by any process. new laid and fresh.

GREASE METHOD A method of preserving eggs. It is important that a pure grease, free from salt, water and impurities is used, for example, Oteg or paraffin wax. The eggs are dipped into the liquid grease and then left to dry. The grease fills up the porous shell which forms a skin to exclude air. Store as for fresh eggs.

LIAISON A mixture of egg yolks and cream whisked together and used to enrich sauces and soups.

LONG HUNDRED A measure of purchase applied to eggs.

NEW-LAID EGGS Recently laid.

SABAYON Whisked egg yolks used as a thickening agent.

SYNERESIS The result of overcooking certain egg mixtures, causing the protein to harden and the liquid to seep out.

THICKENING Sauce anglaise, ice cream, milk puddings, bavarois. These preparations are thickened by the coagulation of the egg protein.

WATERGLASS A solution of sodium silicate used to preserve eggs. A solution is made from sodium silicate and boiling water. It should only be used cold. The eggs are packed point downwards in an earthenware bowl or galvanised pail and the solution is poured over them. To prevent evaporation, cover with a secure lid.

Activity

1. Briefly explain how eggs should ideally be stored.
2. Name two varieties of eggs other than hens' eggs.

   (a)

   (b)
3. Name the bacteria which is most likely to affect eggs and cause food poisoning.
4. Find out how eggs are purchased in your establishment.
5. Using your cookery book find three methods of cooking eggs in water.

   (a)

   (b)

   (c)
6. Find out which chef is responsible for cooking egg dishes in your establishment.

NVQ SVQ 2

Prepare and cook basic shellfish dishes

ELEMENT 1

Prepare basic shellfish dishes

INTRODUCTION

The term shellfish covers an extensive variety of marine and fresh water creatures (all without a backbone).

Shellfish were once the stable diet of urban Londoners who couldn't afford anything to eat so they had to go fishing for their supper! Nowadays, shellfish are a food prized by gourmets. Their delicate constitution lends itself to simple preparation and cooking while maintaining maximum flavour. It offers a wealth of opportunity for chefs to express themselves creatively.

The seas off the British Isles are rich in seafood: lobsters, prawns, shrimps, crabs, mussels and oysters. Unfortunately though, it is necessary to import shellfish from the warm waters of exotic locations where supplies are plentiful; shrimps and prawns are imported from Thailand, India, Taiwan, Nigeria, the Gambia and the USA.

NOTE: Shellfish from these countries are always purchased frozen and tend to be larger in size.

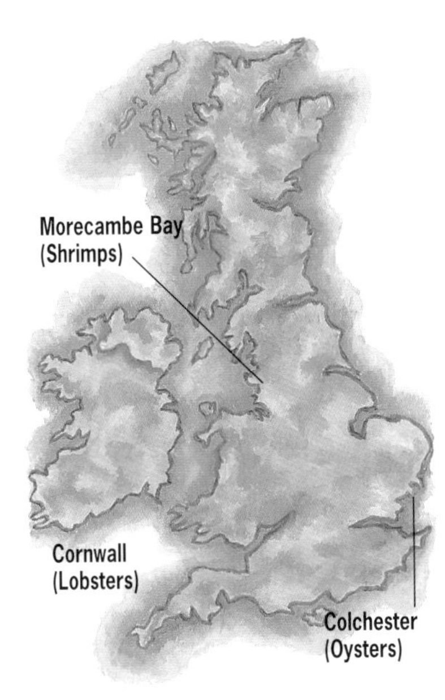

Figure 162 Map of Britain showing shellfish centres

NOTE: Cephalopod are grouped as molluscs although they have an internal transparent shell or bone (quill) instead of a hard external shell. Cuttlefish, squid and octopus are cephalopods.

CLASSIFICATION OF SHELLFISH

For culinary purposes shellfish are divided into two main categories: crustaceans and molluscs.

- Crustaceans: lobsters, crabs, crayfish, prawns, shrimps and scampi.
- Molluscs: clams, mussels, oysters, cockles and scallops.

NOTE: Squid are included in this group.

Crustaceans have jointed limbs and a tough shell covering the body. All are taken from salt water with the exception of the crayfish. A great deal of the flavour and quality is concentrated within the shell which is usually pulverised and used for sauces and/or soups.

Molluscs are soft-bodied shellfish and may be divided into two main categories: univalve and bivalve.

- Univalves have one shell and include whelks, cockles, winkles and snails.
- Bivalves have two shells joined together and include mussels, scallops, clams and oysters.

QUALITY POINTS

The following should be observed when purchasing shellfish.

Fresh crustaceans should:

- whenever possible be purchased live;
- not have any missing claws (lobster or crabs);
- have black and glossy eyes;
- have a lustrous and fresh-looking shell.

Fresh molluscs should:

- have a pleasant sea smell;
- have tightly closed shells (if open, they are dead or nearly dead and should be discarded);
- not have excess barnacles and mud.

STORAGE OF SHELLFISH

WARNING! To prevent cross-contamination never store cooked and uncooked shellfish together.

Always purchase fresh shellfish from a reputable supplier. Ideally, they should be stored in a seawater or freshwater tank, however, this is usually only possible in establishments specialising in shellfish. Under usual conditions, shellfish should be kept in a separate refrigerator, at a temperature of between 1° C and 5° C and stored separate from other foods.

Lobster, crabs, mussels and oysters must be bought live. This not only ensures freshness, but is a safeguard against possible contamination: dead shellfish may be poisoned and might cause food poisoning and in extreme cases even death.

Lobsters and crabs can be kept alive for up to 12 hours provided they are kept in a cool place and covered with a damp cloth. Mussels and oysters are at their best for up to 24 hours, but under the right conditions, may be kept for up to three days.

HYGIENE

Shellfish are highly susceptible to contamination and poisoning. One of the major hygiene risks is buying from dubious sources.

An EEC directive (effective 1993) covers live molluscs, oysters, mussels, scallops, cockles, whelks and winkles and it extends the strict hygiene controls in the UK. It states that all live shellfish for human consumption must comply with the following.

- They should be fresh, alive and free from dirt.
- They should contain low levels of bacteria.
- They should contain no salmonella or toxic or other objectionable substances.
- They should not contain dangerous levels of paralytic or diarrhetic shellfish poisoning.

The directive does not, however, cover crustaceans, prawns, lobsters and crabs, which are controlled by a fishery product directive.

Shellfish are scavengers and are often caught living at the end of sewage outfalls. Oysters and mussels in particular, need to be thoroughly cleaned as they are 'filter feeders' and thrive and grow fat on human sewage. Unless they are scrupulously cleaned before being eaten they can cause serious and even fatal cases of food poisoning.

Always:

- prepare shellfish in a clean and hygienic environment (away from other foods);
- do not leave them to lie around in hot kitchens for longer than is absolutely necessary;
- wash all preparation surfaces, equipment and utensils thoroughly before and after use.

(See Maintain and promote hygiene in food storage, pp. 48–50.)

PREPARATION OF LIVE (RAW) SHELLFISH

Shellfish require little preparation other than a careful, thorough washing and cleaning before being cooked. Specialised crustacean preparations will require some expertise in cutting.

Figure 163 A lobster

Lobster

There are several varieties of lobster available. When alive they are black or dark blue in colour and only turn bright red when cooked. The female is known as a 'hen' lobster and can contain eggs in the form of red roe or coral.

Preparation of lobster

1. Thoroughly wash the lobster.
2. Place lobster flat on a board. To kill, insert point of knife in the centre of the natural line of the head just behind the eyes and cut through to the board.
3. Remove claws and crack them.
4. Starting near the head, cut the tail into its natural segments and remove the black trail from each segment.
5. Split the head section into two halves and discard the sacs and grit.
6. Remove creamy sections (tomalley) and coral if any.
7. Place in a bowl of fresh water to clean.

NOTE: This preparation is used for Lobster à l' Américaine and should only be prepared just before cooking.

Crab

Light brown in colour, they have powerful claws (larger in the male than female). When cooked they turn bright red.

Preparation of crab

Using a trussing needle to kill the crab:

1. Firstly, stab underneath just above the mouth.
2. Lift up the tail flap and stab in a number of directions in the centre of the exposed sections.

NOTE: The edible crab will shed its claws if not killed before cooking.

Dublin Bay prawns, prawns and shrimps

These crustaceans are small and have little or no meat in the claws. Only the flesh from the tail is used.

Preparation of Dublin Bay prawns (scampi), prawns and shrimps

1. Gut: hold the middle tail flap and twist to dislodge from the shell, carefully pull to remove trail (gut) in a whole piece without breaking.
2. Remove head and claws in one piece.
3. Lay tail sideways on a cutting board and strike with the hand to break the bony connecting tissues on the underside.
4. Pull open, extract flesh in one piece.

Dublin Bay prawns are also known as:

- saltwater crayfish (America);
- scampi (Italian);
- Norway lobster.

When alive they are pale in colour and go pink when cooked.

Figure 164 Mussels

Mussels

Closely related to the clam, mussels are found in both salt and fresh water. They are bluish black in colour.

Preparation of mussels

Always discard any mussels with open shells.

1. Thoroughly scrub to remove any sand or mud. Scrape away any barnacles and attached hairy fibres.
2. Place in a bowl of salted water for 2 to 3 hours to disgorge the sand in the shell.
3. Give a final rinse under cold running water before cooking.

Oysters

Native oysters come principally from Whitstable, UK, although a great number of oysters and mussels are now farmed in parts of the UK and Ireland. France produces in the region of 175,000 tons of oysters (Marennes and Portuguese) annually, mostly off the Brittany coast.

Types of oysters

British:	Royal Natives, Royal Whitstable, Colchester, Whitstable, Poole, Helford
Irish:	Shannon
Continental	
French:	Marennes Vertes, Marennes Blanches, Belons, Gancale, Brittany
Dutch:	Natives
Belgian:	Victorias
Portuguese:	Blue points (Gryphas)

Preparation of oysters

1. Open carefully with an oyster knife. Insert the edge of the knife at the hinged end and lever open.
2. Cut through the muscle close to the shell to release the oyster from the deep shell.
3. Turn the oyster over in the deep shell and place it on crushed ice.
4. Discard the flat shell.

Scallops

So named for their fluted shaped shell, there are two basic varieties:

1. delicately flavoured small bay scallops or 'Queenies' (Isle of Man);
2. the larger deep-sea scallops.

Preparation of scallops

1. To remove scallop from shell, place scallop, round side down, on the side of a hot stove (fish will detach itself from shell and the top flat shell will spring open with the fish attached).
2. Carefully slide a sharp knife between the flat shell and the fish.
3. Discard flat shell.
4. Discard dark frill (edible, however, rarely eaten) leaving the white round centre (scallop) with the orange tongue (roe) attached.
5. Thoroughly wash the scallops and use as required.

KEY WORDS

AU GRATIN Coated with cheese sauce, sprinkled with grated cheese and breadcrumbs and browned under a salamander.

À LA FRANÇAISE Moistened with milk and lightly coated in seasoned flour.

À L'ORLY Marinaded in lemon juice, parsley and passed through seasoned flour and batter.

BROILING American term for grilling.

BROCHETTE On a skewer.

PANÉ (À L'ANGLAISE) Passed through seasoned flour, egg wash and breadcrumbs.

Activity

1. Find out if there are any shellfish farms in your area.
2. How long does it take shellfish to mature in their natural habitat as opposed to farming.
3. Make a list of shellfish used in your establishment or college. Find out their purchasing unit (per lb/kg or each) and record their market price on the chart below.

Shellfish	Purchasing unit	Price per each, lb/kg

4. What are the main contamination threats when preparing and cooking shellfish?
5. Why is it important to wash shellfish prior to cooking?

ELEMENT 2
Cook basic shellfish dishes

INTRODUCTION

Oysters and mussels have been enjoyed by people as a prime source of food since prehistoric times. Shellfish are prized for their tender, fine-textured flesh and are prepared simply in a variety of ways. However, they have a tendency to deteriorate rapidly because they contain quantities of certain proteins and amino acids which encourage bacterial growth.

Only purchase shellfish from a reputable supplier to ensure a high-quality product.

QUALITY POINTS

It is important that cooked crustaceans:

1. have their shells intact with no visible signs of damage;
2. have no signs of discoloration;
3. do not have an unpleasant smell;
4. should not be too heavy for their size (if they are they could be diseased and full of fluid).

STORAGE OF COOKED SHELLFISH

The fine eating quality of shellfish depends on absolute freshness. Storing cooked shellfish for too long must be avoided as it increases the risk of harmful bacterial growth and possible food poisoning. Cooked shellfish should be stored separately from other foods (especially raw shellfish) to avoid cross-contamination, at a temperature of between 0°C and 3°C.

HYGIENE

(*See* Maintain and promote hygiene in food storage, pp. 48–50.)

Always:

- ensure that cooked shellfish are prepared in a clean, hygienic environment (away from other foods);
- ensure that they are not be left lying around in hot kitchens for prolonged periods of time;
- ensure that all preparation surfaces, equipment and utensils are thoroughly washed before and after use.

LOBSTER

Cooking lobster

To cook the lobster place it in a pan of boiling salted water and simmer for 15 min for the first pound and 10 min for each subsequent pound, up to a maximum of 40 min.

Menu uses

- soups, bisques;
- sauces: sauce Américaine;
- grilled: barbecued or under a salamander;
- boiled: in court bouillon, cooled and served cold on salads;
- mousses and soufflés: hot or cold.
- pâté.

CRAB

Cooking crab

NOTE: Discard Dead Man's Fingers on a crab.

Crabs are killed before cooking using the method recommended by the RSPCA.

Place the crab in a pan of boiling salted water and allow 15 min for the first pound and 10 min for each subsequent pound up to a maximum of 35 min.

Dressing a cooked crab

Figure 165 Cooked and dressed crab

Cooked crab should be cooled completely and stored in a fridge for 3 to 4 hours before dressing.

Crab is prepared for presentation (dressing) by placing the cooked crab on its back and twisting off the legs.

Discard the dead man's fingers (gills) and sac. Remove the white meat from the claws (after cracking them open with the back of a knife) and the breast. Season with salt, a drop of lemon juice or vinegar and milled pepper. Remove the soft brown meat, sieve. Mix with breadcrumbs, mayonnaise and mustard, and season.

Menu uses

- soups, bisques;
- dressed for salads;
- pâtés, mousses and hot soufflés.

DUBLIN BAY PRAWNS (SCAMPI)

Dublin Bay prawns can be cooked in a similar way to lobster: grilled or barbecued single, kebabs or panéed and deep fried. In their shells, scampi make excellent garnishes. When cooking frozen scampi always make sure that the flesh is defrosted thoroughly to permit even cooking.

Menu uses

- soups, bisques;
- shallow fried, meunière style;
- deep fried, panéed;
- poached in court bouillon and/or white wine.

PRAWNS AND SHRIMPS

Prawns and shrimps usually come pre-cooked (boiled) and frozen with the exception of king or jumbo prawns.

Menu uses.

- soups, bisques;
- sauces;
- hors d'œuvre, bound in mayonnaise sauce and made into cocktails and salads;
- potted (shrimps only);
- grilled and shallow fried (jumbo and king prawns only);
- passed through pané, deep fried (jumbo and king prawns only);
- garnishes for fish, egg, meat, poultry and rice dishes.

MUSSELS

Mussels are best poached in the minimum of liquid. They are cooked in their shells in a heavy pan for as long as it takes the shells to open. Overcooking causes the mussels to be rubbery in texture. The most famous mussel dish is moules marinières.

Menu uses

- soups, as the main ingredient or as a garnish;
- poached and grilled;
- garnishes for fish, pasta and rice dishes.

OYSTERS

Raw oysters are prepared and served on a bed of crushed ice, with lemon juice and Tabasco sauce. They can also be cooked by poaching or sautéed.

Menu uses

- as an hors d'œuvre, raw;
- garnish for beef steaks, beef pies and fish dishes;
- steamed, poached, grilled and baked.

SCALLOPS

Scallops may be poached, sautéed or baked. Care must be taken not to overcook as they become rubbery in texture and lose their flavour.

Scallops used to be served in a sauce (in their shells which were cleaned) with a line of piped duchesse potato as a decorative border before being glazed under a salamander.

Menu uses

- hors d'œuvres, hot or cold;
- poached and deep fried;
- mousses, hot or cold.

KEY WORDS

AU GRATIN Coated with cheese sauce, sprinkled with grated cheese and breadcrumbs and/or browned under a salamander or in the oven.

À LA FRANÇAISE Moistened with milk and lightly coated in seasoned flour.

À L'ORLY Marinaded in lemon juice, parsley and passed through seasoned flour and batter.

BROILING American term for grilling.

BROCHETTE On a skewer.

PANÉ (À L'ANGLAISE) Passed through seasoned flour, egg wash and breadcrumbs.

Activity

1. Find out if there are any shellfish farms in your area.
2. How long does it take shellfish to mature in their natural habitat as opposed to farming?
3. Make a list of shellfish used in your establishment or college. Find out their purchasing unit (per kg) and record their market price on the chart below.

Shellfish	Purchasing unit	Price per each, lb/kg

4. What are the main contamination threats when preparing and cooking shellfish?
5. Why is it important to wash shellfish prior to cooking?

NVQ SVQ 2

Prepare and cook basic cold and hot desserts

ELEMENT 1

Prepare, cook and finish basic cold desserts

INTRODUCTION

Cold and hot desserts are produced by the pastry section in the kitchen. Great care must be taken in the preparation of cold and hot desserts as they are the final part of the meal and, as such, will leave the lasting impression of the cuisine. They must be as good as, if not be better than, those courses that have preceded them.

HYGIENE

(*See* Maintain and promote hygiene in food preparation and cooking, pp. 51–4.)

Strict standards of hygiene must be maintained when preparing and cooking hot and cold desserts as the ingredients used, such as fresh cream, eggs and milk are susceptible to harmful bacteria which multiply, becoming a potential health risk. All work areas, surfaces, equipment and utensils should be thoroughly cleaned. Always ensure that any sugar or sweet mixture that has fallen on surfaces or floors is removed and the area or surface cleaned thoroughly, otherwise it will attract insects and flies.

STORAGE

(*See* Maintain and promote hygiene in food storage, pp. 48–50.)

Cold desserts need good refrigeration and should be covered whenever possible to avoid cross-contamination. Ideally they should be stored in a separate refrigerator away from other foods. If this is not possible they should be kept separate from savoury foods and especially strong-flavoured commodities. Ensure that only the freshest of ingredients are used in strict rotation. Never used old or stale foods and always discard out-of-date products.

Figure 166 Jelly

TYPES OF COLD DESSERT

Jellies

In the main, most establishments use convenience jellies. However, some still prepare fresh jellies producing superior varieties and flavoured jellies from fresh fruits, juices and liqueurs. A basic jelly is made from gelatine, sugar and water.

Trifles

Trifles are very much a traditional British dish and are made with sponge, ratafia biscuits or sponge biscuit, fresh fruits or jam and jelly. There are five basic sweets known as trifle: fruit trifle, sherry trifle, fruit and sherry trifle, Scots trifle and jelly trifle.

Trifles are topped in one of two ways:

1. cold thick custard sauce, piped with whipped cream and decorated with glacé cherries, angelica and/or small macaroon biscuits;

COOKING TIP: The Italian version of trifle is *'Tiramisu'*.

COOKING TIP: Most chefs whenever possible will use fresh milk for making egg custards, but there are other milk products on the market that may be used, either when there are shortages or when special circumstances dictate.

2. piped with whipped cream and decorated with glacé cherries, angelica and/or small macaroon biscuits.

Egg custards

A true baked custard mixture is made from milk, egg yolk, sugar and is flavoured with vanilla (Crème anglaise). It is thickened by gently heating it in a bain marie in the oven. The mixture slowly coagulates to produce a firm mass. If the mixture is not cooked in this manner the direct heat would cause the custard to scramble and overcook. The temperature of custard must not exceed 149°C, otherwise the mixture will boil, trapping bubbles, and it will be watery.

Cream caramels

Cream caramels are made with a fresh egg custard mix which is poured on top of a 'set' layer of caramelised sugar. They are then placed in a bain marie and baked in an oven.

Meringues

The term 'meringue' covers all forms of beaten egg whites and sugar, almost irrespective of the proportions used and the additions. The best meringues are made from fresh or frozen egg whites and a hard-grained caster sugar. Meringues can be coloured and flavoured to enhance the flavour and appearance of an otherwise sweet but bland product. Care must be taken when adding these ingredients so that the stability of the meringue is not lost. Meringues are best made in a stainless-steel or copper bowl and whisked with a fine whisk. However, when a bulk meringue mixture is made in a mixing bowl, the bowl should be scalded with boiling water to remove all traces of grease, otherwise the meringue will not aerate.

Meringues can be divided into three groups:

COOKING TIP: Meringues may be made from reconstituted dried albumen or meringue powder.

- Cold — shells, vacherins, toppings, pavlova
- Hot — petit fours, fancy meringues, shapes
- Italian — (also known as boiled meringue) used in omelette soufflés, butter cream, biscuit glacé, fruit meringues

Stabilizers

For bulk meringue a stabiliser may be added to prevent the meringue from 'flowing'. Ethyl methyl cellulose (EDIFAS) and tapioca starch are used.

Baking meringues

Meringues are baked in a slow oven between 110 °C and 132 °C, the optimum temperature being 121 °C.

A lighter, crisper product is achieved if the meringue is left in an oven overnight on the pilot light or alternatively dried out for at least three hours in an oven with the door ajar to release the steam. Powder meringues only require drying and not baking. They are white, powdery, crumble easily and tend to have an inferior flavour.

Meringue toppings on flans, Queen of Puddings and Baked Alaska-style sweets are flashed through a very hot oven to tinge the meringues with colour and leave the inside of the meringue soft.

A baked meringue should be a delicate fawn colour and have a slight caramel flavour.

Cold rice dishes	Moulded Creams	Flans/Tarlets	Fruit based
Pear/Fruit condé	Bavarois	(Sweet and short pastry)	Poached pears
Empress Rice	Petits-pots	Apple	Compote of fruit
	Crème brulée	Fruit tarts/Flans	Fruit salad
	Blancmange	Lemon meringue	
		Jam tart	

Cream

Pastry cream (crème patissière)

Pastry cream can be described as a cooked vanilla-flavoured filling made from egg yolk, sugar, flour, flavouring and milk and is used to fill flans, gateaux and pastries.

Types of milk

The following types of milk are used for cream fillings:

- UHT
- sterilised
- condensed
- evaporated
- dried milk.

Types of cream used in cold and hot desserts

Types of cream	*Colour codes*	*Legal minimum fat %*	*Uses*
Single cream	Red	18	For pouring over pies, cakes and fruit salad and to enrich sauces
Whipping cream	Green	35	Used in sauces and puddings to enrich and is ideal for trifles and in sponge cakes
Double cream	Blue	48	For sauces, pouring over pies, cakes and fruit salad. It can also be whisked and piped for decorating
Double cream 'extra thick'	N/A	48	For pouring over pies, cakes and fruit salad, but with extra thickness. It cannot be whisked.
Clotted cream	Gold	55	Served on pies and puddings and with scones and jam.

Aerosol cream

Aerosol cream is made with UHT milk that is filled into tins under sterilised conditions; nitrous oxide is used as the propellant. A disadvantage is that the cream starts to collapse soon after application so it should only be used on desserts that are for immediate consumption and never used as a filling.

Cream substitutes

Cream substitutes are mainly based on vegetable fats or oils which are emulsified in water with other permitted substances. A variety of these products are available under the descriptions:

- imitation cream;
- non-dairy cream;
- dessert topping.

Storage of cream

Fresh cream should always be kept cool, clean and covered. It will store successfully unopened at optimum temperature under refrigeration for a maximum of 10 days. A guide to its shelf life is the date stamp on the label, which should always be checked before buying and using the product.

ELEMENT 2

Prepare, cook and finish basic hot desserts

INTRODUCTION

Hot and cold sweet and pastry dishes are generally prepared in a separate department from the main kitchen due to their specialised nature. It is essential that all ingredients are accurately weighed, mixed and cooked at the correct temperature to produce the perfect dessert.

STORAGE

Hot desserts for service should be kept at a temperature of above 65°C. Should the temperature of hot desserts that contain dairy products (eggs and cream) fall below this temperature for any length of time, they might become a potential health risk, i.e. dangerous to eat and capable of causing food poisoning.

(See Maintain and promote hygiene in food storage, pp. 48–50.)

Cooked hot desserts for consumption at a later date should be chilled as quickly as possible after they have been cooked. Never leave hot desserts to cool in a kitchen environment: apart from potential health risks from bacteria they might also attract vermin, e.g. mice, cockroaches and flies.

TYPES OF HOT DESSERT

Pancakes/crêpes

Generally sweet pancakes are made from a thin, light and delicate batter. The only exceptions are where a double layer of batter is used to enclose fruit or another sweet mixture. A pancake batter is a mixture of milk, eggs, flour, fat or oil and sugar. American pancakes, Welsh drop scones and Scotch pancakes have baking powder added to aerate the mixture.

The following should be observed when making pancakes.

- The batter should be made with a soft flour; strong flour will make the mixture tight and tough.
- Do not use too much egg, otherwise the pancakes will have an over-soft spongy texture.
- The prepared batter should be of a flowing consistency which should quickly cover the bottom of the frying pan in an even coat.
- Use oil and clarified butter to fry pancakes to ensure maximum taste.
- Do not make the pancakes too soon in advance. They are best when made fresh and served immediately.

Fruit pies and puddings

Fruit pies and puddings can be made from any fresh fruit singly or from a variety of mixed fruits. Whenever possible always use fresh fruits. However, tinned fruit may be used, provided the cooking time is reduced to take into account the fact that the fruit is already cooked.

Basic milk puddings

Milk puddings are sweet and easy to produce desserts. They can be made from a number of starches such as rice, semolina, tapioca and sago.

COOKING TIP: Synaeresis (weeping). On standing, many gelatinised products (e.g. rice) release their liquid and the 'gel' structure shrinks. This phenomen is commonly known as 'weeping'. It can be recognised when the liquid collects around the top edge of the custard or a cornflour mould.

Baked The starch is washed, drained and placed into cold milk along with a knob of butter and sugar in a suitable dish and placed in the oven to cook.

Boiled The washed and drained starch is 'rained' into the hot milk and stirred back to the boil. The mixture is covered and allowed to simmer, preferably in a bain marie to prevent the mixture from burning. Sugar, eggs, butter and cream are added to enrich.

Pre-cooked (instant) The powder is sprinkled onto cold milk and whisked for a few minutes to prevent lumps from forming. The starch has been pre-cooked and modified so cooking is not necessary.

THICKENING LIQUIDS USED IN HOT AND COLD DESSERTS

Liquids may be thickened for desserts by the following methods:

- using one or a number of starch commodities;
- mixing;
- cooking.

The type and quantity of the thickening agent and the length of cooking time determine the finished consistency of the product. All starch-based desserts must be 'cooked out' to prevent the unpleasant taste of raw starch. Always allow sufficient time for cooking hot desserts.

COOKING TIP: Starched-based desserts should be cooked in a thick-based pan to prevent burning.

Starch powders

The following starch powders are used for thickening:

flour	pastry cream
cornflour	blancmanges
riceflour	milk puddings

COOKING TIP: For soufflés and crème patissière a kneaded butter is used to thicken the mixture. This is made with equal quantities of flour, butter (*col roux*) and sugar to flavour, which is gradually whisked-in in small amounts into a boiling liquid. As the fat melts the flour is dispersed evenly and the mixture thickens without forming lumps.

Bread and butter pudding

(× 4 portions)

Ingredients

600 ml	milk
60 g	granulated sugar
3	eggs
4 slices	thin, buttered, slices of white or brown bread
60 g	sultanas
	vanilla essence/pod
1 tspn	ground nutmeg

Figure 167 Bread and butter pudding

Method

1. Place the eggs and sugar into a large mixing bowl and whisk. Whisk in the boiling water and pass through a chinois.
2. Remove crusts from the sliced bread. Cut into fluted 5 cm rounds using a pastry cutter and dip them into melted butter.
3. Arrange the trimmings in an ovenproof dish and sprinkle over the washed sultanas.
4. Place fluted roundles on top overlapping.
5. Pour over the custard mixture and stand for 10 min.
6. Sprinkle caster sugar and freshly grated nutmeg on top.
7. Cook in a bain marie in a moderate oven.

Crème caramel

(× 6 portions)

Ingredients

600 ml	milk
60 g	caster sugar
4	eggs
	vanilla essence/pod

Caramel

120 g	granulated sugar
150 g	water

Method

Caramel

1. Place 90 g of the water in a sugar boiler. Add the sugar and dissolve completely.
2. Carefully bring to the boil and cook until the sugar takes on a golden colour.*
3. Gradually add 60 g cold water. Do not allow to boil up – a little cold water will halt the colouring of sugar.
4. Reboil and pour a little of the caramel in each of six dariole moulds.
5. Reserve a small quantity of the caramel and dilute with more cold water.

* NOTE: Temperature should be 175°C

Custard

1. Place the milk in a thick-bottomed saucepan with the vanilla pod and bring to the boil.
2. Whisk the eggs and sugar together.
3. Whisk in the hot milk into the egg and sugar mixture.
4. Strain mixture and leave to stand.
5. Pour custard into the prepared dariole moulds and place the dariole moulds into a warm bain marie.
6. Cook in a moderate oven for about 30 min until the custard is set.
7. Allow to cool completely before turning out on to a serving dish. Pour over the remaining caramel.

Pancakes

(× 8 portions)

Ingredients

240 g	flour, soft
2	eggs
600 ml	milk
30 g	butter, melted
pinch	salt
120 g	oil, for frying

Method

1. Place the eggs, milk and salt into a mixing bowl and whisk well.
2. Gradually sieve in the flour and whisk after each addition to ensure a smooth consistency.
3. Mix in the melted butter.
4. Allow to stand for an hour before use. Adjust consistency if necessary.
5. Place a little oil into the pan and heat to smoking point (177°C).
6. Pour in just enough batter to cover the bottom of the pan with a very thin layer.
7. Cook until the top of the pancake has set and the underside is a light golden colour.
8. Using a palette knife turn pancake over and cook until underside is the same colour.
9. Stack on top of each other in between layers of greaseproof paper. Finish as required.

Fritters (*Beignets*): basic batter

(× 4 portions)

Ingredients

120 g	flour, soft
30 g	egg yolk
150 ml	water
30 g	salad oil
60 g	egg white
25 ml/120 g	oil, for frying
pinch	salt

Method

1. Sieve flour and salt into a confectioner's bowl and make a bay.
2. Add egg yolk and water and mix to a smooth paste.
3. Gradually beat in the oil. Cover and allow to stand before using.
4. Just before using, whisk the egg whites to a stiff foam and fold gently into the batter mixture.

Apple fritters

Ingredients

Apples	½ apple per portion

Method

1. Prepare the apples: wash, peel, core and slice the apples into 6 mm rings and place them in a bowl of acidulated water.
2. Pass apple rings through flour and shake off any excess flour.
3. Dip them in the batter mixture and place into the hot oil.
4. Cook until golden brown on both sides (about 6 to 8 min).
5. Drain thoroughly and place on a baking sheet.
6. Dredge with icing sugar and glaze under a salamander.
7. Serve hot.

COOKING TIP: Other fruits may be substituted.

Banana fritters (*Beignets de bananes*)

Split four bananas in half lengthways and cut in half across to produce 4 pieces from each banana.

May be spread with hot thick pastry cream first and allowed to cool, then finish as from stage 2 of apple fritters.

Pineapple fritters (*Beignets d'ananas*)

Sprinkle 4 pineapple rings with kirsch (cut large rings in half), then finish as from stage 2 of apple fritters.

Meringue (boiled)

Ingredients

150g	egg, white
300g	sugar, granulated or cubed
90g	water
pinch	cream of tartare
	colour and flavour as required

Figure 168 Pavlova

Method

1. Place the sugar, water and cream of tartare in a clean copper saucepan.
2. Carefully dissolve the sugar and boil to 118°C to 121°C (hard-boil).
3. Whisk the egg whites to a stiff snow consistency.
4. Add the boiled sugar in a steady stream, while continuously whisking until the meringue is firm.
5. Add colour and flavour and/or fruit pulp as required.

NOTE: For fruit meringue add up to 150g fruit pulp (strawberry, apple etc.) at stage 5.

Meringue (cold)

Ingredients

150g	egg, white
300g	sugar, granulated or cubed

Method

1. Thoroughly scald the mixing bowl and whisk to remove any grease.
2. Place the egg whites and sugar in the cleaned bowl and whisk to a stiff snow consistency.
3. Add two-thirds of the sugar gradually while continuously whisking. Whisk until the meringue is very stiff.
4. Carefully stir in the remaining one-third of sugar with a spatula.

Baked rice pudding (*Pouding de riz*)

(× 4 portions)

Ingredients

100 g	rice, short or wholegrain
½ litre	milk, whole or skimmed
50 g	sugar, caster or unrefined
10 g	butter or margarine
	vanilla essence
	grated nutmeg

Method

1. Thoroughly wash the rice and place it in a pie dish.
2. Add the milk and sugar and mix well together.
3. Add butter or margarine, vanilla essence and grated nutmeg.
4. Place on a baking sheet and wipe clean the rim of the dish.
5. Place in a preheated oven 180°C to 200°C, Reg. 4 to 6, until the pudding begins simmering.
6. Reduce heat and cook the pudding slowly for about 1½ to 2 hours.

Pastry

Choux paste (*Pâte à choux*)

Ingredients

½ litre	water
100 g	butter, margarine or oil
125 g	flour, strong
4	eggs
pinch	sugar

Method

1. Place the water, sugar and fat in a saucepan and bring to the boil. Remove from heat.
2. Sieve the flour. Add mixing with a wooden spoon.
3. Return to a moderate heat and stir continuously until the mixture leaves the sides of the pan. Remove from heat and cool.
4. Gradually add the beaten eggs, mixing well after each addition. The paste should be of a dropping consistency.

KEY WORDS

BOMBE MOULD A domed copper mould with a lid.

CHARLOTTE MOULD A multi-portion metal mould.

CHINOIS A conical strainer.

COUPE A small ice-cream dish.

DARIOLE MOULD A small metal mould.

FLASHING To cook quickly either in the oven or under a salamander.

FLOWING When a meringue looses its shape because it has been left for a time before using.

PANACHÉ A mixture.

PASTEURISED EGGS Whites or beaten whole eggs are available frozen or chilled in various quantities and used for large productions of sponges, cakes and cold desserts.

PROVE, A PAN To make non-stick.

SOUFFLÉ MOULD A china ribbed dish.

VACHERIN A nest shape made from meringue.

Activity

1. Using a cookery book, find the following recipes and give a brief description of the dish below.

   (a) Baked apple
   (b) Lemon meringue pie
   (c) Empress rice
   (d) Bavarois

2. Why should liquid egg custard be strained?
3. Using a cookery book, find **four** fruit purées that could be used to flavour a basic jelly.
4. Speak to your supervisor or head chef and ask them for their recipe for sherry trifle and meringues. Copy out the recipes below:

Sherry trifle	Meringue

5. Why is it necessary to take extra precautions when storing dairy ingredients for hot and cold desserts
6. Name **three** forms in which eggs can be purchased.
7. Research the vegan alternative to gelatine and copy your results below.

Prepare and cook basic dough products

ELEMENT 1
Prepare basic dough

INTRODUCTION

A basic dough is usually made from strong flour, a pinch of sugar, salt and a warm water and yeast solution. Some doughs, known as unleavened breads, do not need yeast or sugar and rely on the natural yeasts present in flour for a little fermentation and rise.

Flour is made from milling the wheat grain. There are three strengths of flour which are as follows.

1. **Strong flour** (hard or bread flour) Best suited for dough-making. It comes from a variety of wheat flour, mainly from Canada and America, and has a high gluten content. Gluten is a muscular substance of great elasticity that strengthens the cellular structure of bread.
2. **Soft flour** (weak flour, biscuit or cake flour) Milled from predominantly British wheat, this is ideally suited for cakes, sponges and pastry making.
3. **Medium strength flour** A combination of equal quantities of strong and weak flour, it is used as an all-purpose flour, mainly for pastries.

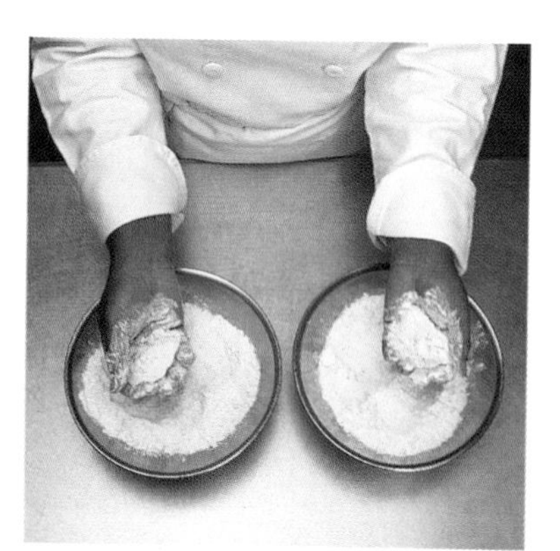

Figure 169 Hand test of flour

Hand test to determine the strength of flour

The strength of flour can be determined by squeezing a small quantity in the hand. A weak flour will cling together when the hand is opened while a strong flour will crumble to a powder.

PRODUCTION OF FLOUR AND USES IN DOUGH MAKING

Flour is made from milling the wheatgrain: the grain is ground separating the parts, sifted and blended to create the required type of flour. The three types of flour are as follows.

- **Wholemeal flour** This contains 100% whole grain and includes the wheatgerm that contains oils and because it is likely to become rancid, it should not be stored for more than two weeks. It is best used to make loaves, rolls, nan bread and pizza bases.
- **Wheatmeal flour** This contains up to 95% whole grain and is best suited for making loaves, rolls and pizza bases.
- **Whiteflour** This contains up to 85% whole grain and is used to make loaves, rolls, buns, pizza bases, nan bread and doughnuts.

YEAST

Yeast is a living organism that liberates/gives off carbon dioxide gas when mixed with warmed water and a little sugar. The primary function of yeast is to change sugar into carbon dioxide and aerate the dough during proving. Secondly, it is used to ripen and condition the gluten in a dough so that the gas is retained during expansion.

Types of yeast available

Yeast used in baking may be either dried or in compressed form.

Dried yeast will keep for several months provided it is kept in cool, dry conditions. When frozen, it will keep for even longer.

Compressed fresh yeast has a sweet, clean, fruity smell and crumbles easily. It will keep for two weeks in the refrigerator or, if frozen, for two months.

Yeast needs four conditions for growth:

1. Moisture;
2. Warmth/temperature;
3. Food;
4. Time.

Moisture

The moisture is usually water, though milk is sometimes used. Milk, however, has the effect of retarding growth.

Temperature/warmth

For the best yeast action, the temperature should ideally be between 25° and 29°C. Above 52 °C and the reaction slows down and the yeast begins to die off. Above 60 °C it is killed, below 20°C its growth is retarded, and at 0°C it is dormant. Some doughs, for example, brioche, Danish and croissant, need to be fermented at a low temperature (15° C to 20 °C). The temperature and the moist conditions can be achieved by using a prover oven.

Food

The food requisite is sugar. The yeast converts the sugar into dextrose which ferments to produce carbon dioxide, which in turn inflates the dough. Flour contains roughly 2½% of sugars such as sucrose, maltose and dextrose. It is not necessary to add sugar to flour to make dough; however, it does help in so far that it cuts down on the time factor.

Time

Yeast needs time to convert the sugar into carbon dioxide which in turn aerates the dough.

Adding salt to your dough

Apart from adding flavour salt has the affect of stabilising the gluten and has a controlling effect on fermentation.

Yeast needs time to work and produce the required amount of carbon dioxide to give optimum size. Too much time and the yeast will over-prove the dough product, causing it to deflate. The dough may also have a sour taste and smell.

COOKING TIP: Never add salt directly to the yeast as it would kill it off and the dough would not rise

STAGES OF DOUGH MAKING

Mixing

When the yeast, liquid and flour have been combined, the dough is then ready for kneading.

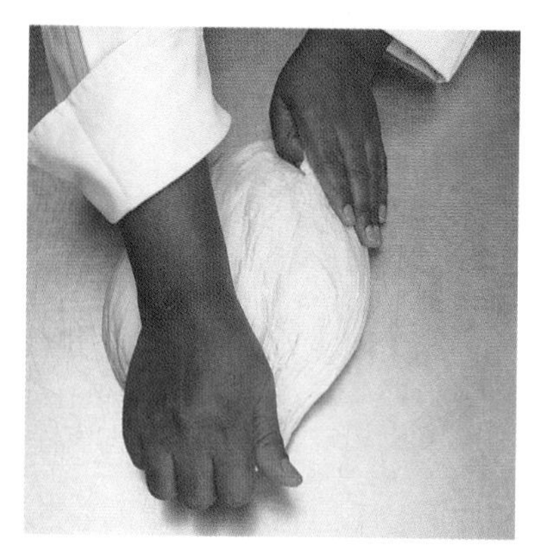

Figure 170 Hands kneading dough

Kneading (knocking-back)

Kneading is continued until the dough has a shiny surface and is no longer sticky to the touch. After fermentation the dough is kneaded back to remove the gases after bulk fermentation time and return it to its original size.

Proving (bulk fermentation time, BFT)

Proving is the action of allowing the dough to condition and double in size, under warm conditions. The most suitable environment for this to occur is in a 'prover' cabinet (this warms water which in turn warms the interior to between 21°C and 27°C). When the dough is fully expanded it will not spring back when pressed.

Over-proving it will result in a distorted, uneven and excessively raised product.

Portioning/weighing

The dough mixture is divided, weighed and placed in baking tins. This can be done manually (by hand) or by using an electrical dough divider which cuts the dough into the correct size.

Moulding

This can be done by hand, on a clean table, or alternatively by using an electrically operated machine which shapes the dough. Hand moulding produces a more superior finish than machine moulding. A well-shaped product should not only have a good shape, but also have an even and unbroken skin.

Folding

This is the action of layering unleavened breads to create a little aeration.

Final proving

This is the final fermentation stage. The yeast produces gas which expands the pockets in the dough. These pockets expand further during baking.

Finishing

Before dough products are baked they might be required to undergo the following finishes.

- **Dusting** They are dusted with flour, rice flour or semolina to give a dulled finish.
- **Egg (with egg yolk)** They are washed with egg yolk to give a deep colour and shiny appearance.
- **Egg (with egg white)** A whisked egg is brushed over the bread roll and then sprinkled with poppy seeds, rock salt, cracked wheat, or sesame seeds to decorate the item further.

COOKING TIP: Alternatively, dough products may be baked without a coating, but finished after cooking with melted butter or a sugar glaze.

Roll shapes

Examples: Round, baton, twist, plait, button, rosette, knot.

Figure 171 Roll shapes

Unleavened bread

This is a very ancient and basic form of bread popular in many different cultures around the world. This particular type of bread has no raising agent and has a flat appearance like a pancake, for example, pitta bread.

Figure 172 Products made from McDougall's range of dough pre-mixes

CONVENIENCE PRODUCTS

Pre-prepared dough

The pre-prepared dough should have undergone bulk fermentation and been knocked back to its original bulk. The finished result should appear to be dry and stretch easily. During the weighing and shaping process it is important that the dough is kept warm and covered with a clean cloth to stop a skin from forming on the surface.

Dough pre-mixes

A range of pre-mixes are available for both the domestic and industrial markets. These may be purchased in both small and bulk quantities. The catering industry tends to purchase such mixtures in bulk. These mixtures are of great value to the busy caterer for the following reasons.

1. They allow a greater range of doughs to be produced with the minimum of skill and labour.
2. They guarantee a standard result.
3. They save a great deal of time.

When using pre-mixes of all types it is important that the manufacturer's instructions are adhered to closely. In real terms the mixes need to be formed into a dough by adding a measured quantity of liquid. Both bulk fermentation and proving are necessary after the product has been formed, to achieve a similar product to traditionally prepared goods.

THE IMPORTANCE OF GOOD HYGIENE

A good standard of hygiene must be maintained at all times to prevent the risk of cross-contamination. The following must be adhered at all times.

- A high standard of personal hygiene is required (hands must be kept scrupulously clean at all times, sticky dough will draw out any dirt from the hands and from under the nails).
- All equipment must be clean before use.
- All working surfaces must be clean before use and cleaned down thoroughly after use.
- All food stuffs should be stored correctly in a safe and hygienic manner.
- All waste food and other debris must be disposed off in accordance with laid-down procedures.

(*See* Maintain and promote hygiene in food storage, preparation and cooking, pp. 48–54.)

PREPARATION OF WORK AREAS

It is essential that the food production area and relevant equipment to be used is correctly prepared. In doing so it will enable the work to be carried our in an efficient and safe manner.

Preparation check list

- Keep work surfaces clean and dry at all times.
- Ensure that all mechanical equipment is clean, safe and kept in full working order with the necessary safeguards in place.
- Prepare and assemble the necessary moulds, tins and baking sheets.
- Assemble and measure required ingredients.
- Check that recipes and methods are clear and fully understood.

KEY WORDS

BFT Bulk fermentation time. This is the period of time from when the dough is made to the time when it has doubled in size and ready to knock back.

KNOCK BACK Also known as kneading. This is the process of conditioning the dough by removing the gases after BFT.

MDD Mechanical dough development. This is a means of reducing or eliminating the bulk fermentation time by mixing the dough in special high-speed mixers.

ADD Additive dough development. This is when chemicals are added to speed up the proving time.

GLAZING Glazing is done with a liquid made from boiled sugar and water and is carried out on some dough products to give them a gloss finish.

DOCKER A wooden disk with protruding points used to make small holes in pizza bases to prevent them from over-rising

DREDGER A container with small holes used to dust dough items with flour or icing sugar.

RIPE DOUGH A dough that has risen to the required size.

ROLLING Using a special rolling machine (also called a pastry brake) for rolling and shaping dough for pizzas.

ELEMENT 2
Cook basic dough products

INTRODUCTION

Dough can be cooked by baking and deep frying. Whatever method of cookery is applied, it is important that the temperature is preset and correct before cooking the dough.

BAKING DOUGH PRODUCTS

(*See* Baking, pp. 79.)

It is essential that ovens are prepared properly and set to the correct temperature before beginning to bake. The dough should be baked at the correct temperature and for the stated recipe time. The usual temperature to bake a bread dough properly is between 200°C and 245 °C. A lower temperature of 175 °C to 195 °C is used for enriched doughs.

COOKING TIP: When a crust forms, this is an indication that the bread is usually cooked. To test: loaves, rolls and buns should have a hollow sound when tapped. If they sound dense and feel heavy, there is still liquid inside and they will need to be baked longer.

Types of baked doughs products

Rolls and loaves These are produced from white, wholemeal or wheatmeal flour. Made with a basic dough they can be any size or shape.

Bun dough/enriched dough This is a basic dough enriched with egg yolk and sugar.

Pizza Originally from Italy, pizza is a savoury tart-like dish filled and finished in a multitude of ways to suit any particular taste.

Pitta and nan These are an unleavened breads mainly used in Eastern and Indian cooking.

Figure 173 Range of baked dough products

DEEP FRYING (DEEP FRIED DOUGH PRODUCTS)

(For more information on deep frying, see pp. 64–75).

Deep frying is the cooking of dough by submerging it in pre-heated oil or clarified fat. It is a fast process with temperatures of up to 190°C. The temperature must be sufficiently hot to brown the outside lightly as well as cooking the inside at the same time.

Doughnuts

Doughnuts are made with an enriched dough. Once cooked they are removed from the fryer and placed on absorbent paper on a wire rack to drain. They can be filled with jam or custard then finished by rolling them in caster sugar. The caster sugar can be flavoured with cinnamon or mixed spice.

COOLING

Remove food items from their containers (tins/trays) immediately and allow to cool on racks or wires. Air needs to circulate around the hot surface of the bread. As the bread cools the temperature will even out and the starch in the bread will solidify.

SAFETY

(See Maintain a safe and secure working environment, pp. 10–23.)

When working in a hot area, accidents can easily occur.

Always:

- use dry oven gloves/cloths to handle hot tins and trays;
- be aware of steam building up in ovens - stand back when opening the oven door;
- follow the manufacturer's instructions when lighting gas ovens.

Never: Overload the oven with dough products

STORAGE OF COOKED DOUGH PRODUCTS

Cooked dough products should be cooked completely before storage. Rolls, loaves, pitta and nan can be stored in sealed plastic bags in a refrigerator or in a dry store room. Enriched dough products should be stored on trays in a refrigerator and kept separate from raw and strong smelling/flavoured foods.

Bread rolls (*Petits pains*)

(approx 20 × 50 g)

Ingredients

500 g	strong flour
20 g	yeast
2 tspn	salt
25 g	fat or margarine, melted, not hot
300 ml	water or milk (37 °C to 38 °C)

Method

1. Separate ferment method. Sift the flour and salt in a mixing bowl or on a table. Cream the yeast and a little of the warm liquid in a separate bowl. When the yeast is completely dissolved, add approximately a quarter of the flour to make a very soft or slack dough or 'ferment'.
2. Knead well for 5 to 8 min. Place the mixture into a prover or in a warm place and cover with a cloth to allow it to rise until it doubles its original size.

Figure 174 Rolls cooling on a wire rack

3. Melt the fat or flour. When the ferment is ready, add it to the remaining flour along with the melted fat or margarine. Work into a dough, kneading for approximately 10 min.
4. Return the dough to the prover or in a warm place and allow to prove to 10 times its original size. When ready, cut into 50 g pieces, and mould into the required shape.
5. Place on baking sheets and eggwash carefully before allowing to prove again until 1½ times the starting size.
6. Cook in a moderately hot oven for 10 to 12 min until golden brown on top.

Bread loaves, small (*pains*)

Ingredients

750 g	good strong flour
25 g	yeast, fresh
25 g	fat or margarine
400 ml	water, warm
Pinch	salt

Method

1. Make a similar dough as for petits pains (as per bread roll recipe).
2. Knead well for 5 to 8 min. Place the mixture into a prover or in a warm place and cover with a cloth to allow it to rise until it doubles its original size.
3. Mould into the required size and shape.
4. Place on baking sheets and eggwash carefully before allowing to prove again until 1½ times the starting size.
5. Cook in a moderately hot oven for 10 to 12 min until golden brown on top.

Basic bun dough

(approx. 50 × 50 g buns)

Ingredients

1½ kg	strong flour
40 g	yeast, fresh
250 g	fat or margarine
150–250 g	caster sugar
4	eggs
500 ml	milk
Pinch	salt

Method

1. Place the yeast, sugar, liquid (temperature approx. 37°C) and roughly a quarter of the flour in a mixing bowl to make a ferment. Mix thoroughly and leave in a prover or warm place and allow it to rise.
2. Sift the remaining flour and salt and rub in the fat or margarine. Make a well in the centre and add the ferment (when ready) and eggs. Knead the dough well until it is completely smooth.
3. Leave and allow to rise for approximately 15 min, knock back and prove again for a further 15 min.
4. Scale and mould into 50 g pieces and place on a lightly greased baking sheet. Prove for a further 10 to 15 min in a prover or for 20 min in a warm place. Allow to rise to 1½ times their original size.
5. Bake in a moderately hot oven for 8 to10 min. Once removed from the oven, brush immediately with a bun glaze or bun wash.

Doughnuts (*Boules de Berlin*)

(approx. 25 × 75 g doughnuts)

Method

1. Make a dough mix (as per bun dough recipe on p. 262) and cut into 75 g portions. Mould into ball shapes and place on a well-floured surface or floured cloth.
2. Allow to prove fully. When ready, remove carefully with a palette knife and immerse in clean, deep fat or cooking oil (temperature 170 °C to 185 C). Test with a small piece of dough to make sure it is hot.
3. If the doughnut immediately rises to the surface of the fat the fat/cooking oil is not hot enough to use; if it sinks, the temperature is not hot enough. Turn regularly to avoid the float time.
4. Remove from fryer and place on absorbent paper on a wire rack to drain.
5. They can be finished by rolling in caster sugar flavoured with cinnamon or mixed spice.

Bun wash

Ingredients

Sugar
Water

Method

1. Boil together equal amounts of water and sugar.
2. Simmer until a light syrupy consistency is achieved. Cool immediately.

KEY WORDS

PROVERS Steam cabinets used to ferment yeast products.

LOADING The term given to the organising of oven space to maximise efficiency and economic use.

OVEN TRAYS Usually made from black wrought iron, steel or aluminum. They are never washed, but scraped and wiped clean as washing removes the non-stick surface. New trays are made non-stick by coating with a thin layer of oil and heating in a very hot oven.

DECK OVENS Specially designed ovens with top, bottom and front heat regulators used specifically for bread-making.

Activity

1. Name **five** dough products and specify what type of flour is used for each.
2. List and briefly describe each stage of dough-making.
3. Name **three** strengths of flour and give an example of what each might be used for.
4. What effect do the following finishing methods have on the final product:

   (a) dusting

   (b) egg wash

   (i) with egg yolk

   (ii) with egg white
5. What are the advantages of using pre-mixes?
6. What points of hygiene should be observed to prevent cross-contamination?
7. List **three** points of safety to observe when working in a hot area.

   (a)

   (b)

   (c)
8. In your own words, explain why it is important to keep cooking areas and equipment hygienic when preparing and cooking dough products.
9. Why is time and temperature important when preparing dough products?

NVQ SVQ 2

Prepare and cook basic pastry dishes

ELEMENT 1
Prepare basic pastry

Figure 175 Cooked pastry product

(See Maintain and promote hygiene in Food storage preparation and cooking, pp. 48–54.)

INTRODUCTION

The term pastry covers a wide range of products, both sweet and savoury. Pastry preparation is a specialised activity which should be carried out in a separate area of the kitchen for two main reasons:

1. to minimise the spread of infection through cross-contamination;
2. temperature control is critical to ensure that a good paste is achieved.

HYGIENE

The following rules **must** be adhered to at all times when preparing pastry.

- Ensure that a high standard of personal hygiene is maintained.
- All equipment and materials and areas must be clean before use.
- Cooked pastry products containing meat or fish, any meat or fish substitutes or vegetables encased in pastry should be stored below 8 °C preferably 3°C–5°C.
- All waste food and other rubbish is disposed of in accordance with laid-down procedures.

FLOURS USED IN PASTRY MAKING

It is important that the correct strength of flour is chosen when making pastry. The best choice for short and sugar pastry is a soft flour.

Sometimes a medium-strength flour is used in pastry making. This is a combination of equal quantities of strong and weak flour. It is mainly used in puff-pastry-making where the mellowness of British flour and the strength of Canadian flour combine to make a perfect product. Some cooks prefer to use strong flour for puff pastry. Choux paste is made with strong flour.

(For more information on flour see Dough, pp. 254–8.)

FATS USED IN PASTRY MAKING

Butter Butter is the most popular fat for pastry making as it gives the finest flavour. A disadvantage of butter is that it has a low melting point, making it difficult to blend and hard to handle.

Lard Refined from mainly pork fat, lard is excellent for shortcrust and for savoury pastries. It is seldom used in modern kitchens as it precludes certain sects and vegetarians.

Suet Originally prepared from the kidney fat of beef, it comes shredded and mixed with a little flour to stop it sticking together. It is used for suet pastry. A vegetarian alternative made from vegetable fat can now be purchased.

Margarine Produced from hydrogenated oil, it can be animal, vegetable or fish.

Pastry fat Specially prepared margarine ideal for use in the production of puff pastry. It has a higher melting point than normal margarine and is suited to excessive handling.

NOTE: When making vegetarian products always read the manufacturer's label to ascertain the origins of the oil.

Compound white fat This is a specially prepared fat used in the production of pastry. Compound white fats are based on vegetable oils that have been treated to raise their melting point.

Shortening This is a specially prepared fat, used in short pastry production to replace traditionally used lard.

TYPES OF PASTRY

Shortcrust This is normally made with two parts soft flour to one part mixture of lard and butter/margarine. It can also be made with equal measures of wholemeal flour and soft flour.

Sugar pastry (also known as sweet paste) This pastry is made by one of two methods:

1. the rub-in method – for pastry products such as tarts, pies and flans;
2. the creaming method – which can also be used for pastries, but is best suited to biscuit recipes.

Suet pastry This is made with plain flour, baking powder, suet, water and salt, which is lightly bound into a dough.

Choux This is made with a boiled dough and butter mixture, beaten with eggs.

Puff pastry Made with a medium or strong flour dough and laminated layers of fat, in total there are between 80 and 240 alternating layers of fat and dough. Puff pastry can be made in various ways.

- **French or star method** The basic dough is shaped into a ball. A cross is cut half way through the dough and the corners pulled out with a rolling pin to form a star shape, leaving the centre thick. The fat is placed in the centre and the star flaps folded over the top. It is then rolled out 1 cm thick and twice as long as it is wide, keeping the corners square. The dough is allowed to rest and relax in the refrigerator for 25 min before it is rolled out and folded as previously described. At this stage one half turn has been completed. Repeat the rolling and folding process until six half turns have been completed, allowing the pastry to rest and relax in between each turn.

- **Book or three fold method** The dough is rolled out 1 cm thick and twice as long as it is wide, keeping the corners square. The fat is evenly spread over two-thirds of the rolled-out dough. The remaining third is folded onto half of the covered piece and folded once more to form two fat and three dough layers. The edges are pressed down to secure. The dough is allowed to rest and relax in the refrigerator for 20 min the rolled out and folded as previously described. At this stage one half turn has been completed. Repeat the rolling and folding process until six half turns have been completed, allowing the pastry to rest and relax in between each turn.
- **Rough Puff (also known as Scotch puff)** This is made by lightly mixing pieces of fat into flour without rubbing in, adding water and mixing to a fairly stiff dough. Puff pastry can be made as full puff (using equal quantities of fat to flour), three-quarters puff (three-quarters fat to flour) and half puff (half fat to flour)

Figure 176 Making puff pastry

CONVENIENCE PASTRY PRODUCTS

Convenience pastries are readily available: frozen, chilled, packet mix. Always follow the manufacturer's instructions (on the packet) when using these products.

Figure 177 McDougall's range of convenience pastry products

KEY WORDS

RESTING/RELAXING The period (usually around 20 min) to relax the pastry in between each stage of production. Resting is important as it allows the gluten to relax.

GLUTEN An elastic substance that strengthens the cellular structure of bread.

RUBBING IN Lightly mixing the flour and fat into a breadcrumb texture.

KNEADING Vigorous manipulation of pastry to bring it to the correct texture.

CUTTING Using pastry cutters to shape pastry.

DUSTING Spreading a fine layer of flour or sugar over a pastry product to enhance presentation.

NOTE: Using too much flour to dust the product will cause an imbalance in the recipe.

ROLLING The action of lightly pinning or spreading out small amounts of pastry with the aid of a rolling pin.

SHAPING To mould pastry to the required shape.

LINING Lining is to make a pastry case from pastry that is rolled to a size slightly bigger than the case, ring or dish you are lining. The pastry needs to be held in shape with a removable inner liner filled with dried beans, peas or lentils and baked blind.

BLIND BAKING Baking pastry cases with a removable inner liner made from greaseproof paper or silicone paper which is filled with dried beans, peas or lentils. Forms a cooked or semi-cooked empty pastry case ready for filling.

GLAZING Brushing pastry with beaten egg yolk or sugar syrup in order to enhance the presentation.

COUCHES Cla sic term which refers to the layers in puff pastry.

FOLDING Folding is the action of creating a layering effect in pastry making (puff pastry).

COOKING TIP: Always select a good rolling pin without dents, bends and bows. Never push with a rolling pin as this stretches the pastry and will distort the shape and may also cause the pastry to crack during cooking. Try to roll pastry only once; the more it is re-rolled the tougher it will become.

ELEMENT 2
Cook basic pastry dishes

INTRODUCTION

For hygiene reasons it is paramount that the work area is properly prepared before starting work.

When cooking care must be taken with temperature: too high and the product will brown before cooking in the centre; too low and the fat in the pastry will melt and seep, ruining the appearance of the product.

The location of the items in the oven is critical. If they are placed too close to each other, the hot air will not be able to circulate around the pastry products properly and therefore they will be unevenly cooked. Too much top or low heat will result in burning, while placing certain pastry products (puff pastry and choux paste products) too near to the oven door will result in their collapsing (due to the loss of heat).

Short (savoury)	Short (sweet)	Sugar	Choux	Suet	Puff
Quiche	Fruit pies	Flans	Buns	Sweet/Savoury puddings	Sweet/Savoury pies
Pastries	Fruit tarts/tartlets Flans	Tarts	Eclairs Profiteroles	Roly Poly	

FILLING

When filling pastry products the following must be followed.

- Never overfill; always allow extra space for expansion during cooking.
- Always crimp the edges well to seal the pastry product.
- If a vent is called for, make sure that it is created. A vent allows steam to escape; if it is not made the pastry might explode.
- Make sure that baked pastry items are placed on a solid tray in the oven. If the tray is inadequate it might warp, spilling the contents.
- If filling before cooking ensure that the pastry has no cracks which might result in the filling leaking out during cooking.

COOKING TIP: If filling after cooking, do not over-fill. If using convenience fillings, i.e. custards etc., follow the manufacturer's instructions and make sure the filling is the right consistency.

COOKING

Pastry products are usually cooked by one of two methods:

1. baking;
2. steaming.

NOTE: Certain pastry goods such as choux may also be deep fried or shallow fried.

(For more information on baking see Baking, pp. 76–81.)

Baking

This is the cooking of foods in an oven by dry convected heat. The moisture within the food is heated sufficiently to produce steam which in turn modifies the dry air. Some pastry products and in particularly choux pastry, benefit by the introduction of steam as it helps to form the desirable surface crust.

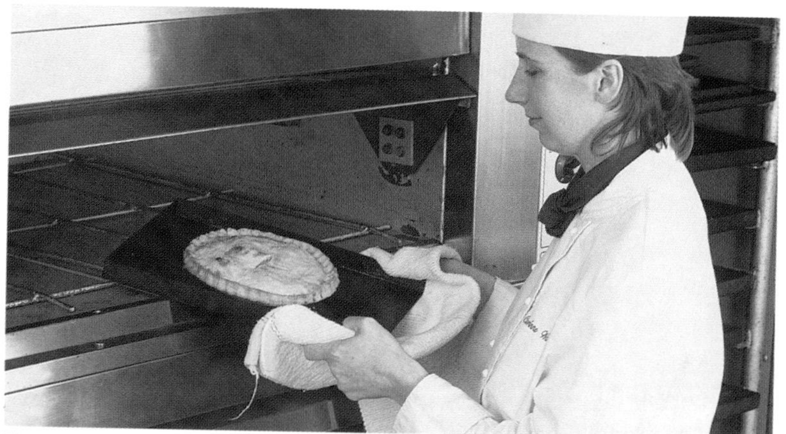

Figure 178 Taking cooked pastry product from oven

(For more information on steaming see *see* Steaming, pp. 87–8.)

Steaming

This is the cooking of food in vapourised water (100 °C) under varying degrees of pressure. Heat is transferred from the steam to the surface of the suet paste which enables it to cook.

Figure 179 Piping meringue

FINISHING

Pastry products can be finished off for presentation in a variety of ways.

Dusting

- Dusting can be done before or after baking. Dusting with icing sugar before baking has the effect of glazing the pastry product. Dusting after baking gives a light sugar coating.

Piping

Piping is sometimes called for in certain products, éclairs, buns, flans. Piping is a skill that needs to be practised often to ensure the best possible finish to the product.

- Semolina may be used to dust certain items, but only if stated in the recipe.
- Flour is sometimes used to dust some pastry items to give them a rustic effect. Use the minimum of flour as too much can affect the quality of the finished product.

Glazing

Glazing is achieved by one of the following methods:

- before baking lightly dust with icing sugar ;
- brushing with water, milk or egg or a mixture of all three before baking (a mixture of beaten egg yolk gives the best glazed effect);
- brushing with a boiled sugar and water mixture after baking;
- brushing with strained jam or jelly after baking.

Puff Pastry (*Pâte feuilletage*)

Ingredients

500 g	strong flour
500 g	unsalted butter
2½–3 dl	water, cold
5 g	salt
1 tspn	lemon juice

Method

1. Sift the flour and salt into a large bowl and rub in 50g butter. Make a well in the centre, add the water and lemon juice and mix together.
2. Knead to a smooth dough and roll into a ball. Cover with polythene or a damp cloth and place in the refrigerator to rest for 30 min.
3. Cut a cross in the dough half-way down, pull out the four corners (star-shape) leaving the centre fairly thick. Carefully roll out each corner to approximately a quarter of the thickness of the centre.
4. Knead or work the remaining butter to the same consistency and shape as the centre of the paste and place it on the centre. Fold over the rolled-out corners and enclose the butter completely to exclude any air.
5. With a rolling pin, press the paste to flatten it then roll it out in an oblong shape (60 cm × 20 cm), keeping the sides straight.
6. Fold the pastry into three, seal edges and roll out in the opposite direction and fold again in three. Wrap it in polythene again and place in the refrigerator for a further 30 min. The pastry has had two turns.
7. Remove pastry and repeat stages 5 and 6 twice more. The pastry would then have had six turns in all and a resting period of 30 min between each two turns.
8. Allow pastry to rest again before using or alternatively place it in polythene and refrigerate.

COOKING TIP: The pastry may be made with only four double turns by folding the two ends of the rolled-out paste to the centre and folding it over together.

Short pastry (*Pâte à foncer*)

Ingredients

500g	soft flour
120g	butter
120g	lard
pinch	salt
1 dl	water, cold

Method

1. Sieve the flour and salt into a large mixing bowl and rub in the butter and lard to a sandy texture.
2. Make a well in the centre and add enough water to bind the ingredients into a smooth paste.
3. Allow pastry to rest, covered, for 30 min, prior to use.

Sweet pastry (*Pâte sucré*)

Ingredients

500g	soft flour
250g	butter
2	eggs
120g	sugar
pinch	salt

Method

1. Sieve the flour and salt into a large mixing bowl and rub in the butter to a sandy texture.
2. Make a well in the centre and add the sugar and eggs and bind the ingredients into a smooth paste.
3. Allow pastry to rest, covered, for 30min, prior to use.

Suet paste

Ingredients

500g	medium flour, sieved
25g	baking powder
250g	prepared beef or vegetarian suet, chopped
pinch	salt
250ml	water, cold

Method

1. Sieve the flour, baking powder and salt into a large mixing bowl. Add the suet and mix in lightly. Make a well in the centre.
2. Add the water to the mixture and mix lightly to achieve a firm paste. If necessary add a little more water.

Chou paste (*Pâte à chou*)

Ingredients

300g	strong flour, sieved
250g	butter
15g	sugar
pinch	salt
½ litre	water
8	eggs, beaten

Method

1. Place the water, butter, sugar and salt in a saucepan. Bring to the boil slowly, the butter should be melted by the time the water is boiled.
2. Remove pan from heat and add the flour, mix in well. Return pan to heat and continue mixing until the mixture is smooth and does not stick to the sides of the pan. Allow to cool slightly.
3. Add the beaten eggs, a little at a time to the mixture and mix thoroughly.

Figure 180 Choux pastry in finished dish

KEY WORDS

HIGH RATIO FATS AND SUGAR
Specially manufactured to absorb higher than normal moisture content.

HIGH RATIO FLOUR
Special flour that is milled to a very fine particle size in order that it will absorb maximum moisture. When combined with high ratio fats and sugars it produces very economical pastry.

SLEEVES Specially designed moulds used to steam suet pastry items.

Activity

1. Name **four** types of pastry

2. Describe the method for making French or star pastry.

3. Pastry products are usually cooked by one of two methods, which are
   (a)
   (b)
4. Describe the cooking process or method.
5. How should:
   (a) cooked pastry cases be stored?
   (b) filled pastry products be stored?
6. Convenience pastries may be purchased either:
   (a)
   (b)
   (c)
7. List **four** points to observe when filling pastry products.
   (a)
   (b)
   (c)
   (d)
8. Explain the following.
   (a) kneading
   (b) baking blind
   (c) loading

(d) resting/relaxing

(e) couches

(f) dusting

9. Why is prepared pastry stored at a 'safe' temperature before cooking?

10. Explain how you can increase the fibre content of basic pastry and how it contributes to a healthier diet.

Prepare, cook and finish basic cakes, sponges and scones

ELEMENT 1
Prepare basic cakes, sponges and scones

INTRODUCTION

The preparation and production of cakes, sponges and scones is a specialist process and requires a wide range of skills and techniques, the essence of which is patience and attention to detail. Always read recipes thoroughly beforehand and select and measure all ingredients carefully and accurately to achieve the correct balance.

Most cakes, sponges and scones need to go into the oven as soon as they are mixed so always ensure that the oven is preheated otherwise the item will spoil.

HYGIENE

(See Maintain and promote hygiene in food storage, preparation and cooking pp. 48–54.)

The highest standards of general hygiene and personal hygiene must be adhered to at all times to guard against the possible risk of contamination and cross-contamination.

Always:

- ensure that all areas, equipment and utensils are clean before use and thoroughly cleaned after use;
- use the correct cleaning materials for their specific job and ensure that they are safely stored after use;
- ensure that all commodities and foodstuffs are stored in a safe and hygienic manner;
- dispose of waste produce and other rubbish in accordance with the laid-down procedures.

STORAGE

Dry commodities, e.g. flour, sugar, cereals and nuts, are prone to contamination and infestation by insects. It is vital that such items are always stored in well-sealed containers. Dry items must always be used in rotation.

Figure 181 Dry commodities

COOKING TIP: For the best possible results only use fresh, high-quality ingredients.

Fresh commodities used in the production of cakes, sponges and scones, e.g. eggs, cream, fats, are extremely prone to contamination so care must be taken to ensure that they are stored in a refrigerator or in a hygienic manner at all times.

TYPES OF FLOUR

It is important in the production of cakes, sponges and scones that the correct flour is always used otherwise the product will be ruined. Most cakes are made with plain, soft or self-raising flour; however, in some cases strong flour or a mixture of soft and strong flours may be used.

Soft flour

This is also known as cake flour and is made from weak flour which is low in gluten. It develops a lot less gluten than other flours and is ideal for sponges and cakes where a high degree of manipulation is not required.

Strong flour

This is made from a flour that has a high gluten content which is developed by manipulation giving a high tensile strength to any dough or paste which is made from it.

Self-raising flour

Self-raising flour is made from flour with the addition of baking powder. The baking powder reacts with the moisture to produce carbon dioxide. The bubbles of gas expand during baking making the product rise.

Scone flour

This specially prepared flour is made specifically for scone mixes. The basic scone flour recipe is made from 1 kg flour, 30 g cream of tartar or cream powder to 15 g of bicarbonate of soda, sifted together several times.

High-ratio flour

This is a flour which has been specially milled to produce a fine flour particle. It is this fineness of the grains which makes it more absorbent.

All-purpose or general flour

This is a blend of both strong and soft flours. It may be used for a wide range of products; however, it does not produce the same quality as single or unblended flour.

COOKING TIP: Always sift white flours before using them to incorporate air and make them easier to mix in.

Wholemeal and wheatmeal flours

These flours consist of the whole wheat grain and have a brown, grainy appearance. They have a much coarser texture than other flours and tend to absorb more liquid than white flour.

TYPES OF FATS

Fats used in baking are usually called 'shortening'. Fat has the effect of 'tenderising' the gluten and also adds flavour and moisture to the finished product.

Fats are used in recipes for the following reasons.

1. They enhance the flavour of the product, especially butter which is transferred to the finished item.
2. They shorten the gluten, giving the product a 'crisp' finish.
3. They help give a better yield. The addition of fat in the mixing process helps to hold air which when heated expands to give more volume.
4. They improve the overall appearance of the finished product.
5. They assist with the 'keeping' quality which enables the product to stay fresh for a longer period.

Butter

Butter is the most popular of fats used in baking because of its rich flavour. It has excellent creaming qualities; however, a disadvantage is that it has a low melting point.

Margarine

Margarine is produced by blending oils. It has an inferior flavour to butter but is easier to handle.

COOKING TIP: Fat can also add nutritional value to a product.

High ratio fats

These are specially prepared fats with the ability to absorb more liquid and sugar than normal fats. They cream more easily and in turn produce a lighter sponge and are more economical.

SUGAR

Primarily sugar is used to add sweetening to cakes, sponges and scones, however, it also has the following uses.

- **It tenderises and moistens** Sugar has the ability to absorb liquid from the mixture, preventing the formation of gluten and reducing the potential for evaporation. There are high-ratio sugars available that are very finely refined to absorb even more moisture.
- **It adds lightness** The creaming of fat and sugar creates air pockets. Caster or soft brown sugar give the best results.

Figure 182 Finished dish with browning

Browning

Cooking at high temperatures caramelises the sugar which gives the finished product a distinctive and attractive colour. Brown sugar gives a richer, darker colour than white sugar. A similar browning effect can be achieved using golden syrup, honey or treacle.

EGGS

These are available in four forms.

(See Prepare and cook basic egg dishes, pp. 225–32.)

- **Fresh hens eggs** Size 3 are generally used for baking. Never use stale eggs.
- **Frozen eggs** These are available as yolks, whites or mixed whole eggs. They save time but they need to be handled and stored carefully.
- **Dried albumen** This is used as a substitute for fresh egg white.
- **Dried, complete egg** – a substitute for fresh, whole egg.

RAISING AGENTS

Raising agents are required to give lift during the cooking process. The proportion of raising agent to mixture must be accurately calculated. If too much is used, the product will rise excessively and have a distorted shape. If too little is used, there will be little or no rise resulting in a flat and solid product.

Sodium bicarbonate (baking soda)

Baking soda starts a chemical reaction once liquid is added to a mixture. Carbon dioxide is produced forming bubbles which give rise to the mixture as it bakes. Baking soda can alter the taste and colour of the finished item, hence the use of cream of tartar.

Baking powder

Baking powder is made from baking soda and cream of tartar and has the same effect as baking soda. Baking powder does not affect the taste or colour of the finished product.

WARNING! Baking soda and baking powder have a limited shelf life and should not be kept for more than two to three months. They must always be stored in containers with tight-fitting lids.

MEASURING INGREDIENTS

In order to achieve the correct balance of ingredients it is essential that all quantities of ingredients are weighed accurately.

TIP: When using a measuring spoon for dry ingredients always level the surface with a knife.

Always:

- only use one set of measurements, i.e. metric or imperial;
- use weighing scales when measuring dry ingredients over 25 g;
- use a measuring jug for larger quantities of liquids with millilitres or fluid ounces.

TIP: Measure small quantities of liquid at eye level for an accurate measure.

Dry ingredients under 25 g may be measured using standard measuring spoons which are available in sets of 2.5 ml, 5 ml, 10 ml and 15 ml (or ¼ tspn, ½ tspn, 1 tspn, and 1 tbspn).

PREPARATION METHODS

Creaming

Cakes made by this method will be rich, moist, firm to the touch and light-textured. Creamed cakes contain half as much fat as flour, or more than half as much. The butter and sugar are beaten together with a wooden spoon or spatula until they are as pale and fluffy as whipped cream.

It is best to use caster or soft brown sugar when creaming mixtures as these have smaller crystals and blend quicker to produce a lighter texture to the finished product.

Method

1. Place the fat into a mixing bowl and using a non-metallic spatula or wooden spoon beat until it softens.
2. Add the sugar and beat until light and fluffy.
3. Add the beaten eggs gradually (ideally in four additions).
4. Add sieved flour, salt and spices.
5. Fold into the mixture carefully.
6. Add remaining ingredients if required by recipe, e.g. milk, fruit.

Figure 183 Creaming fat and sugar

Figure 184 Creaming fat, sugar and eggs

Figure 185 Folding in the flour

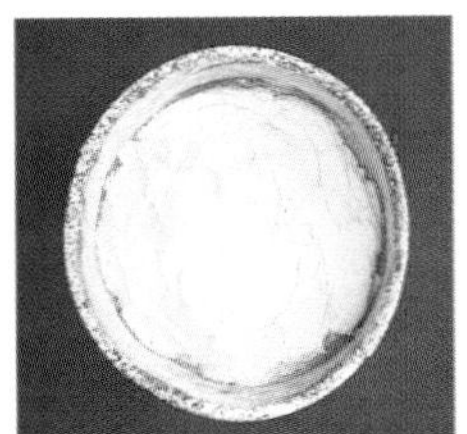

Figure 186 Finished mixture in cake tin

Figure 187 Removing cake from oven

Whisking

Cakes made by this method are the lightest of all sponge cakes e.g. Genoese. The cake rises simply because of the air incorporated during whisking. The eggs and caster sugar are whisked together before the flour is folded in. Whisked cakes should be eaten on the day they are baked as they do not keep well.

Method

1. Place sugar into a mixing bowl and add the egg.
2. Whisk briskly over a bowl of hot water (bain marie) until the mixture thickens and is lukewarm.
3. Remove bowl from hot water and whisk until it reaches the ribbon stage.
4. Gradually fold in the sieved flour lightly to form a smooth and fluffy blend.

Rub-in

This method produces cakes that have a soft, open texture (plain cakes). The proportion of fat to flour is half or less. The fat is rubbed in to the flour with the fingertips and thumbs. Cakes and scones made by this method may have the ingredients altered in order to make more economical or 'low-fat' cakes and scones.

Batter is used to make drop scones, cooked on a griddle.

Method

1. Sieve the flour into a mixing bowl and add the dry ingredients (with the exception of sugar), mix well.
2. Rub in the butter or margarine with the fingertips until mixture resembles fine breadcrumbs.
3. Add sugar and any fruit, stir well.
4. Make a well in the centre and add beaten egg and milk. Beat well.

ELEMENT 2

Cook and finish basic cakes, sponges and scones

INTRODUCTION

It is very easy to ruin prepared products by careless baking so it is essential to ensure that the correct oven temperature is preset and that the cooking time is adhered to. This should reduce the possibility of spoiling the finished product.

SAFETY

Items removed from the oven will be exceptionally hot.

Always:

- use thick, long, dry oven cloths;
- balance the baking sheet/tray properly;
- ensure that no part of the hand or arm comes into contact with hot baking sheets or trays.

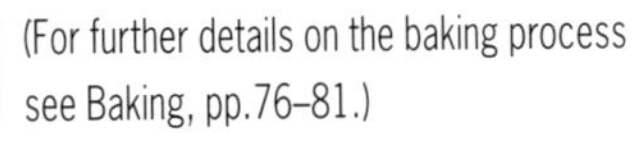

(For further details on the baking process see Baking, pp.76–81.)

Never: Use damp oven cloths, tea towels or cloths for removing items from the oven.

Common faults when cooking cakes, sponges and scones:

Problem	*Caused by*
Coarse/open texture	• too much raising agent • temperature too high during cooking • insufficient mixing
Close texture	• mixture not beaten enough • too much flour added • temperature too high or not high enough during cooking
Cracked crust	• temperature too high during cooking
Sunk in the middle	• temperature too high during cooking • oven door opened too frequently during cooking • product removed too soon from oven – undercooked
Large holes/uneven texture	• insufficient mixing • too much raising agent added • temperature too high during cooking
Crust too thick	• over-cooked • too much sugar used • oven temperature too low during cooking

CAKE TINS

Always choose a good-quality, strong cake tin. Cake tins are available in a variety of different shapes and sizes and some have non-stick surfaces with loose bases, making it easier to remove the cake.

It is essential to use the correct size cake tin specified in the recipe. If the tin is too big, the finished product will most likely be pale, flat and shrunken-looking. If it is too small, the cake will bulge over the sides and lose its contours.

When using a cake tin that is a different shape from that stated in the recipe, it is best to choose a tin that holds the same liquid capacity. If the correct-sized tin is not available use a slightly larger cake tin, however, the mixture will be shallower and will require less cooking time (test the cake approximately 5 to 10 min early).

Types of cake tins

Standard cake tins The most common everyday tins used are available in various sizes: 15 cm, 18 cm and 20.5 cm. For specialised celebration cakes larger tins are available.

Figure 188 Flan ring

Sandwich tins These are shallow, round tins with straight sides for making sandwich and layer cakes.

Moule à manaque tin This is a deep sandwich tin with sloping sides.

Spring-release tin These are available with alternative bases.`

Small cake tins and moulds These are available individually or in sheets of 6, 9 or 12. They contain shapes for sponge fingers and eclairs etc.

Flan rings (Savarin tins) These are available in a variety of forms. Round flan tins with plain or fluted sides and removable bases are generally used for pastry flan cases. A special flan tin with a raised base is used for making sponges.

Loaf tins These are used for cakes as well as breads and are available in 450g and 900g sizes.

Swiss roll tin This is a rectangular shallow tin.

Types of cakes

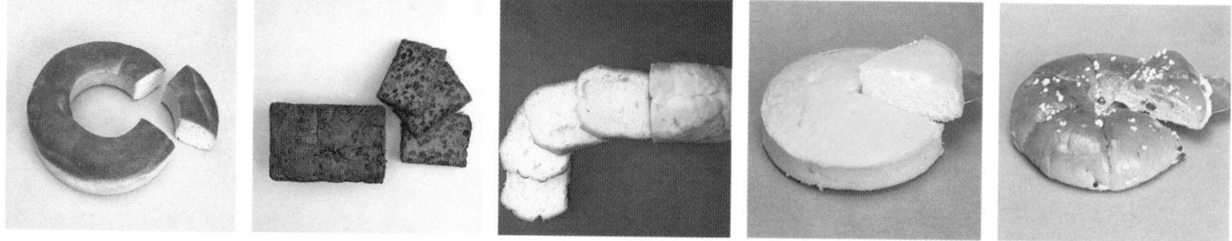

Figure 189 Different types of cake

LINING A CAKE TIN

Cake tins without a non-stick surface should be greased and lined prior to use. Non-stick cake tins do not need to be lined; however, they should be lightly greased and coated with sifted flour and caster sugar.

Line a sandwich tin as follows.

1. Place the tin on a sheet of greaseproof paper and draw around the base with a pencil.
2. Cut out the circle and fit into the base of the cake tin.

Line a deep tin as follows.

1. Lightly grease the tin with a little oil or fat.
2. Cut out a strip of greaseproof paper long enough to reach completely around the tin and wide enough to extend approxi mately 5 cm above the top of the tin.
3. Fold up one edge of the long strip approximately 2.5 cm, snip the folded portion at intervals.
4. Neatly place the strip in the tin with the cut edges in the base of the tin. Carefully place circle in the base over the cut edges to make a neat lining.

Testing the cake

Test whether the cake is done in the following way.

1. Insert a warmed skewer into the centre of the cake.
2. If it comes out clean the cake is ready. If not, the cake should be returned to the oven and re-tested at 10 min intervals.

Turning out and cooling products

NOTE: Some cakes are finished before cooking, e.g. Dundee cake (with almonds on top), chocolate chip cake, buns with glacé cherries.

When the product has been baked it should be removed from the baking tin or sheet and placed on an open cooling wire, in a cool and hygienic area, to allow air to circulate freely around the product. Any lining paper should be left on the hot item and removed once the item has completely cooled.

Storing cakes, sponges and scones

TIP: Store cakes and biscuits separately otherwise the biscuits will go soft.

Cakes should be stored as follows.

- When completely cold, place in a tin with an airtight seal.
- Fruit cakes should be wrapped in greaseproof paper and tin foil before being placed in an airtight container and stored.
- If the cake contains a fresh cream filling or decoration, store it in a refrigerator.

Freezing cakes, sponges and scones

TIP: Always unwrap cakes before thawing completely.

Undecorated cakes freeze relatively well. The cake should be wrapped in freezer wrapping paper and sealed tightly. Decorated cakes should be placed in the freezer without wrapping until they become firm to the touch and then wrapped in freezer paper and placed in a suitable container, e.g. polythene.

ELEMENT 3

Decorate basic cakes, sponges and scones

(For further details on the baking process see Baking, pp.76–81.)

TIP: Practice makes perfect!

(See Maintain and promote hygiene in food storage, preparation and cooking, pp. 48–54.)

INTRODUCTION

Decorating cakes and sponges is a highly skilled craft which takes considerable time and patience to learn properly.

The following should be remembed when decorating.

- Have the proper equipment to hand.
- Plan designs beforehand.
- Start with simple ideas.
- Do not use too many colours.
- Allow sufficient time for drying.
- If possible, practise your design and techniques on a cake board or cake dummy.

HYGIENE

The fillings, coatings and toppings on cakes and sponges can be made from fresh cream or butter cream and require special attention during preparation.

Always:

- wash hands thoroughly before starting work;
- only use clean equipment and utensils;
- use the freshest, quality products;
- do not handle the fillings too much.

STORAGE

It is important that finished sponges and cakes are stored properly. Fruit cakes with simple jam, marzipan and royal icing should be stored in air tight containers. Fresh cream or cream-substitute products should be stored in refrigerators or chilled display units.

TYPES OF FILLINGS, COATINGS AND TOPPINGS

Filling	Coating/Topping
Cream based	Fondant
Fruit based	Royal icing
Butter cream	Water icing
Boiled buttercream	Cream
Chocolate/ganache	Cream and additions
	Butter cream
	Boiled butter cream

Jam

Jam should be beaten thoroughly and, in most cases, strained through a sieve to remove the seeds to give a smooth texture. It is generally used for spreading over cakes and sponges and may be spread with a straight-edged palette knife or alternatively piped in a pattern using a piping bag and nozzle.

Piping gel

This is a convenience product available in a number of colours and used in a similar way to jam or icing sugar.

Fondant

This may be purchased in convenience form or made fresh. Boiled sugar and glucose are mixed together at a temperature of 102°C and worked to a soft white cream or a marble slab. Fondant is heated to blood temperature to spread.

Sugarpaste

This may be used to ice all types of cakes. It is soft and pliable enough for moulding into all types of sugar decorations.

Royal icing

A traditional icing used to cover celebration cakes, it may be used for flat, peaked icing or piping, according to the consistency.

Convenience icing

This is a ready-made product which may be purchased in slab form and used to cover cakes and sponges.

NOTE: Some butter cream recipes use eggs. However, in cases where the cakes or sponges are stored above 10°C this is not good practice due to the risk of salmonella in uncooked eggs.

Butter cream

A butter cream filling should be as smooth as possible and 'lump' free. The best results can be achieved in the following ways.

- Use unsalted butter to enhance the overall flavour.
- To correct butter creams that have separated, beat gently over a low heat.
- Use correct temperatures to give a better consistency.
- Store butter creams covered and separate from strong-smelling foods.
- Only keep butter creams for the minimum of time.

Fresh cream

Fresh cream may be whipped by hand or with an electric whisk.

The following must be adhered to at all times:

- All equipment, utensils, tools, piping bags, nozzles etc. must be kept scrupulously clean.
- All dairy cream products should be stored under cool conditions, preferably in a refrigerator.
- Fresh cream may be frozen, but the emulsion will break down and it will not be able to be whipped to a foam upon defrosting.

- Fresh cream can be a source of food poisoning. Care must be taken when handling it.
- Store fresh cream at 4°C for a maximum of five days.
- Keep containers of cream hygienically covered until required.
- Maintain high standards of personal hygiene.

NOTE: A high temperature can cause cream to turn to butter.

Types of fresh cream

Whipping cream This contains 35% butterfat and when whipped produces a light high-yield firm foam.

Double cream This contains 48% butterfat. It produces a lower yield but has a firmer foam.

Synthetic cream This is a convenience non-dairy product used as a substitute for fresh cream.

Creaming method

Victoria Sandwich

Ingredients

100g	butter or margarine
100g	caster sugar
2	eggs
100g	self-raising flour

Filling

4 tbspn	jam
	caster sugar to dredge

Method

1. Grease two 18cm sandwich tins and line the base of each tin with greaseproof paper.
2. Place the butter or margarine and sugar into a mixing bowl and cream together with a wooden spoon until pale and fluffy.
3. Add the egg a little at a time and beat well after each addition.
4. Gradually sift the flour onto the mixture and fold in quickly.
5. Divide the mixture between the two sandwich tins and lightly smooth the surface of the mixture with a palette knife.
6. Place both cakes in a preheated oven for approximately 20 min or until they are well risen and begin to shrink away from the sides of the tins.
7. Allow cakes to cool completely before sandwiching them together with the jam. Dredge caster sugar over the top.

Rub-in method

Scones

Ingredients

225g	self-raising flour
30g	butter or margarine
5ml	baking powder
150ml	milk approx
Pinch	salt
1	egg, beaten to glaze

Figure 190 Scones on a plate

Method

1. Sift together the flour, baking powder and salt into a mixing bowl. Cut the butter or margarine into small pieces and add to the flour.
2. Rub in the butter or margarine until the mixture resembles fine breadcrumbs. Make a well in the centre and stir in a little milk to make a fairly soft dough.
3. Place the dough on a floured work surface and knead lightly to remove any cracks.
4. Roll out the dough to approximately 2cm thick. Cut into rounds with a cutter or cut into triangles with a sharp knife.
5. Place on a preheated baking shet and brush with beaten egg to glaze. Bake for approximateley 20 mins.
6. Remove from oven. Allow to cool on a wire rack. Variation: To make fruit scones add 60g of washed and dried sultanas, raisins, currants or mixed fruit to the basic mixture.

Whisked method

Swiss roll mix

Ingredients

4	eggs
100 g	caster sugar
100 g	plain flour

Method

1. Place the eggs and sugar in a mixing bowl and stand over a saucepan of hot water.
2. Whisk the eggs and sugar together until they have doubled in volume and are thick enough to leave a thick trail on the surface when the whisk is lifted.
3. Remove bowl from heat and continue whisking for five minutes until the mixture is cooler and creamy.
4. Sift half the flour over the mixture and fold in lightly, using a metal spoon. Sift and fold in the remaining flour.
5. Pour mixture into the prepared Swiss roll tin and tilt to distribute the mixture evenly. Do not smooth the surface of the mixture as this will force out the air bubbles.
6. Place in preheated oven for approximately 6 min until firm but springy to the touch.
7. Turn out on to a sheet of greaseproof, silicon paper sprinkled with caster sugar. Trim sides and ends with a sharp knife. Evenly spread with warm jam.
8. Roll into a fairly tight roll in the paper. Allow to cool completely on a wire rack and remove from the paper.

Royal icing

Ingredients

2	egg whites
1 ml	lemon juice
500 g	Icing sugar, sieved
5 ml	glycerine

Figure 191 Cake iced with a royal icing

Method

1. Place the lemon juice and egg whites in a large mixing bowl.
2. Sift some of the icing sugar into the bowl. Using a wooden spoon, stir the icing sugar into the egg whites and lemon juice.
3. Add more icing sugar until the mixture resembles the consistency of thick cream. Beat well.
4. Leave to stand to allow air bubbles to surface.

* Best prepared well in advance of use to ensure there is no air left in the mix.

Sugarpaste

Ingredients

1	egg white
30 ml	liquid glucose
600 g	icing sugar, sieved

Method

1. Place the egg white in a mixing bowl and add the liquid glucose.
2. Sift the icing sugar into the bowl and stir the icing sugar, egg white and liquid glucose together.
3. When the mixture begins to bind together use the fingers to form the mixture into a ball shape.
4. Transfer to a lightly covered icing-sugared surface and knead until it is smooth and silky.

Rich fruit cake

Ingredients

450 g	currants
225 g	seedless raisins
100 g	sultanas
225 g	plain flour
5 ml	salt
225 g	soft brown sugar
225 g	butter, unsalted
4	eggs
100 g	almonds, blanched
100 g	candied orange peel
4 tbspn	brandy
1 orange	grated rind and juice
1 tspn	cinnamon
1 tspn	grated nutmeg

Method

1. Place the currants, sultanas, raisins, and orange peel into a large mixing bowl, stir well. Stir in the brandy. Cover and leave overnight.
2. Sift the flour, spices and salt together into a large mixing bowl.
3. Cream the sugar and butter until it is pale and creamy.
4. Beat the eggs individually into the butter mixture, beat well after each addition.
5. Fold in the flour and spices. Stir in the soaked fruit, almonds and orange rind and juice until all ingredients are combined.
6. Transfer the mixture to a prepared cake tin and level the top. Place a sheet of non-stick paper over the top of the cake and bake for approximately 4 to 4½ hours in a preheated oven, 1½ hours at 160 °C, 1 hour at 150 °C and 1½ hours at 140 °C.
7. Allow to cool completely on a wire rack before removing the cake from the tin.

KEY WORDS

BAKING POWDER Made with one part bicarbonate of soda and two parts cream of tartar.

BLOOM The term used to measure the quality of the surface appearance of a finished product.

COAGULATION The solidification of protein during the cooking process.

COATING The process of applying coatings to a cake or sponge.

CUT AND FOLD The method of gently mixing flour into a light mixture without losing any lightness.

COATING The process of applying coatings to a cake or sponge.

DUSTING/DREDGING Shaking icing sugar through a fine chinois, sieve or dredger over cakes and sponges to produce an attractive effect.

FILLING A chosen filling is piped or spread on the layers of sponge to add flavour and moisten.

GLUTEN The protein formed when water is added to wheat flour.

RAISING AGENT An ingredient added to a mixture that allows it to rise. The agent may be mechanical (whisking), chemical (baking powder) or biological (yeast).

RECOVERY TIME The time required for the oven to reach the correct temperature between bakes.

SHORTENING Fats used in the baking process.

SPLITTING Using a long knife to cut a sponge or cake into a number of layers

SPREADING Applying cream or jam to the surface of a sponge or cake.

SMOOTHING To level off cream or butter cream on the surface of a sponge or cake with a palette knife.

TRIMMING It is essential that cakes and sponges are trimmed to ensure that they are uniform.

Activity

1. Name **six** types of flour and their uses:

   (a)
   (b)
   (c)
   (d)
   (e)
   (f)

2. Why should flour be sifted before use?

3. List **three** reasons why fats are used in baking:

   (a)
   (b)
   (c)

4. Why must all ingredients be accurately measured?

5.List four points of hygiene to observe when using fresh cream:

   (a)
   (b)
   (c)
   (d)

6. How do you store:

   (a) Dry commodities

   (b) Fresh commodities

7. Temperature control levels are determined by which two factors:

   (a)

   (b)

8. State the preparation methods for the following:

   (a) Creaming:

   (b) Whisking:

   (c) Rub-in:

Receive, handle and store food deliveries

ELEMENT 1
Receive and handle food deliveries

INTRODUCTION

Most large kitchens have a stores with an appointed storekeeper in charge. The stores should stock a sufficient supply of non-perishable commodities. Some foods, in particular fresh produce, should be ordered and purchased, whenever possible, on a daily basis.

The stores is a major department and its role it is to receive and issue stock to other departments.

Figure 192 Kichen stores (A)

Figure 193 Kichen stores (B)

Figure 194 Kichen stores (C)

THE STOREKEEPER

The storekeeper is responsible for:

- coordinating orders;
- sorting orders for various suppliers;
- procuring the best prices;
- checking quality and quantity of incoming and outgoing stock.

Other duties include:

- maintaining accurate records;
- keeping up-to-date with current commodity prices;
- keeping an ample supply of goods in store;
- maintaining adequate storage space for in situ and incoming provisions;
- disposing of all expired stock and recording accordingly;
- ensuring that orders are delivered and despatched on time;
- maintaining a good standard of hygiene in stores.

NOTES:

- **All chilled and frozen foods must be checked for temperature on delivery and the temperature recorded.**
- **All deliveries must be checked for quantity and quality against the order.**
- **Records should be kept of orders placed over the telephone.**

SAFETY

Storing commodities can be hazardous. Large and heavy sacks and boxes may be required to be lifted onto shelves or into fridges and freezers and should be carried properly so as to not cause an accident or personal injury. They should also be stacked safely and securely so as not to fall and cause injury.

(*See*: Maintaining a safe and secure working environment, Element 3, pp. 17–20

CONTROL SYSTEMS IN STORES

For a stores to function effectively there must be a system for recording:

- incoming stores;
- stores held in stock;
- outgoing stores.

INTERNAL ADMINISTRATION

Departmental requisition forms Usually in duplicate, the chef de partie fills them in to order supplies from stores. They must have the date, quantity and an authorisation signature.

Order book This is used by the storekeeper to record provisions ordered (usually in triplicate). The top copy goes to the supplier.

Stocksheets These are used for recording the actual stock held in the stores. They can be easily audited to ensure there is no loss through unnecessary wastage, pilfering or deception.

Stores ledger This is a loose leaf file allocating one ledger sheet per item, to record quantities held in stock.

Bin cards These are displayed on bins, buckets or in areas where an item is stored in stock. Each time an item is drawn from stores, it is recorded on a bin card.

EXTERNAL ADMINISTRATION

Delivery note This is sent with the goods supplied. Always check that:

- everything ordered has been delivered;
- correct quantity/weight/item(s) are received.

NOTE: Accurate records must be maintained regarding any amendments made.

Credit note This advises clients on any allowances or adjustments to be made, for example, for over-charging or returned goods.

Invoice Usually sent on the day the goods are dispatched, this is a bill sent to the customer, setting out goods supplied together with costings.

Statement This is a summary of all invoices and credit notes detailing monies outstanding and credits for previous accounting periods.

Activity

1. State what procedures are followed for issuing stores in your establishment.
2. Make a list of fresh meat, poultry, fish and vegetables, that your establishment uses. Speak to your supervisor or chef and add the price per unit.
3. What food items should be delivered:
   daily?
   weekly?
   other?
4. Find out which goods are delivered in:
   sacks;
   boxes;
   plastic packaging;
   paper packaging.

ELEMENT 2
Store food deliveries

INTRODUCTION

A great deal of care must be taken when planning and equipping a storeroom area. The layout should be planned according to the flow of raw materials in and out of the storeroom area. Storage requirements for the range of commodities stored must also be taken into account.

PLANNING THE STORES

A well-planned stores should include the following features:

- It is secure to prevent unauthorised entry.
- It is conveniently situated for receiving and distributing provisions.
- It is easy to clean and maintain a good standard of hygiene to prevent the infestation of pests.
- It is kept cool and well ventilated.
- It has sufficient lighting, away from direct sunlight.
- It faces north and is free from dampness.
- It has adequate shelving and refrigeration space.
- It has sufficient and adequate storage containers.
- Appropriate sets of scales are available.
- There is an adequate and comfortable area for the paperwork to be done.

Foods for storage can be divided into two categories:

Perishable foods all meats, poultry, game, offal, vegetables, fruit and dairy produce;

Dry goods cans, jars, bottles, bulk powders, bread and confectionery produce.

Storage containers

One of the most important ways to prevent contamination of food is to use the correct storage containers. Ideally, storage containers should be modular with wheels for easy manoeuvring and be made from plastic or coated metal (so as not to corrode), have tight-fitting lids (to prevent infestation from pests) and be labelled to record the contents.

Perishable storage

Food must be stored immediately and in the correct manner on arrival to prevent the deterioration of commodities and the risk of cross-contamination.

Perishable storage can be divided into five main areas:

1. Deep-freeze storage

Frozen foods should be checked on arrival to ensure that they are properly frozen and then stored away immediately. Chest cabinets or walk-in freezers are best suited for supplies of vegetables, meat, fish and shellfish.

Manufacturers guaranteed times are as follows.

Figure 195 Fish refrigerator with drawers

Freezer type	Most foods	Ice-cream
−6 °C (*) (domestic)	1 week	1 day
−12 °C (**) (commercial)	1 month	1 week
−18 °C(***) (commercial)	3 months	1 month

2. Cold room storage

The food is kept chilled and in peak condition for preparing and cooking. It should be stored correctly to prevent the risk of cross-contamination. Raw foods should be placed on the bottom shelves and must **never** be allowed to come into contact with cooked food. Cooked foods should be carefully wrapped and labelled with the date, a brief description of the food and be initialled.

3. Fresh fish storage

Ideally, fish should be stored in a separate refrigerator in trays on ice.

4. Vegetable storage

Vegetable stores should be cool and well-ventilated. Large establishments have cool rooms designed specifically for vegetable storage which keep a constant, even temperature.

Bins and racking facilities should be readily accessible for root vegetables

5. Dairy product storage

Dairy products should be refrigerated as soon as possible.

Rotating stock

Stock must be rotated so that old stock does not accumulate and perish. The golden rule is 'first in, first out'. Always make sure that foods are properly labelled.

STORAGE OF MEAT, POULTRY AND OFFAL

Bacon storage Bacon has a longer shelf life than fresh meat and may be stored for longer periods under refrigeration conditions. It should be kept separate from strong smelling foods (it tends to take on strong flavours). Freshly bought bacon cannot be frozen successfully; however, you can purchase frozen bacon which has been specially treated.

Lamb storage Joints and small cuts of lamb should be kept in meat trays in a refrigerator with the blood drained regularly.

Pork storage Pork should be kept in a refrigerator at between 3 °C and 5 °C, on meat trays, for a maximum of four days. The blood should be drained regularly.

Offal storage Offal should be stored on meat trays, in a refrigerator at between 3°and 5 °C for up to five days. The trays should be drained regularly to remove excess blood.

Poultry and game storage Poultry should be kept away from other foods to prevent cross-contamination. It should be kept refrigerated at a temperature of 3°C for a maximum of three days.

Most game is improved after a period of hanging and maturation. This helps to tenderise and develop the 'gamey' taste. Game is allowed to mature for between 2 and 10 days before consumption. Once it has 'matured' it should be drawn to remove the innards and either skinned if it is furred game or plucked if it is feathered game. It can deteriorate if it is not handled and stored correctly, ideally at a temperature of between 2 °C and 3° C. Once prepared, game birds should be placed in single layers on trays and not stacked on top of each other. Venison is hung and can be stored after drawing and skinning for up to 10 days at a temperature of between 2 °C and 3 °C. Hare and rabbit can be kept up to 3 days.

Frozen meat, poultry, game and offal

Frozen meat, poultry, game and offal should always be kept wrapped to avoid freezer burn. They should be kept at a temperature of below –18°C. Defrost on meat trays in a refrigerator at a temperature between 3 °C and 5 °C.

THAWING FROZEN FOODS

Always:

- allow plenty of time for the food to thaw;
- thaw the food on a dish or on a tray as this helps to collect any drips and stop the spread of cross-contamination;
- use thawed food quickly: it is more perishable than fresh food.

Hygiene hazards in refreezing

Refreezing is dangerous if the thawed food has spent any time at room temperature.

- Food can be refrozen provided there is still ice in the wrapping.
- If food is thawed in the fridge below 5 °C there is no risk of food poisoning

STORAGE OF FRESH FISH AND SHELLFISH

Fresh fish and shellfish are highly perishable. They should be kept at a temperature of 0 °C in separate fish refrigerators, which are less likely to be opened frequently, spoiling the fish and shellfish.

NOTE: Fresh fish and shellfish will keep fresh for a maximum of three days, after which time they will deteriorate rapidly.

STORAGE OF COOKED FOOD ITEMS

Cooked food should be cooled properly, wrapped and labelled with the contents and date when refrigerated, and then initialled.

STORAGE OF FRESH VEGETABLES

Observe the following rules to ensure that vegetables are kept at their best under storage conditions.

- If possible have vegetables delivered daily.
- Always use vegetables in rotation: use up older stock before using new.
- Storage rooms should be kept at a temperature of below 10°C, preferably between 4° C and 8°C.
- Root vegetables should be removed from sacks and plastic bags and stored in bins or racks away from direct sunlight.
- Green vegetables should be stored in a cool, well-ventilated room on racks.
- Salad items may be left in their containers and stored in a refrigerator.

AMBIENT STORAGE OF DRY GOODS

- Bread should be kept in a well-ventilated container with a lid. Cakes and biscuits should be kept in air-tight tins.
- Bottles, cans, jars and packets should be unpacked from boxes, inspected for damage and stacked on shelves.
- Canned foods should be inspected to make sure they have not blown and are in perfect condition. Dented cans should be used as soon as possible because, if left, they will rust and eventually puncture.
- Flour, cereal, dried fruits and pasta should be stored in containers with tight-fitting lids as they are prone to infestation from insects.
- Always check for expiry dates and discard all out-of-date stock immediately.

NOTE: Always store cleaning materials away from food, ideally in a separate store.

KEY WORD

BLOWN TINS The presence of gases either caused by bacterial action on the food or the enzymes in the food attacking the tin plate.

Activity

1. Why should frozen food be thawed in the refrigerator?
2. Find out or ask your supervisor why food should not be packed too tightly in a refrigerator.
3. Why must old stock be used before new stock?

Prepare and present food for cold presentation

ELEMENT 1

Prepare present sandwiches and canapés

INTRODUCTION

Sandwiches can be a dainty component of afternoon tea, or substantial enough for a meal. It was the fourth Earl of Sandwich (1718–92), a keen gambler who was credited with inventing the sandwich. He came up with the idea of taking sustaining nourishment quickly without having to vacate the gambling tables. Cheese or cold beef was placed between two slices of buttered bread and became so popular that it became known as the 'sandwich'.

HYGIENE

Sandwiches for presentation are best made as near to the time they are required as possible. If they are prepared early they should be properly wrapped and refrigerated.

All fillings used in sandwich-making must be:

- of a high quality;
- always fresh;
- thoroughly washed before use in the case of salad foods.

(*See* Maintain and promote hygiene in food preparation and cooking, pp. 51–4.)

Avoid cross-contamination by minimising the handling of foods. To avoid spoilage between preparation and consumption, sandwiches should be prepared quickly. Potential dangers are from cooked fillings which might become infected and in turn cause food poisoning.

Preparation areas and all equipment/utensils used in the preparation of sandwiches must be kept scrupulously clean at all times.

Sandwiches, rolls and similar bread products with fillings that contain meat, fish, egg, soft cheeses, vegetables and substances used as substitutes for meat, fish or egg must be kept at a temperature not exceeding 5°C.

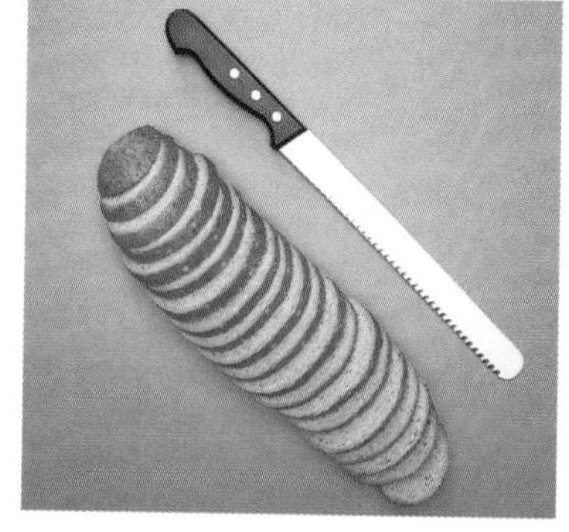

Figure 196 Bread with carving knife

SANDWICHES

The word sandwich also applies to other similar light snacks, some made with only one slice of bread (rye bread, pitta, crisp bread, French stick) in the form of an open sandwich, while others can be made with three or even four slices of bread or toast (a triple-decker sandwich).

Breads

(*See* Prepare cold and hot sandwiches and rolls, pp.121–2, for examples of bread.)

There is an enormous variety of different breads for sale that may be used in sandwich making and which come in a variety of shapes, sizes, flavours, textures and even colours!

Spreads

(*See* Prepare cold and hot sandwiches and rolls, pp. 122 for alternative spreads.)

The traditional sandwich spread is plain butter, flavoured butter or mayonnaise. Nowadays there are a number of 'healthy' options to choose from, such as low fat spreads and flavoured olive oil.

DIFFERENT TYPES OF SANDWICHES

Different types of sandwiches include:

- conventional sandwich;
- tea sandwich;
- buffet and reception sandwich;
- open sandwich (Smørrebrød);
- pinwheel (roulade) sandwich;
- continental sandwich (French sandwich);
- canapés;

Figure 197 Range of sandwiches

Conventional sandwiches

Also known as 'closed' or 'lunch-box' sandwiches these can be served for any occasion. They consist of two slices of bread (white, brown or white and brown), spread with a flavoured butter spread, filled and garnished.

Conventional fillings Seasoned meat (roast beef, lamb or pork); poultry (roast chicken, turkey, duck); cooked hams (smoked ham, boiled ham); cooked meat (corned-beef, salami, mortadella, liver-sausage, blood-sausage); tongue; chicken liver; liver pâté; gammon; game; fish (smoked salmon, fresh salmon, smoked trout, smoked herring, sardines, smoked eel); shellfish (prawns, lobster, shrimps); dry and creamed cheeses or eggs.

Some meats,e.g. cooked ham, may be served with a pickle or chutney. Other meats and fish may be flavoured with a thin spreading of plain or flavoured (tomato, tartare or anchovy) mayonnaise and/or mustard.

Garnishes Lettuce, tomatoes, watercress, mustard and cress, spring onions, radishes, gherkins, pickled and fresh cucumber, parsley.

Presentation Sandwiches can be cut into triangles, squares and fingers.

Tea sandwiches

Served for afternoon tea, they consist of two thin slices of (white, brown or white and brown) bread, spread with a plain butter, a light filling of thinly sliced cucumber, creamed and dry cheeses, pickles, sliced hard-boiled eggs, meat or fish pastes, meat or fish spreads, tomatoes or fresh tomato pureé, preserves or thinly sliced fruit.

Garnish This is as for conventional sandwiches.

Presentation Tea sandwiches usually have the crust removed (not always) before being cut into a variety of small shapes, for example, triangles, squares and fingers.

Buffet and reception sandwiches

These are served at buffets and receptions and consist of two slices of bread (white, brown or white and brown) spread with flavoured butter. Fillings are as for conventional sandwiches plus potted meat and fish.

Garnish This is as for conventional sandwiches.

Presentation The crusts are removed and they are cut into a variety of small neat shapes, for example, triangles, round, fingers, fluted, square or plain, using pastry cutters. This method, however, is extremely wasteful. Never re-use sandwiches that have been displayed on a buffet as they may be contaminated with germs, i.e. from sneezing, dust or coughing.

NOTE: Sandwiches for buffets used to be sprayed with aspic jelly or a similar gelatinous material to flavour and keep the sandwiches looking fresh. Caution should be observed when using aspic jelly as it is a favourable medium for bacterial growth.

Pinwheel or roulade sandwiches

These are sandwiches made from loaves of white or brown bread thinly sliced lengthways and spread with butter and a filling. Fillings consist of paste spreads or thin slices of meats, fish, vegetables or cheese. The roll is then sliced into individual 'wheels'.

Garnishes These include lettuce, tomatoes, watercress, mustard and cress, spring onions, radishes, gherkins.

Presentation These sandwiches are cut into rounds.

Continental sandwiches (French sandwich)

Usually served as a lunch-time snack and made with slices of baguette (French stick) cut in half lengthways or with slices of cottage loaf. These are spread with a flavoured butter and they are usually filled with either a single filling or a combination of various fillings.
Fillings and garnish This is as for conventional sandwiches.

Presentation Cut into small strips,these sandwiches may be eaten easily with one's fingers.

Open sandwiches

Also known as 'Smørrebrød', they are usually served as lunch-time snacks or on buffets. They may be made with sliced baguette (French stick), pumpernickel, bread rolls, rye, Vienna or regular loaves (flavoured bread may be used). The fillings are arranged on the slices of bread in a decorative style.

Fillings and garnish This is as for conventional sandwiches.

Presentation They may be attractively arranged on a serving flat or go straight onto a plate without covering.

Canapés

These are served at buffets and receptions. They may be made with a variety of thinly sliced toasts, crackers, water and/or cheese biscuits and short or puff pastry shapes (boats, squares or rounds). They may be arranged by hand or piped on top. They may be topped with piped plain or flavoured (tomato, tartare or anchovy) mayonnaise coloured butter, meat, fish or egg paste, cream cheese, smoked meat or fish, or exclusive cheeses.

Fillings and garnish This is as for conventional sandwiches.

Note: Traditional cold canapés were glazed with an aspic to enhance the colour and prevent the filling from drying out. This practice has diminished over the years for two reasons.

1. **Health and hygiene The temperature fluctuation involved in putting warm aspic onto chilled food provides excellent growth conditions for bacteria.**
2. **The distinctive flavour of aspic (made from gelatine and clarified stock) is considered to detract from the true flavour of the sandwich filling.**

PRODUCTION OF SANDWICHES

To produce large quantities of sandwiches for cold presentation the following rules should be observed :

1. Using a sandwich loaf, cut off the top, two sides and one end crust (leaving one end and the bottom crust attached).
2. Cut through the end crust down to the bottom (not right through).
3. Cut slices horizontally through the loaf (using a long bread knife) and use the end crust as a guard, piling the slices on top of each other on the top crust.

4. Spread half of the slices with butter, layering them out, and place the filling on top, arranging it near to the edge.
5. Butter the remaining slices and invert each onto the filling and press together.
6. Pile on the crust and trim the edges evenly.

To serve: cut into triangles, fingers or squares ready for garnishing.

If the sandwiches are to be stored for later use, wrap them in a clean damp cloth or dampened greaseproof paper.

Always:

- have fillings prepared and in separate containers;
- soften and cream the spread;
- have a container on hand for crusts and trimmings.

Prepare and present food for cold presentation

ELEMENT 2

Prepare and present cooked, cured and prepared foods

Figure 198 Cold presentation of food

(*See* Maintain and promote hygiene in food storage, preparation and cooking, pp 48–54.)

INTRODUCTION

Cold preparation involves the performance of any task from making canapés to presenting and arranging magnificent items of food for a buffet table. Whole joints of meat, poultry and whole fish may be carved by a chef in attendance.

In some establishments buffets are prepared every day for display in a refrigerated unit where people can help themselves in the knowledge that every measure has been taken to ensure that the food is not contaminated. However, other establishments lay buffets on ordinary tables in a restaurant where there is the risk of food becoming contaminated from exposure to the excessive heat, falling ash or coughing and sneezing.

HYGIENE

It is imperative that strict hygiene standards are maintained at all times during the preparation and storage of cold preparations. Particular attention should be taken regarding temperature controls. All food used in cold preparations (cooked or uncooked) will require to be refrigerated prior to being served.

When preparing food for cold preparation the following rules of hygiene should be followed.

1. Keep all preparation areas, equipment and utensils in a clean and hygienic manner at all times.
2. Due care and attention must be paid to the cleaning and trimming of all items for cold presentation. Ensure that vegetables and fruit are rinsed thoroughly in cold water to remove dirt and any insects. Only use the finest quality ingredients and never use old or stale food. Prepare ingredients and only use ingredients for immediate use, refrigerate other items for use later.
3. Cooked food for cold presentation, especially meats, needs to be cooked thoroughly to minimise the risk of contamination.
4. Once food has been arranged on or in serving dishes/bowls it should be garnished or dressed appropriately and placed in a refrigerated cabinet or fridge for service.

STORAGE

Food for cold presentation should be kept refrigerated at all times. When preparing food for cold presentation it should not be left for prolonged periods of time in the warm kitchen environment or at temperatures above 10°C. Some kitchens have special preparation rooms where the temperature never rises above 10°C. If the buffet table is not displayed in a refrigerated unit any unused food should be discarded. Never place unused food back in the fridge to be eaten later.

TYPES OF COLD PRESENTATIONS

Types of food to be served in cold preparation fall into the following categories:

- sandwiches, all filled bread rolls and canapés;
- cooked or cured fish and meats;
- pasta, rice, pulses;
- fruit salads;
- vegetables salads;
- savoury and sweet mousses, terrines, pâtés etc.;
- frozen or chilled cream and fruit mixes.

Cold preparation may form the following part of a meal:

- hors d'œuvre;
- buffet;
- sweet course.

Hors d'œuvre

Hors d'œuvre are intended as a first course, an appetiser to stimulate the appetite. They are usually served at luncheon and may be an individual portion of, or a selection of, hard-boiled eggs napped with a cold sauce, usually mayonnaise; pasta, pulse or rice salad; raw fruit bound in a dressing or cold sauce; cooked or raw vegetable salad; cooked, pickled, raw or smoked fish; cooked or smoked meats; poultry or game; pâtés or terrines. Some non-vegetable-type hors d'œuvre such as cantaloupe melon, caviar, smoked salmon and oysters are also served at dinner. There are two different types of hors d'œuvre.

1. Single hors d'œuvre (*hors d'œuvre singulier*) This is a single side dish usually served at dinner.
2. Selection of hors d'œuvre (*hors d'œuvre variés*) A selection of side dishes usually served at luncheon. Most salads can be served as part of *hors d'œuvre variés*.

NOTE: Hors d'œuvre variés may be displayed in a static refrigerated cabinet.

There is a third classification of hors d'œuvre, hot hors d'œuvre (*hors d'œuvre chauds*). These are usually seen on buffet menus though they are also be served for lunch or dinner. In Britain they are usually referred to as a 'hot savoury'.

Meat, poultry, game

Pâté

Pâté is a highly seasoned preparation of lean pork, streaky bacon, fat pork and liver served accompanied with hot melba toast.

Goose liver pâté

Pâté de foie gras is a delicacy made from goose liver, originally from Alsace, France.

Salami, cooked and smoked sausage

Salami and cooked and smoked sausages are sliced thinly and served cold either separately or as an assortment.

Mortadella (Italy)

This is a large oval shaped sausage, made from pork and veal with large pieces of pork fat.

Salami (Italy and Hungary)

Made from bacon, pork and beef, salami is highly seasoned and coloured with red wine. It is dried and cured.

Frankfurt

There are many varieties which are made from pork or ham. They are first dried, then smoked before boiling.

Liver sausage

This is made from a mixture of highly seasoned pigs' or calves' liver and minced pork.

Parma ham (*jambon de parme*)

A special Italian ham which is cut very thinly, Parma ham can be served with melon.

Smoked or cured ham

Jambon de Bayonne/Jambon de Westphalie is similar to, and treated as for, Parma ham.

Gulls' eggs

These are usually bought in already hard boiled and are accompanied by brown bread and butter.

Quails' eggs

Can be bought hard boiled and are usually served in aspic.

Vegetable hors d'œuvre

Figure 199 Vegetable hors d'œuvre

Most vegetable salads can be used as *hors d'œuvre variés*. Certain vegetables can be blanched in water then cooked 'al dente' in an *à la grecque* or Portugaise marinade.

Fish

Smoked eel

Smoked eels are served accompanied by prepared lemon wedges, brown bread and butter and horseradish sauce.

Caviar

Prepared from the roe of the various types of sturgeon, caviar originates from Russia, Iran or Romania. The best-known and most expensive varieties are Beluga, Ocietrova and Sevruga. It is imperative that caviar should be stored between 0 °C and 1 °C.

Caviar is served in a timbale or in its original jar on a bed of ice and accompanied by melba toast, butter, sieved egg yolks and egg whites, and prepared lemon wedges.

Smoked salmon

Smoked salmon is purchased ready prepared either as sides of smoked salmon or thinly sliced. It is served accompanied by prepared lemon wedges, brown bread and butter.

Smoked trout/smoked mackerel

Purchased ready prepared, smoked trout and mackerel are skinned, the heads removed and filleted. They are served accompanied by prepared lemon wedges, brown bread and butter and horseradish sauce.

Dressings and sauces

Dressings and sauces are used to bind ingredients together, add flavour, retain a fresh look to dishes and make dishes look attractive.

Examples are: mayonnaise, sour cream sauce, vinaigrette, French dressing, English dressing, Roquefort, lemon, fines herbes.

Chaudfroid sauce

This is a mixture of two parts béchamel, velouté or demi-glace to one part aspic jelly. The sauce and aspic is mixed thoroughly and used to coat items for cold buffets.

Marinades

Marinades are used to preserve, tenderise and give flavour to meat, game, fish and vegetables.

Examples of marinaded food are: soused herrings, rollmops, Greek-style and Portuguese-style vegetables, pickled beef, ham.

Buffets

Traditionally buffets were decorated with sculptured fats and carved ice images and the foods given height and prominence by using socles made from rice or semolina.

All buffet items should be attractively arranged, decorated and displayed in a refrigerated cabinet in the restaurant for the customers to choose from.

Buffets should consist of a selection of:

- meats: roast ribs of beef, pressed ham, gammons, ox tongues, legs of lamb, suckling pig;
- poultry: roast turkey breast, mousses, pâtés, galantines, spring chicken, supremes of chicken;
- fish: poached salmon, smoked trout, smoked salmon mousses;
- game: pheasant, venison;
- salads;
- eggs;
- cold sweets.

Some meats and fish are coated with a chaudfroid sauce and decorated with thin-cut vegetables, truffles and egg white, and, if required, glazed with aspic jelly.

Figure 200 Prepared salad

Salads

A salad is an agreeable combination of vegetables and/or fruit and/or meat, poultry, game or fish. It can be served as an hors d'œuvre, a main course, or an accompaniment to a main course.

There are two basic types of salads, broadly known as:

1. Simple or plain salad which consists of one main item, e.g. beetroot, tomato, cucumber bound with a dressing or sauce.
2. Compound or mixed salads which consist of several items marinaded and bound in a dressing or a sauce.

NOTE : There is a conflict of opinion as to which salads go into which category. Some chefs class coleslaw as a simple salad because traditionally it has a main vegetable, cabbage with a little shredded carrot, similar to potato salad.

(See Prepare and cook cold and hot desserts, pp.243–53.)

Cold sweet preparations

PRESENTATION

The presentation of cold preparations is of the utmost importance and all food should be attractively arranged and decorated and look appealing so as to stimulate the appetite.

Any mixtures, fillings or stuffings should be well seasoned and well flavoured.

KEY WORDS

ASPIC A clear jelly made from meat stock, gelatine and egg white.

CONCASSÉ Roughly chopped tomato flesh.

CURE To preserve items of food by smoking, salting or pickling.

GELATINE A preparation obtained from the bones, connective tissue, and collagen of calves and other animals. Available in powder or leaf form and used to set jelly, bavarois and mousse.

NAPPER To coat with sauce or aspic.

MAYONNAISE Made from an emulsion of egg yolks and oil and seasoned with English mustard, vinegar, salt and pepper.

SMØRREBRØD Scandinavian open sandwich.

Activity

1. What is the ideal method of presenting cold preparations?

2. Make a list of six hors d'œuvre that might complement each other on the same plate.

   (a)
   (b)
   (c)
   (d)
   (e)
   (f)

3. List eight smoked or cured continental sausages.

   (a)
   (b)
   (c)
   (d)
   (e)
   (f)
   (g)
   (h)

4. Using your cookery books or after discussion with your supervisor find out three uses for chaudfroid sauce.

   (a)
   (b)
   (c)

5. Describe what you consider to be a good selection for a buffet.

NVQ SVQ 2 Cook-chill food

ELEMENT 1

Portion, pack and blast-chill food

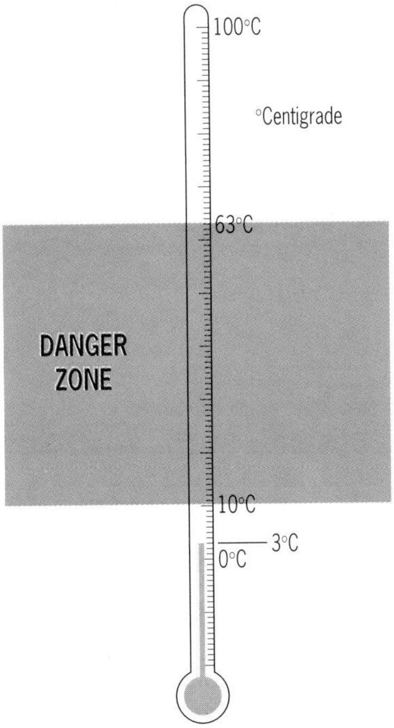

INTRODUCTION

Cook-chill is a procedure where food is cooked, chilled rapidly and stored in a controlled, low-temperature environment, between 0 °C and 3 °C at a central unit. It is then transported under refrigeration to satellite units for thorough reheating and consumption. Under normal temperature conditions the actions of micro-organisms, enzymic and chemical reactions on food cause rapid deterioration. Cook-chill prolongs the storage life of food by inhibiting the multiplication of bacteria and other micro-organisms and slowing down the chemical and enzymic reactions. Though food poisoning bacteria cannot be killed by chilling, the low temperature ensures that they cannot grow or reproduce.

100°C
°Centigrade
63°C
DANGER ZONE
10°C
3°C
0°C

Figure 201 Temperature zones: low temperatures that ensure food-poisoning bacteria cannot grow or reproduce

USES OF COOK-CHILL

Cook-chill foods are extensively used in industrial catering for multi-sited operations: night service and weekends, conference centres, banqueting, room service and staff catering. It is also used on a wide scale in aircraft and shipping operations, welfare catering, school meals and leisure centres.

SAFETY AND HYGIENE

The following rules of hygiene must be followed at all times when preparing cook-chilled foods.

- Maintain a high standard of personal hygiene.
- Clean all equipment, materials and areas before use.
- Take temperature checks and record regularly.
- Foods must be stored in the correct manner; if not, dispose of them.
- Discard food not consumed by its 'eat by' date.
- Dispose of all waste food and other rubbish in accordance with the laid-down procedures as prescribed in the Food Hygiene Safety Regulations (1995).

(See Maintain and promote hygiene in food preparation and cookery, pp. 51–4.)

The following rules of safety should be adhered to:

- Personnel should be trained to operate the equipment in a safe working manner.
- All equipment must be regularly serviced to ensure it is in safe working order.

Nutrition

With cook-chill the nutritional loss to vegetables (in particular Vitamin C) is greater and the loss increases the longer vegetables are cooked and held in store.

Health

The Department of Health (DoH) have designated guidelines for the production and storage of cook-chill foods. For details and further information refer to their leaflet entitled 'Guidelines on pre-cooked chilled foods'.

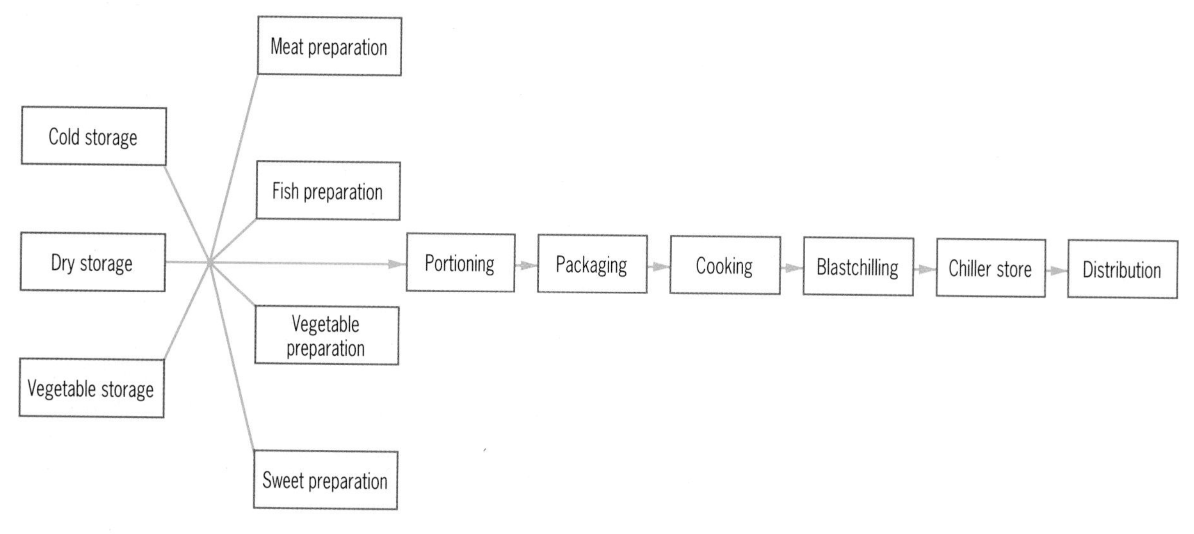

Figure 202 Cook-chill flow chart

COOK-CHILL PROCESS

The four processes are:

1. basic preparation;
2. initial cooking and portioning;
3. chilling and storage;
4. reheating/regenerating.

Basic preparation

It is essential that only top-quality raw ingredients are used and that they are stored at the correct temperature and humidity levels, under strict conditions of hygiene. All equipment used for temperature controlled storage should be fitted with accurate −5° C to +5°C thermometers.

All food items are suitable for the cook-chill process; however, particular combinations can withstand the changes in temperatures better than others and have an improved appearance and taste after reheating.

To avoid the possibility of cross-contamination, the food preparation area should be separate from the cooking area, as should the portioning and packaging area. Equipment and utensils for raw and cooked foods must be kept separate and identified by colour code.

Initial cooking and portioning

Careful planning must go into a cook-chill operation to ensure that foods are only kept for a minimum period of storage.

The maximum nutritional value of the food must be preserved. The method of cookery chosen must produce the most acceptable flavour and texture of the final product.

Particular care must be taken to ensure that the core/centre temperature of the cooking food reaches a minimum temperature of at least +70 °C; however, +75 °C is recommended by most of the experts in this field as a safer minimum temperature. Portioning should be carried out quickly (within 30 min), hygienically and in a separate working area from the cooking area and the temperature should not exceed +10°C.

Containers used in cook-chill

Once food has been cooked it can be placed in re-usable metal or ceramic containers or disposable ones made from foil, or special laminated plastic containers.

As well as portioning food to individual requirements, the size and shape of the container should be selected for fast chilling. The containers must be clearly labelled with the contents, net weight, date of cooking, number of portions, storage information and reheating instructions. The depth should be no more than 5 cm. The majority of this information must be put on using a bar-code system which may be read with a light pen.

Chilling

The DoH guidelines recommend that the chilling process commence within 30 min of cooking and that the food is reduced to a temperature of between 0°C and 3°C within a further period of 90 min. Temperatures should be monitored regularly and immediately adjusted to meet requirements.

The food must always be left uncovered while chilling, otherwise it may not reach its optimum temperature within the regulation time and will therefore have to be discarded.

Chilled foods must be stored in a special refrigeration area, apart from, and never next to, conventionally prepared foods.

EQUIPMENT USED IN COOK-CHILL OPERATIONS

To facilitate the passage from cooking to chilling, the equipment used to cook the food should match the capacity of the chilling equipment.

Cooking equipment

Figure 203 Steamer oven

Figure 204 Forced-air convection oven

Figure 205 Microwave

Atmospheric and high pressure steamers These steamers are ideal for reheating large quantities of cook-chilled foods

Bratt pans for boiling These pans are used for stewing, shallow frying and poaching.

Combination ovens These are ovens using more than one source of heat, usually convection and microwave or convection and infra-red grill.

Convection steamers These steamers use convected, super-heated steam to reduce baking, roasting, steaming and braising times.

Conveyor belts Conveyor belts help with portioning and speed up production cycles.

Forced-air convection ovens These ovens are used for baking, roasting and braising.

Infra-red ovens These ovens are specifically designed for regenerating foods and use high-intensity infra-red heat radiating from elements at the top and bottom of the oven. They are suitable for reheating individual or small quantities of chilled foods.

Microwave ovens These ovens are suitable for reheating individual or small quantities of chilled foods rapidly.

Pressure and automatic fryers These fryers have integral oil filters, basket lifting mechanisms and programmable controls for high performance in deep frying.

Régéthermic ovens These ovens are specially manufactured for the reconstitution/regeneration of cook-chilled foods.

Re-usable containers These containers store and protect the cooked, portioned item.

Steamed jacket kettles or boilers These are used for boiling. Temperature probes should be used to ensure that the centre/core of the food reaches a temperature of at least 70°C.

Tilting kettles These kettles are similar to steamed jacket kettles, with a tilting action from the vertical to the pouring position. They are ideal for continued batch cooking.

Chilling equipment

Blast chiller These chillers are sometimes known as air-blast chillers and are capable of taking large trolley loads of cooked foods. Low temperature air is passed along the trolley's shelves to chill cooked foods evenly and rapidly.

Cryogenic batch chilling tunnels These chilling tunnels use carbon dioxide (CO_2) or liquid nitrogen at a temperature of -196°C, which is sprayed into a chilling cabinet containing the warmed foods. The heat is quickly absorbed by the cold liquid or gas. The disadvantage of using carbon dioxide (CO_2) is that it is expensive.

Tunnel chillers/roll through chillers These chillers use a conveyor belt system to move the warm foods through rapidly-moving cold air.

Water chilling baths These baths are used to cool foods that are sealed in special plastic bags.

ADVANTAGES AND DISADVANTAGES OF COOK-CHILL

Advantages

1. **Prolonged storage life** The method enables a greater range of dishes to be produced without excessive wastage. Even though a temperature of 0 °C to 3 °C does not give a storage life comparable to frozen foods, it can ensure the preservation of cooked products in batches and, therefore, production can be scheduled to maximise use of equipment, staff, space and time.
2. **Bulk buying** Commodities can be bought in bulk for batch cooking, thereby reducing the food costs without lowering the quality.
3. **Staff costs** As fewer staff are required, cook-chill operations are less costly. Production, at more economic times, straight shifts, i.e. Monday to Friday daytime instead of split shifts and weekends etc., can be operated for skilled staff. This reduces energy costs, e.g. equipment is on only when it is being used and it is being used to its full capacity.
4. **Working conditions** Cook-chill operations allow the staff to prepare the food in a more methodical and relaxed atmosphere unlike in conventional kitchens, with peaks of activity leading up to and during service times.
5. **Equipment** Space is kept to a minimum thereby reducing capital costs.

Disadvantages

The specialised equipment required for cook-chill is very expensive to install.

The cook-chill process can affect the flavour and appearance of particular foods, for example:

- dishes containing starch can taste stale;
- fresh vegetables tend to discolour and take on a strong aroma;
- delicate meats, e.g. poultry and veal deteriorate after 2 to 3 days;
- meat dishes without sauces can develop acidic tastes;
- meat dishes in sauce nearing the end of their storage life tend to acquire a 'flat taste. If spiced, the spicey flavour can overwhelm the taste of the meat;
- oil oxidisation causes fatty meat and fish to develop 'off' flavours.

ELEMENT 2

Store cook-chill foods

INTRODUCTION

Personnel involved with the storage of cook-chilled foods must be appropriately trained (at NVQ Levels I and II in Food Preparation and Cooking) and able to uphold strict standards of professional practice.

Department of Health guidelines on storing hot and cold cook-chill foods state that:

1. Food should be held at or below +3 °C and never above +10 °C until reheated. If the food is at +5 °C, it must be consumed within 12 hours. It should not be held at below 0°C or it will freeze with a deterioration in appearance for presentation.
2. Reheating of the food should take place at or close to the point of consumption, as reheated food is as vulnerable as conventionally prepared food to contamination and loss of nutritional quality and palatability.
3. Under no circumstances should the food be reheated at a central point and then distributed hot unless the distribution times are less than 15 min from the commencement of service.
4. Suitable types of reheating equipment include infra-red, forced air ovens and steamers and steam convection ovens. Special chill reheat trolleys used in conduction and forced air convection ovens may be used but traditional types of hot-air ovens tend to dehydrate exposed areas of the food during reheating so care must be taken when using them.
5. Reheating of chilled food should begin as soon as possible and no longer than 30 min after the food is removed from the chiller. The food temperature should reach +70 °C and be maintained at this temperature for at least 2 min.

(For information on reheating equipment see Element 1, pp. 312–13.)

FOOD SERVICE

For quality reasons the service of food should be as soon as possible after reaching optimum temperature. The temperature must never be allowed to drop below +63 °C.

It is essential that any meals not consumed are destroyed and not reheated or returned to chilled storage.

Figure 206 Transportation of cook-chill food

COLD STORAGE EQUIPMENT

Refrigerators and cold storerooms maintain a temperature of below +3°C but not below 0 °C. These should be capable of taking complete trolley loads of food directly from the blast-chiller. They are usually fitted with special alarms to indicate any rise in temperature.

TRANSPORTING CHILLED FOODS

Food has to be transported from the central production kitchen to the satellite units, either hot or chilled. Hot food should be stored at a temperature of above +70°C and consumed within 2 hours of reheating. If the temperature of chilled food rises above +10°C during transport it should be destroyed.

Ideally, refrigerated vans (refrigerated eutectic holdover vans) should be used to distribute chilled foods between the central kitchen and the satellite units. These are heavily insulated vans which have a number of large eutectic (brine-filled) plates situated in the ceiling of the interior and, a refrigeration compressor motor that reduces these plates to the desired temperature. In most cases this compressor is run from a single or three-phase electricity supply in a 'plug in overnight' operation. While in transit a petrol or diesel motor is used to power the compressor. Alternatively there are two other methods provided the distribution period is fairly short.

1. **Insulated boxes** These are purpose-built and are used to transport and hold chilled food between the central kitchen and a satellite unit. With increased insulation the boxes are capable of holding the temperature, hot or cold for up to 3 h, however, this figure will depend on ambient temperature, traffic conditions and the initial temperature of the food.
2. **Insulated vans** These are, in fact, motorised insulated boxes, utilising either polystyrene insulation to keep food hot or cold or 'dry ice' to keep the foods chilled.

COLD STORAGE AFTER DELIVERY

To avoid the risk of contamination, it is essential that cook-chilled food be stored immediately on delivery and in a refrigerator which must be at a temperature between +1 °C and +3 °C. The refrigerator must be used solely for chilled foods as the constant opening and closing of normal refrigerators would increase the possibility of contamination from the fluctuation in temperature.

There are purpose-built chillers on the market designed specially to take régéthermic baskets and some are built to accommodate régéthermic trolleys that wheel in and out.

If the chilled food temperature rises above +5°C (below +9°C) it must be consumed within 12 hours. If the temperature rises above +10°C it must be discarded as instructed in the guidelines laid down by the Department of Health.

WARNING! Regenerated chilled foods that have not been consumed should be destroyed and never, under any circumstances, be reheated or returned to a chilled storage.

REHEATING, RECONSTITUTING AND REGENERATING

Cook-chill foods must be heated as quickly as possible to a minimum temperature of 70°C but, as with initial cooking, a more ideal temperature would be 75°C. This can be carried out in combi-ovens, infra-red ovens, microwaves and régéthermic ovens or steamers.

STOCK ROTATION

Cook-chill products have a very short life. It is therefore paramount that all food is appropriately labelled and an efficient and effective stock rotation system set in place.

MONITORING AND RECORDING TEMPERATURES

This can be carried out manually, by a person checking the temperature from a thermostat (hot foods) or with a thermometer (chilled foods) at regular intervals. This information must be correctly recorded on a chart.

Alternatively, there are a number of electronic devices available to do this job which are more efficient and precise. These are:

- a needle probe which is inserted into the food and read at regular intervals; some models provide a digital read-out and have an audible alarm fitted which sounds if the temperature rises;
- a device that can be fitted to a refrigerator and read from a 24 hour chart
- an appliance which is placed in a refrigerator and can be read with an infra-red device. This also gives a printed read out. The device is sometimes known as the 'plastic chicken'.

TEMPERATURE CONTROL RECORD SHEET

TEMPERATURE CONTROL RECORD SHEET

Equipment	Rec'd Temp	Date am pm	Date am pm	Date am pm	Date am pm	Date am pm	Date am pm	Date am pm
Hot Display Unit	+110°c							
Hot Food on Display	+73°c							
Cold Display Unit	<+5°c							
Cold Food on Display	+5°c							
Refrigerator (1)	<+5°c							
Refrigerator (2)								
Refrigerator (3)								
Refrigerator (4)								
Deep Freeze (1)	−18°c							
Deep Freeze (2)								
Deep Freeze (3)								
Deep Freeze (4)								
Walk-in Freezer	−18°c							
Walk-in Fridge	<+5°c							
Hot Food Sample*	>+70°c							

*Random sample of food as it is taken out of the oven/microwave.

PLEASE NOTE: The recommended temperatures are meant as guide only. You should refer to the manufacturer' instructions as equipment temperatures may vary slightly.

Figure 207 Temperature control record sheet

KEY WORDS

BLAST CHILLING
The rapid chilling of food in special chiller.

TIME BUFFER The term used for the extra time between preparation and service that the cook-chill systems can provide.

Activity

1. Give reasons why chilled food might be discarded.
2. What is the most effective method of distributing cook-chilled food?
3. Find out how effective your blast chiller is. Using the chart below, plot the decrease in temperature of a batch of hot cooked food to the optimum chilled temperature.

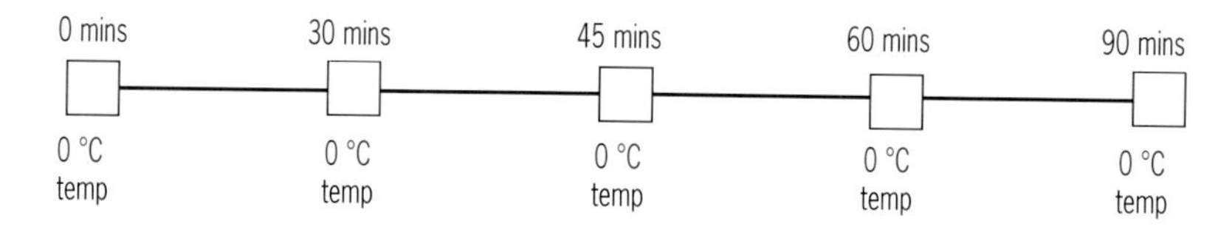

4. List six pieces of equipment suitable for the production and regeneration of cook-chilled foods.

NVQ SVQ 2

Cook-freeze food

ELEMENT 1
Portion and pack blast-freeze foods

INTRODUCTION

Cook-freeze is the procedure where food is centrally prepared, cooked, chilled and then frozen to a temperature of -18°C for distribution to satellite units for regeneration. The process is governed by the Department of Health (DoH) guidelines due to the considerable risks involved if the cook-freeze operation is not conducted properly.

The preparation and cooking process is the same as for cook-chill, though some recipes need to be modified to account for the action of freezing on cooked food.

Once the food is cooked, the freezing process must commence within 30 min of cooking and portioning. The food should reach a core temperature of at least –5 °C within 90 min of entering the freezer and –18 °C to –21°C subsequently but not below this.

Once the food has been frozen, it is stored in a cold store room at a temperature of between –18 °C and –20 °C from where it is distributed to satellite kitchens for regeneration and consumption.

COOKING TIP: The faster the freezing process the superior the food will be when regenerated.

USES OF COOK-FREEZE

Cook-freeze foods are extensively used in industrial catering for multi-sited operations: night service and weekends, conference centres, banqueting, room service and staff catering. It is also used on a wide scale in aircraft and shipping operations, welfare catering and school meals and leisure centres.

Figure 208 Aeroplane food

COOK-FREEZE: THE PROCESS

Not all foods can be successfully frozen and regenerated. In some foods, the changes in moisture dispersement within the raw material lead eventually to moisture losses on thawing, also bringing about certain irreversible physical changes in the constituted product. These products have to be treated with stabilisers. For example, the protein gel in untreated egg whites becomes de-natured, resulting in a toughened gel and yielding free water.

Recipes need to be reformulated to allow for changes in freezing. Sauces, gravies and soups are subject to similar problems and need to be specially prepared. Natural gums and modified starches are used as alternative thickening agents. They prevent curdling and separation of fats from solids and liquids.

COOKING TIP: A recirculation grinding mill is used to mix sauces, soups and gravies. This machine blends the thickened liquid into a smooth mix, thus eliminating large particles which could speed up separation.

Once cooked, the food needs to be portioned quickly. The DoH specify that once the food is cooked it should take no longer than 15 min (with the exception of meat which needs to 'set' for 15 min before being carved or sliced) to be portioned. When the food has been portioned and packed it is loaded onto trolleys which are then wheeled into a freezer.

THE EFFECTS OF FREEZING ON FOODS

Freezing prolongs the life of food by stopping or at least slowing down the processes of deterioration, and the lower the temperature, the more effective this is. To ensure that the frozen foods are kept at their peak and reduce the chance of spoilage the storage temperatures should be at a constant minimum of –18 °C and preferably as low as –30 °C.

Cook-freeze demands care and understanding to ensure that the benefits of the process outweigh the potential damages that can be caused, which are as follows:

- Some foods change in flavour, texture and colour.
- Meat eventually turns brownish grey if stored too long.
- Food structure can be severely damaged during the critical period when the ice crystals are forming.
- Freezing must be rapid to avoid damage to the food.

The processes that cause food to spoil or deteriorate are:

1. temperature;
2. exposure to air;
3. exposure to moisture.

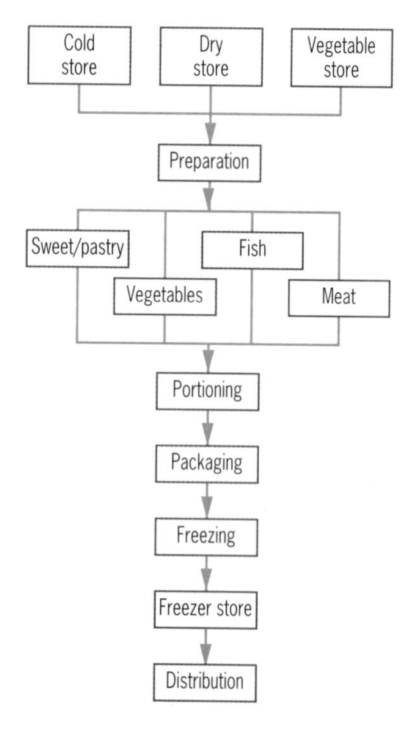

Figure 209 Cook-freeze flow chart

EQUIPMENT USED IN COOK-FREEZE

As in conventional catering, the equipment requirements in both the production and finishing kitchens need to be 'tailor-made' to match the menu.

Cooking equipment

(*See* Portioning and packing cook-chill foods, pp.312–313.)

PORTIONING AND PACKAGING

Pre-cooked frozen food must be protected from oxidisation (contact with excessive amounts of air) and from moisture loss.

The actual style and type of package used is governed by the use to which the product will be put and how regeneration will take place. Packaging comes in single-portion packs, complete meal packs and bulk packs.

Containers used to store frozen foods can be made from :

- special plastic compounds – vacuum-sealed pouches consisting of plastic made from materials that will withstand temperatures of up to 100°C;
- pressed aluminum foil – ideal for regeneration in conventional

NOTE: Labels are important for ensuring that different dishes can be identified by date of production and use-by date.

ovens, but not suitable for microwaves as they tend to distort and bend easily. Ideally they should be placed in ceramic dishes during regeneration;

- cardboard plastic laminates – made from high-density polythene over cardboard. These are suitable for microwave but they can also be used in conventional ovens.

FREEZING EQUIPMENT

Air-blast freezer

An insulated refrigerated tunnel in which refrigerated air is 'blasted' over the food at a velocity of approximately 5.0 m/s (metres per second). Blast freezers, sometimes known as air-blast freezers, are capable of taking large trolley-loads of cooked foods. The process involves passing low temperature air (between –32 °C and –40 °C) along the trolley's shelves freezing foods evenly and rapidly within 90 min.

Cryogenic freezers

An alternative method used for freezing is to spray carbon dioxide or liquid nitrogen at –196 °C over the food while it is being conveyed through a freezing tunnel absorbing the heat and quickly freezing the food. This is especially useful for freezing soft fruits as this process has the effect of almost instantaneous freezing.

NOTE: CO_2 freezing tunnels were originally designed for the freezing of fresh poultry. The disadvantage of using carbon dioxide (CO_2) is that it is expensive.

Tunnel freezers/roll through freezers

A conveyor belt system is used to move foods such as peas and sliced vegetables through rapidly-moving cold air.

THE PLATE SYSTEM

This is used to freeze fragile foods such as asparagus, broccoli, spinach. The food is held between hollow plates through which special refrigeration liquid is circulated.

THE FREEZING OF FOODS

Freezing meat and poultry

Freezing does not give an infinite life to foods, it merely extends the life. Even when the product is frozen, the enzymes present in the fat of meat and some poultry oxidise and deteriorate. Chicken fat on the other hand contains a natural antioxidant and does not spoil as quickly.

Covering the cooked food with a sauce or gravy can help to prolong the beneficial effects of freezing by excluding air, however, in general, cooked meats and poultry should never be kept frozen for more than three months.

Sauce recipes have to be modified as wheat flour has a tendency to split when frozen. A specially manufactured starch can be obtained commercially, or a waxy starch made from rice, maize or tapioca may be used. Egg yolks can also be used to thicken sauces, but care must be taken when regenerating not to use too high a temperature, otherwise they will break down and split.

Figure 210 Whole fish

Freezing fish

Fish has a delicate flavour and in freezing is prone to flavour loss while oily types of fish are likely to spoil due to fat oxidisation. The best way to preserve the delicate flavour of fish is to cover it with a sauce or a coating such as breadcrumbs or batter. Batter recipes also have to be modified, adding a waxy starch.

Protecting cooked fish dishes as recommended will give an expected freezer life of eight weeks. After that time the fats in the sauces and coating become rancid.

Freezing vegetables

Not all vegetables are suitable for freezing. The cellular structure of cucumber, tomatoes, lettuce and other salad vegetables disintegrates. Vegetables are only suitable for cook-freeze if they have been purchased and processed within 3 to 4 hours of harvesting.

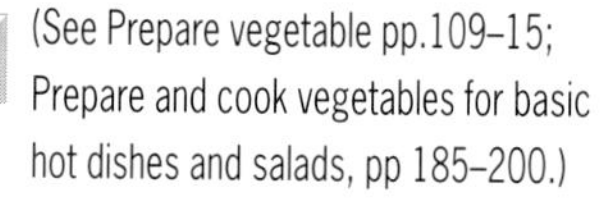

(See Prepare vegetable pp.109–15; Prepare and cook vegetables for basic hot dishes and salads, pp 185–200.)

The vegetables are blanched in a high-pressure steamer sufficiently to arrest the actions of enzymes and prevent them from creating an acidic flavour at a later stage. Blanching for too long will destroy the structure of the vegetables and make them appear limp; the green colour in vegetables fades and cauliflower goes yellow. Over-blanching will also destroy the vitamin content of the vegetables.

Cooked potato dishes are ideal for freezing. French fries and roast potatoes need to be blanched in a deep fryer before freezing. Duchesse potato extensions such as croquettes freeze particularly well.

Freezing fruit

(*See* Prepare fruit, pp. 116–20.)

Freezing has the effect of softening the texture of fruits. Fruits such as grapes or strawberries have a tendency to collapse when defrosted and lose their appeal. Sliced apples and peaches go brown unless they have been frozen in an acidulated liquid or syrup.

Freezing eggs, pasta and rice

Though frozen pasteurised scrambled eggs and hard-boiled eggs are commercially available, soft-boiled egg yolk changes into a stiff paste when frozen.

Pasta and rice should be frozen undercooked so that they do not overcook during regenerating.

Freezing desserts

In most cases, 'regular cooked' deserts that include cream, custard and fruit cannot be frozen successfully. The cream curdles, custard separates and the fruit tends to 'leak' and loose form when frozen. Frozen food companies use modified starches, natural gums and thickening agents and other chemicals to ensure that products freeze and thaw successfully.

ADVANTAGES AND DISADVANTAGES OF COOK-FREEZE

Advantages

1. Food production planning is easier and food wastage should be

NOTE: Frozen food must be protected against dehydration and oxidation by the use of moisture–vapour–proof, air-tight packaging. If ice builds up on the surface of the cooked food, it will suffer freezer burns. The ideal packaging is sealable plastic pouches into which the food is placed. The air is vacuumed out and in its place is placed an inert gas, usually CO_2, which helps to prevent spores from developing.

FACT: In 1928 Clarence Birdseye while on holiday in Labrador in Alaska noted how Eskimos preserved fish and meat by freezing it in the open air. The food froze quickly and kept indefinitely. Finding that the food was tender and fresh-tasting after months of storage he proceeded to experiment and found out how to recreate the same fast freezing action and so began the frozen-food industry.

cut down or eliminated. Production can be scheduled to optimise the use of equipment, reduce staff and maximise space and time. In addition, bulk or quantity buying of commodities for each batch cooking session greatly reduces costs without lowering quality.

2. Production times are not geared to services as straight shifts for skilled staff at more economic times can be operated. Conditions are also improved for staff; unlike conventional kitchens, with activity leading up to and during service times, cook-freeze operations allow the staff to prepare the food in a more orderly and relaxed atmosphere.

Disadvantages

1. Specialised cook-freeze equipment is very expensive to install and to run.
2. Some dishes containing starch can taste stale.

Figure 211 Eskimos in Alaska

KEY WORDS

BLAST FREEZING The rapid freezing of food using high-speed cold air to reduce the temperature quickly.

DEFROSTING Raising the temperature of the food slowly until it has reached its pre-frozen state.

INSTABILITY Some foods have a tendency to separate during the cook-freeze process and are deemed as 'unstable'.

RECRYSTALLISATION This is where similar, thawing ice crystals attach themselves to larger ice crystals and refreeze damaging the food. When frozen food is heated from its frozen state, unless it is to be served cold then it should only be thawed in the refrigerator.

REGENERATON The final stage in the cook-freeze process when the thawed food is quickly heated to a safe temperature for consumption.

INTRODUCTION

ELEMENT 2
Store cook-freeze foods

Department of Health guidelines state that cooked-frozen food should be held at –18 °C or lower. Personnel involved with the storage of cook-freeze operations must be appropriately trained and able to uphold strict standards of professional practice.

FREEZER EQUIPMENT

Figure 212 Insulated food transportation

1. Deep freezers or freezer rooms are used. These are capable of storing foods at temperatures of between –20 °C and –30 °C.
2. Special insulated boxes, purpose-built, are used to transport and hold frozen food short distances between the central kitchen and a satellite units. They are capable of holding the temperature for up to 3 hours, however, this figure will depend on ambient temperature, traffic conditions and the initial temperature of the food.
3. Refrigerated vans (refrigerated eutectic holdover vans) must be used to distribute chilled foods between the central kitchen and the satellite units. These are heavily insulated vans which have a number of large eutectic (brine-filled) plates situated in the ceiling of the interior and a refrigeration compressor motor that reduces these plates to the desired temperature. In most cases this compressor is run from a single or three-phase electricity supply in a 'plug in overnight' operation. While in transit a petrol or diesel motor is used to power the compressor. Alternatively there are two other methods provided the distribution period is fairly short:

   (a) insulated vans, which are in fact motorised insulated boxes, utilising polystyrene insulation;

   (b) 'dry ice' to keep the foods frozen.

STOCK ROTATION

Stock rotation is of paramount importance with frozen food. Products should be appropriately labelled and systems set up to ensure a good stock rotation.

MONITORING AND RECORDING TEMPERATURES

Monitoring and recording of temperatures must be carried out manually, by a person checking the temperature from a thermostat (hot foods) or thermometer (frozen foods) at regular intervals and recording this information on a chart.

Alternatively there are a number of electronic devices available to do this job. These are more efficient and precise.

(See Fig 265, p. 317 cook-chill food.)

One such device is a needle probe which is inserted into a sample from a batch of cooked food and read at regular intervals. Some models provide a digital read-out and could have an audible alarm fitted to sound if the temperature rises. Other devices can be fitted to a freezer and read from a 24 hour chart.

RE-HEATING/RECONSTITUTING/REGENERATING EQUIPMENT

1. **Infra-red ovens** are specifically designed for regenerating foods and use high-intensity infra-red heat radiating from elements at the top and bottom of the oven. They are suitable for reheating individual portions or small quantities of frozen foods.
2. **Infra-red grill or microwave combination ovens** These are used for regenerating or thawing frozen foods.
3. **Microwave ovens** These are suitable for reheating individual and small quantities of frozen foods rapidly.
4. **Régéthermic ovens** These are specially manufactured for the reconstitution/regeneration of frozen foods.
5. **Steamers** These are ideal for reheating large quantities of frozen foods.
6. **Thawing cabinets** These operate at a temperature of 10 °C and are used to speed up the thawing of frozen delicate foods before regeneration.

KEY WORDS

BATCH COOKING Splitting large quantities of particular commodities into batches to cook when the cooking equipment is not large enough to process the entire quantity at once.

CPU The abbreviation used for the Central Production Unit where the food is initially prepared and chilled.

CRYOGENIC Producing low temperature using carbon dioxide or liquid nitrogen.

SATELLITE KITCHEN The term given to the unit(s) where the final stage of the cook-freeze process is carried out and the food is served to the customer.

TIME BUFFER The term used for the extra time between preparation and service that the cook-freeze systems can provide.

Activity

1. What is carboxy methyl celluoluse used for?
2. Why is rapid freezing better?
3. Find out what modified starches are used in the establishment for cook-freeze sauces.
4. List foods that might not thaw successfully.
5. Why is speed important when cook freezing foods?
6. How can the destruction of pathogenic micro-organisms be ensured?

Clean and maintain cutting equipment

ELEMENT 1
Clean cutting equipment

Figure 213 Trainee cleaning parts of a machine (A)

(See Clean food production equipment, pp. 35–6.)

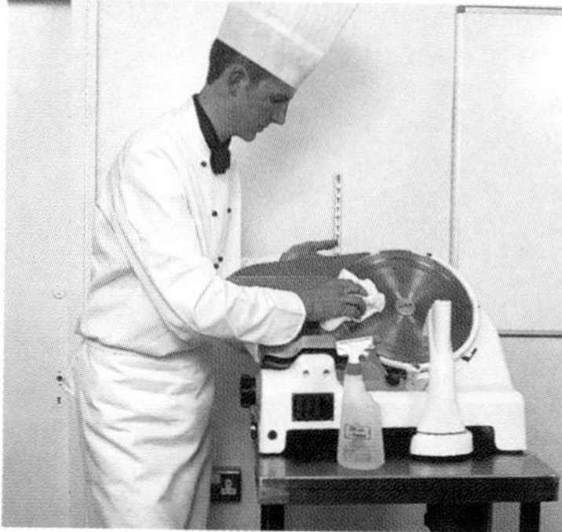

Figure 214 Trainee cleaning parts of a machine (B)

WARNING! Under the Dangerous Machine Order no person under the age of 18 may clean any machinery used as, or forming part of the equipment of the premises if this would expose them to risk of injury from a moving part of that or any adjacent machinery.

INTRODUCTION

By definition, cutting equipment is dangerous and due care and attention must always be observed when cleaning dangerous machinery/equipment. The Health and Safety at Work Act 1974 imposes a duty on all employers of five persons or more to prepare a written statement of their general policy with respect to the health and safety at work of their employees and the organisation and arrangements for carrying out that policy. The policy must be brought to the attention of all employees and must be reviewed and amended accordingly. The policy must also cover the guarding of machinery, cleaning procedures of cutting equipment as well as the inspection and maintenance of the plant and equipment.

CARE WHEN CLEANING DANGEROUS EQUIPMENT

To avoid injury when cleaning cutting equipment always follow the manufacturer's instructions and guidelines.

Cleaning procedure

1. Switch off the machine and isolate the power, i.e. mains connection.
2. Dismantle the machine (pay particular attention to any exposed blades). No blade must be moved without its guard.
3. Set all cutting blades to zero setting.
4. To remove grease and debris, thoroughly wash in a hot water and detergent solution.
5. Thoroughly dry all parts with a soft cloth.
6. The main body of the machine should be wiped clean with a damp cloth containing an appropriate detergent.
7. Reassemble machine and check that it is operating correctly.
8. Reset blades to zero and reconnect to power source.

To prevent accidents occurring from negligence, never attempt to clean an item of machinery unless the appropriate training has been given. If in doubt, consult a supervisor or head chef for professional advice and guidance.

CLEANING AGENTS

Detergents

There are three basic methods of cleaning:

1. dispersion/suspension;
2. chemical reaction;
3. abrasion.

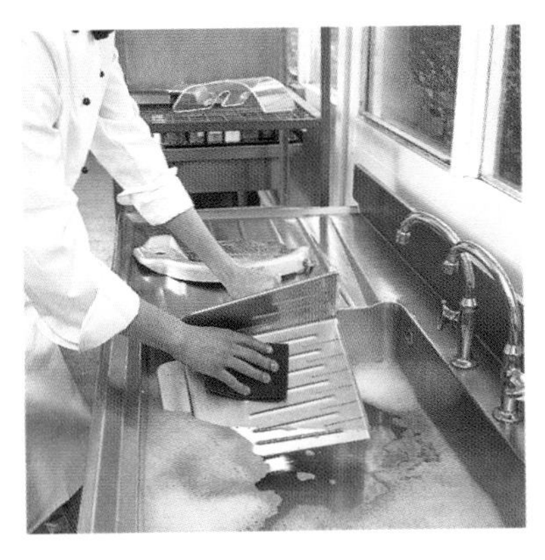

Figure 215 Cleaning a part in the sink

Dispersion/suspension cleaning This is the most common method of cleaning. The dirt is removed by wetting, penetration, lifting, dispersing, suspending and rinsing.

1. **Wetting** The cleaning solution wets the article and lifts some of the dirt.
2. **Penetration** Thick dirt is removed by chemicals which break the surface tension of the water and allow it to spread through the dirt.
3. **Lifting** The detergent lifts the dirt.
4. **Dispersing/suspending** The dirt must be suspended in the bulk of the cleaning solution and not re-deposited on the clean article or on the bottom of the container.
5. **Rinsing** Finally, the article is rinsed in clean water.

Chemical reaction It is possible by chemical means to alter the structure of some types of water-insoluble soils so that they become soluble in water and are easily removed. The clean article is finally rinsed in clean water.

Abrasive cleaning A method which uses a mechanical process rather than a chemical application, for example, domestic scouring powders and creams and sand blasting.

There are six basic groups of chemicals used in the formulation of detergent products. These are:

1. inorganic builders;
2. solvents;
3. sequestrants;
4. natural soaps;
5. synthetic surface active materials (surfactants);
6. acids.

Disinfectants

Disinfectants kill most micro-organisms or inhibit their growth, with the exception of bacterial spores. Where there is a risk of cross-contamination, disinfectant should be used on all machine surfaces. Some disinfectants double-up as sanitisers, a single product incorporating both a detergent and a disinfectant. Disinfectants are broken into the following groups:

- **Bleach (sodium hypochlorite)** This is compatible with the majority of detergents and does not leave a taste on metal surfaces, however, it may cause damage to metal surfaces.
- **QACs (Quaternary Ammonium Compounds)** These synthetic detergents with anti-bacterial qualities are quick-acting and easily mixed with all detergents. They are also non-corrosive.

- **Iodophors** These are quick-acting and used for cleaning floors. Iodophors can corrode metals.

COSHH

To clean equipment correctly and remove dirt and bacteria it is often necessary to use chemicals in the form of a solution. Some cleaning chemicals, however, are a health hazard if not used properly. It is therefore vital that adequate training is given to all employees and that the manufacturer's instructions are adhered to at all times.

The Control of Substances Hazardous to Health Regulations (COSHH), effective from 1October 1989, placed a duty on all employers to 'reduce employee exposure to hazardous substances to within, and preferably below, acceptable limits' For further details refer to 'The Control of Substances Hazardous to Health Regulations 1988' (SI 1988 No. 1657).

SUMMARY OF THE HEALTH AND SAFETY AT WORK ACT 1974

The law imposes a general duty on the employer 'to ensure so far as is reasonably practicable, the health, safety and welfare at work of all employees'. It insists on certain factors being identified in a company statement policy as follows:

- The policy statement is personalised, in order that all employers and employees of the establishment are covered and protected under the Health and Safety at Work Act.
- There must exist an exact line of responsibility and command initially from the most junior to the most senior personnel with overall responsibility.
- The constitution of any safety or staff committee together with the names of any appointed safety representatives must be clearly set out.
- There must be clear arrangements for implementing the health and safety policy.

For further details refer to the Health and Safety at Work Act 1974 (Section 2(3)).

ENFORCING THE HEALTH AND SAFETY LEGISLATION

Health and Safety regulations are enforced by the local authority under the guidance of the Health and Safety Executive. However, most catering establishments fall within the responsibility of the Environmental Health Officer (EHO). The EHO has the authority to:

- issue a Prohibition Notice which in effect immediately prevents a business from functioning until remedial action has been taken;
- issue an Improvement Notice which must be acted upon within stated time parameters;
- prosecute any person not complying with the Act and, if

necessary, seize and render harmless or destroy anything that they consider may be of imminent danger.

HYGIENE

All equipment must be thoroughly cleaned at the end of each working session. They should also be cleaned during the day if there is a risk of bacteria cross-contaminating food.

STORAGE

(See Maintain and promote hygiene in food storage, pp. 48–50.)

Cleaning materials and equipment must not be stored in any food room. It must be kept in a separate store used only for this purpose. It should be well-ventilated, cool and dry. When storing cleaning materials which require specialist training for safe handling, it is of the utmost importance that they are stored in a secure, safe place away from unauthorised access.

REPORTING ACCIDENTS

NOTE: All switches, including safety cut-out switches on all machinery must be checked before the machines are used each day to ensure they are in safe working order.

All accidents in the workplace must be reported to the employer who is responsible for maintaining accurate records of all accidents which are entered in an Accident Book. If an accident results in the person sustaining a major injury or in the death to an employee/customer it must be reported to the Environmental Health Officer.

Never use machinery with faulty or broken parts

Any person injured at work while operating or cleaning equipment must report the accident to the employer who is duty bound to notify the appropriate authorities. The 'Reporting of Injuries, Diseases and Dangerous Occurrences Regulations 1985' (RIDDOR) imposes duties on persons responsible for the activities of people at work to report to the enforcing authority (generally either under the Health and Safety Executive (HSE) or the local authority) the following :

- fatal accidents;
- major injury accidents/conditions;
- dangerous occurrences;
- accidents causing more than three days' incapacity from work;
- certain work-related diseases;
- certain matters dealing with the safe supply of gas.

Employers or any people who have sole responsibility for the workers or the premises in which they are working are obliged to maintain accurate written records of 'reportable' incidents.

Dangerous parts of machinery must be securely guarded either with a permanent guard or a removable guard with an automatic cut-out that will not allow the machine to be operated without the guard being correctly fitted. Guards are specifically designed to prevent any part of a person or their clothing from coming into contact with any moving part of the machine.

Figure 216 Mincing machine

Figure 217 Slicing machine

Guards appropriate to the type of danger caused by equipment

Equipment	*Potential danger*	*Guarding*
Worm-type mincing machines	Fingers coming into contact with the cutters or worm when the machine is in motion	A tray is fitted over the feed opening; the opening in the tray to be not more than 2 inches in diameter and the distance between the top of the opening and the worm of the machine to be not less than 5 inches. When feeding products into the machine use a suitable, hygienic plunger
Rotary knife bowl-type chopping machines	Fingers and hands coming into contact with chopping blades	Interlocked cover over rear half of bowl extending forward a short way over the centre. If the cover is lifted, the machine must stop operating. A brake may be fitted to ensure the knives stop immediately the cover is lifted. Alternatively, a time-delay interlock may prevent the cover from being lifted until the blades have stopped
Dough brakes (dough rolling tables)	Hands or clothing being drawn into the in-running rollers	A fixed or automatic guard extending along either side of the table from the rollers to prevent contact with them. If the guard is not fixed it must be interlocked so that the machine stops when the guard is removed or raised The guard should be sufficient to prevent contact along the conveyer and also from above or to the side of the roller
Power operated rotary bowl mixer	Trapping of hands, arms, clothing, etc., in between the beater or hooks and the bowl	A device that fits around the bowl and spindle mechanism preventing contact with the moving parts (guards should be interlocked). Many catering establishments, however, do not have guards fitted
Food mixers with slicing or chopping attachments	Contact with rotary knives, cutting edges, in-running rollers or rotary worms	A hopper fitted to the front of the machine into which the food is placed. A pressure-plate must be fitted to the front of the hopper to push food into the cutting mechanism.
Circular knife slicing machine/Gravity feed slicers	Contact between hand and cutting blades.	Enclosure around top and back of blade closely fitting, following the contour of and overlapping the blade. This guard should be interlocked. A metal or plastic guard fitted over the carriage to enclose partially or totally the product being sliced. This guard may also be interlocked An end or last slice device to provide pressure against the product, particularly useful when slicing shorter pieces

Equipment	Potential danger	Guarding
Horizontal feed machines	As for gravity feed machines	The top and rear of the blade should be enclosed. Fixed guards should be fitted in front of the blade. On some machines, the blade may be crescent shaped or planetary. On such machines a brake should be fitted and interlock guards provided on the feed and delivery sides of the blade **NOTE:** A special precaution required when cleaning either of the above machines is to ensure that the blade is turned down to zero thickness

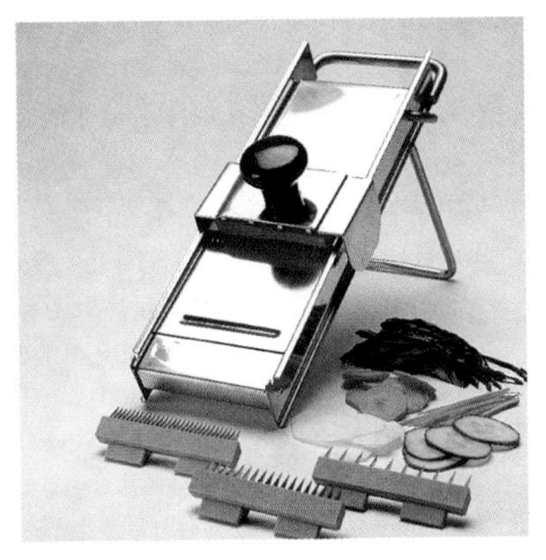

Figure 218 Mandolin

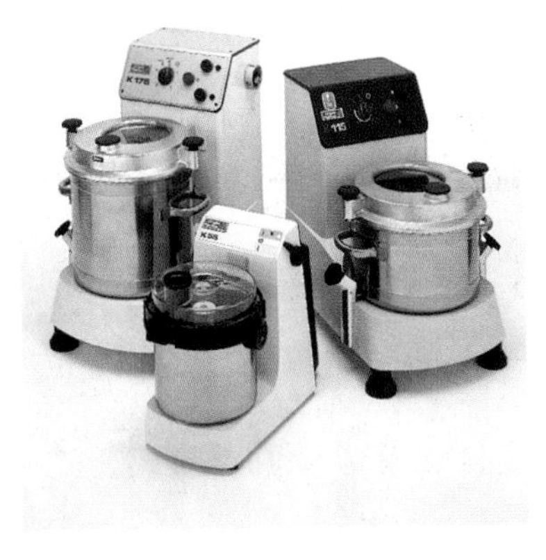

Figure 219 Food processor

ELEMENT 2

Maintain cutting equipment

INTRODUCTION

It is the responsibility of both the employer and employee to observe all health and safety regulations. The Environmental Health Officer (EHO) regularly carries out inspections to all establishments to ascertain whether these are being enforced. The EHO will advise and assist on any health and safety issues.

SAFETY OF CUTTING EQUIPMENT MACHINERY

Most accidents usually occur as a result of insufficient training, careless cleaning, inadequately guarded machinery or the guards not been used during operation. There are three basic methods by which machinery may be made safe:

1. **By virtue of construction** The machine is constructed in such a way as to make it as safe as possible and also that it is supplied in a condition in which all the moving parts are enclosed and access to them is not necessary to operate it.
2. **By means of position** The law allows moving parts of machines to be exposed if they are in such a position that they can never be approached.
3. **By fencing or guarding** The guards are suitable for the purpose for which they are used and strong enough to withstand any treatment. They must be constructed and positioned in such a way that the machine can continue to be effectively operated. When the guard is removed the machinery should be rendered unusable until it is replaced.

(See Maintain a safe and secure working environment, pp.10–23.)

CARE IN MAINTAINING CUTTING EQUIPMENT

Cutting equipment

Before using any power-driven machinery always check that :

- the machine is switched off;
- the power supply is switched off using the isolation switch;
- the guards are safely in place;
- the cutting blades are set as required;

Once these checks have been made, connect power and switch the machine on.

Every machine is potentially dangerous and must therefore be cared for in a responsible manner. Procedures for the use and cleaning of cutting equipment is outlined in the Health and Safety at Work Act 1974.

The act outlines:

- securing the health, safety and welfare of persons at work;
- protecting other persons against risk of harm from activities carried out in the workplace.

It also controls:

- the purchases, storage and handling of dangerous articles and substances;
- the emission of noxious or offensive substances into the atmosphere.

Figure 220 Staff safety training in front of a machine

WARNING! Always check that blades are completely covered.

SAFETY TRAINING

Ensure that the correct training has been received before using equipment and that manufacturer's instructions are carefully followed. If guards are fitted they must be used, as they are designed to prevent any part of a person or clothing coming into contact with any moving part of the machine. Machinery should be checked regularly by the Health and Safety Executive to ensure that it is functioning in a safe manner.

When cleaning machinery it must be isolated from the mains supply and stripped down following the manufacturer's instructions. All machinery to be stored away must be stored in a safe manner so as not to cause an accident.

PRESCRIBED DANGEROUS MACHINES ORDER 1964

The following catering machinery and equipment fall within this act.

Power-driven

1. worm-type mincing machines;
2. rotary knife bowl choppers;
3. dough brakes;
4. rotary bowl mixers;
5. food mixers, when used with attachments for mincing, slicing, chipping or any cutting operation;
6. automatic tart or pie making machines;
7. vegetable slicing machines;
8. potato chipping machines;
9. wrapping machines;
10. machines of any type equipped with a circular saw blade;

Power-driven or not

1. circular knife-slicing machines;
2. potato chippers.

All employees must co-operate with the employer and comply with any duty or instruction given within the Health and Safety at Work Act. Employees must act in a responsible manner and take reasonable care of the health, safety and welfare of other persons in the workplace.

NOTE: Staff should not intentionally or recklessly interfere with or misuse any safety literature provided by the employer in the interests of Health and Safety in the workplace.

All staff should have:

- organised training sessions on cleaning and maintaining equipment and machinery;
- access to manufacturer's operating manuals for reference regarding the cleaning and maintenance of specific machinery and equipment.

KEY WORDS

ALKALIS Substances present in cleaning agents/detergents and used to remove greasy food residues.

BACTERIOCIDES Substance capable of killing bacteria.

COSHH Control of Substances Hazardous to Health Regulations 1988.

EHO Environmental Health Officer.

HASAWA Health and Safety at Work Act 1974.

HSE Health and Safety Executive.

HSR Health and Safety (First Aid) Regulations 1981.

ISOLATION SWITCH A wall-mounted switch which cuts off electrical power to a machine.

RIDDOR Reporting of Injuries, Diseases and Dangerous Occurrences Regulations 1985.

SANITISE To reduce the load of micro-organisms to an acceptable level.

Activity

1. With the assistance of a chef or supervisor, draw up a cleaning schedule for the dangerous equipment where you work.
2. Find the following words in the grid:
   (a) COSHH
   (b) RIDDOR
   (c) HASAWA
   (d) Sanitise
   (e) Disinfectant
   (f) Detergent
   (g) QAC
   (h) Bleach
   (i) Cross-contamination
   (j) Accident Book

S	W	R	R	E	I	L	N	N	R	E	G	G	S	H	C
A	T	T	Y	P	B	L	E	A	C	H	S	M	Z	R	A
N	A	W	Z	M	M	U	R	U	R	R	M	C	O	H	C
I	R	U	D	D	Z	R	I	D	D	O	R	S	I	O	C
T	A	R	E	D	C	D	B	I	O	Y	S	L	I	O	I
I	A	E	S	D	R	E	T	I	U	C	M	M	O	I	D
S	I	E	S	E	E	A	T	C	O	S	H	H	I	O	E
E	U	S	G	G	T	E	S	N	C	Y	I	N	I	O	N
T	S	G	G	I	A	A	T	U	N	C	N	Y	H	Z	T
N	B	A	L	U	L	A	B	S	S	S	N	O	A	Z	B
Y	Y	Y	Y	L	M	C	T	T	G	C	D	O	S	O	O
T	T	O	U	I	C	B	U	Q	E	B	N	N	A	B	O
E	J	T	N	E	G	R	E	T	E	D	O	T	W	N	K
T	N	A	T	C	E	F	N	I	S	I	D	L	A	B	U
N	T	D	D	Y	I	H	E	E	W	T	Q	W	L	A	U
I	U	R	D	N	W	T	B	U	E	T	Q	U	A	A	L
O	J	R	S	S	S	W	U	C	C	C	A	L	A	A	L
S	J	G	G	H	G	M	U	C	N	H	C	C	E	L	B

3. Compile a list of dangerous equipment in your establishment.

Prepare and cook battered fish and chipped potatoes

ELEMENT 1
Prepare batter for frying

FACT: One of the earliest, if not the first, reference to fried fish was during the last century when Charles Dickens refers to a 'fried fish warehouse' in *Oliver Twist* (1838).

INTRODUCTION

Deep-fried battered fish and chips are a great traditional British dish. The hallmark of a good fryer is the quality of the fried fish it produces. The main ingredient apart from the fish is the batter. Batter can be made fresh with flour, eggs, milk plus a raising agent or alternatively a convenience mix may be used which involves adding water or milk to a powder to complete. Whichever way the batter is made there must be consistency in the finished product. If not, the flavour and appearance will be inferior. Making fresh batter properly is time-consuming whereas with convenience mixes, large or small quantities can be made quickly.

Convenience mixes should only be used in situations where there is insufficient skilled staff or a shortage of staff.

PREPARING THE BATTER

Fish is battered for the following reasons:

- to protect the fish from extreme heat during cooking;
- to minimise the absorption of oil/fat;
- to enhance the appearance and texture of the finished dish.

It is important that when preparing batter all the ingredients are weighed correctly and, when using convenience products, the manufacturer's instructions are followed carefully.

COOKING TIP: Ideally, only make the batter when required and only sufficient for your immediate needs.

Equipment

1. a mechanical mixer with a paddle and whisk (ideal method for preparing batter);
2. a stainless-steel bucket and a durable whisk (for manual operations);
3. Measuring equipment.

HYGIENE

When preparing batter the strictest hygiene standards must be adhered to at all times. Preparation areas and equipment must be thoroughly cleaned before and after use, in order to prevent contamination of the batter and fish.

WARNING! Never mix old batches of batter with fresh batter, as this might pose a contamination threat.

STORAGE

Only make sufficient batter for immediate need. However, any excess batter should be stored in stainless-steel or plastic containers and covered with either a tight-fitting lid or cling film. It should be labelled to show the product, date stored, and the use-by date.

QUALITY POINTS

COOKING TIP: When making fresh batter only use the tried and tested standard recipes for the best results.

It is vital that freshly made batter is carefully mixed: too thin a batter will not hold on to the fish and will leave scraps of batter: too thick and the batter will not cook properly. Extra care should be taken when using a frozen batter which should always be cooked from its frozen state. If the batter is allowed to thaw and become warm during storage, it will spoil during frying.

When batter is left to stand it becomes thinner, it is therefore best to make the batter slightly thicker, and thin it down as necessary.

Fresh batter recipes: Yeast batter and egg batter

Yeast batter

Ingredients

500 g	medium flour (i.e. half strong, half soft)
25 g	yeast
500 ml	water, tepid
Pinch	salt

Method

1. Sieve the flour into a bowl and add a pinch of salt. Make a well.
2. Place the yeast in a clean bowl.
3. Add the tepid water to the yeast and dissolve completely in the water.
4. Add yeast mixture gradually to the flour to form a smooth batter. Cover the bowl and allow the mixture to ferment in a warm place for 1 hour.
5. Pass food through seasoned flour prior to passing through the batter.

Egg batter

Ingredients

500 g	flour
500 ml	milk and water
2	eggs
Pinch	salt

Method

1. Sieve the flour into a bowl and add a pinch of salt. Make a well.
2. Add the tepid water to the flour.
3. Add the egg and form a smooth batter. Cover and set aside to rest in a cool place and allow the batter to thicken.
4. Pass food through seasoned flour prior to passing through the batter.

Figure 221 McDougalls convenience batter

Portions	Flour	Yeast	Eggs	Water	Salt
10	500 g	25 g	2	500 ml	5g
20	1 kilo	50 g	4	1 litre	10 g
40	2 kilo	100 g	8	2 llitre	20 g
50	2½ kilo	125 g	10	2½ litre	25 g
100	5 kilo	250 g	20	5 litre	50 g

ELEMENT 2
Prepare and cook battered fish

(*See* Prepare and cook basic fish dishes, pp. 171–84.)

INTRODUCTION

The most common fish used for frying are cod, haddock, whiting, plaice, codling, dogfish, hake and various species of ray. It is important that, whether fresh or frozen, only the finest quality fish is used for frying.

PREPARING FISH FOR FRYING

Prior to deep frying fish, always pat the surface dry before coating with seasoned flour and batter.

PORTIONING

COOKING TIP: The average-size portion of fish is 120 g.

For continuity of size most establishments purchase fish already pre-portioned for frying. These are usually frozen, though they may be fresh. Fish purchased unportioned is filleted and skinned by skilled personnel. When cutting fish it is best to cut equally sized portions of the same thickness, which ensures even frying. For maximum retention of natural mineral salts which give fried fish its particular succulent flavour it is best to cut and prepare the fish as close to frying time as possible.

Cutting boards

A separate chopping board must be used when preparing fish. Blue-coloured chopping boards (usually) signify fish only and should be made from a hardened non-porous material, for example, high density polyethylene which is non-absorbent, non-toxic and complies with all hygiene regulations.

Figure 222 Cooked fish in batter

Fish storage containers

Raw fish should ideally be kept in a separate refrigerator at a temperature of between 3 °C and 5 °C.

Frying range

Fish should be fried at between 180 °C and 220 °C. If fried at a lower temperature the batter will absorb too much oil and the fish will be soggy, while a higher temperature will burn the batter before the fish is cooked.

FLASHPOINT

All oil has a recommended frying temperature. Beyond that temperature the oil begins to break down and deteriorate. Initially it reaches smoking point (which is obvious from the smoke) and shortly after flashpoint. A blue haze forms over the hot oil just before the oil ignites and catches fire.

Type of frying medium	Recommended frying temperature	Smoke point (°C)	Approx. flashpoint (°C)
Vegetable oil[1]	180	220	324
Vegetable fat[1]	180	220	321
Vegetable oil[2]	180	204	324
Pure vegetable fat	175	215	318
Pure vegetable oil	170 to180	220	330
Maize oil[1]	180	215	224
Finest fat	180	202	321
Dripping[1]	163[3]	165	300
Lard	190		320
Finest olive oil	170	148 to 165	275

NOTES: [1]Finest quality [2]High class [3]Without chemical modification

SAFETY

(See procedure in the event of a fire, pp. 14–16.)

Should a fire occur, immediately sound the alarm and, if possible, throw a fire blanket over the fryer before calling the fire brigade and evacuating the building.

To prevent fires, regularly check the thermostat to ensure that the oil is not overheating. Another practice is to filter the oil regularly to remove food particles from the oil.

NOTE: If moisture seeps into the oil it might spit when heated.

Storage of cooking oil/fat

Oil and fat should be stored with the lid tightly closed (to prevent the oil from going rancid) in a cool place.

ELEMENT 3

Prepare and cook chipped potatoes

INTRODUCTION

Potatoes became a popular food in Britain in the late eighteenth century. There are several varieties that are favoured for frying but, generally, Maris Piper, Maris Bard, Wilja, King Edward, Premiere, Pentland Dell, Pentland Squire, Desirée and Estima are the most popular ones. Potatoes should be purchased from a good reputable potato merchant who will ensure that they are appropriate for your needs and are of a good standard.

Figure 223 Potatoes

STORAGE

Fresh potatoes should be stored at least 20 cm from the ground, on pallets, in a cool dry room away from direct sunlight and at a temperature of between 7° C and 10 °C. Once the potatoes are peeled and chipped they should be stored fully submerged in stainless steel or plastic buckets in water until required. If the potatoes are not kept in water and are exposed to oxygen, a chemical reaction will cause the potatoes to discolour.

NOTE: A sulphite preservative can be used to prevent the formation of the browning chemical 'Melanin'. It works by inhibiting the enzymic reaction when peeled potatoes are exposed to oxygen. When using such products always follow the manufacturer's instructions.

Figure 224 Potato peeler

Hygiene

To ensure a maximum standard of hygiene a cleaning rota should be organised and adhered to. All surfaces should be made from stainless and equipment and utensils should be made of plastic or stainless steel. Potato peelings and trimmings should not be allowed to accumulate in or around equipment and must be discarded regularly.

EQUIPMENT REQUIRED FOR PREPARATION OF CHIPS

Chipped potatoes should be prepared in an area with adequate drainage facilities and situated close to sufficient power points. The basic equipment required:

- potato rumbler/peeler;
- a container of a suitable size to store the peeled potatoes;
- a chipping machine (to cut the potatoes);
- two water baths (one to store the potatoes and an additional one for the prepared chips).

It is also necessary to have tools for removing the eyes from potatoes and containers to transport potatoes from the preparation area to the frying area.

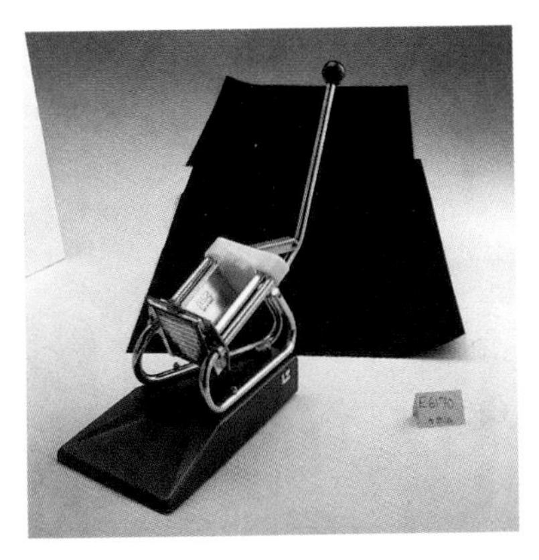

Figure 225 Chipper

EQUIPMENT USED FOR FRYING POTATOES

The best frying ranges are heated by gas (gas is easier to regulate) and there should ideally be three frying units. Professional fryers use only the best equipment fitted by range manufacturers, after the appropriate permission has been obtained from the local authority. All ranges have temperature regulators and monitoring devices on each fryer to record and ensure that the fat does not overheat.

The ideal cooking medium for frying is beef dripping. With the increased emphasis on 'healthy eating' polyunsaturated fat or oil can be substituted, though this might affect the overall flavour of the chipped potato. The temperature of the fat or oil should never exceed 195°C, if it does it will spoil more rapidly.

It is essential that the frying medium be kept in as near perfect condition as possible. This ensures a perfectly fried product with the correct taste. To increase the life of oil it should be filtered at the end of each shift. Filtering involves passing the oil through a fine mesh strainer to collect food particles (if left in the oil they would accelerate decomposition, lowering the flash-point and increasing the risk of fire). Some frying ranges are fitted with electrical filters.

CAUTION: Take care that water or cleaning fluid does not find its way into the fryers as it will ruin the fat and could possibly, if the fat is hot, cause it to overflow.

Correct ventilation is also very important. Flue outlets must be fitted to remove fumes from burning gases and fryers. Fumes passing through flue outlets must be discharged so as not to cause a nuisance to the public. A coarse wire mesh filter should be incorporated in the flue system to collect coalesced fat particles. The filter should be easy to remove and clean and this should be done regularly to prevent the build-up of fat which would increase the risk of fire.

All ranges should be equipped with a heated display cabinet for the customers to view the produce on sale. The temperature of hot cabinets should not drop below 65°C.

Ranges should be cleaned after each shift with warm water and detergent and finished with a steriliser.

SAFETY

When preparing and frying it is paramount that all electrical power points and switches are water-resistant.

(For further information see Maintain a safe, secure working environment, pp.14–16. *See also* Carry out procedures in the event of a fire, pp. 14–16.)

Preventing fat fires

Most fires occur because a thermostat has failed and/or the fryer has been left unattended. They can also be caused by the frying medium frothing over (usually because of the continued frying of wet food).

If noticed early enough, many fires can be extinguished by cutting off the source of the heat and closing the lid of the equipment and/or covering the burning oil with a fire blanket.

COOKING TIP: Usually chips are finished by sprinkling a little salt over them to enhance the flavour. However, in recent years there has been a trend to use low salt 'sodium substitute', as a healthier option.

Activity

1. Make your own cleaning rota for your establishment.
2. What fat(s) do you use to fry food?
3. What standard recipe do you use for batter in your place of work?

Prepare, assemble and cook pizza products

ELEMENT 1
Prepare pizza products ready for cooking

INTRODUCTION

The pizza originated in one of the poorest regions of southern Italy, where food was so scarce that nothing was ever wasted. It is thought they were invented by bakers as a means of utilising 'leftovers' (pieces of dough) at the end of a bread-making session. Italian immigrants to the USA and the UK opened the first pizza houses or pizzerie (special pizza bakeries with exceptionally hot ovens).

Traditional pizzas are made from a bread dough circle base with a basic tomato filling and a cheese topping. Nowadays, they not only come with numerous toppings to suit individual tastes, but come in a variety of sizes from single to multiple portions. Modern-day pizzas include enclosed and folded pizzas and might have a sweet filling and topping as well as a savoury. Pizzas make the perfect light snack, cut into wedge slices and eaten with the fingers or alternatively a plate-sized pizza makes a substantial meal.

QUALITY POINTS

Only the finest ingredients should be used when making pizza. The success of a pizza depends on the quality of the bread dough which should be light and not 'stodgy'. The best base is made from a yeast dough, but it can be made from a scone dough or a convenience mix. Canned chopped tomatoes are ideal for the filling and many brands have added ingredients: garlic, chilli, onion, basil and mixed herbs which will enhance the overall flavour to the filling. Fillings and toppings should be plentiful.

HYGIENE

Always ensure that pizzas are prepared in a clean, hygienic environment.

(See Maintain and promote hygiene in food storage, preparation and cooking, pp. 48–54.)

All preparation surfaces, equipment and utensils should be washed thoroughly before and after use. Never compromise by using old or stale ingredients for the base or fillings. Keep foods refrigerated at all times. Wash hands thoroughly before, during and after handling ingredients.

STORAGE

Always ensure the following:

- Store dried pizza ingredients in a cool, dry place.
- Store chilled and frozen ingredients in suitable hygienic containers in a fridge or freezer.
- Seal convenience mixes tightly after use and store in a cool, dry place.

FREEZING

Pizza dough and complete pizzas may be frozen. Pizza dough may be frozen after the first kneading. It should be wrapped in catering film and labelled with the date and quantity before freezing. To defrost, place on a tray in a fridge. Remove from the fridge to allow it to rise before baking.

Alternatively, allow the pizza dough to rise and prepare pizza in the normal way. Bake pizza for 10 min only, cool, ideally in a blast chiller, wrap in a polythene bag and freeze immediately. Remove and cook straight from the freezer.

SPECIALIST EQUIPMENT

Figure 226 Pizzeria oven

FACT: Pizza Hut uses more than 400 million pounds of tomatoes each year and 50 million pounds of pepperoni.

ELEMENT 2
Assemble and cook pizza

INTRODUCTION

The pizza market has grown rapidly in the 1990s to become one of the most popular 'eating-out' activities in the UK.

Pizzas are made from a basic bread dough circle base, a basic filling and a combination of mouthwatering toppings of your choice: any combination of cheeses, Parma ham, mushroom, olives, shellfish, pepperoni, sweetcorn, pineapple, anchovy fillets etc. Whatever your dietary requirements a pizza may be made with a selection of favourite ingredients.

FACT: The Margherita pizza is named after the 19th century Queen of Italy.

QUALITY POINTS

Pizzas may be baked in a conventional oven, however, they have a somewhat inferior quality to those baked in a pizzeria oven. The pizzeria oven reaches an exceptionally high temperature (essential for 'setting' the dough) and so the pizzas, when baked, always have a good, light dough, whether thin and crispy or thick and traditional.

ASSEMBLING PIZZAS

Always:

- avoid using starchy topping ingredients, as the pizza base is very substantial and the pizza will end up being too 'heavy';
- ensure that ingredients are appropriately seasoned before assembling the pizza;
- drain all ingredients before they are used, to prevent the pizza from becoming too 'soggy';
- arrange the heavier topping ingredients to the edge of the pizza rather than in the middle, to prevent it from sagging at the point when it is cut into wedges;
- brush with oil before assembling to prevent the absorption of moisture from the toppings.

COOKING TIP: Push up the edge of the dough to form a rim; this will prevent the topping from spilling over during cooking.

Never overfill the pizza otherwise it will overflow in the oven and ruin the appearance. It will also make it difficult to eat.

BASIC PIZZA INGREDIENTS

Flour Traditional pizzas are made from a bread dough, derived from a strong plain bread flour. For a brown bread base, use stoneground wholemeal or wholemeal and granary. Alternatively, mix equal quantities of white flour and wholemeal. Always sift the flour first to ensure a light dough.

Salt Add the required amount to the flour when sifting. Salt gives flavour and helps to develop the gluten in the flour which produces the elasticity of the dough.

Yeast This is a living micro-organism (raising agent). Always follow the manufacturer's instructions when using dried yeast.

Water Always use tepid water (at the optimum temperature for the yeast to grow). Only use the amount stated in recipe: too much water and the dough will be difficult to handle and the base will be hard.

Figure 227 Cooked pizza

Tomato sauce Every pizza has a tomato sauce as the basis of the topping. The sauce should be well seasoned before it is added to the pizza base.

Cheese The most common cheese used is Mozzarella as it melts to produce the strings of cheese when a slice is cut. Other cheeses used include Parmesan and Cheddar. Always use a milder flavour cheese when using a combination of strong flavoured toppings.

Herbs Fresh herbs are best. The most commonly used include basil, parsley and oregano.

Toppings Most ingredients are suitable for a topping.

Kneading

Kneading mixes all the ingredients together and strengthens the gluten, which holds the bubbles of air created by the yeast, which causes the dough to rise. Dough will require kneading until it becomes smooth and pliable. Extra ingredients may be added to the dough when kneading, e.g. olives, herbs for added flavour.

Pizza scone (biscuit) base

(one 25 cm/10 in round)

Ingredients

175 g	self-raising flour
½ tspn	salt
30 g	butter
120 ml	milk

COOKING TIP: For a more interesting flavour, olive oil, grated cheese or mixed herbs may be added to the mixture after rubbing in the butter.

Method

1. Sift the flour and salt into a mixing bowl.
2. Rub in the butter until it resembles fine breadcrumbs.
3. Make a well in the centre of the mixture and pour in nearly all the milk at once. Knead lightly to a soft dough, if necessary add the remaining milk.
4. Transfer dough to a floured surface and knead.
5. Roll out or press the dough into a lightly greased baking sheet or pizza pan. Push up the edge to form a ridge. Use immediately.

Basic pizza (*Pizza Romana*)

Ingredients

100 g	bread dough
50 g	tomato concassé
1 tspn	pinch chopped basil
1 tspn	pinch chopped marjoram
50 g	chopped oregano
50 g	Mozzarella cheese
10 g	Parmesan cheese

Method

1. Knock back the bread dough and roll out into the appropriate rounds and dock (i.e. prick with a fork or baker's docker).
2. Spread the tomato concassé over the top. Sprinkle over the top the chopped basil, marjoram and oregano and season with salt and pepper.
3. Grate or slice the Mozzarella cheese thinly over the top of the concassé.
4. Sprinkle over the Parmesan cheese.
5. Leave to prove for 30 min before placing in a preheated oven for the appropriate time.
6. Remove pizza from oven and serve immediately.

Extensions of the basic pizza recipe

Dish	*Additional ingredients per portion*	*Action*
Capricciosa	25 g sliced cooked ham	Cut into 1 cm squares and place on top of the concassé. Cover with cheese
	10 g cooked sliced mushrooms	Sprinkle over the cheese
	10 g chopped cooked artichoke bottom.	Sprinkle over the top.
	2 olives	Arrange on top
Funghi	50 g cooked sliced mushrooms	Sprinkle over the top of the cheese
Mare	15 g cooked scampi	Place on top of the concassé
	15 g prawns	As above
	15 g cooked mussels	As for scampi. Cover with the cheese
Margherita	50 g pecorino cheese	Slice and use in place of the Mozzarella cheese
Napolitana	2 anchovy fillets	Cut in half lengthways and arrange on top of the cheese
	2 black olives	Place in between the anchovies
Prosciutto	50 g Parma ham	Slice thinly and place on top of the concassé. Cover with the cheese
Siciliana	50 g tuna fish	Chop finely and place on top of the concassé. Cover with the cheese
	2 olives	Cut into slices and arrange over the cheese
Wurstel	50 g sliced German sausage	Arrange on top of the concassé and cover with the cheese

Figure 228 Pizza being served (slice being lifted)

FACT: Pizza Hut is the world's largest pizza restaurant chain with more than 7,600 restaurants and delivery units.

Storage of cooked pizza

Freshly baked pizza bases can be cooled on wire racks and frozen when cold to be used later. Care should be taken not to overbake the base, otherwise the dough will become too dry for reheating. Prepared pizza dough ready for baking may be stored in the fridge for a maximum of 2 hours.

Serving pizza

To ensure quality of product, always serve a pizza as soon as it leaves the oven. It should be transferred to a warm plate to prevent it going cold too quickly. If it is allowed to go cold, the cheese will set and lose its elasticity and the base will become too wet.

KEY WORDS

CALZONE In Italian the word 'calzone' means trousers! But in this case it refers to a reverse pizza resembling a large pastry with the dough on the outside and the filling on the inside.

KNEADING To work the dough for the purpose of strengthening the gluten while making it soft and pliable.

PIZZA PAN A special baking tray used to bake pizza in.

PIZZERIE OVEN Specialised oven used for baking pizzas.

PIZZA PEEL Specialist serving tool for transferring the baked pizza for portioning into serving dishes.

PIZZA CUTTER A cutting wheel used for portioning pizza

Activity

1. List four points to take into consideration when assembling pizzas.
   (a)
   (b)
   (c)
   (d)
2. Name two bread doughs used for making pizzas.
   (a)
   (b)
3. Explain how you would go about freezing:
   (a) a pizza dough
   (b) a complete pizza

4 Glossary of terms

à la	In the style of.
à la crème	Served with or coated with a cream sauce or fresh cream.
à la menthe	With fresh mint leaves; garnished with whole or chopped blanched leaves.
Aboyeur	Shouter' – person who calls out the orders in the kitchen.
Africaine (à l')	With flat mushrooms, tomatoes, egg plants and chateau potatoes.
Aigre-doux	Sweet and sour.
Ail (gousse d'ail)	Garlic (clove of garlic).
Alaska	Omelette soufflé (baked Alaska).
Alphonse XIII	Garnish, egg plant, tomato sauce and pimento.
Algérienne	Garnish, small peeled tomatoes, artichokes and croquette of sweet potatoes.
Alsacienne (à l')	Sauerkraut in small tartlets.
Amandes mondées	Shelled almonds.
Amandine	Garnish, sliced sautéed almonds and finely chopped parsley.
Ambassadeur (à la)	Garnish, artichokes and duchess potatoes.
Américaine (homard à l')	Lobster cooked American style, chopped onions, shallots, garlic, parsley, tarragon, tomatoes and brandy.
Ancienne (à l')	(a) Garnish, button mushrooms and button onions, heart-shaped croutons and finely chopped parsley. (b) Kidney beans, hard-boiled eggs and braised lettuce.
Anchois	Anchovy.
Andouillète	Chitterling sausages with tripe.
Anis	Aniseed flavour.
Anna, pommes	Thinly sliced seasoned potatoes layered in a special 'Anna' mould and cooked in an oven.
Appareil	Culinary term indicating a basic mixture.
Arlésienne (à l')	Preparation of white wine, garlic, eggplant, onion and chopped tomatoes.
Armagnac	French brandy from the district of Armagnac in France.
Arome	Aroma.
Aromates (aux)	With herbs.
Assaisonnements	Seasonings, condiments.
Assisette (charcutière)	A selection of delicatessen sausages, garlic sausage, salami and mortadella.
Assorti	Assorted.
Au beurre	With a light coating of melted butter.
Baba	An enriched dough product, soaked in a light syrup and rum.
Ballotine	Boned, stuffed and rolled chicken leg.
Baron de boeuf	Double sirloin of beef.
Barquettes	Boat shaped pastry case used for canapés

Basse-côte	Spare rib of pork.
Bataille	Potatoes cut into 1 cm dice and deep fried.
Bavette	Thin flank of beef.
Bouquetière	A selection of cooked vegetables, usually carrots, cauliflower, French beans and turnips.
Bûche de Noël	Yuletide log (French Christmas cake).
Byron (pommes)	Potatoes with a hollow top, sprinkled with cheese, covered with cream and glazed.
Cabernet (sauvignon)	Type of grape used in the production of wine.
Cabillons	Small type of cheese made from goats' milk.
Cacao	Cocoa.
Coc (noix de)	Coconut.
Calon segur	Wine from Medoc district of Bordeaux, France.
Calvados	Apple brandy.
Campagne (de)	Country (from the).
Campagne (pâté de)	Country-style pâté.
Canapé	Hors d'œuvre or savoury presented on a small slice of toasted bread or pastry case sometimes covered in aspic jelly.
Cannelle	Cinnamon.
Cantaloup	Melon, originally grown at Cantaupo near Rome.
Capitolade	Chicken stew, demi glaze, with white wine.
Câpres	Capers.
Caprice	Fish served dipped in butter and breadcrumbs and garnished with half a banana cooked in butter and grilled with sauce Robert. Sometimes served with a spoonful of mango chutney
Capucine	Coffee with cream and sprinkled with powdered chocolate.
Cardinal	(a) Béchamel sauce and fish stock, truffle essence. (b) Lobster butter and cardinal sauce.
Cardon	Cardoon, similar to an artichoke.
Carème	(a) Famous chef of the early nineteenth century and dishes named after him. (b) Hard-boiled egg, artichoke bottoms, truffles and Nantura sauce.
Carotte (rapée)	Grated carrot
Caroline	Medium-grain rice.
Carte du jour	Menu of the day.
Carte (à la)	Dishes chosen from the menu card.
Cassata	Neopolitan ice-cream with glacé fruit.
Casserole (en)	Saucepan (cooked in a fireproof dish).
Cassis	Blackcurrant or blackcurrant liqueur.
Cassoulet	A stew dish originating from the Languedoc region of France, prepared from port, lamb, or goose with haricot beans.
Castillane (à la)	Chopped tomatoes cooked in oil with small onion rings, croquette potatoes and pieces of meat.
Catalane	(a) Garnish of aubergines sautéed in oil, served with pilaw of rice and large pieces of meat. (b) Artichoke bottoms.
Caviare	Caviar-roe of sturgeon fish.
Célestine	Consommé thickened with tapioca garnished with julienne of savoury pancake.
Cèpes	Type of edible mushrooms.

Cerfeuil	Chervil.
Cérises (glacées, et ubilées au maraschino)	Cherries (sugared, soaked in kirsch syrup, flamed, soaked in maraschino).
Cervelas	Saveloy, type of sausage.
Chambey	Thin slices of potatoes, bacon and grated cheese.
Chambord (à la)	Fish garnish, mushrooms, fish quenelles, soft fish roe tossed in butter, crayfish tails, slices of truffles and fleurons.
Champeaux	Garnish for sauté chicken, white wine and meat glaze, garnished with small onions and cocotte potatoes.
Chantilly (à la)	Whipped cream and sugar.
Chapelure	White breadcrumbs used for coating dishes cooked 'au gratin'.
Charcuterie	Meat delicatessen such as sausages and pates.
Chassagne	Montrachet Wine from Burgundy, France.
Châtaigne	Sweet chestnut.
Charentais	Type of melon from Charentes (France).
Châtelaine	Garnish for large joints, artichoke bottoms, tomatoes, braised celery and château potatoes..
Chauchat	Garnish for fish (border of cooked potato round fish).
Cheval	Horse (horsemeat).
Chèvre	Goat (usually refers to cheese made from goats' milk).
Chevreuil	Toebuck (venison).
Chicorée	(a) Vegetable: Belgian endive or chicory. (b) Used as a flavouring essence in coffee.
Choix (au)	Choice of.
Choron	(a) Sauce Béarnaise with tomato puree. (b) Garnish (garnish of artichoke bottoms, peas and noisette potatoes).
Choucroute	Sauerkraut.
Chou de mer	Sea kale.
Ciboulettes	Chives.
Civet de lièvre, de lapin	Brown hare stew, rabbit (jugged hare).
Clairet	Bordeaux wine (English claret).
Clarmart	Garnish of artichoke bottom with puree of pea and château potatoes.
Cléopatre (truite)	Garnish for shallow fried fish: shrimps, capers, soft herring roe.
Clermont	Garnish for tournedos: chestnuts, soubise sauce covered with egg yolk and onions.
Cocotte (en)	Cooked and served in small, round earthenware or porcelain dish (as for eggs).
Coeur de laitue	Lettuce heart.
Compote	Poached fruit, fresh and dried.
Compris (service)	Included (service included).
Concassé (tomato)	Roughly chopped tomato flesh.
Conde (poire)	Bed of sweet rice covered with apricot glaze.
Confiserie	Confectionery goods.
Confit	Crystallised.
Confiture	Jam
Conserves (au vinaigre)	Preserved foods (pickles).
Contrefilet	Boned out sirloin of beef.
Cooked out	Usually describes flour that has been cooked to the stage when it loses its starchy taste.
Coq de bruyère	Wood grouse.
Coquille Saint Jacques	Scallops.

Corbeille (de fruits)	Basket (of fruit).
Coriandre	Coriander spice.
Cornet de York	Ham moulded in the shape of a cone.
Cornichon	Gherkin (pickled cucumber).
Coulibiac	Hot fish and chicken pie (Russian cookery).
Couronne (en)	In a crown shape.
Court bouillion	A cooking liquor for fish consisting of water or stock, wine, vinegar and root vegetables.
Couscous	North African speciality – meat and grain stew.
Crapaudine	Pigeon or chicken cut up and flattened in the shape of a toad, grilled and garnished with sliced gherkins.
Crème – acidulée	Cream, soured.
– fouetté	Whipped.
– pâtissière	Pastry cream.
Crepinetta	Little flat sausage.
Cresson de fontaine	Watercress.
Crevette grise, rose	Shrimp, prawn.
Croissant	Crescent-shaped bread made of puff pastry.
Croquembouche balls	Crisp pastries, made of small chou paste.
Croquette	Food in a cylindrical shape and deep fried, e.g. croquette potatoes, meat/fish croquettes
Croustade	Pastry case (puff pastry).
Croûte (en)	In pastry.
Croûtons	Shaped pieces of bread, shallow fried.
Crudités	Raw vegetables (assorted).
Crustaces	Shellfish.
Cuisse	Leg of.
Cuire	To cook.
Culinaire	Culinary.
Cumin	Dried seed used for flavouring.
Curaçao	Orange liqueur.
Dariole	Small cylindrical mould (for puddings).
Dartois	(a) Two puff pastry layers with almond or pastry cream in-between. (b) Garnish: turned carrot, turnip, celery and rissoled potatoes.
Daube, en	Method of braising meat (usually beef) in red wine and stock.
Dauphine (pommes)	Chou paste mixed with potato deep fried.
Dauphinoise (à la)	Dauphine method of preparing vegetables with grated Gruyère.
Déglacer	To swill out a pan or roasting tray in which food has been cooked with water, wine or stock in order to extract the flavourings from the sediment to make an accompanying sauce or gravy.
Dégraisser	The process of skimming off fat from a liquid.
Déjeuner (à la fourchette)	Lunch (knife and fork meal).
Delmonico (pommes)	Cubes of potato coated in milk, covered in breadcrumbs and grilled.
Demidoff (consommé)	Chicken consommé garnished with dices of vegetables, truffles, quenelles, mushrooms and chervil.
Demi sel	Type of cream cheese.
Derby (croûtes)	Garnish: ham puree and pickled walnuts.
Désosser	To bone out.

Diable (à la)	Usually applied to poultry. Battered, seasoned, grilled, sprinkled with breadcrumbs, browned and served with devilled sauce, shallots, pepper, white wine reduced and cayenne.
Diable à cheval (canapé)	Prunes stuffed with chutney wrapped in bacon served on toast.
Dièppoise	Garnish: shrimps' tails, mussels, mushrooms. Brushed with beaten egg to brown. Garnish for fish dishes, cucumber turned into 'clove of garlic shape' cooked slowly in butter.
Dubarry (crème)	(a) Cauliflower (soup). (b) Cauliflower with cheese sauce.
Du jour (plat)	Of the day (dish).
Draining	Draining or drying of all the cooking liquor from the food before coating with sauce. Usually done by placing the poached food on a clean cloth or absorbent paper. This is important as the undrained liquor mixing with the masking sauce will spoil both appearance and consistency.
Elbarde	Bearded, shellfish
Écarlatte	Shallot.
Éclair	Chou pastry good filled with cream or pastry cream.
Écossaise (à l')	Scotch egg sauce, thin béchamel garnished with white and yolk of eggs.
Écrèmé (lait)	Skimmed milk.
Égyptienne (à l')	Pureé egyptienne is prepared from yellow split peas.
Emmenthal	Cheese from Switzerland.
Émincé (de volaille)	Thin slice (of chicken).
En branche	Whole (spinach) as opposed to purée.
En buissons	Crayfish cooked in court bouillon, cooled in their juice, served hung by the tail on a stand, garnished with parsley.
En cascade	Shellfish, usually prawns arranged in a dish like a waterfall.
En robe chambre (pommes)	In their jacket (potatoes): steamed.
Entrée	The first meat dish to figure on the menu.
Entremets	(a) *sucres* – sweet course. (b) *de legumes* – vegetables.
Épices	Spices (word 'condiments' is also used).
Épicure (canapé)	Roquefort cheese, butter with chopped onions.
Escalope	Thin slice usually of veal (scallop).
Escargot	Snail.
Estouffade	(a) Food slowly stewed. (b) Basic brown stock.
Esturgeon	Sturgeon (caviar-producing fish).
Étuvée (à l')	Method of cooking food in tightly covered container with little or no water.
Envoyez	Order from *aboyer* (shouter) 'to send up/away'.
Excelsoir	Garnish for tournedos and noisettes. Fresh lettuce or fondantes potatoes.
Farce (farci)	Stuffing (stuffed).
Farine	Flour
Faubonne	Puree of green peas or haricot beans with julienne of vegetable, chervil, butter and cream.
Favourite (salade)	Crayfish tails with truffles, asparagus tips, seasoned with lemon juice, olive oil, salt, pepper, celery and parsley.

Fécule	Potato starch used to thicken soups and stews, subistute for gluten based starches.
Fermière (à la)	With vegetables, i.e. carrots, turnips, onions and celery cut roughly. Usually applies to large joints of meat or poultry, also with soup and omelettes.
Fève	Broad bean.
Filet (d'Anvers)	Without bone, of meat, fish or poultry.
Filet mignon	Thin end of fillet.
Fines herbes	Mixed herbs (parsley, chervil, chives, rosemary).
Flageolet	Small kidney bean.
Flamande (à la)	(a) Carbonnade made of slices of beef cooked in beer with slices of onions. (b) With the inclusion of Brussels sprouts.
Flambé	Flamed.
Fleurons	Quarter moon-shaped puff pastry used as a decoration for various dishes.
Florida (cocktail)	Cocktail of orange and grapefruit segments.
Foie	Liver.
Foie gras	Fatted liver of geese with truffles.
Fondantes (pommes)	Potatoes cooked in stock in an oven.
Fonds de cuisine	Basic stocks.
Fondue (au fromage)	Melted cheese with wine and seasonings.
Forestière (à la)	(a) Morels tossed in butter, dices of bacon and parmentière potatoes. (b) *Cèpes* tossed in butter, mushrooms and pommes cocottes. (c) *Crème forestière* (cream of mushroom soup garnished with julienne of mushrooms).
Four (au)	Baked in the oven.
Fraise (des bois)	Strawberry (wild strawberry).
Fraise (Romanoff)	Strawberries with curaçao and fresh cream.
Framboise	Raspberry.
Frangipane	Pastry made of butter, sugar, eggs, almonds and flour.
Frappé	Chilled.
Fritot de chou-fleur	Cauliflower bouquet dipped in batter and deep fried.
Friture	(a) Fried food (small fish). (b) Vessel for deep frying.
Fromage (au)	Cheese (with).
Fromage de tête de porc	Pork brawn.
Fruits confits	Crystallised fruit.
Fumé (anguille, saumon)	Smoked (eel, salmon).
Fumet	A concentrated fish stock used to flavour fish dishes.
Galantine	Cold poultry or game that has been boned, stuffed, rolled and glazed.
Garbure	Soup, vegetable pureé, butter and cream and fried croutons.
Garnir (garniture)	To garnish (garnish).
Gazpacho	Chilled soup of Spanish origin made of cucumber, pimentos, garlic, tomatoes, oil, onions.
Gaufre	Waffle.
Gelée (en) (gelée d'aspic)	Jelly (in) (savoury jelly for coating chaud-froid dishes and for decorating).
Gendarme	Type of pickled herring or sausage.

Génoise	(a) Sponge pastry; also entrements made with sponge pastry. (b) Purée of herbs, pistachios, almonds cooked with yolk of eggs, lemon juice, salt and pepper and finished with oil.
Gervais	Cheese producer from France.
Gibier (à poils, à plume)	Game (furred, feathered).
Gingembre	Ginger.
Girolle	Type of mushroom. Iced, glazed.
Glacé de viandes	Meat juices or meat glaze.
Gnocchi (Romaine)	Semolina with egg yolk, cheese and butter.
Gnocchi (Parisienne)	Chou pastry and béchamel sprinkled with cheese and browned.
Goujon de sole (goujonnette)	Gudgeon (small strips of fish).
Grand Duc	Garnish, asparagus heads, slices of truffles for chicken.
Grand-mère	Garnish, button onions, mushrooms and diced bacon.
Grand Veneur	Poivrade sauce with venison flavour, redcurrant jelly and cream.
Grenobloise (poisson meuniere)	Cooked 'meunière' with capers and peeled wedge of lemon.
Grenouille (cuisses de)	Frog (legs).
Gribiche	Oily sauce made of yolk of eggs and hard-boiled eggs, oil and vinegar seasoned with mustard, capers and chopped gherkins, parsley and tarragon and dices of white of hard-boiled eggs.
Groseille	Redcurrant.
Groseille à maquereau	Gooseberry.
Gruyère	Waxy textured cheese from France and Switzerland: distinctive appearance on account of its large holes.
Haché	Minced.
Haut Brion	Red wine from Medoc district of Bordeaux.
Haute cuisine	Cooking at its best.
Havanaise	Salad lettuces, shrimps, asparagus heads, mayonnaise thinned with cucumber purée.
Hélène	Salad-green pimentos, truffles, asparagus heads, tangerines, vinaigrette with brandy.
Henri IV	Garnish for tournedos and noisette-Pont-Neuf potatoes and watercress.
Hochepot	Stewed meat.
Hollandaise	Yolks of eggs and butter sauce.
Homard	Lobster.
Hors d'œuvre (au choix, variés)	Hors d'œuvre (choice of, variety of)
Huile (à l')	With oil.
Hussarde	(a) Garnish for large joints: potatoes and eggplants stuffed with horseradish. (b) Sauce: minced onions and shallots, fried in butter with wine.
Impératrice (riz à l')	Cooked rice with salpicon of mixed fruit soaked in liqueur, red jelly on top of dish.
Impérial (à l')	Mushrooms, truffle and foie gras.
Infusion	Infusion, steeping in liquid.
Italienne (à l')	(a) Italian style, usually with cooked spaghetti , butter, cream and grated Parmesan cheese. (b) Duxelles sauce, brunoise of ham and herbs. (c) Mayonnaise with lemon juice, garnished minced brain and chopped parsley.

Ivanhoe (canapé)	May be shaped like Ivanhoe shield; purée of haddock with cream and grilled mushrooms.
Ivoire (sauce)	Ivory: a supreme sauce with a meat glaze to give it an ivory colour.
Jalousie	Flaky pastry slice filled with jam and baked in oven.
Japonaise	(a) Garnish for meat: croustade filled with Japanese artichokes and croquette potatoes. (b) Tomato and dice of pineapple served on lettuce leaves with an acidulated cream dressing (lemon juice, castor sugar and cream).
Jeanette	(a) Usually with forcemeat and foie gras. (b) Cold chicken, decorated and covered with aspic jelly.
Jubilées (cérises)	Poached and stoned cherries, flambéed with kirsch.
Jus	Juice.
Jus lié	Gravy thickened with arrowroot.
Jus de rôti	Roast gravy, unthickened
Kebab (Brochette)	Lamb or mutton cut into small pieces/cubes and cooked on a skewer, served with rice, peas and onions.
Kirsch	Liqueur made from cherries; also used for flavouring or flambes.
Kummel	Liqueur flavoured with cumin.
Langue (de chat)	Tongue (pastry in the shape of a cat's tongue).
Lapin (domestique, de Garenne)	Rabbit (tame, wild).
Lard (gras, maigre)	Bacon (fat, lean).
Lardon	Small dice of bacon.
Laurier (feuillies de)	Bay leaves.
Levure	Yeast.
Liaison	(a) A binding ingredient such as egg yolk or cream. (b) A mixture of egg yolks and cream whisked together and used to enrich and thicken sauces.
Lier	To bind.
Lièvre (levreau)	Hare (young hare).
Limande	Lemon sole.
Limousine	Garnish, cooked chestnuts, from the Limousin district of France
Longschamps (crème)	Fresh pea soup garnished with vermicelli, sorrel and chervil.
Lorette (a) pommes	(a) as 'dauphine': cigar-shaped (potatoes).
(b) salad	(b) Corn salad with beetroot and celery.
Loup de mer	Sea bass.
Louisiane (à la)	Louisiana style: creamed sweet corn, rice, fried bananas cut in roundels.
Lucifer	Poached oysters, rolled, in English mustard, egg and breadcrumbs, deep fried.
Licine	Clam (type of mollusc).
Lucullus (tournedos)	Garnish, fried crouton: truffle, mushrooms, cock's combs, kidney, asparagus tips, half-glaze sauce, truffle essence and Madeira wine.
Macérer	To soak, usually fruit in liqueur to give flavour.
Macis	Mace, dried shell of nutmeg, used to flavour marinades, brines and sauces.
Madeleine	Small light cake.

Madère (au)	(a) Madeira wine from island of same name. (b) Half glazed sauce with Madeira. Magnum Bottle twice the normal size.
Maintenon	Suprême sauce, slices of truffle and chopped mushrooms, sweetcorn.
Maison	House speciality.
Manie (beurre)	Butter and flour kneaded and used as a thickening or binding agent.
Marbré	Marbled: used in connection with certain sweet and pastry dishes.
Maréchale	(a) Asparagus tips and slices of truffle garnish. (b) Quenelles, truffles, cock's combs.
Marengo (poulet sauté)	Garnish for sautéed chicken, half glazed with tomatoes, white wine, mushrooms, truffles croutons, fresh water crayfish.
Marie Thérèse	Garnish for tournedos or noisette, cooked in butter, half glazed, tomatoes, risotto and truffle.
Marignan	Type of savarin pastry: small boat-shaped.
Marinade	Liquor to tenderise meat: root vegetables, bouquet garni, white wine, vinegar and oil.
Mariner	To keep meat in a marinade to make it more tender.
Marinière	(a) Marine style. (b) White wine sauce with mussels. Marivaux Oval nests of duchesse potatoes.
Marjolaine	Marjoram (aromatic herbs).
Marmelade	Purée of cooked fruit.
Marsala	Fortified wine from Sicily (very sweet).
Marron (marron glacé)	Chestnut (chestnut glazed in sugar).
Marseillaise	(a) Fish stew speciality from Marseilles. (b) Tomatoes, stuffed olives, garlic, anchovy, potatoes.
Maryland (suprême de volaille)	Breadcrumbed chicken, shallow fried, sweetcorn, pancake, bacon and half-fried banana.
Mascotte	Garnish for meat and poultry: artichoke bottoms, truffle slices, cocotte potatoes.
Médaillon	Medallion of meat and other round-shaped preparations.
Médicis	Garnish for meat of artichoke bottoms, peas, carrots and turnips, noisette potatoes, sauce Choron: béarnaise sauce with tomato purée.
Mélange	Mixture or assortment.
Mercedes	Garnish of tomatoes, mushrooms, braised lettuce and croquette potatoes.
Meunière	Fish, Miller's wife style: floured, shallow-fried, noisette butter, lemon slices, lemon juice and parsley, honey.
Mignon	(a) Thin end of fillet of beef. (b) Poultry and sweetbread, artichoke bottoms, halved tomatoes, braised lettuce and chateau potatoes.
Mignonette	(a) Poivre – roughly chopped peppercorns. (b) Pommes – potatoes chopped in small batons.
Mijoter	To simmer gently.
Miroton	A type of dish made of boiled slices of beef and covered with a sauce; usually reheated.
Mode à la	In the fashion of.
Moelle (de boeuf)	Marrow (of beef).
Monaco	Poached fish, fine herb sauce with tomato-flavouring, poached breaded oysters, truffle slices.
Mont Blanc (crème)	Whipped cream mixed with chestnut purée.

Monter au beurre — The process of incorporating chilled butter pieces into sauces to thicken and improve the glaze.

Monte Carlo — (a) Poached haddock, cream sauce, poached egg and roughly chopped tomatoes.
(b) Mousse with chantilly and meringues.

Monter — To whip up cream.

Montmorency (caneton) — (a) half-glazed sauce and cherries.
(b) Garnish for noisette and tournedos; artichoke bottoms, carrots, noisette potatoes.

Montpellier — A savoury herb butter.

Morelle — Type of mushroom.

Mortadelle — Italian type of sausage served as an hors d'œuvre.

Morue — Salted cod.

Moscovite (canapé) — Moscow style: various appetisers on toast cut into different shapes and covered with aspic jelly.

Moulin à poivre — Peppermill.

Mousse — Whipped white of egg with cream; various flavourings, savoury and sweet.

Mousseline — (a) Hollandaise sauce with whipped cream.
(b) Mashed potatoes with whipped cream.

Moutarde — Mustard.

Mure — Mulberry.

Muscade (noix) — Nutmeg.

Napper — To coat or cover with a sauce.

Nature — Plainly cooked. Also applies to wine to which nothing has been added.

Navarin — Brown lamb stew.

Navet — Turnip.

Newburg (homard) — Cooked, sliced lobster, cream, Madeira or sherry, crab served with rice.

Niçoise — (a) Usually indicates presence of tomatoes, French beans, olives and peppers.
(b) Fish garnish: chopped tomatoes, garlic, capers, slices of lemon, anchovy butter.

Noisette — (a) Hazelnut.
(b) (Potatoes) small hazelnut-size roasted in clarified butter.
(c) Hollandaise sauce with noisette butter.

Noix (de Brésil, de coco) — Walnut (Brazil nut, coconut).

Noix de veau — Cushion of veal.

Nouilles — Noodles.

Nuits St Georges — Côtes de nuits; famous red Burgundy wine.

Nymphes — Frog legs. Also poached in white wine, served cold with chaudfroid and aspic jelly.

Oie (oison) — Goose (Gosling).

Oignon — Onion.

Olivette (pommes) — Roast potatoes cut the size of a small olive with special cutter

Opéra (crème) — (a) Cream caramel cooked in a circular savarin mould, strawberry soaked in kirsch, crème caprice (whipped cream mixed with small pieces of meringue) placed in the centre.
(b) Noisette and tournedos garnish: tartlets filled with chicken liver, scallops, Madeira sauce, duchesse potatoes, asparagus tips.

Orange sanguine	Blood orange.
Orge (perle)	Barley (pearl barley).
Orloff	(a) Scrambled egg garnished with crayfish tails and a slice of truffle. (b) Meat garnish: braised celery in timbale, celery purée, tomatoes, braised lettuce, chateau potatoes.
Orly (à l')	Fish marinaded in oil, lemon juice and parsley, passed through seasoned flour, dipped in batter and deep fried. Served with tomato sauce.
Oseille	Sorrel.
Osso Buco	Italian dish of knuckle of veal served with rice.
Paillettes de fromage	Cheese straws.
Palmier (coeurs de)	Palm hearts.
Panachée (salade, glace)	Mixed (mixed salad, assorted ice-cream).
Panade	A binding agent; may be flour, butter and water.
Paprika	Red and mild Hungarian pepper.
Parisienne (pommes)	Round, ball-shaped potatoes shaped with a special cutter.
Parme (jambon de)	Parma ham (smoked).
Parmesan	Italian hard goat cheese.
Passer	To strain.
Pâtes alimentaires	Pasta (macaroni, spaghetti, lasagne).
Pauillac	Red wine from the commune of Médoc in the Bordeaux district.
Paupiette	Rolled fillet of fish or meat.
Paysanne (à la)	Peasant style.
Peler	To peel.
Perche	Perch, bass.
Perdreau (perdrix)	Partridge.
Périgord (périgourdine)	Region of France renowned for its truffles and pâté de foie gras.
Pernod	Aniseed-flavoured aperitif.
Petit déjeuner	Breakfast.
Petite marmite	Beef and chicken consommé garnished with vegetables, pieces of beef and chicken served in a small earthenware pot.
Petit suisse	Cream cheese.
Piémontaise (Risotto)	Rice dish, garnished with mushrooms, tomatoes, pimentos and truffles.
Piperade	Regional dish: tomatoes, peppers and eggs beaten to a fluffy consistency. Piquante (sauce) Sharp (sauce of demi-glaze, with white wine vinegar, gherkins and herbs).
Pissenlit	Edible dandelion (in salads).
Plat (du jour)	Dish (of the day).
Poivre (de cayenne)	Pepper (cayenne pepper).
Poivron	Pepper (pimento).
Pojarski	Chopped veal or chicken mixed with butter and breadcrumbs, cutlet shape, bone stick inserted, breadcrumbed, shallow fried.
Pont l'Évêque	French cheese.
Port Salut	French cheese.
Portugaise	(a) From Portugal, usually with tomatoes and onions. (b) Entrée: stuffed tomatoes, chateau potatoes.
Pouilly fuisse	Dry white wine from the Côte Maçonnaise in Burgundy.
Poule au pot	Boiling fowl cooked in a pot with vegetables.

Poulet (de grain, reine)	Chicken (corn-fed chicken, young spring chicken).
Printanière	With spring vegetables.
Provençale	(a) Provence style-chopped tomatoes, garlic, cooked in oil, olives. (b) Tomatoes, stuffed mushrooms, garlic.
Quenelles	Finely sieved chicken, game or fish forcemeat. Seasoned and flavoured accordingly, whisked egg whites and whipping cream added.
Quo vadis (canapé)	Soft roes on toast, grilled mushrooms.
Ravier	Oblong deep dish for service of salad or hors d'oeuvre.
Ravigotte (sauce)	(a) Veloute sauce flavoured with wine and vinegar, shallots, chervil, tarragon and chives. (b) Vinaigrette, capers, parsley, chives, tarragon, onions.
Raton	A kind of cheese cake.
Réduction (réduire)	To reduce a liquid by boiling so as to increase or extract the flavour.
Renaissance (à la)	Garnish of artichoke bottoms, carrots, turnips, French beans, peas, asparagus tips, cauliflower and hollandaise sauce: fondantes potatoes.
Richelieu	Stuffed tomatoes, stuffed mushrooms, braised lettuce, château potatoes.
Rillettes	Cooked meat or poultry cooked and minced, eaten cold as pâté.
Romanoff (fraises)	(a) Strawberries, whipped cream and curaçao. (b) Meat garnish: stuffed cucumbers, duchess potatoes, croustade filled with celery, rare salpicon and mushrooms, horseradish sauce.
Romarin	Rosemary (herb).
Roquefort	French blue cheese.
Rosbif	Roast beef.
Rossini	(a) Garnish of foie gras, truffle, half glaze and Madeira wine. (b) For tournedos and noisette: foie gras scallops sautéed in butter, truffles.
Reducing	The cooking liquor is strained after use and rapidly boiled. It is then added to the accompanying or coating sauce.
Saindoux	Lard
Saint Paulin	French cheese.
Saint Pierre	John Dory (fish).
Saison (de)	Season (of the).
Salpicon	Mixture of fruit of vegetable cut into dice and covered with sauce.
Sandlier	Wild boar.
Sarah Bernhardt	Garnish of demi glaze, port wine, meat marrow, croutons, tomatoes, braised lettuce.
Sardine	Sardine.
Sarladaise (pommes)	(a) Sliced potatoes and truffles cooked in stock in the oven. (b) Garnish for meat.
Schneider (pommes)	Potatoes in the style of, cooked in milk, cream, meat glaze, butter and chopped parsley.
Schnitzel	Term used to denote a thin slice of meat, usually veal.
St Émilion	Red wine from the borders of the Pomerol district in Bordeaux.
Table d'hôte	Meal at a set price.
Tamiser	To sieve
Tasse (en)	Cup (in a).

Théodora (salade)	Artichoke bottoms, oysters, mushrooms, crayfish, mayonnaise.
Thérèse	Poached fillets of fish, noisette potatoes, truffle, white wine sauce.
Thermidor (homard)	Lobster in half shelf, white wine sauce, with mustard and Mornay sauce.
Timbale	(a) Small round dish with a double container used for cooking delicate fruit and soufflés. (b) Presented in timbale dish.
Tortue	(a) Turtle (turtle soup). (b) Entrée: quenelles, mushrooms, gherkins, garlic. (c) Scallop of veal tongue and brain, fried egg, crayfish, croûton, truffles.
Tranche (mince, épaise)	Slice (thin, thick)
Tripe	Tripe.
Truffe	Truffle.
Valenciennes	Garnish of risotto valenciennes (rice cooked in meat stock) and served with croquette potatoes.
Viroflay	Garnish for meat, spinach balls Viroflay style, artichoke quarters, château potatoes
Voline	Veil of spun sugar.
Winterthur (à la)	Lobster dish served with peeled shrimps and a salpicon.
Xérès (au)	With sherry.
Yaourt	Yoghurt.
Yvette	Scrambled egg with asparagus tips, crayfish tails, truffles, in tartlet, Nantua sauce.
Zabaglione	Italian sweet made with a sabayon of yolk of egg, sugar and Marsala wine; finger biscuits.
Zingara	Tarragon-flavoured half glaze sauce, julienne of ham, tongue, mushrooms, truffles; Madeira.
Zucchini	Small vegetable marrow.

Index

Page numbers in bold denote Level II. Entries in italic denote recipe. t denotes table. f denotes figure